THE WARRIOR AND THE PACIFIST

This book looks at two contradictory ethical motifs—the warrior and the pacifist—across four major faith traditions—Buddhism, Judaism, Christianity, and Islam—and their role in shaping our understanding of violence and the morality of its use. *The Warrior and the Pacifist* explores how these faith traditions, which now mutually inhabit our life spaces, bring with them across the millennia the moral teachings that have traveled from prehistoric humanity, embedded in the beliefs, rituals, and institutions socially constructed by humans to deal with ultimate concerns, core aspects of daily personal and social life, and life transitions.

Lester R. Kurtz is Professor of Sociology at George Mason University Korea. He is the editor of the *Encyclopedia of Violence, Peace, and Conflict* (2nd ed., 2008), co-editor of *Women, War, and Violence* (2015), *The Paradox of Repression and Social Movements* (2018), *Nonviolent Social Movements* (1999), and *The Web of Violence* (1997), and author of books and articles including *Gods in the Global Village* (4th ed., 2016), *The Politics of Heresy* (1988), and *The Nuclear Cage* (1988).

THE WARRIOR AND THE PACIFIST

Competing Motifs in Buddhism, Judaism, Christianity, and Islam

Edited by Lester R. Kurtz

NEW YORK AND LONDON

First published 2018
by Routledge
711 Third Avenue, New York, NY 10017

and by Routledge
2 Park Square, Milton Park, Abingdon, Oxon, OX14 4RN

Routledge is an imprint of the Taylor & Francis Group, an informa business

© 2018 Taylor & Francis

The right of Lester R. Kurtz to be identified as the author of the editorial material, and of the authors for their individual chapters, has been asserted in accordance with sections 77 and 78 of the Copyright, Designs and Patents Act 1988.

All rights reserved. No part of this book may be reprinted or reproduced or utilised in any form or by any electronic, mechanical, or other means, now known or hereafter invented, including photocopying and recording, or in any information storage or retrieval system, without permission in writing from the publishers.

Trademark notice: Product or corporate names may be trademarks or registered trademarks, and are used only for identification and explanation without intent to infringe.

Library of Congress Cataloging-in-Publication Data
A catalog record for this book has been requested

ISBN: 978-1-138-58543-0 (hbk)
ISBN: 978-1-138-58544-7 (pbk)
ISBN: 978-0-429-50526-3 (ebk)

Typeset in Bembo
by Apex CoVantage, LLC

Printed in the United Kingdom
by Henry Ling Limited

CONTENTS

Note on Contributors   *viii*
Foreword   *xiv*
Kevin P. Clements

1 Rethinking Religion and Violence   1
   Lester R. Kurtz

PART I
The Buddhist Tradition   **11**

2 Buddhism and Violence: An Oxymoron? Text and
    Tradition in Buddhist Just-War Thinking   13
    Iselin Frydenlund

3 Engaged Buddhism East and West: Encounters with the
    Visions, Vitality, and Values of an Emerging Practice   36
    Paula Green

4 Aspects of Social Engagement Within the Southeast
    Asian Buddhist World   57
    Jordan Baskerville and Somboon Chungprampree

PART II
The Jewish Tradition — 67

5 War and Peace: Intertwining Threads in the Jewish Tradition — 69
   Rabbi Tirzah Firestone, PhD

6 Jewish, Israeli, and Zionist Traditions of War and Peace — 86
   Paul Scham

7 "Purity of Arms": Educating Ethical Warriors in the Israeli Army — 104
   Noam Zion

PART III
The Christian Tradition — 133

8 Peace and War in Christian Thought: A Partisan Guide — 135
   Nigel Biggar

9 Nonviolence: A Style of Politics for Peace — 162
   Pope Francis

10 Christianity and Islam in an Age of Transition: Violence or Healing? — 169
   Joseph A. Camilleri

PART IV
The Islamic Tradition — 193

11 Making Peace with Islam: The Muslim as Peacemaker — 195
   Afra Jalabi

12 Transforming Terrorism with Muslims' Nonviolent Alternatives? — 216
   Chaiwat Satha-Anand

13 Islamic Approaches to Nonviolence and Peacebuilding: A Critical Examination — 242
   Mohammed Abu-Nimer

PART V
Addressing the Issues Cross-Culturally 263

14 Building Peace with Religious Support: The Case
    of Sri Lanka 265
    Jehan Perera

15 Interreligious Dialogue 284
    Lisa Schirch

16 Warriors and Pacifists: Dilemmas, Paradoxes, Alternatives 298
    Lester R. Kurtz

Index *332*

CONTRIBUTORS

Mohammed Abu-Nimer, of the International Peace and Conflict Resolution program at American University, served as Director of the Peacebuilding and Development Institute. He holds a PhD in Conflict Analysis and Resolution from George Mason University. Professor Abu-Nimer has been intervening and conducting training workshops and courses all over the world in conflict zones such as: Sri Lanka, Mindanao-Philippines, Palestine, Egypt, Northern Ireland, Bosnia, Chad, Niger, and Kurdistan-Iraq, as well as other areas including the United States and Europe. He is the founder of Salam Institute for Peace and Justice and co-founder and co-editor of the Journal of Peacebuilding and Development. As a scholar, he has published many books and articles, including: *Nonviolence and Peacebuilding in Islam: Theory and Practice* (2003); *Post-Conflict Power-Sharing Agreements: Options for Syria* (with Salamey, Imad, Abouaoun, Elie, eds., 2017); *Peace-Building By, Between and Beyond Muslims and Evangelical Christians* (Abu-Nimer and Augsburger, eds., 2009); *Unity in Diversity: Interfaith Dialogue in the Middle East* (Abu-Nimer, Khoury, and Welty, 2007); *Interfaith Dialogue: A Guide for Muslims* (with Muhammad Shafiq, 2007); and *Reconciliation, Coexistence, and Justice: Theory and Practice* (ed., 2001).

Jordan Baskerville is a PhD candidate in religions of Asia at the University of Wisconsin-Madison, focusing on the history of socially-engaged Buddhism in Southeast Asia, especially Thailand and Vietnam. He spent more than a year in Thailand completing dissertation research and has published in the Kyoto Review of Southeast Asia, and Rian Thai: International Journal of Thai Studies.

Nigel Biggar is Regius Professor of Moral and Pastoral Theology at the University of Oxford, where he also directs the McDonald Centre for Theology, Ethics, and Public Life. He is a former President of the Society for the Study of Christian Ethics (UK). Among his publications are *In Defence of War* (2013), *Burying the Past: Making Peace and Doing Justice after Civil Conflict* (2003), and most recently *Between Kin and Cosmopolis: An Ethic of the Nation* (2014). He has written on the possibility of a truth commission for Northern Ireland for the *Irish Times*, on the Iraq war for the *Times* (London) and the *Financial Times*, and on Scottish independence for *Standpoint* magazine. His hobbies include reading history, playing cards, and making pilgrimage to military cemeteries.

Joseph A. Camilleri, OAM, is Emeritus Professor at La Trobe University, Melbourne, and Executive Director of Alexandria Agenda, a new venture in ethical consulting. In a teaching career at La Trobe spanning forty years, he taught some thirty-five subjects at either undergraduate or postgraduate level. In 2005, he founded the La Trobe Centre for Dialogue. Under his leadership, the Centre quickly established a national and international reputation for research, training, and policy development. He has authored or edited over twenty-five books and written some 100 book chapters and journal articles. His research has centered on five key areas: security and peace studies, culture and religion in international relations, international political theory, the foreign policies of the great powers, and the international relations of the Asia–Pacific region. Over the past ten years, Camilleri has convened some twenty major international dialogues and conferences, and appeared before several parliamentary and government inquiries, most recently the parliamentary inquiry into Multiculturalism in Australia in 2013. He serves on several editorial and advisory boards and recently coedited a Special Issue of the scholarly journal *Global Change, Peace and Security* on the recently adopted nuclear ban treaty. For further details, see his personal website: www.josephcamilleri.org.

Somboon Chungprampree is a Thai social activist working for peace and justice in Asia. Even as a university student, he was involved in the student movement in Thailand, which focused on environmental justice. Since 1997, he has worked in different positions with key Thai/regional/international civil society organizations. Presently, he serves as Executive Secretary of International Network of Engaged Buddhists (INEB). He is a civic leader and serves on the board of a number of international and national foundations. He has a great interest in photography.

Kevin P. Clements is Foundation Chair of Peace and Conflict Studies and Director of the New Zealand Centre for Peace and Conflict Studies at the University of Otago, Dunedin, New Zealand. He is also Secretary General of the Toda Institute for Global Peace and Policy. Prior to taking up these positions, he was Professor of Peace and Conflict Studies and Foundation Director of the Australian Centre for Peace and Conflict Studies at the University of Queensland, Brisbane, Australia. He went to Queensland from International Alert, where he was Secretary General from January 1999 to September 2003. During his time there he was on the Board of the European Centre for Conflict Prevention, and was previously President of the European Peace Building Liaison Office in Brussels. Prior to becoming Secretary General of International Alert, Kevin was the Vernon and Minnie Lynch Chair of Conflict Resolution at the Institute for Conflict Analysis and Resolution at George Mason University in Fairfax, Virginia, from 1994 to 2000, and Director of the Institute from 1994 to 1999. His career has been a combination of academic analysis and practice in the areas of peacebuilding and conflict transformation. He was formerly Director of the Quaker United Nations Office in Geneva and Head of the Peace Research Centre at the Australian National University in Canberra. He has been an advisor to the New Zealand, Australian, British, Swedish, and Dutch governments on conflict prevention, peace, defense, and security issues, and advised the German government and the OECD on states and violence. He was President of the International Peace Research Association (IPRA) from 1994 to 1998 and Secretary General from 2008 to 2010; President of the IPRA Foundation from 1995 to 2000; and Secretary General of the Asia Pacific Peace Research Association. Professor Clements has been a regular consultant to a variety of nongovernmental and intergovernmental organizations on disarmament, arms control, conflict resolution, development, and regional security issues. He has written or edited eight books and over 165 chapters/articles on conflict transformation, peacebuilding, preventive diplomacy, and development with a specific focus on the Asia–Pacific region.

Tirzah Firestone, PhD, is Emerita Rabbi of Congregation Nevei Kodesh: Jewish Renewal Community of Boulder, Colorado; a Jungian psychotherapist; and an author. She was ordained in 1992 by Reb Zalman Schachter Shalomi and holds a doctorate in depth psychology from Pacifica Graduate Institute (2015). Her studies and cutting-edge work in cultural trauma, ancestral healing, and the intergenerational transmission of injury are the focus of her counseling and group practices and the topic of a forthcoming book (Adam Kadmon, 2018). Tirzah served for seven years on the board of Rabbis for Human Rights, North America, currently known as T'ruah: The Rabbinic Call for Human Rights. She is the founder of the Muslim–Jewish Alliance of Boulder County, Colorado.

Iselin Frydenlund is Associate Professor in Religious Studies at MF Norwegian School of Theology and is affiliated to the Peace Research Institute Oslo. She has published numerous book chapters and articles on Buddhism and politics and violence in Sri Lanka and Myanmar, most recently in *The Journal of Religious and Political Practice* (2018), *Oxford Encyclopedia of Religion* (2018), *Military Chaplaincy* *in a Pluralist Age* (ed. Brekke and Thikonov, 2017), *Buddhist Modernities* (ed. Havnevik et al., 2017), the *Nordic Journal of Human Rights* (2017), and the *Journal of Religion and Violence* (2017). She has also been engaged in Buddhist dialogue work concerning religious minorities in Buddhist majority states.

Paula Green is Emerita Professor of Conflict Transformation at the School for International Training Graduate Institute in Vermont, where she founded and directed the CONTACT (Conflict Transformation Across Cultures) programs, bi-annual intensives held in the US and South Asia for international peacebuilders. Dr. Green also founded and directed the US-based NGO Karuna Center for Peacebuilding in Amherst, Massachusetts, which offers training, mentoring, and education in peace and conflict in war-torn and war-recovering countries around the world. In 2009 she received an award from the Dalai Lama as an "unsung hero of compassion." Dr. Green has been active with the International Network of Engaged Buddhists (INEB), the Buddhist Peace Fellowship, the Insight Meditation Society, and the Nipponzan Myohoji New England Peace Pagoda, as well as the US and International Fellowships of Reconciliation. With graduate degrees in psychology and intergroup relations, she has taught peacebuilding in many countries in Asia, Africa, Eastern Europe, and the Mideast. Her interests are in increasing skills for preventing and responding to conflict and fostering civil society initiatives that humanize relations across perceived differences. She is currently developing a national people-to-people model for bridging differences within the US, beginning with communities in New England and Appalachia.

Afra Jalabi is a Montreal-based Syrian writer. Jalabi is currently finishing her PhD at Concordia University in Montreal in the Department of Religions and Cultures. She is a frequent lecturer on issues related to Islam and nonviolence. She has participated in international conferences and appeared in Arab, American, and Canadian media, having also worked as a columnist in the Arab Press for the last eighteen years. She has a master's degree in journalism from Carleton University and a BA in Anthropology and Political Science from McGill University.

Lester R. Kurtz is Professor of Sociology at George Mason University Korea, and holds an M.A.R. from Yale and a PhD from the University of Chicago. Editor of a three-volume *Encyclopedia of Violence, Peace, and Conflict* (2nd ed., 2008), he co-edited with Mariam M. Kurtz the two-volume *Women, War, and Violence* (2014); *The Paradox of Repression and Social Movements* (with Lee A. Smithey, 2018); *Nonviolent Civil Resistance* (with Sharon Erickson Neptstad, 2012); *Nonviolent Social Movements* (with Stephen Zunes, 1999); *The Web of Violence* (1997); and *Third World Peace Perspectives* (with Shu-Ju Ada Cheng, special issue of *Peace Review*). He is author of *Gods in the Global Village* (4th ed., 2016), *The Nuclear Cage* (1988), and *The Politics of Heresy* (1988). He is a past chair of the Peace and Justice Studies

Association as well as the Peace, War, and Social Conflict Section of the American Sociological Association, which awarded him its Robin Williams Distinguished Career Award. He has been a visiting professor at the European Peace University, the University of Chicago, Northwestern University, Delhi University, and Tunghai University, as well as Distinguished Researcher at the Institute of the Nanjing Massacre and International Peace. Lester and Dr. Mariam Kurtz have three children at home with them in South Korea, Amina, Amani, and Brian; his daughter Patience is a graduate student at DePaul University in Chicago.

Jehan Perera is Executive Director of the National Peace Council of Sri Lanka (NPC). The organization was established in 1995 as an independent and nonpartisan civil society organization to facilitate a citizen's movement for reconciliation. A key objective of the organization is to support efforts to find a negotiated political settlement that would lead to reconciliation and nation building. Perera was part of the government delegation at the UN Human Rights Council session in Geneva in March 2017, as the civil society representative. He writes a regular weekly political column for the Sri Lankan media. He has a BA in Economics from Harvard College, an LLB from the Open University of Sri Lanka, and a JD from Harvard Law School.

Chaiwat Satha-Anand is Professor of Political Science and Director of Peace Information Center at Thammasat University and Chairperson of the Strategic Nonviolence Commission, Thailand Research Fund—a think tank that proposes nonviolent policy alternatives to deadly conflicts in Thai society. He has written, edited, or co-edited some forty books published both in Thailand and abroad. Some of his writings have been translated and published in Arabic, Bahasa Indonesia, Chinese, German, Italian, Japanese, and Korean. His most recent publications include: editor, *Nonviolent Space/Thailand's Future* (2016—in Thai); author, *Barangsiapa Memelihara Kehidupan* (*Essays on Nonviolence and Islamic Imperatives*; 2016—in Bahasa Indonesia); co-editor (with Olivier Urbain), *The Promise of Reconciliation?: Examining Violent and Nonviolent Effects on Asian Conflicts* (2017); author, *Nonviolence and Islamic Imperatives* (2017). He was named "Thailand's Best Researcher in Political Science and Public Administration" by the National Research Council and Thammasat University's Kiratiyajaraya Distinguished Professor in 2006. He also received the National Sri Burapha Distinguished Writer Award in Bangkok and the International El-Hibri Peace Education Prize in Washington, DC, in 2012.

Paul Scham is Research Associate Professor of Israel Studies and Executive Director of the Gildenhorn Institute for Israel Studies at the University of Maryland, where he primarily teaches courses on the history of the Israeli–Palestinian conflict. He is co-editor of *Shared Histories* (2006) and *Shared Narratives* (2013) and has authored a number of articles, blogs, and op-eds on the conflict, Hamas, historical narratives, Jordan, and the peace process. From 1996 to 2002, he coordinated Israeli-Palestinian joint research projects at the Truman Institute for Peace of the Hebrew University. He is Managing Editor of the *Israel Studies Review*, an interdisciplinary academic journal, and blogs at http://progressiveisrael.org/blog/.

Lisa Schirch is North American Research Director for the Toda Peace Institute and Senior Policy Advisor with the Alliance for Peacebuilding. A former Fulbright Fellow in East and West Africa, Schirch has conducted conflict assessments and participated in peacebuilding planning alongside local colleagues in over 20 countries, including Afghanistan, Pakistan, Iraq, Sri Lanka, Indonesia, Kenya, Ghana, and Fiji. Schirch has published seven books and dozens of chapters and articles on a range of themes, including the design and structure of a comprehensive peace process in Afghanistan, civil–military relations, and the role of the media in peacebuilding. In 2015, Schirch finished a three-year project coordinating a global network to write a *Handbook on Human Security: A Civil-Military-Police Curriculum* and a set of forty peacebuilding case studies on *Local Ownership in Security*. Schirch also is a member of several advisory and research review panels for the Global Community Engagement and Resilience Fund (GCERF) in Geneva, Switzerland; the UN Development Program International Advisory Group on Infrastructures for Peace; and the Ministry of Foreign Affairs of the Netherlands' International Advisory Committee of Security and Rule of Law (SRoL) in Fragile and Conflict-Affected Settings (FCAS) and the Knowledge Platform on Security & Rule of Law, and served as the co-chair of the working group on engagement with religious actors by the US State Department Office on Religion and Global Affairs. Schirch has worked as a consultant on conflict assessment and peacebuilding planning for the United Nations Development Program, the World Bank, several branches of the US government, the US Foreign Service Institute, and many local civil society organizations.

Noam Zion has been Senior Research Fellow at the Shalom Hartman Institute since 1978. He studied philosophy at and graduated from Columbia University and the Hebrew University; and Bible and Rabbinics at the Jewish Theological Seminary of America and the Hartman Beit Midrash. He is on the faculty of the Hartman Rabbinic Enrichment Center, the Beeri teacher training program on democratic and Jewish values for Israeli high school teachers, and the Muslim Leadership Institute. As an educator, his popular publications and worldwide lectures have focused on Passover, Hanukkah, and Shabbat. His academic research includes a trilogy on the intellectual history of philanthropy, charity, and tzedakah entitled *Jewish Giving in Comparative Perspectives* (2013) and a nine-volume work on *Talmudic Marital Dramas* and *The Talmudic Kama Sutra* (2018).

FOREWORD

It gives me great delight to write the Foreword to this book edited by Dr. Lester Kurtz. In 2016, I convened a workshop in Tokyo, on behalf of Otago University and the Toda Peace Institute, to try and understand how four world religions accommodated, and endeavored to reconcile, competing warrior and pacifist positions within their different traditions. To this end, I brought together religious leaders, theologians and religious studies experts to analyze and discuss these issues so that we might better understand some of the relationships between religious belief, practice and violent behavior.

Way back in social science pre-history(!), Glock and Stark (1965) *Religion and Society in Tension*, proposed that there were five dimensions of religiosity. These are ideological (belief), intellectual (knowledge or cognitive), ritualistic (overt behavior traditionally defined as religious), experiential (experiences defined as religious in the sense of arousing feelings or emotions) and consequential (the effects of the other four dimensions applied in the secular world). I wanted the 2016 workshop to explore these factors so that we might understand better the precise relationships between such religiosity and spontaneous or organized violent behavior.

As a Christian Pacifist, I have no problem in asserting that my ethical choices in relation to violence are driven by my religious ideological belief in the transformative power of love and by an intellectual appreciation of how love has manifested itself through time. There are plenty of Christian rituals that reinforce my pacifist beliefs through their celebration of love, life, forgiveness, redemption and reconciliation. All of these qualities are capable of generating altruistic, self-sacrificing feelings and emotions. I am hopeful because of my beliefs and because of the positive historical consequences of empathetic, loving people promoting the common good, often at considerable personal loss and suffering. I have absolutely no difficulty, therefore, in identifying with texts, beliefs, practices and behavior that highlight the pacifist tradition within Christianity.

I am aware, however, that there are many others who share my Christian beliefs and practices who do not adopt my pacifist position. On the contrary, these people believe that Christianity can legitimate just and holy wars and acts of violence in defense of the faith or in pursuit of social justice. We share a faith tradition but derive very different ethical imperatives from our beliefs, doctrines and practices. If Christian communities can bring together individuals who are united in the central tenets of faith but differ deeply on their ethical and political consequences, so too can other religious traditions. There are, of course, many believers from all religions who aspire to sacrificial love and a life of nonviolence but get caught up in the demands of different violent contexts. It is important, therefore, that we not lapse into simplistic dualisms about the warrior and pacifist traditions within contemplative and confrontational faiths. The reality is that believers array themselves on complex war-peace spectrums and are never fully pacifist or fully warrior. It is the task of books such as this to understand how we can embrace complexity and live with deep and challenging ethical questions. If we can do this, then we have a chance of giving expression to values, beliefs and actions that will enable individuals and groups to engage the better angels of their nature and generate cultures and structures of peacefulness instead of cultures and structures of violence.

The workshop chose to focus on the Abrahamic Religions (Judaism, Christianity and Islam), as these have been at the heart of much violence over the centuries. But since one of the sponsors of the meeting was Buddhist, we thought it important also to understand how a contemplative religious tradition based on compassion dealt with questions of internal and external violence. All religious traditions have in fact succumbed to violence at some stage of their evolution. A recent book by Douglas Pratt (2017), *Religion and Extremism: Rejecting Diversity*, demonstrates clearly that all religions, but especially the Abrahamic, have had violent pasts and paths. The challenge for social scientists is to understand whether this is because violence is inherent in religion or because religion has been instrumentalized by secular power to sanction violent means in the achievement of secular goals.

What is clear is that where there is no intentional separation of synagogue / church /temple /mosque from state power or, worse, where there is a theocratic fusion of both, violent conflict is more probable than where there is a separation of the sacred and the secular.

While this book considers ways in which Buddhism has been involved in a range of violent conflicts and has utilized violence to preserve the integrity of the Sangha, the vast majority of twentieth- and twenty-first-century "religious conflicts" have occurred within and between the Abrahamic Religions—Jewish-Jewish, Jewish-Muslim, Muslim-Christian, Muslim-Muslim, Christian-Christian. The question is: what are the key issues and incompatibilities that trigger violent animosity among and between diverse religious groups, and how these can be addressed so that they are resolved nonviolently rather than violently? Whether these conflicts were caused by the warrior traditions within each religion or some other cause is the key question.

Hans Kung (1992) distinguishes world religions into three main currents: (i) The Confrontational Religions: Judaism—17.4 million adherents; Christianity—1.6 billion members; and Islam—1 billion adherents; (ii) The Religions of Self Communion: Hinduism—700+ million adherents; Buddhism—300 million+ adherents; and (iii) The Religions of Harmony: Confucianism—emphasizing the unity of the world, nature, society and cosmos, which has 800+ million adherents. The reason why Kung argues that confrontational religions are that way is because of singularism and universalism. Singularism argues that there is only one valid faith, and universalism argues that this faith applies to the whole world. Religions making truth claims that are exclusive seek to persuade believers and non-believers alike of their validity. This proselytization can be violent or nonviolent, but because of the exclusive singularity and universal scope of the claims, it inevitably generates confrontation. Oriental religions, particularly those of "Self Communion," can also be violent, hierarchical and patriarchal but are made "softer" by being polytheistic, pluralistic and resting much more on concepts of personal religious experience and enlightenment. It is interesting that most Inter-Faith dialogue takes place between the confrontational religions rather than between those religions and those of self-communion and harmony.

There are some very deep structural and cultural drivers of violent and nonviolent behavior within all religions. Many of these triggers flow from the same dynamics that generate unpeacefulness and peacefulness in the secular realm as well. Wherever religion and power combine they tend to reproduce the maladies that bedevil all hierarchical, elitist and unequal systems.

Elise Boulding (2000), in her book *Cultures of Peace: The Hidden Side of History*, argues that one of the major sources of violence within and between religions is a clash between what she thinks of as a Holy War Culture and a Holy Peace Culture. Holy War Culture is a male warrior construct based on the exercise of power. It is characterized by a patriarchal warrior God who demands the subjection of women, children and the weak to men who she thinks of as the proto-patriarchs. Patriarchy exerts a strong influence on conflict within Hinduism, Buddhism, Judaism, Christianity and Islam.

The challenge facing those of us interested in more pacific cultures and institutions is exactly the same as those facing women seeking an end to male domination and harassment in the workplace: namely, how to articulate and re-emphasize the values of the feminine in religion and how to do this while challenging the patriarchal dominance of religious leaders.

Boulding's idea of a Holy Peace Culture was intended to provide a critical counterpoint to Holy War Culture. Holy Peace Culture seeks to elevate love as the prime mover of all behavior. In doing so, it promotes the equality of women and men and makes a radical preference for the poor, the dispossessed and the marginalized. It builds on all the nonviolent holy peace communities that exist within all the major religious traditions, e.g., the peace churches within Christianity—the Quakers, Mennonites, Brethren, etc., and similar groups within Islam (e.g., the Sufi traditions), Judaism and Buddhism.

Boulding's preference for a Holy Peace tradition faces many contemporary and historical challenges. In the first place, the Holy-Just War tradition has dominated most religious discourse and practice, and Holy Peace traditions are seen as utopian, naïve and impractical. Religious extremists or religious actors committed to harnessing their faiths to coercive capacity have all emphasized warrior rather than pacifist traditions and have been supported in this by the development of close links between sacred and secular actors. Religious values, beliefs and practices have been repeatedly invoked to legitimate patriotism, nationalism and the political status quo. Every US president, for example, feels inclined to finish off major political speeches by invoking God's blessing of America. This is not that unusual within Christianity. Religious leaders through time have all been active supporters of national wars. In the First World War, German soldiers had God with us, "Gott mit uns" in German on their belts, while British tanks and warships were blessed by priests before being sent into battle. The replacement of Holy War Culture by a Holy Peace Culture, therefore, is not an inevitability. Given the current resurgence of atavistic nationalism, reactionary populism and the election of cynical and autocratic leaders in many parts of the world, it seems even more utopian now than it did in 2000 to promote such an idea. Yet this was one of the primary motives for the workshop out of which this book has emerged.

I wanted the Tokyo group to identify and understand Holy Peace Cultures within each religious tradition; think about what might be needed to elevate these in a world of ruthless power; and figure out how to ensure that love, compassion and the values associated with these were given space to grow, nurture and sustain nonviolent alternatives, even as tribalism and nationalism seem to be reasserting themselves. My desires were not universally accepted by all participants, but the papers that were presented and are reproduced here indicate some of the positive and negative dynamics affecting the development of a more empathetic and compassionate world.

The reinforcement of cultures of peace has to be accompanied by an enlargement of what I call boundaries of compassion. Religious institutions are critical to both enterprises, and the question, therefore, is how to advance these virtuous dynamics in a largely cynical and dispirited world? Our survival as a species depends on advancing species identity and what it means to be fully human, rather than retreating into narrow xenophobic notions of national identity.

The first step in this process is for religious and other institutions to develop a rationale for how states, societies and communities might move from dominatory to collaborative power. If we are to generate a genuine paradigm shift from sovereignties based on "power over" others to those based on "power with" others, it is critical that we have value and normative systems capable of sustaining egalitarian, relatively non-coercive, integrative imaginaries. This means concentrating more attention on social rather than political sources of continuity, change, predictability and order, and it means tapping into the Holy Peace Culture while dismantling the Holy Warrior Culture.

States like to argue that social systems are dependent on their coercive capacity, without which there would be anarchy. It is important to reverse the optics on these assumptions. Social and economic relationships are, arguably, more critical to effective, capable and legitimate governance than coercive capacity. When states reveal the iron fist behind the velvet glove of enlightened governance, it is normally because their economic, social or political policies have failed and large numbers of citizens no longer believe that the state is acting in their better interest. Most political theory and politicians with authoritarian inclinations, therefore, concentrate on the state as the principle ordering agent, with coercive agency as its major weapon. It is time to focus attention on more fundamental social dynamics if we are to develop paradigms capable of doing justice to diversity and inclusive, resilient democratic polities. Religious institutions have traditionally focused a lot of their attention on what is likely to generate integration and community rather than polarization and division. This has always been considered one of the major positive functions of religion.

The second step, is to focus attention on what currently delivers unity, stability and harmony. Religious institutions that are inclusive, welcoming, altruistic and egalitarian have a crucial role to play in guaranteeing social continuity through time. The most fundamental social dynamic governing most relationships, and the DNA for peacefulness, is the norm of reciprocity. It has been systematically isolated and marginalized from the realm of the political by those who want to argue the primacy of the state, yet it is the norm of reciprocity that holds most communities and societies together through time. Without it, political systems would have to depend almost completely on their monopoly of force. Predictable social relationships are much more important than "imposed" political order. Reciprocity is the glue that governs the millions of social exchanges that take place every day, most of which have nothing to do with the realm of politics. The norm of reciprocity—sometimes known as the golden rule in theological terms—generates altruism among kin and non-kin groups; it limits selfishness and challenges freeloaders and dominators. It creates the sociological and social psychological basis for equality, integration and harmony and is capable of providing a critical frame for anti-authoritarian resistive politics. To do this effectively, however, means linking this fundamental theological and social value to what I call the politics of compassion. This is the opposite of dominatory, pathological, fear-driven, xenophobic politics based on a monopoly of force and coercion. It has the capacity to be a new political paradigm for an interdependent world. It starts with compassionate citizens, who elect compassionate politicians capable of utilizing political mechanisms for a more compassionate world. These compassionate individuals will be integrated in religious and educational systems that focus on values as much as achievement.

The politics of compassion is radical because it hinges on making social (rather than economic and political) criteria the major foci of political decision making. (e.g., by asking how religious, economic, political and military decisions will impact social wellbeing and community). It is inclusive rather than exclusive, egalitarian rather than hierarchical and it rests on sociation instead of domination. It aims at resolving problems nonviolently, collaboratively, empathetically and altruistically.

The challenge, however, is understanding and combating all the dynamics that threaten to undermine these values, e.g., possessive individualism, neo-liberalism and elite-driven politics. Compassionate citizens do not occur by accident. They need to be nurtured and rewarded. In the first instance, this might mean paying as much attention to emotional intelligence as intellectual. This is a quality that is at a distinct premium in many advanced democracies at the moment. The promotion of compassionate politics by religious institutions should reinforce positive relationships; decrease the prevalence of toxic negative emotions and behavior; increase optimism and hope; build resilience and energy levels; and counter fear-based politics.

Compassionate politics is loving kindness in action. It pays particular attention to health, education and welfare, which are key to life and societal happiness and are critical reinforcers of reciprocity. This is why welfare states have been so successful on most wellbeing indicators, even though these systems are not immune to authoritarian impulses if subject to the politics of fear.

For a new socially driven imaginary to replace tired Westphalian sovereignty-driven imaginaries, it must first, however, analyze and negate dominatory politics and practices everywhere. This means analyzing relationships of domination and subordination at the personal, social and religious as well as the formal political levels. The #metoo movement is a wonderful example of women challenging patriarchal domination, entitlement, harassment and dominant relationships in workplaces and in homes. The global struggles for the recognition of women as religious leaders is also part of this movement. It is around these kinds of movements that political respect is forged and compassionate politics become possible.

Second, there can be no compassionate politics that does not place equality and inclusion at its heart. This means a radical critique of the ways in which our own governmental and nongovernmental processes produce and reproduce patterns of hierarchy, power and privilege. But it also means giving priority to the weakest and poorest and, as mentioned above, an identification and reinforcement of individuals and groups who are willing to sustain the social fabric in the face of economic and political subversion.

Third, it means focusing on inclusive participatory processes capable of doing justice to the concrete experiences of those who are victims of domination, violence, marginalization and humiliation. This new paradigm rests on personal transformation and a willingness to live courageous, hopeful and loving lives. These are critical ingredients for speaking "truth" to power, challenging dominatory power force and coercion.

John Paul Lederach, in his book *The Moral Imagination: The Art and Soul of Building Peace* (Lederach 2010), proposes a pocket mantra to guide those interested in generating a more humane and more peaceful world. These are absolutely perfect proposals for those of us interested in promoting the politics of compassion and for ensuring that religious institutions can do justice to their Holy Peace traditions. He suggests that all human beings should learn the capacity *to reach out to those we fear*. This is vital advice in a world that seems hell-bent on moving in the opposite direction and retreating behind real and imagined walls. Second, he thinks it vital that we all start transcending simplistic dualistic thinking so that we might *touch the heart of complexity*. This is also critically important if we wish to develop more empathetic consciousness and eliminate unproductive naming and blaming of others for our own mistakes. Third, he is committed to *imagining beyond what is seen*. This quality is at the heart of what this book has been investigating. How do we (whoever the we is) develop new imaginaries suitable for the twenty-first century? Finally, he suggests that we might want to *risk vulnerability one step at a time*. This advice is eminently sensible for all of us seeking to overturn outmoded concepts of power and politics and who want religion to be a source of peacefulness in the twenty-first century. How do we quietly start replacing the old paradigms with something new—how do we ensure that the risks we take will be transformative rather than ineffective? If we wish to enhance the dignity of every single human being in the planet, it is critical that we take the first steps fully aware of their risks but emboldened by the imperative of a radical alternative to the status quo.

Kevin P. Clements

References

Boulding, E. *Cultures of Peace: The Hidden Side of History*, Syracuse, NY: Syracuse University Press, 2000.
Glock, Charles Y. and Stark, Rodney. *Religion and Society in Tension*, Chicago: Rand McNally and Company, 1965.
Kung, Hans. Project Weltethos Munich, 1992. www.global-ethic-now.de/gen-eng/0b_weltethos-und-religionen/0b-00-einleitung/0b-00-religionen.php
Lederach, John Paul. *The Moral Imagination: The Art and Soul of Building Peace*, New York: Oxford University Press, 2010.
Pratt, Douglas. *Religious Extremism*, London: Bloomsbury Press, 2017.

1

RETHINKING RELIGION AND VIOLENCE

Lester R. Kurtz

Violence moves back and forth in space, but also in time. Our rituals of violence—and moral legitimations of and objections to it—are diffused geographically and chronologically, within and across cultures and human history. At the core of our understanding of violence are the faith traditions that now mutually inhabit our life spaces. They bring with them across the millennia the moral teachings that have traveled from prehistoric humanity, embedded in the beliefs, rituals, and institutions socially constructed by humans to deal with ultimate concerns, core aspects of daily personal and social life, and life transitions.

The goal of this volume is to look at two contradictory ethical motifs—the warrior and the pacifist—across four major faith traditions—Buddhism, Judaism, Christianity, and Islam—and their role in shaping our understanding of violence and the morality of its use. Every era must wrestle with the issue of violence, but ours has a particular responsibility because our means of destruction are now god-like. For the first time, apparently, we have the ability to destroy not only our sworn enemies, but the ecosystem that sustains all life on our planet. Indeed, our struggle with violence has become not simply an individual or community concern, but an ultimate and universal one.

Buddhists have been addressing these issues for 2,500 years; they brought us together in Tokyo in spring of 2016 with generous funding from the Toda Foundation. Kevin Clements and Olivier Urbain selected and invited a group of scholars of religion and violence for an intensive session. Facilitated by Kevin Clements and Paula Green, we explored our differences and commonalities, our intellectual and personal responses and experiences with these two contradictory motifs. The chapters that follow grew out of that dialogue, combined with the years of research on this topic that the participants brought to the table.

A key feature of our understanding of violence is the idea of the ambivalence embedded in these motifs: humans tend to condemn and condone it at the same time, often using violence as a means for combating violence or punishing those who use it, as in incarcerating or executing criminals or military retaliations against invasions. This bi-valent—simultaneously positive and negative—attitude toward violence requires a distinction between good and bad violence, the legitimate and illegitimate. Those who choose violence, as does the warrior, are required to provide accounts for it, to others but also to themselves (see Bandura 1999).

That is where religious traditions enter the picture—the beliefs, rituals, and institutions of the faith traditions become major arbiters, either directly or indirectly, in the process of determining the ethical status of the decision to go to war and specific acts of war. What are the criteria for the "just" use of warfare and violence, and what are the taboos around its use?

As I argue in the final chapter of this book, both warrior and pacifist motifs and paths of action present serious dilemmas. The warrior is faced with taboos against killing that run through the world's ethical traditions, and what appear to be some inherent tendencies among humans (and other animal species) to avoid killing their own (Grossman and Siddle 2008). The clearest evidence of this dilemma is the phenomenon now identified as Post-Traumatic Stress Disorder (PTSD) or, more precisely, Perpetrator-Induced Traumatic Stress (PITS; see MacNair 2002, forthcoming).

Gandhi tries to address these dilemmas by paradoxically combining the warrior and the pacifist in the nonviolent activist, who fights like the warrior but—like the pacifist—avoids harming.

Religion and Conflict[1]

A primary feature of religion's role in a conflict is that it can intensify adversarial dynamics and lead to violence . . . or committed, radical nonviolence. In both cases, people are willing to sacrifice themselves—and others—when participants turn to violence. As Georg Simmel notes, the intensity of religious conflict is related to the fact that the parties to the dispute view themselves as

> representatives of supraindividual claims, of fighting not for themselves but only for a cause, [which] can give the conflict a radicalism and mercilessness which find their analogy in the general behavior of certain very selfless and very idealistically inclined persons. Because they have no consideration for themselves, they have none for others either; they are convinced that they are entitled to make anybody a victim of the idea for which they sacrifice themselves.
>
> *(Simmel 1971: 87)*

All conflict is relational, whether carried out by violent or nonviolent means; as Simmel (1971; cf. Kurtz 2005) notes, conflict is an intense form of interaction that often brings people together, even when the valence of the relationship is negative.

Sheldon Ekland-Olson (2012, 336) observes that there is a "paradox of community in which the ties that bind us together become the ties that keep us apart."

Religion is often the content of a conflict, though not its basis (Kurtz 2005). The conflict may be political, economic, class-based, familial, or even psychological, but religious issues become the content around which the conflict evolves and how it is articulated by the partisans. When fighting breaks out between Protestants and Catholics in Northern Ireland, or Hindus and Muslims in India, the conflict is as much economic as religious, even when it is framed by the media, politicians, or participants as religious. Conflicting parties and the media that report on them need an issue on which to focus their disagreement, especially if it is diffuse, complex, or particularly self-serving. Religion often provides potent content for battles, because it acts as a catalyst and can therefore change the properties of social forms, such as relationships. Moreover, if the cause is sacred—rather than self-interested or profane—it is easier to justify violence against the adversary or self-sacrifice in nonviolent resistance. Religious symbols become a lightning rod for conflict, as the 2017 burning cross of the KKK has in Charlottesville, Virginia.

Sometimes conflicts are truly religious, even when they contain other elements, and the conflict itself is sacralized. These conflicts often appear intractable, because adversaries invest so much of themselves and their identity in the conflict itself and its outcome that they will risk everything to perpetuate or escalate it until they win or lose. Religious controversy shares many characteristics with conflict in general, but has its own uniquenesses. First, because it deals with "unrestricted values" (Cavanagh 2009) or "ultimate concerns" (Tillich 1957), it is charged with great passion and meaning, and takes place on an abstract level. Second, religious conflicts are carriers and concealers of other forms of conflict. Sacred conflicts are likely to be extremely passionate, and are ironically those most likely to be carried out for profane purposes. It is not just the most holy causes that provoke religious conflict: the intensity of reaction provoked by a truly dastardly deed means that the act requires an exceptional account. Evil deeds therefore require sacred legitimation if the perpetrator is to avoid punishment or self-sanctioning (Bandura 1999; Kurtz 2005).

The more visible religious conflicts—or conflicts carried by religion—often recruit warriors committed to using violence to carry them out, but the same is true of nonviolent conflicts and even pacifism, both of which require a commitment that has religious characteristics even when not represented in the traditional language and rituals of a faith tradition. A Mohandas K. Gandhi, Martin Luther King, Jr., or Dorothy Day have an intense commitment to action and self-sacrifice that rivals that of any warrior. Long-term nonviolent campaigns are often sustained between major public events like mass demonstrations, strikes, and boycotts, by people of faith who work from a long-term, sometimes even "otherworldly" perspective, and their discipline and energy are motivated by their belief in a higher power, which often gives the conflict staying power.

The Plan

In the chapters that follow, we journey through the four major faith traditions of Buddhism, Judaism, Christianity, and Islam, then explore some trans-tradition approaches to peacebuilding and interfaith dialog. In my concluding chapter I draw upon the other contributions and fold them into my own research on this topic, which focuses on Gandhi's efforts to address the warrior-pacifist dilemmas. Collectively, we hope to make a contribution to our understanding of this tension between the warrior and the pacifist with and across the traditions that we have now all inherited and that exist in the space we collectively inhabit.

We begin with Buddhism, generally perceived as the most peaceful of these traditions. The Buddha seems quite clear in his condemnation of violence, even hatred. In verse 5 of the Dhammapada, the Buddha says, "Hatred does not cease through hatred at any time. Hatred ceases through love. This is an unalterable law" (see Bodhipaksa 2015 for a discussion of its various translations).

Iselin Frydenlund challenges that common perception of Buddhism as pacifism, however, in her chapter, "Buddhism and Violence: An Oxymoron?" At times—especially when the community itself is threatened—even the Buddha appears to sanction violence in self-defense, a contradiction of his apparent pacifism that subsequent Buddhists have singled out to justify their use of violence. Frydenlund begins with monastic support for state violence in the Sri Lankan civil war, and then explores both canonical and traditional sources regarding the use of force in public affairs. She concludes that nonviolence is crucial in the tradition, especially for self-understanding, but that Buddhist ethics is particularistic and there is no systematized treatment of whether and when force and war are justified. Instead, various narratives in the Buddhist canon and literature play a crucial role as "discursive sites" where the use of force is often discussed as a necessary evil and the nonviolent state is only an ideal.

The other two chapters on the Buddhist tradition are more concerned with how contemporary Buddhists are addressing the causes of violence through a movement of "Engaged Buddhism." Paula Green's "Visions, Vitality, and Values of an Emerging Practice" provides an overview of that movement and how it places greater emphasis on the social implications of a tradition that has focused more on individual spirituality. She discusses its history and some key figures, noting how they emphasize the social implications of the Buddha's teachings, and the role of such practices as meditation, mindfulness, sharing of authority, and reflective thinking in addressing problems of violence. In "Aspects of Social Engagement Within the Southeast Asian Buddhist World," Jordan Baskerville and Somboon Chungprampree focus especially the part of that movement in which they are themselves involved. (Chungprampree serves as executive director of the International Society of Engaged Buddhists). The INEB attempts to apply the teachings of the Buddha on "overcoming suffering through the cultivation of ethics, wisdom and compassion" (Baskerville and Chungprampree) in the contemporary world, sometimes very concretely, as with the creation of the International Forum on Buddhist-Muslim Relations, which has a website at www.facebook.com/buddhistmuslimforum.

All three chapters on the Jewish tradition explore what Tirzah Firestone calls its "intertwining threads" of war and peace over a 4,000-year history. Stories of retribution and injunctions to conquer, annihilate, and kill in self-defense exist side by side with the principle that life must be saved at all costs. Murder is forbidden because humans are created in the Divine image, an idea that "provides the foundation for human rights and social justice within Western civilization." Paul Scham identifies the uniqueness of Jewish thought on these issues, since it was purely theoretical during most of its long history, laying the groundwork for its spiritual descendants, Christianity and Islam. Noam Zion explores the complicated efforts to apply that abstract tradition in the real world, with the Israeli Defense Force's (IDF) mixed effort to set limits on the use of force. The IDF uses the term "purity of arms" in an honor code designed to set legal limits on the use of force by Israeli soldiers in "ambiguous and dangerous field conditions." Rather than evaluate how effectively this code works in practice, he explores the ways in which soldiers are given "non-militaristic virtue education" designed to cultivate a "warrior ethos that teaches compassion rather than vengeance."

Nigel Biggar explores a similar idea in Christianity, with centuries-long efforts to set boundaries on the use of violence with a "just war" tradition that specifies when and how violence might be employed. He develops a carefully documented critique of the idea of Jesus as a pacifist by analyzing a major advocate of that position, Richard Hays (1996), and his book *The Moral Vision of the New Testament*. Biggar concludes that "the New Testament does not bear Richard Hays' pacifist reading" and that "Christian opinion and practice in the early church were divided at least from the end of the second century." The church does not go as far as the Israeli Defense Force's "purity of arms," however; Biggar contends that "Christian just warriors agree with their pacifist *confreres* that vengeance is not a proper motive for fighting" and that "the idea of a morally pure war" is not what the Christian "just war" doctrine means.

In order to round out the picture of Christianity in the volume, we have added a chapter from a different genre and by an author not attending our Tokyo gathering, but a piece most relevant to the task of this volume: Pope Francis's message on World Peace Day, New Year's Day, 2017. Although he ties his message firmly to previous papal and official pronouncements, he takes on not only war, as previous popes have done, but violence itself, and provides some good sociological analysis of what he calls "a horrifying world war fought piecemeal." Moreover, he contends,

> we know that this "piecemeal" violence, of different kinds and levels, causes great suffering: wars in different countries and continents; terrorism, organized

crime and unforeseen acts of violence; the abuses suffered by migrants and victims of human trafficking; and the devastation of the environment.

What is the solution? It is not more violence, the pontiff declares: "Violence is not the cure for our broken world. Countering violence with violence leads at best to forced migrations and enormous suffering." That path leads to "death, physical and spiritual, of many people, if not all."

Instead, Pope Francis insists, the answers to the problem of violence lie with active nonviolence, which he finds consistent with the teachings of Jesus. "To be true followers of Jesus today also includes embracing his teaching about nonviolence," he says, including the love of enemies, which is the nucleus of the Christian revolution, citing his predecessor Pope Benedict. Pope Francis does not mince words: "Violence profanes the name of God."

Joseph Camilleri's "Christianity and Islam in an Age of Transition: Violence or Healing" bridges our exploration of Christianity with that of Islam, situating the high-stake issue of the role of religion in a context of profound transition, one characterized by the "globalisation of insecurity" (Camilleri and Falk 2009). In addressing such questions as "Can it help to establish the normative foundations for a peaceful and ecologically sustainable world order?," he compares two core traditions in this quest: Christianity and Islam. Camilleri observes that "the most serious shortcoming of just war principles is their elusiveness. They don't easily translate into a coherent course of action either for the individual or the polity," and notes that the two traditions share many of the same ambiguities. Mainstream Christianity has ample examples of the condemnation of warfare, however, and despite the acceptability of force under strict circumstances in Islam, "the weight of Islamic scholarship across the different jurisprudential schools portrays Islam as a religion deeply committed to justice and peace."

All three chapters focusing on the Islamic tradition emphasize the peaceful and nonviolent possibilities of Islam, without ignoring obstacles and misunderstandings surrounding the tradition. Two of the authors are veterans of what we might call the "Islam as nonviolent" school; the third is an eloquent newcomer to the scholarly literature. Afra Jalabi, a native Arab speaker, suggests that

> the word Islam, often mistranslated as "submission," could more accurately be translated as peace-activation or peace-making, since it is a verb noun referring to the active moving or spreading of peace. In contrast, the word for submission, which in Arabic is *Isstislam*, which is a state of peacefulness that has been imposed externally.

A Muslim, however, is "an active peacemaker;" to be a Muslim "in the pure grammatical sense, is to be an active agent of peace," which is why "nonviolence is a central teaching in the Quranic text as well as compatible to Muhammad's own conduct." In her chapter, Jabali then focuses "on some nonviolent possibilities often hidden in the buried trenches of our victorious religious histories and narratives." We all "tend to exoticize others while redeeming our own cultural and religious practices," so that paradoxically "we are the same in rejecting our sameness." All four traditions in this volume are, she claims, "about breaking free from attachments," and offer "liberation from false beliefs."

In the Qur'an, according to Jabala, the message goes back to the creation story, when the angels had two central concerns about the new creation of humanity: corruption and bloodshed. Indeed, shortly thereafter in the narrative, the two sons of Eve and Adam engage in a conflict that leads to bloodshed. But already here the lesson of nonviolence shines through the tragedy: it is Abel who shows courage in the conflict, and devotion to God, refusing to raise his hand against his brother even in self-defense. His brother gives way to the path of violence and becomes humanity's first criminal. "Abel's voice in the Quran is the voice of all those who actively choose peacefulness even when threatened."

Mohammed Abu-Nimer explores "Islamic Approaches to Nonviolence and Peacebuilding: A Critical Examination," identifying the religious foundations for nonviolent action but also the difficult context within which the Muslim community exists, rife with Islamophobia, media misrepresentations of the tradition, and different schools of interpretation. Some studies represent an "offensive Islam" that is inherently violent; others see a "defensive Islam" that allows for the use of force under certain strict conditions to defend the faith and justice. A third, less studied but now emerging approach "reinterprets Islamic teaching" by emphasizing the values of peace, the unity of humankind, nonviolence, justice, patience, and the sacredness of human life. Abu-Nimer also frankly addresses the challenges that the third approach faces, both internal and external to the tradition, from authoritarian political systems to cooptation of religious leaders by the government, widespread corruption, and patriarchal and hierarchical social structures that limit participation. Moreover, the residues of colonial domination and a widespread belief that peace is a tool for cooptation and nonviolence a form of passivity in the face of injustice inhibit many from seeing the religious foundations and political effectiveness of nonviolent action to address their grievances.

Chaiwat Satha-Anand is no stranger to the issues we are wrestling with in this volume, having written and taught about them—as well as acted on them—for decades. He jumps right to the heart of the matter in the contemporary context by confronting terrorism from a Muslim scholar's point of view. He suggests that "terrorism, seen as a form of political violence, grounded in its own reasons yet producing destructive results to all concerned, needs to be transformed into more productive/creative conflicts with Muslims' nonviolent alternatives." When he looks at how terrorism works, rather than what it is, he finds that the similarities between that path and "principled nonviolence" are in many ways similar (beyond their obvious differences), which is what makes the transformation possible. Both approaches agree on fighting injustice and the willingness to die for a just cause. The obstacles that remain, however, are the absence of innocents for terrorists and the instrumental logic governing terrorism. In exploring how Abdul Ghafar Khan fought British colonialism from a position of Muslim nonviolence, Satha-Anand demonstrates how Islam can fight against injustice while allowing the opponents to remain distinctively human, instead of turning humans into objects like acts of terror do, which he claims contradicts the Islamic worldview.

The final section of this volume moves beyond the analysis of specific faith traditions and addresses interfaith and trans-faith perspectives, from Jehan Perera's discussion of interfaith peacebuilding in Sri Lanka to Lisa Schirch's work on interfaith dialog, both examples of concrete actionable alternatives that go beyond debates about the meaning of scriptures, traditions' histories, and contemporary dilemmas. In these chapters, people of faith are acting to construct a peaceful world.

In Sri Lanka, in the midst of a long and destructive civil war when the government restricted space for action in civil society, district level interreligious committees (DIRCs) played a major role in addressing community level conflicts and building up trust across the barriers that the civil war had erected in the nation. Buddhists, Hindus, Muslims, and Christians came together with a focus on problem-solving actions, made possible in part because of the status of religious clergy in Sri Lankan society as moral arbiters, especially at the community level. After the war, facing a legacy of human rights violations, war crimes, and severe inequalities in economic and political resources, religious organizations worked to mitigate divisions and promote peace, despite the politicization of religion that had taken place during the war. Perera offers accounts of specific interfaith projects that facilitated the post-war healing process and discussed the interfaith role in building consensus for the government's transitional justice and reconciliation process.

Lisa Schirch, who has worked as an interreligious dialog facilitator and participant in dozens of countries worldwide, brings her expertise to the question of how faith communities can come together safely to share their traditions and come to understandings that result in the kind of collaboration that Perera describes in Sri Lanka. In her chapter, she summarizes the lessons from her experience and her own publications in the area (Schirch 2004, 2005). She explores the structure and common models of interreligious dialog, noting that they often include "a sharing of experience, confession and repentance of wrongdoing, as well as acts to symbolize forgiveness and reconciliation." She paints the landscape of such dialogs, highlighting key elements and discussing their varied outcomes, which can include improved understanding, reduced antagonism, or collaborative actions.

In the final chapter, I draw upon many of the insights from these other contributions and add them to my own efforts to understand the role of faith traditions in promoting or mitigating violence. As I alluded to earlier, my own insights are largely a result of studying Gandhi, and the legacy he left in his wake, as nonviolent activists—many rooted in faith traditions—attempted to address the contradictory dilemmas of the warrior and the pacifist by engaging in nonviolent activism. It is not simply a matter of organizing protest demonstrations or even civil disobedience against injustice, but of going deeper—as the faith traditions themselves have—to construct nonviolent social structures, peaceful cultures, and sustainable ecologies. Although often the source of the most brutal violence, the faith traditions—acting together in this time of crisis—can construct a way out that leads to a better future or, as Dr. King put it, one of community rather than chaos.

Note

1 For a more thorough discussion of these issues, see Kurtz (2005), on which this discussion draws heavily, excerpted by permission from the journal *Ahimsa Nonviolence*.

References

Bandura, Albert. "Moral Disengagement in the Perpetration of Inhumanities." *Personality and Social Psychology Review* 3, no. 3 (1999): 193–209.
Bodhipaksa, Author. "Hatred Does Not Cease Through Hatred at Any Time: Hatred Ceases Through Love. This Is an Unalterable Law." *Fake Buddha Quotes*, April 13, 2015. http://fakebuddhaquotes.com/hatred-does-not-cease-through-hatred-at-any-time-hatred-ceases-through-love-this-is-an-unalterable-law/.
Camilleri, Joseph A., and Jim Falk. *Worlds in Transition: Evolving Governance Across a Stressed Planet*. Cheltenham; Northampton, MA: Edward Elgar, 2009.
Cavanaugh, William T. *The Myth of Religious Violence: Secular Ideology and the Roots of Modern Conflict*. Oxford; New York: Oxford University Press, 2009.
Ekland-Olson, Sheldon. *Who Lives, Who Dies, Who Decides? Abortion, Neonatal Care, Assisted Dying, and Capital Punishment*. London: Routledge, 2012.
Grossman, Dave, and B. K Siddle. "Psychological Effects of Combat." In *Encyclopedia of Violence, Peace, and Conflict*, edited by Lester R. Kurtz, 3: 139–149. Amsterdam: Elsevier, 2008.
Hays, Richard B. *The Moral Vision of the New Testament: Community, Cross, New Creation, A Contemporary Introduction to New Testament Ethics*. 1st edition. San Francisco: HarperOne, 1996.
Kurtz, Lester R. "From Heresies to Holy Wars: Toward a Theory of Religious Conflict." *Ahimsa Nonviolence* 1 (2005): 143–157.
MacNair, Rachel. *Perpetration-Induced Traumatic Stress: The Psychological Consequences of Killing*. West Port, CA: Praeger Publishers, 2002.
MacNair, Rachel. "The Psychology of Agents of Repression: The Paradox of Defection." In *The Paradox of Repression and Its Management*, eds. Lester R. Kurtz and Lee Smithey. Syracuse, NY: Syracuse University Press, 2018, pp. 74–101.
Schirch, Lisa. *Little Book of Strategic Peacebuilding*. Intercourse, PA: Good Books, 2004.
Schirch, Lisa. *Ritual and Symbol in Peacebuilding*. Connecticut: Kumarian Press, 2005.
Simmel, Georg. *Georg Simmel on Individuality and Social Forms*. Edited by Donald N. Levine. University of Chicago Press, 1971.
Tillich, Paul. *Dynamics of Faith*. New York: Harper & Row, 1957.

PART I
The Buddhist Tradition

2

BUDDHISM AND VIOLENCE: AN OXYMORON?

Text and Tradition in Buddhist Just-War Thinking

Iselin Frydenlund

Buddhist Monks and the Sri Lankan Civil War

In April 2009, only three weeks before the fall of the Tamil insurgency group Liberation Tigers of Tamil Eelam (LTTE) in Sri Lanka, Buddhist monks belonging to a Sinhala Buddhist nationalist party called the Jathika Hela Urumaya (JHU) staged a demonstration outside the offices of the British High Commissioner in Colombo. At this point, the army was engaged in a full-scale war, and a population of more than 250,000 Tamil civilians (mostly Hindu and Catholics) was trapped within an area of 250km² area in the northern parts of the island. The civilians faced intense fighting and lacked food, water, sanitation and health care. The Buddhist monks outside the British High Commissioner staged their protest, not against the war activities of the State, but against a visit by the British Foreign Secretary and the French Foreign Minister to discuss the humanitarian situation in northern Sri Lanka and push for a ceasefire.[1] The monks resented what they saw as unduly foreign intervention in the country's internal affairs. Moreover, they expressed their support to the army's military efforts against the LTTE and asked the government to 'continue the protection of the motherland'. While these Buddhist monks belong to a particularly pro-Sinhala section of the Buddhist monastic order (Sangha), support for a military solution to Sri Lanka's 'terrorist' problem was common among Buddhist monks and Buddhist lay people alike. In fact, pacifism—here defined as no-warism—was only favoured by a small minority of Sri Lanka's Buddhist monks (Frydenlund 2005). Rather, the great majority of the monks deemed the use of state force as legitimate in order to secure the integrity of the state, as well as to protect Buddhism on the island. Support for the military effort was expressed through formal politics (as seen in JHU's support of the Rajapaksa government), but also through a myriad of activities carried out outside of formal politics, like the many demonstrations outside of the Norwegian embassy in Colombo against the Norwegian-facilitated peace process (2000–2008). Furthermore, sections of the Sangha contributed moral support to the Sri Lankan Armed Forces—and its pre-dominantly Buddhist military personnel—through various forms of ritual interaction, serving as 'military chaplains' or actively recruiting soldiers, even though the latter was considered controversial by 'mainstream' monks (Kent 2010; Frydenlund 2017a and 2017b). In short, although to a varying degree, the Buddhist monastic order in Sri Lanka opted for a military solution to the ethnic conflict on the island.

Thus, empirical material from the Sri Lankan civil war (see, e.g. Tambiah 1992; Bartholomeusz 2002; Frydenlund 2005, 2013; Kent 2010; Degalle 2013), together with similar material from Thailand (see, e.g. Jerryson 2009; Satha-Anand 2013), leaves the question of 'Buddhist militarism' in Theravāda Buddhism an intriguing puzzle.[2] In this chapter, I wish to move beyond ethnographic material that empirically demonstrates Buddhist justifications for war, including the many intersections between military structures and organized Buddhism, and ask questions about how we are to *theorize* about Buddhist militarism and just-war ideology. As the Sri Lankan case clearly demonstrates, Buddhist just-war ideology certainly exists, but the burning question is how to locate this ideology within Buddhist textual and historical traditions. Is the contemporary scene a historical exception due to modern nationalism and wartime radicalization, or can we discern a wider historical pattern that would justify the use of the term 'Buddhist just-war tradition'? If so, how would such 'tradition' relate to canonical texts?

The Construction of Buddhism as Pacifist

In spite of an increasing bulk of research that investigates 'Buddhist violence', we are still represented with the simplistic view that Buddhism is, or at least *should* be, pacifist.[3] Surprisingly, many academic introductions to Buddhism, as well as volumes on comparative ethics of war, still uncritically reproduce the view that 'true' Buddhism is pacifist. Take, for example, the entry on 'War and Peace' in the *Encyclopedia of Buddhism*, where Damian Keown (2010, 812) writes that

> Buddhist teachings strongly oppose the use of violence, analyzing it in psychological terms as the product of greed (*rāga*), hatred (*dveśa*) and delusion (*moha*). . . . The pacifist ideal of the classical sources has not prevented Buddhists from fighting battles and conducting military campaigns from a mixture of political and religious motives.

According to Keown, Buddhist violence is the result of a tension between precept and practice, but he offers no explanation as to how his notion of 'pacifist' would actually correspond to assumed similar ideas in the classical sources, or how Buddhists have rationalized—and still rationalize—the use of armed force. Along similar lines, the scholar-monk Ven. Mahinda Deegalle argues in *Religion, War, and Ethics: A Sourcebook of Textual Traditions* (2014, 544) that

> Buddhism is rather well known for its explicit and uncompromising pacifist foundations with regard to warfare . . . When Buddhist communities have been drawn or forced into warfare, their engagement in the battlefield has drawn the attention of scholars concerned with the pacifist foundations of Buddhist doctrines and its celebration of the ideals of nonviolence.

Similarly to Keown, Ven. Deegalle asserts the 'uncompromising pacifist foundations' of Buddhism, but without any further analysis of what pacifism could have meant in early Buddhism, or to what extent 'pacifism' is at all the right term for a discussion of nonviolence in Buddhism. Moreover, Ven. Deegalle argues that historically, Buddhists have only been 'drawn' or 'forced' into war, implying that Buddhists have not engaged in aggressive warfare. Such a statement ignores the many expansionist wars between Thai and Burmese kings, between Arakanese and Burmese Buddhist kings or between Sinhala Buddhist kings (to name but a few), glossing over—not illuminating—tensions and ambiguities when it comes to Buddhist warfare.

Another academic tradition I believe has contributed in significant ways to the prevalent perception of Buddhism as pacifist is in fact peace and conflict studies. One of the leading figures within peace research—and the co-founder of the International Peace Research Institute, Oslo (PRIO)—is Johan Galtung (1930–). An explicit interest in Buddhism clearly emerges in his writings from the 1980s onwards, when titles such as 'Peace and Buddhism', 'The Role of Buddhism in the Creation of Peace' and 'Buddhism: A Quest for Unity and Peace' begin to appear (see PRIO report 1980). In these works, Galtung clearly regards Buddhism as the most valuable source for world peace. Moreover, in his introductory work to peace and conflict studies, *Peace by Peaceful Means: Peace and Conflict, Development and Civilization*, Galtung (1996) applies the Buddhist concepts of the Four Noble Truths and the Eightfold Path. As far as I can see, Galtung does not critically engage in discussions about the place of violence and militarism within Buddhism, but has introduced Buddhist concepts to peace and conflict studies, and to peace activism in general, as tools for world peace. Thus, Buddhist notions of nonviolence have been used in a specific political environment in postwar Europe, and subsequently contributed to the perception of Buddhism as a *pacifist* religion.

'Degeneration Theory': From 'Ethical' to 'Political' Buddhism

The discourse of Buddhism-cum-pacifism is also the normative position in the Sri Lankan debate, and violence is generally regarded as un-Buddhist. For example, leading monks such as the late Ven. Madhie Pannasiha (1985, 6) have argued that 'Buddhism, more than any other religion, has indeed contributed most towards world peace. It is the teaching of tolerance and love'. According to highly respected Buddhist scholar P.D. Premasiri, nonviolence is one of the core virtues in Buddhism, and the ultimate goal of Buddhism is to overcome conflict in the consciousness of the individual. Moreover, in line with the psychologizing tendency within Buddhist philosophy and ethics, conflicts at both the mental and the social level are traced to psychological causes. Consequently, wars originate in the minds of people. Moreover, as conflict is regarded as the result of an unenlightened response to one's sensory environment, Premasiri (2006, 81) holds that 'there could not be a righteous war from the Buddhist point of view'. However, he also points out that there are different degrees of moral development within any Buddhist community, and that ordinary lay Buddhists are involved in the pursuit of pleasures of the senses (*kāma*). This pursuit of *kāma* is seen as the immediate psychological cause of conflict. As most people are attached to their possessions, Buddhism 'considers conflict as an unavoidable evil in society' (Premasiri 2006, 82). Nonetheless, Premasiri concludes, the ultimate religious goal of *nibbāna* is antithetical to acts of violence.

A similar view is held by the Sri Lankan scholar-monk Mahinda Deegalle (2001, 2), who argues that 'Buddhist teachings maintain that under any circumstance, whether it is political, religious, cultural or ethnic, violence cannot be accepted or advocated in solving disputes among nations'. Based on narratives that emphasize loving, kindness and compassion in a violent world, Ven. Deegalle rejects the suggestion that Buddhism can be a source for just-war ideology. In this view, the true pacifism of Buddhism is unquestionable, and violence committed in Buddhist societies is due to violations of the norm of nonviolence. Ven. Deegalle (2001, 2) holds that 'whatever violence found in the so-called Buddhist societies is merely a deviation from the doctrine of the Buddha and a misinterpretation of Buddha's valuable message'. This is based on the interpretation that 'the Pali canon of Theravada Buddhists completely lacks any textual resource that could be used as the basis for developing a just war theory' (Deegalle 2009, 75). The famous anthropologist Gananath Obeysekere (1992, 158) also questions the Buddhist identity of those who advocate violence, holding that such arguments represent a 'perversion of Buddhism' and a rejection by those who make them of their 'Buddhist heritage'. Later, he even calls for a 'fundamentalist turn'—that is, a return to the original scriptures, to find the perceived original truth of nonviolence (Obeyesekere 1995, 254). Thus, a distinction is made between the Buddhist doctrinal tradition and Buddhist history, where violence committed in Buddhist Sri Lanka is explained as a result of the growth of ethno-nationalism so that 'the substantially soteriological, ethical, and normative components of doctrinal Buddhism qua religion were weakened, displaced, even distorted' (Tambiah 1992, 58). In this separation between 'ethical' and 'political' Buddhism, doctrinal Buddhism remains a religion of absolute nonviolence.

These strong condemnations during the civil war must, I suggest, be understood as a particular *normative* positioning whereby Sri Lankan intellectuals sought to challenge militant Sinhala nationalism. In the context of the civil war, they draw upon the abundant sources in the Pāli canon that advocate nonviolence. However, while I acknowledge that the direct encouragement of the use of violence for a just cause seems to be absent in the Pāli canon, I do find the distinction between Buddhist soteriology/doctrinal Buddhism and Buddhist history problematic in this regard, simply because the texts that are considered key elements of doctrinal Buddhism are not self-contained in terms of meaning: their interpretation is always a product of history. In Sri Lanka, the same texts (e.g. the *Cakkavattisīhanāda Sutta*) have given rise to both pacifist and just-war interpretations. Thus, what I call the 'degeneration theory' is profoundly essentialist and reductionist. It ascribes certain meanings to texts in the Pāli canon, leaving little room for different textual interpretations. In my view, radical readings of Buddhist doctrine, like those presented below, cannot simply be explained away as 'un-Buddhist'. The rhetoric of what represents 'true' religion or not belongs to the normative (or *emic*) level, and it is not the task for comparative just-war scholars to judge leading Buddhist monks in Sri Lanka as not representing 'true Buddhism' because they supported state military action.

Buddhism and Comparative Just-War Ethics

In recent years, the scope of the comparative ethics of war has moved beyond the Abrahamic religions and been widened to include Asian civilizations as well (see e.g. Robinson 2003; Brekke 2006; Popovski, Reichberg and Turner 2009). Relevant works discuss the extent to which notions of *jus ad bellum* and *jus in bello* can be identified in the various religious traditions around the world. Apart from providing cross-cultural analysis, several of the contributions in this literature aim to find resources within each tradition that can provide moral restraints of war.[4] Applying Christian and Western-based vocabulary to Buddhism gives rise to serious challenges, and it is not clear to what extent Western concepts can be legitimately used to understand the nature of Buddhist ethics. For example, and as I argue in more detail later, Buddhist ethics is largely psychological in nature, and deals with the social realm to a far lesser degree than do Christian, Judaic, Islamic or Hindu ethics. Also, comparative just-war ethics may seem far more problematic with regard to Buddhism compared to other world religions, since Buddhist canonical texts are believed to advocate pacifism. As I will discuss in length in this chapter, the view that canonical texts advocate pacifism is widely held by Buddhists as well as by scholars of Buddhism, but it is my contention that this 'discourse of nonviolence' ignores ambiguities concerning violence in the canon.

The field of Buddhist ethics is vast and complex, and it is not possible to give a detailed survey of it here. The Pāli term closest to *ethics* is *sīla*, which is translated as 'morality'. *Sīla* is considered to be a vital prerequisite for meditation, wisdom and enlightenment, and therefore plays an important role in Buddhist soteriology. Although the expression *ethics* is an *etic* term foreign to Pāli Buddhism, it is now applied and regarded as a useful analytical category within Buddhist studies.[5] Efforts have been made by various scholars to conceptualize Buddhist ethics in terms of the Western ethical vocabulary as either consequentialist (actions are bad because they bring an undesired end); intentionalist (it is the intention behind a certain act that is decisive for its moral status);[6] utilitarian (meaning that the moral worth of an action is determined by its outcome); deontological (according to which the consequences of an act are not a determinant of its moral worth); or as virtue ethics (with emphasis on the moral character of the agent). Broadly speaking, Buddhist studies scholars are divided into two camps when it comes to the nature of Buddhist ethics: on the one hand, scholars such as Damien Keown (2013) hold a 'meta-theoretical position', claiming to identify an underlying moral theory of Buddhist ethics. On the other hand, scholars such as Charles Hallisey (1996, 34) argue that there is no 'moral theory underlying or structuring Buddhist ethics, one which, once identified, would provide a global justification for the specific parts of Buddhist ethics'. This discussion on ethical theory is of importance to the question of the very possibility of a 'Buddhist just-war tradition': if one adopts Keown's position, Buddhism and violence would necessarily become an oxymoron. Particularism, on the other hand, opens up analysing militarism from *within* Buddhism itself, as one legitimate possibility among many.

As the Buddhist textual material analysed in this chapter will show, it seems plausible to side with Hallisey and to emphasize the fact that like other 'world religions', Buddhism is diverse, and that Buddhists have at all times resorted to more than one kind of moral theory. Therefore, the quest to categorize Buddhist ethics as belonging to one or other of the families of ethical theories is futile. Following this line of thought, Buddhist ethics are best understood as a kind of 'ethical particularism', which implies no underlying moral theory, but rather different *prima facie* duties that can be overridden if the context allows. The particularist position is, among other things, justified with reference to the role played by narratives for conveying ethics.[7] Stories provide us with knowledge analogous to personal experience, and they make us sensitive to the *context* within which a choice for action has to be made. This theoretical framework informed the late Tessa J. Bartholomeusz (2002) in her book *In Defense of Dharma*. This was the first academic work on Sri Lankan Buddhism that applied the framework of comparative just-war ethics to discussions on the role of Buddhism in the Sri Lankan civil war. Her work brings to our attention the ways in which Buddhist narratives that allow for war are resorted to, identifying the development of a 'Buddhist just-war ideology' during the civil war. This context-sensitive position goes against Kantian ethics, showing that moral decisions are not made in a vacuum; it is 'not an ahistorical activity of the rational mind', to borrow the words of James Turner Johnson (1981, x).[8] Both history and context inform moral values in Buddhist societies in relation to military action, and Bartholomeusz showed us an array of possible positions along the pacifism–just-war continuum during Sri Lanka's civil war. Yet, exactly how this just-war ideology stands in relation to Buddhist texts and traditions needs further analysis.

In general, we can say that compared to Islamic jurisprudence, Christian just-war theory or the Hindu manuals of statecraft, Buddhist cultures across Asia have no *systematized* tradition of ideas or practices in relation to the use of military force. There are canonical accounts—for example, in the *Umagga Jātaka*—that emphasize that the righteous party in a war should not resort to unnecessary acts of violence and that the innocent should not be harmed (Premasiri 2006), which resemble the Christian notions of *jus in bello*. Yet there are few systematic treatments about the justified use of force, or *jus ad bellum*. Rather, Buddhist ideas about the justified use of force are conveyed through canonical and post-canonical narratives, in addition to the interpretation of history, but it does not constitute a theoretical field of its own. This fragmentation makes it reasonable to argue that we cannot speak of a just-war tradition in a way similar to Western religions. Exactly for this reason, in practise, Buddhist kings in Sri Lanka often resorted to the Hindu manuals of law (*dharmaśāstra*).

On a brief comparative note, it is worth mentioning that the most explicit examples of Buddhist justification for violence are found in the Mahāyāna tradition(s), where compassionate murder can be justified from a doctrinal position, with some texts describing *bodhisattvas* killing persons who were about to commit serious crimes, most notably the *Upāyakauśalya Sūtra*. By being killed before the wrongful act is carried out, the potential wrongdoer is saved by the *bodhisattva* from going to hell. As the *bodhisattva* kills out of compassion, she or he will not suffer the karmic effects of that act, but rather acquire merit.[9] The doctrinal position that justifies this is the particular Mahāyāna doctrine of skilful means (*upāya-kauśalya*), which implies that spiritually advanced beings, such as the *bodhisattvas*, may in some cases break the precepts out of compassion. Historically, this tradition has been used to justify killings, as for example in the case of the assassination of the Tibetan king Glang-dar-ma by a Buddhist monk in 842, an event still celebrated in monasteries in the so-called Black-Hat Dance (Kværne 1984). Also, the Mahayāna notion of the emptiness of reality (*sunyatā*) has been used to justify violence from a Buddhist perspective by arguing that neither the killed or the killer in reality exist (Victoria 1997).

Examples of compassionate murder with reference to Theravāda doctrines are harder to find, probably owing to the fact that the Therāvada tradition did not accept the Mahāyāna interpretation of skilful means. Therefore, transgression of the precept of nonviolence has been justified in a somewhat different manner. For example, in Thailand in the 1970s the Buddhist monk Kitthiwuttho argued, with reference to scriptures, that soldiers who killed communists gained 'more merit for protecting the nation, the religion and the king than demerit from taking life' (Swearer 1999, 214). This position, no matter how controversial it might look today, expresses an *ethical* position that is in fact widely accepted in Theravāda Buddhist societies, namely that one's good intentions of protecting Buddhism from danger might reduce (or even override) individual negative consequences of violence. Above all, this is of relevance to Buddhist soldiers, as well as of the Buddhist military chaplains, serving in Buddhist majority armies in Asia.

Buddhist Just-War Ideology during Sri Lanka's Civil War

During the civil war in Sri Lanka, Buddhist monks and laypeople represented a wide range of positions along the pacifism–just-war continuum. In September 2002, Ven. Bellanwila, one of Sri Lanka's most influential monks, presented a paper at a conference in Oslo arranged by the Buddhist Federation of Norway. In it, he emphasized that 'just-war' was an oxymoron, and that under no circumstances was war justifiable on Buddhist grounds. However, he admitted the possibility that war is unavoidable under certain circumstances. The question of unavoidability is a key concern here. If Sri Lanka and Buddhism are perceived to be under threat, is violence then unavoidable? The actions taken by monks against the peace process indicate that during the Tamil uprising violence was deemed unavoidable by the great majority of Buddhist monks in Sri Lanka. In fact, my interviews with Buddhist monks during the war indicate that hardly any supported absolute pacifism.

Rather, as the civil war continued, a 'Buddhist utilitarianism' developed and gained prominence. On the basis of particular interpretations of the *Mahāvaṃsa*, it was argued that *in certain cases* violence may be permissible. Thus, nonviolence was not considered as absolute, but rather a *prima facie* duty (Bartholomeusz 2002). This implies that the duty of nonviolence can be overruled at times when Buddhism is perceived to be in peril. Nonetheless, Buddhism-cum-pacifism is the hegemonic discourse in Buddhist Sri Lanka, making outright demands by Buddhist monks for a military solution problematic. Therefore, prominent monks suggested that they preferred to ask the government 'to *protect* the country'. In the political climate during the war, *protection* of Sri Lanka normally implied opposing the Norwegian-facilitated peace process and support for military action against the LTTE.

Even though Buddhism-cum-pacifism was the normative discourse for most, a minority of radical monks was explicit in their demands for a military solution. For example, according to Ven. Rathana (2002) of the Sinhala National Heritage Party, the Jathika Hela Urumaya (JHU), terrorism had to be eradicated by military means. With a clear reference to the Buddhist tradition, he stated that

> there are two central concepts of Buddhism: compassion and wisdom. If compassion was a necessary and sufficient condition, then the Buddha would not have elaborated on wisdom or prajna. Hitler could not have been overcome by maitriya alone. Today there is a discourse about peace in Sri Lanka. It is an extremely artificial exercise and one that is clearly being orchestrated under the threat of terrorist attack.

In contrast to monks like Ven. Pannasiha or Ven. Bellanwila, however, Ven. Rathana in fact applies Buddhist doctrinal concepts to justify the use of armed force. To him, compassion (in this case nonviolence) needs to be complemented (or overruled) by wisdom, understood as the use of armed force. Along with other militant monks like Ven. Elle Gunawansa (who actively engaged in active recruitment of soldiers) or Ven. Rambukkana Siddharta (who composed the lyrics of the Army Song), Ven. Rathana belongs to a minority within the Sangha, among whom the normative discourse of nonviolence is set aside.

However, while the above militaristic positions should be understood as specific responses to Sri Lanka's civil war, it cannot solely be explained away as contemporary radical innovation, or exceptionalism. For example, looking back at the writings of highly respected monks such as Ven. Walpola Rahula (1907–1997), we find early on articulations of the view that Buddhist monks could (or should) support state military action. In *The Heritage of the Bhikkhu* (1974 [1946], 21) Ven. Rahula discusses monastic support for the great hero of Sinhala nationalism, King Duṭṭhagāmaṇi (161–137 BCE), stating that 'blessed and inspired by the presence of *bhikkhus*, the warriors fought with great courage and determination'. In a footnote to this sentence, Ven. Rahula clarifies his position on monastic relations to the army further:

> It should not be understood here that the *bhikkhus* went to fight in the war. Some are of the opinion that the *bhikkhus* were invited to go to the army in order that the warriors could offer them alms. Undoubtedly the *bhikkhus* were offered alms. However that is not the main import of the occasion. When *bhikkhus* accompany the army the war appears to be of religious significance, and more and more people support the war effort. The assistance of the *bhikkhus* was also necessary to establish peace and order in the areas liberated. It is mentioned that King Rājasiṃha II (1635–1687 A.C.) took *bhikkhus* with him when he went to war. Mvh. xcv 16.

In Ven. Rahula's text, three important elements in army-Sangha relations can be identified. First, he explicitly states that army and Sangha are two different institutions and that their distinctive roles have to be maintained. Thus, violence is not carried out by Buddhist monks themselves. Second, he refers to the idea that monks need to relate to armies in order to care for the soldiers' religious 'needs', indicating reciprocal ritual interconnectedness between soldiers and monks. Third, and most important for our purpose here, *bhikkhus* are instrumental in ensuring popular support for state war. The war in question is presented in the *Mahāvaṃsa* as just-war from a Buddhist point of view, and its legitimacy is axiomatic in Buddhist Sri Lanka, although it deserves mentioning that the tendency to ethnicize this story along contemporary nationalist lines has been met with some criticism. In his discussion of the war, Ven. Rahula does not raise a debate about the justified use of force; its justification is taken for granted. Moreover, the above quote clearly indicates that he thought monastic support for state war was not limited to this given historical case, but applicable to other contexts as well.

Violence and Political Paradigms in the Pāli Canon

In any case, even if we were to accept the idea of a distinction between doctrine and history, would a 'return to the canon' really give unequivocal answers? Kings flourish in both canonical and post-canonical Buddhist literature; the historical Buddha was himself a prince who abandoned his own political career to seek enlightenment; the tales in the *Jātaka* recall the life of the Buddha as a king in previous lives; and the canonical texts reflect many meetings between the Buddha and various kings during the former's lifetime. Although the Buddha was generally silent about political affairs, a Buddhist ideology of kingship (different from that of Hinduism) gradually developed. Different interpretations were made of the various texts (different versions of the canons, as well as Buddhist texts in the vernacular) in each of the cultures where Buddhism established itself, giving rise to different political paradigms throughout the Buddhist world.

In the following I shall pay attention to certain principles of royal ideology discernable in the Pāli canon that are relevant for our understanding of Buddhist justifications of violence in Sri Lanka. According to Gokhale (1969, 731), early Buddhist views on the state passed through three distinct phases. Since Buddhists today refer to principles found in all three phases, I have chosen not to focus on the assumed historical development of these principles, emphasizing instead that all three phases present political paradigms that later Buddhists could and would base their political thinking and practices upon.

The early Buddhist view of the state begins as a quasi-contractual arrangement under which the king performs certain functions (protection) in return for certain rights (shares of the crop). The *Aggañña Sutta* in the *Dīgha Nikāya* (*DN*, 27) tells of a dim past, when humans fell from a state of happiness into a state of greed and violence. To save themselves from anarchy, they elected an outstanding individual, the *mahāsammata* (meaning the 'Great Elect'). This *sutta* rejects the Divine basis of the caste system, as well as the Divine right of kings. For our purpose here, the *Aggañña Sutta* is of importance as it recognizes the use of force in order to re-establish order and to protect human lives. Moreover, if read as an early form of a social contract, the ideal of the *mahāsammata* acknowledges the use of force within a 'quasi-democratic' political structure. Noticeably, in this Buddhist myth of origin the word *ahiṃsā* is not used, and ideals on nonviolence are not easily identified. In post-canonical literature, like the *vaṃsa*-literature found throughout Buddhist South and Southeast Asia, the *mahāsammata* ideal is fused with royal ideology so that the Buddha (himself of royal origin) is depicted as a descendant from the *mahāsammata*, and moreover, that historical Buddhist kings, particularly in Burma/Myanmar and Sri Lanka, trace their descent from the *mahāsammata*.[10] To what extent the *mahāsammata* represents a republican or a monarchic political ideal in early Buddhism is of less relevance. Here, suffice to say that in what was to become one of the most significant models for exemplary Buddhist rule the use of violence in public affairs is clearly recognized.

The second paradigm articulates the 'two wheels' theory that became the basis of much early Buddhist political theory. This view was first articulated by King Ajātasattu, who reputedly said that while the Sangha was *dhammacakka* (the wheel of law), he (as king) was *āṇācakka* (the wheel of command). This implies a clear distinction between the temporal and the spiritual, although their interdependence is also acknowledged (Gokhale 1969, 732–733). The *mahāsammata* figure and the 'two wheel' theory clearly testify to the importance of royal power in early Buddhism. Without royal power, anarchy and *a-dhamma* would prevail. The importance of kingship is also reflected in the fact that several of the rules in the monastic code (*Vinaya*) were amended to accommodate royal needs.[11]

However, kings are also often described as greedy and autocratic, and canonical texts refer to fear of royal tyranny. The *Vinaya* (I 40) specifically prohibits monks from entering the political sphere, so the only protest possible was for them to leave the territory of a despotic ruler. The need for social order—which was granted by the king—and royal support of the Sangha, on the one hand, and the fear of abuse of power, on the other, created a paradox that the early Buddhists sought to solve through ethicizing the state (Gokhale 1969). Early Buddhists thus asserted the power of *dhamma* (righteousness, norms, justice) over *āṇā* (the state). Moreover, *dhamma* was seen as a cosmic force that also regulates the order of nature. Therefore, if the king followed the *dhamma*, he would be able, after observing particular rites, to master nature (e.g. rain-making).

It is within the third political paradigm that the ideal Buddhist king is shaped. Only a few sermons in the canon deal explicitly with kingship, the most famous being the *Cakkavattisīhanāda Sutta*. This is the *locus classicus* of the doctrine of the ideal king, the *cakkavatti* ('wheel-turning king'). The political principle laid down in the *Cakkavattisīhanāda Sutta* is that of the righteous ruler who conquers territory through the principles of righteousness and morality. He is the 'secular' counterpart of the Buddha, and both are said to bear the 32 marks of the superhuman on their bodies. The ideal king, the *cakkavatti*, rules according to ten royal virtues (*dasarājadhamma*): alms-giving, morality, charity, justice, penitence, peace, mildness, mercy, meekness and patience. The prototype of the *cakkavatti* is the mythical King Mahāsudassana, mentioned in the *Dīgha Nikāya*. Like the Buddha, he has all the marks of a 'great man' (*mahāpurisa*).[12] He is spiritually advanced and suffuses the universe with the four *brahmavihāras* (a key set of four meditative practices: love, compassion, sympathetic joy and equanimity). He rules without recourse to violence, since his power is based on the *dhamma* and not the stick (*daṇḍa*). Furthermore, he leads a happy life owing to the vast stores of merit he has accumulated in previous lives. The issue of merit is crucial to Buddhist ideas of kingship, as its legitimacy is traditionally understood as depending on the ruler's merit status. The logic behind this is that the person who ranks highest in the social hierarchy can be no other than the person with the largest store of merit. The primeval contract we saw in the *Aggañña Sutta* is now substituted by *dhamma*, and the state is perceived as a quasi-divine institution. Moreover, *dhamma* constitutes the necessary royal charisma, but a king's failure to observe the *dhamma* will result in the loss of this charisma. As Gokhale (1969, 738) notes, there is a balance of forces between *āṇā* and *dhamma*; this 'limits the potential despotism of the state', while 'subordination to the *dhamma* makes it an instrument of morality'.

This is in clear contrast to the doctrine set out in the *Arthaśāstra*, the famous Hindu manual of statecraft,[13] in which violence is portrayed as a necessary tool for the maintenance of an ordered society. Moreover, the *Arthaśāstra* presents a Machiavellian state where the monarch has absolute power, based on economy and law enforcement. Brekke (2004, 47–48) argues that the *Arthaśāstra*'s realist and cynical political view is different from the religious traditions of the epic literature, where the purpose of war is not victory but to follow the laws of *dharma*. Within the epic literature, war is holy; it is a goal in itself. For the author of the *Arthaśāstra*, however, although the warrior's duty is part of his *dharma*, war is never an end in itself. Early Buddhist texts, as well as Māhāyana *sūtras* such as the Lotus Sūtra, show a clear dislike for the ideology of the *Arthaśāstra*. Moreover, the *Cakkavattisīhanāda Sutta* can be seen as providing an example of a Buddhist nonviolent—and in fact pacifist—alternative to Hindu kingship ideology, and can be understood as an attempt within canonical Buddhism to harmonize ethics and politics.

However, it removes the problematique from the real world, as the *Cakkavattisīhanāda Sutta* presents a 'fantasy world in which royal rule is possible without violence' (Collins 1996, 242). The ideal, then, is nonviolence, but this ideal rarely seems to have been used as a charter for the art of politics. Also, it is remarkable that in the *Cakkavattisīhanāda Sutta* the activities of the righteous Buddhist king are described in military metaphors: the king *conquers*, and he is flanked by an army. This can be interpreted metaphorically as the righteous king's effort to conquer greed, hatred and delusion, but another possible interpretation is that even the righteous king has to protect his subjects through defensive war. In fact, the *Cakkavattisīhanāda Sutta* served as a literary source for just-war ideology to sections among Buddhist monks and lay people during the Sri Lankan civil war (Bartholomeusz 2002).

Ahiṃsā *and the Question of Pacifism*

Leaving Buddhist political ideology aside, an important question to address is to what extent the precept of abstaining from taking life is explicitly discussed in relation to war in the canon, or whether no-harm *ahiṃsā* is considered to be self-evident. At first sight, Lambert Schmithausen (1999) points out, this would seem to be a simple issue as the first precept to be observed—by lay Buddhists and monastics alike—is to abstain from inflicting harm. Participation in warfare, therefore, seems incompatible with this precept. Indeed, in three (almost) identical sermons, the Buddha tells military leaders that they will go to hell, and not heaven, as the Vedic tradition held. In the *Yodhajiva Sutta* (ch. XLII), for example, the Buddha tells a soldier (*yodha-ājīvo*) that to one that engages in fighting 'one of two paths is open, either purgatory or rebirth as an animal'. Also, upon hearing the story of the fighting between King Pasenadi and King Ajātasattu, the Buddha seems to argue against military action from a consequentialist position by saying that violence fosters violence in a never-ending circle of action and retribution. This position of radical pacifism is also found in the *Abhidharmakośabhāṣya*, a later systematic treatise, in which it is stated that 'killing is bad karma even in case of *self-defence* or when done for the sake of *defending friends*' (quoted in Schmithausen (1999, 48–49). Similar positions of radical pacifism are also found in the *Jātakas*, where stories are told about rulers who, horrified with the violence connected with kingship, choose the path of asceticism or refrain from military self-defence (Schmithausen 1999, 51–52). Thus, a strict application of the Buddhist ethical principal of nonviolence cannot but lead to the rejection of all kinds of war, including defensive war.

However, while radical pacifism evidently is found in the canon, so is the assumption that violence belongs to a separate sphere of activity, that of the warrior caste (to which kings belong). In fact, the political paradigms discussed above all accept the institution of war, in that they regard it as being within the jurisdiction of the state. As Gokhale (1969, 734) points out, 'the Buddhist works are full of injunctions against violence but these are, more often than not, related to the level of individual and inter-group relations'.

Furthermore, the Buddha appears to be reserved in advocating absolute pacifism with regard to kings. Perhaps the early Buddhists were reconciled to the fact that they could not influence the state beyond giving ethical advice? We can only speculate about the reasons for the Buddha's reservation in this matter, although Bareau's (1993) position—namely, that the Buddha may have considered political interference as detrimental to the future of the monastic order—also seems reasonable.

Karmic Consequences for Soldiers and Soteriological Insecurity

A closer look at the above-mentioned *Yodhajiva Sutta* raises some intriguing questions about what nonviolence means in a given military context. It is clear in this text that the Buddha condemns violent action in war as having negative karmic consequences for the individual soldier (rebirth in hell, not in heaven). In this respect, the text follows the psychologically oriented nature of Buddhist ethics, emphasizing the intention of the soldier when entering the battlefield. The Buddha says that the soldier must have had 'this low, mean, perverse idea: "Let those beings be tortured, be bound, be destroyed, be exterminated, so that they may be thoughts never to have existed'" (*Yodhajiva Sutta*, 217). Implicitly, this leaves the question about intentionality open to Buddhist soldiers and military personnel. Does it imply that killing out of duty, or killing with the right intention, does not bring about negative karmic consequences? The text is silent on this question, but the question about intentionality brings to mind the story, told in the *Aṅguttara Nikāya* (IV: 185), of the general Sīha, who declared, in the context of meat-eating, that he would not intentionally kill a living being. There is no indication, however, that he found his duties as a soldier incompatible with the precept of nonviolence. Therefore, Schmithausen (1999, 53) concludes 'the warrior is conceived as observing the Buddhist norms wherever they do not conflict with his specific duties as a warrior'.

Jus in Bello

Principles of *jus in bello* are not much elaborated in the Pāli canon, although ideals of just treatment of prisoners of war can be discerned in certain narratives. For example, in one of the stories about the war fought between the good King Pasenadi and the evil King Ajātasattu, King Pasendi upon winning the war deprives his enemy of his men and equipment, but lets him live. According to the text "Two Sayings About War" (in the *Saṃyutta Nikāya*, §§4,5, 110), the King thought 'although this king injures me who was not injuring him, yet he is my nephew'. Thus, killing of war prisoners is discouraged, acknowledging (by logical extension) a shared humanity between the warring parties.

Early Buddhist History and Post-Canonical Political Ideals

The greatest historical inspiration for Buddhist kingship, however, is the Indian emperor Ashoka (268–239 BCE). What is often referred to as the 'the Ashokan paradigm' includes ideals of nonviolence, patronage of Buddhism, assistance to the poor and royal purifications of the Sangha. It should be noted, however, that Ashoka embraced the principle of nonviolence only *after* the territories were brought under his control. From Ashoka's edicts we know that he conquered most of his empire through brute force; only afterwards he embraced *dhamma* as the policy of his reign. Ashoka adopted the doctrine of *ahiṃsā*, but this did not imply radical nonviolence or pacifism in the 'public' sphere. For example, although he showed dislike of animal slaughter, slaughter was not abolished in the castle, only reduced. Moreover, capital punishment continued throughout his reign. Finally, Ashoka stated that war was not necessary (at the moment), but, in Thapar's (1998, 202) words, 'if his successors should have to make a conquest in the future, it was to be hoped that they would be merciful where possible and deliver light punishments'. Ashoka's 'pacifism', then, was the result of his empire being secure. When the territory was conquered and made secure, Ashoka developed a policy of government based on *dhamma*, which became an efficacious ideology of security and political stability.[14]

These Buddhist ideals were essential in strengthening royal charisma, but they did not provide a charter for practical politics. In fact, although *bodhisattva* ideals were prominent, most kings in Sri Lanka up to the sixteenth century participated in the battlefield (Kemper 1991, 45). For the *practice* of political power, Buddhist kings in Sri Lanka looked to India for the 'secular' tradition of state craft, namely the *Kauṭilya-Arthaśāstra* (Bechert 1978, 8). For example, the *Cūlavaṃsa* contains indirect references to *Arthaśāstra*-like military tactics used by Sinhalese kings, such as Parākramabāhu, king of Poḷonnaruva (1153–1186 CE). Moreover, Parākramabāhu explicitly refers both to the *Jātakas* as well as to Kauṭilya. In Smith's (1978, 137) opinion, 'the clear blending of Indian and Sinhalese elements is nowhere more present in Ceylon's history than in [Parākramabāhu's] reign'. Moreover, this reign, as related in the *Cūlavaṃsa*, is a perfect example of the 'two-wheel theory' (that of the *dhammacakka* and the *āṇācakka*), discussed above.

Mahāvaṃsa *and Early Just-War Ideology*

One of the most famous examples of Theravāda Buddhist justifications for war is found in the Sri Lankan text *Mahāvaṃsa*, from the fifth century CE. This text tells of the Buddhist king Duṭṭhagāmaṇi (161–137 BCE), who in order 'to bring glory to the doctrine' (*Mhv*. XXV, 3) killed the (Tamil) king Eḷāra, who, in fact, is portrayed as a just king. As he was feeling remorse for the slaughter, eight *arahants* come to comfort him, but the king asks: 'How shall there be any comfort for me, O venerable sirs, since by me was caused the slaughter of a great host numbering millions?' (*Mhv*. XXV, 108). The *arahants* reply that

> from this deed arises no hindrance in thy way to heaven. Only one and a half human beings have been slain here by thee, O lord of men. The one had come unto the (three) refuges, the other had taken on himself the five precepts. Unbelievers and men of evil life were the rest, not more to be esteemed than beasts. But as for thee, thou wilt bring glory to the doctrine of the Buddha in manifold ways; therefore cast away care from thy heart, O ruler of men!
>
> *(Mhv. XXV, 109–111).*

The king is not said to have committed compassionate murder, but through a strategy of dehumanizing the opponent, killing for the sake of the *dhamma* is justified. Therefore, this text shows that to break the precept of not killing is allowed or even required in certain situations. This passage raises the issue of 'Buddhist just war'. Sri Lankan monk Walpola Rahula (1974, 21) has written that 'the religio-patriotism at that time assumed such over-powering proportions that both *bhikkhus* and laymen considered that even killing people in order to liberate the religion and the country was not a heinous crime'. Rahula continues his analysis by stating that this 'is diametrically opposed to the teaching of the

Buddha'. Nonetheless, he does not seem particularly *concerned* about either the king's ethical dilemma or the response of the *arahants*. The main impression given the reader is the impressive nature of the religio-nationalism of the period, as well as the importance of *bhikkhus* in political life (Rahula 1974, 20–22).

By contrast, other monastic scholars—such as Ven. Mahinda Deegalle—are far more critical in their interpretation of the text, even though Deegalle admits the possibility that when the *arahants* consoled the king they applied 'skills-in-means' (Pāli: *upāya-kosalla*), that is the Buddha's skill in expounding the *dhamma*. The Buddhist community would not benefit from having a remorseful king, and the *arahants* were thus implementing a 'rehabilitation strategy' (Deegalle 2001, 4). Nonetheless, Deegalle argues, 'justifying that killing Tamils during war is not a papa [sin] is a grave mistake even if it was used in the Mahavamsa as a skill-in-means'. To my knowledge, only a small number of monks denounce the *Mahāvaṃsa* altogether. Some of the very few pacifist Buddhist monks I have met in Sri Lanka rejected the text as 'un-Buddhist', on the grounds that it is post-canonical and does not represent 'true', canonical teachings.[15] Also within Buddhist studies, this textual passage has been interpreted as being contrary to the 'classical standpoint', and it has been argued that its message is 'convoluted, disturbingly inappropriate for an arahant to suggest, and verges on the scandalous' (Greenwald 1978, 18). Such a view provides a perfect example the 'degeneration theory' (discussed earlier), which points to researchers' disappointment with the lack of congruence of Buddhist teachings and practices. This is not to deny, however, that the Duṭṭhagāmaṇi story is an example of a radical formulation of a king's duty to protect Buddhism. Regardless of its technically defined post-canonical status, the *Mahāvaṃsa* enjoys a *quasi-canonical* status in Sri Lankan Buddhism, and Duṭṭhagāmaṇi was regarded by the *Mahāvaṃsa*, as well as by later tradition, as an exemplary Buddhist king, e.g. he is said to have enjoyed rebirth in the Tusita heaven. Later Sinhala works, such as the *Saddharmālaṃkāra*, dehumanize the Tamils slain by King Duṭṭhagāmaṇi in even more aggressive ways (Obeyesekere 1992, 136). Justification of violence through dehumanization of the enemy, then, was accepted by later generations of Buddhists in Sri Lanka, although pacifist ideals were nurtured in other narratives. Moreover, as has been pointed out by various scholars, the *Mahāvaṃsa* plays an enormously important role in contemporary Sri Lanka, and King Duṭṭhagāmaṇi is a national hero, symbolizing both the Sinhala struggle against foreign invasion and the role of the righteous king who protects Buddhism. King Duṭṭhagāmaṇi's war against Eḷāra serves *par excellence* as a narrative for Buddhist justification for war, and it was often cited during the Sri Lankan civil war.

Buddhist Pacifism: A Utopian Ideal?

Other Buddhist narratives are less clear in their justification for violence. For example, the story of the Sri Lankan king Sirisaṃghabodhi (247–249 CE) shows how the dilemma of reconciling soteriological nonviolence with *realpolitik* have been discussed within certain Buddhist narratives. His story is transmitted and remembered in two texts, the *Mahāvaṃsa* and in a medieval biography known as the *Hatthavanagallavihāravāsa*, both containing multiple and contradictory moral theories. In the biography Sirisaṃghabodhi is portrayed as a *bodhisattva* who is reluctant to accept the throne, since he is said to be—in a way that refers to a story in the *Jātaka*—afraid of committing 'grievous action which brings men to hell' (quoted in Hallisey 1996, 36). However, he is persuaded by Buddhist monks to accept the throne, since they regard him as a wise person. As Hallisey points out, Sirisaṃghabodhi's reluctance can be understood both as consequentialist (actions are bad if they bring an undesired end) and as deontological (the moral worth of an action is not judged by its consequences but by its nature). Moreover, the monks' argument that Sirisaṃghabodhi is a good and wise man suggests virtue ethics. The story of Sirisaṃghabodhi is even more interesting in that it holds that his reign was racked with crime, in spite of the fact that he was thought to be the very personification of the *dhamma*. He ruled without force, which led to chaos and decay.[16] In this case, his virtue was not enough to make him a good ruler. This story thus conveys the ideal of nonviolence, while simultaneously indicating that violence is a prerequisite for royal rule. Moreover, different texts relate different ends to the king's life. In the biography, the king is said to have become an ascetic, while in the *Mahāvaṃsa* (*Mvh*. XXXVI), the king gives his life for the benefit of his kingdom—that is, he kills himself.[17] Reference to historical kings who ruled according to *bodhisattva* ideals, like King Sirisaṃghabodhi of the third century, was explicitly made by later kings up to the sixteenth century.[18] In fact, Holt points out that

> So impressive was this caricature of Sirisanghabodhi's bodhisattva kingship ... that every second Sinhala king from the seventh through the twelfth century included Sirisanghabodhi's name in his official title, while *every* king from the thirteenth through the sixteenth century incorporated his name formally.
>
> *(Holt 1991, 59; emphasis in original)*

Turning once again to contemporary Sri Lanka, we see in the following comment by President J.R. Jayewardene (1978–1989) that the *bodhisattva* ideal of the aforementioned King Sirisaṃghabodhi is still remembered, but that the president does not regard the precept of nonviolence as applicable to him:

> I can not follow [the precept of abstaining from killing any living being] because my duty is laid down in the Constitution.... Sri Sanghabo wanted to follow Buddhism fully after he became King, so he released all the prisoners. And they started robbing and killing and the people started saying 'we can't have you for our King!'. There was big turmoil and unrest and they forced him to resign, to abdicate. And he left Anuradhapura.... I must

be like that then, there is no half fairness, and I am not going to be like that, I wanted to govern this country, I was elected to govern.

(quoted in Horst 1995, 26)

The story of King Sirisaṃghabodhi contains multiple moral positions about the use of violence and military means. Hallisey (1996, 37) suggests that such stories can be seen as 'discursive sites' where 'Buddhists debated the scope and validity of the different ethical theories which they knew'. King Duṭṭhagāmaṇi, too, lamented the carnage his victories on the battlefield had brought about, thus conforming to the Ashokan ideal. However, the resemblance to the Ashokan ideal stops there, as Duṭṭhagāmaṇi proclaimed war with a Buddhist relic in his spear, accompanied by five hundred Buddhist monks (who thus transgressed several *Vinaya* regulations). Moreover, the *arahants* consoled the king; they did not ask him to change his ethical standards.

Ethical Particularism and Compartmentalization of Values

The 'solution' to the 'problem' of reconciling Buddhist ideals of power with *realpolitik* can also be explained in terms of a 'compartmentalization of values' (Schmithausen 1999). According to Schmithausen, this term refers to a specific strategy for dealing with the problem of politics and violence, namely, to have different sets of values: one set of Buddhist values and another set that is local in origin and often strongly influenced by Indian manuals of law and politics. The advantage of this thesis is that it allows for ethical pluralism within a given political culture. However, while Schmithausen's thesis certainly fits well with kings like Parākramabāhu, it has other implications that—at least, as I see it—confuse our understanding of the relationship between Buddhism and political power. It ignores the Buddhist views of the state found in the canon, leaving us with the impression that Buddhist values are apolitical vis-à-vis 'local values'. Another problem is that what is 'local' in this setting is not clear. What would be regarded as 'local' differs from one context to another. In the Sri Lankan context, both Buddhist values and the *Kauṭilya-Arthaśāstra* came from India, and there are few traces of a pre-Buddhist local political culture.[19] Perhaps Schmithausen's model fits better in cases where Buddhism was formally established relatively late—for example, in the Khmer kingdom. In that case, Theravāda Buddhism came to an already existing political culture based upon a synthesis of Mahāyāna Buddhism and Brahmanical practices.

Nonetheless, it was not the *realpolitik* of Kauṭilya but the Ashokan paradigm that was to become the ideal. In essence, this implied that the state was not an end in itself, but rather a means towards a higher end. This resembles one of the three political paradigms found in early Buddhism, as pointed out earlier, namely the ethnicization of the state. Such ideals of a 'Dhamma State' have inspired Sri

Lankan politicians up to the present time, most notably the late president Premadasa and the Jatika Hela Urumaya.

Concluding Remarks

Although nonviolence remains the ideal for Buddhist rulers, there would seem to be few references to pacifism. Kings have nurtured ideals of compassion, and at times have banned hunting within the polity, but only in very few instances does the ideal of nonviolence relate to nonviolence in the political realm. Even the most famous instance of pacifism in Sri Lanka's history—the reign of Sirisaṃghabodhi—lives on in the tradition without leading to a resolution of the conflicting moral stances towards the justified use of force. The reason for this, I have argued, lies in early political paradigms that acknowledge the necessity of royal rule for the subsistence of Buddhism.

Pacifism (derived from Latin *peace-making*) is a complex term, but a common usage of the term refers to the commitment to making peace that rejects violent means for obtaining this end. Thus, war is always considered to be wrong. However, the concept includes a variety of positions, ranging from general and total nonviolence in all societal spheres, to more specific anti-warism. In Western philosophy pacifism can be distinguished between minimal and maximal pacifisms, between absolute and contingent pacifisms and between deontological and consequentialist pacifisms. How wrong war and violence are deemed to be, and at what times, depends upon the position one takes. In Buddhist teachings we find maximalist and absolute pacifist notions, most importantly the notion that the ultimate goal of religious striving is contrary to any use of violence. However, this is restricted to the personal level. In fact, with a few notable exceptions, 'anti-warism', or what we might call 'political pacifism', is largely absent in Buddhism. Seen from a cross-cultural ethical perspective on religion and war, two things are striking in the case of Buddhism: one is the importance of *ahiṃsā* (no-harm); the other is the lack of any systematized thinking about the justified use of force, what in Western tradition is referred to as just-war tradition. My argument is that the lack of systematized thinking on the use of violence in public affairs does not make Buddhism necessarily pacifist. Moreover, if the Pāli canon is classified as pacifist, then later Buddhist justifications of violence would necessarily be deviations of the norm of nonviolence. In my view, this perspective escapes the difficult question of how canonical texts have been used to justify—or to silently accept—state-sanctioned violence.

Buddhism's canonical ambiguity in relation to war has, I believe, made the co-existence of the Sangha and state power possible for more than two millennia. Much of the writings on Buddhism and nationalism/violence in Sri Lanka rests upon a prototypic definition of religion—that is, a constructed original that is compared to later 'deviations' from that original. In this case—and in accordance with the textual emphasis of Buddhist studies—the original is supposedly found in the doctrines of the Pāli canon. Moreover, the Pāli canon is often associated with soteriology and individual ethics, whereas other aspects of the religion are regarded as later deviations. Politics, accordingly, is often viewed as being not part of the doctrine of early, 'pristine' Buddhism. What may be called 'degeneration theory' is no more than normative evaluations of change that provide no explanation as to why and *how* Buddhists themselves base their thoughts and actions on the Buddhist tradition. The crucial point is that for the contemporary monk in Sri Lanka, canonical ambiguity regarding violence leaves open a range of political positions and practices in relation to war.

Notes

1 Colombo Page, 29 April 2009, at www.colombopage.com/ (accessed 14 February 2010).
2 The question of violence in other Buddhist traditions is beyond the scope here.
3 I argue elsewhere that Buddhism-cum-pacifism is the result of a specific reorientation in Buddhist modernism of the late nineteenth century; see Frydenlund (2017c).
4 This political aim is found in James Turner Johnson (1997, 227). Brekke (2006, xii) also suggests that cross-cultural ethics might provide avenues for countering moral relativism.
5 For example, an online journal, *The Journal of Buddhist Ethics*, is devoted to issues related to Buddhist ethics, and its editorial board is made up of leading Buddhist scholars; see http://blogs.dickinson.edu/buddhistethics/.
6 Richard Gombrich (1996), for example, pays particular attention to the role played by intention in early Buddhism. Along similar lines, Rupert Gethin (2004) argues that Buddhist ethics is first and foremost *psychological* in nature. In his view, the *Abhidhamma* is not ultimately concerned with ethical rules or principles. Rather, it seeks to articulate a spiritual psychology focusing on the root causes that motivate action. If you intentionally kill out of compassion, Gethin asks, can you ultimately be sure that your mind is pure?
7 This is true for religion in general, as pointed out by the philosopher Stanley Hauerwas. Indeed, both Hallisey and Batholomeusz draw upon Hauerwas's theories. It should be noted that also in religions with strong legal traditions, such as Islam and Judaism, narratives play a central role in conveying ethical dilemmas.
8 This is an argument against Kantian ethics.
9 In Gethin's (2004) view, the *Upāyakauśalya Sūtra* represents a deliberate challenge to 'mainstream Buddhist ethics' as found in the *Abhidhamma*.
10 These ideas are further elaborated upon in the chronicle literature called *Mahāsammatavaṃsa*.
11 For example, monks were not allowed to eat elephant flesh, as the elephant was regarded a royal animal, and they had to postpone the observance of the rain-retreat if the king so wished.
12 'One born to greatness and destined to be either a Universal Ruler [*cakkavatti*] or a Buddha' (*Dictionary of Buddhism*).
13 Most generally ascribed to Kauṭilya, the adviser to King Chandragupta Maurya, who ruled a great Indian empire from the end of the third century BCE.
14 There is a tension between the Ashoka of the edicts and the Ashoka of the Buddhist textual tradition. Turning to the Theravāda texts, we see that Ashoka embodies the ideal of the *cakkavatti*, who through *dhamma* gives peace and prosperity to his subjects.
15 Interviews with Buddhist monks in Colombo, August 2004 and January 2006.

16 The disastrous effects of the attempt to rule without resorting to the use of force are also described in the *Mahāvaṃsa*.
17 The suicide story is nowadays referred to in discussions about the legitimacy of suicide (Bartholomeusz 2002, 120). Suicide is a serious problem in Sri Lanka, with the country ranking highly in terms of global suicide statistics.
18 Harris (1999) points out that post-canonical texts on the Buddhist polity in the Thai and Burmese traditions unfortunately have been neglected in Western scholarship. In the Sri Lankan case, however, post-canonical texts in the form of the *vaṃsa*-literature have been the subject of considerable academic attention.
19 This is not to say that all political culture in Sri Lanka has been Buddhist. Various political cultures, based upon different political ideals drawn from Theravāda Buddhism, Mahāyāna Buddhism and Śaivism, have developed in the island over the centuries.

References

Aṅguttara Nikāya. 1919. Edited by R. Morris and E. Hardy, 5 vols. London: Pali Text Society.
Bareau, André. 1993. 'Le Bouddha et les rois'. *Bulletin de l'Ecole fransaise d'Extrême- Orient* 80 (1).
Bartholomeusz, Tessa J. 2002. *In Defense of Dharma: Just-War Ideology in Buddhist Sri Lanka*. London: Routledge Curzon.
Brekke, Torkel. 2004. 'Wielding the Rod of Punishment—War and Violence in the Political Science of Kautilya'. *Journal of Military Ethics* 3 (1): 40–52.
———. ed. 2006. *The Ethics of War in Asian Civilizations: A Comparative Perspective*. London: Routledge.
Collins, Steven. 1996. 'The Lion's Roar on the Wheel-Turning King: A Response to Andrew Huxley's "The Buddha and the Social Contract"'. *Journal of Indian Philosophy* 24 (4): 421–446.
Deegalle, Mahinda. 2001. 'Is Violence Justified in Theravada Buddhism?' *Current Dialogue* 39: 8–17.
———. 2009. 'Norms of War in Theravada Buddhism'. In *World Religions and Norms of War*, edited by V. Popovski, G. M. Reichberg, and N. Turner. Tokyo: United Nations University Press.
———. 2014. 'The Buddhist Traditions of South and Southeast Asia'. In *Religion, War, and Ethics: A Sourcebook of Textual Traditions*, edited by Greg Reichberg and Henrik Syse. Cambridge: Cambridge University Press.
Frydenlund, Iselin. 2005. *The Sangha and Its Relations to the Peace Process in Sri Lanka*. Oslo: Peace Research Institute Oslo (PRIO Report 2/2005).
———. 2017a. 'Buddhist Militarism Beyond Texts: The Importance of Ritual During the Sri Lankan Civil War'. *Journal of Religion and Violence*: 27–48.
———. 2017b. '"Operation Dharma": The Sri Lankan Army as an Instrument of Buddhist Nationalism'. In *Military Chaplaincy in a Pluralist Age*, edited by Torkel Brekke and Vladimir Thikonov. New Delhi: Oxford University Press, 81–103.
———. 2017c. '"Buddhism Has Made Asia Mild": The Modernist Construction of Buddhism as Pacifism'. In *Buddhist Modernities: Re-Inventing Tradition in the Globalizing Modern World*. London: Routledge, 204–221.
Galtung, Johan. 1996. *Peace by Peaceful Means: Peace and Conflict, Development and Civilization*. London: PRIO.

Gethin, Rupert. 2004. 'Can Killing a Living Being Ever Be an Act of Compassion? The Analysis of the Act of Killing in the Abhidhamma and Pali Commentaries'. *Journal of Buddhist Ethics* 11.

Gleditsch Nils Petter et al. 1980. *Johan Galtung: A Bibliography of His Scholarly and Popular Writings 1951–80*. Peace Research Monographs 9. Oslo: International Peace Research Institute (PRIO).

Gokhale, Balkrishna G. 1969. 'The Early Buddhist View of the State'. *Journal of the American Oriental Society* 89 (4): 731–738.

Gomrich, Richard. 1996. *How Buddhism Began: The Conditioned Genesis of the Early Teachings*. Jordan Lectures in Comparative Religions, Vol. 17. London: Athlone Press.

Hallisey, Charles. 1996. 'Ethical Particularism in Theravāda Buddhism'. *Journal of Buddhist Ethics* 3: 32–43.

Harris, Ian (ed.). 1999. *Buddhism and Politics in Twentieth-Century Asia*. London: Pinter.

Horst, Josine van der. 1995. *Who Is He, What Is He Doing? Religious Rhetoric and Performances in Sri Lanka during R. Premadasa's Presidency (1989–1993)*. Amsterdam: VU University Press.

Jerryson, M. 2009. 'Appropriating a Space for Violence: State Buddhism in Southern Thailand'. *Journal of Southeast Asian Studies* 40 (1): 33–57.

Johnson, James Turner. 1981. *Just War Tradition and the Restraint of War: A Moral and Historical Inquiry*. Princeton, NJ: Princeton University Press.

———. 1997. *The Holy War Idea in Western and Islamic Traditions*. University Park, PA: Pennsylvania State University Press.

Kent, Daniel. 2010. '"Onward Buddhist Soldiers"'. In *Buddhist Warfare*, edited by Michael K. Jerryson and Mark Juergensmeyer. New York: Oxford University Press.

Keown, Damien. 2010. 'War and Peace'. In *Encyclopedia of Buddhism*, edited by D. Keown and C. S. Prebish. London: Routledge.

Kværne, Per. 1984. 'The Rise and Fall of a Monastic Tradition'. In *The World of Buddhism*, edited by Richard F. Gombrich and Heinz Bechert. London: Thames and Hudson.

Obeyesekere, Gananath. 1992. 'Dutthagamani and the Buddhist Conscience'. In *Religion and Political Conflict in South Asia: India, Pakistan, and Sri Lanka*, edited by D. Allen. Westport, CN: Greenwood Press.

———. 1995. 'Buddhism, Nationhood, and Cultural Identity: A Questions of Fundamentals'. In *Fundamentalisms Comprehended*, edited by M. E. Marty and S. R. Appleby. Chicago: University of Chicago Press.

Pannasiha, Madihe. 1985. *Peace Through Tolerance and Co-existence*. Edited by S. V. Dharmayatana. Maharagama, Sri Lanka: Sasana Sevaka Society.

Premasiri, P. D. 2006. 'A "Righteous War" in Buddhism?' In *Buddhism, Conflict and Violence in Modern Sri Lanka*, edited by M. Degalle. New York: Routledge.

Rahula, Walpola. 1974 [1946]. *The Heritage of the Bhikkhu*. New York: Grove Press.

Rathana Athurliye. 2002. 'A Buddhist Analysis of the Ethnic Conflict'. Paper presented at the Bath conference on Buddhism and conflict in Sri Lanka.

Robinson, Paul (ed.). 2003. *Just War in Comparative Perspective*. Aldershot: Ashgate.

Popovski, Vesselin, Gregory M. Reichberg, and Nicholas Turner. 2009. *World Religions and Norms of War*. Tokyo: United Nations University Press.

Saṃyutta Nikāya, §§4,5., Part 1. 1917. Translated by Caroline A.F. Rhys Davids and Suriyagoda Sumangala Thero. London: Pali Text Society, pp. 109–110.

Schmithausen, Lambert. 1999. 'Aspects of the Buddhist Attitude Towards War'. In *Violence Denied: Violence, Non-Violence and the Rationalization of Violence in South Asian Cultural History*, edited by Houben, J. E. M. and K. R. V. Kooij. Leiden: Brill.

Smith, Bardwell L. 1978. *Religion and the Legitimation of Power in South Asia*. Leiden: Brill.
Tambiah, Stanley J. 1992. *Buddhism Betrayed? Religion, Politics, and Violence in Sri Lanka*. Chicago: University of Chicago Press.
Thapar, Romila. 1998. *Asoka and the Decline of the Mauryas: Revised Edition with New Afterword, Bibliography and Index*. New Delhi: Oxford University Press.

3

ENGAGED BUDDHISM EAST AND WEST

Encounters with the Visions, Vitality, and Values of an Emerging Practice

Paula Green

The latter decades of the twentieth century witnessed the spread of Engaged Buddhism throughout Asia and the West, championed by Thich Nhat Hanh of Vietnam and building on earlier experiments especially in India and Sri Lanka. Based on wide interpretations of traditional Buddhist teachings, these new practices became tools of social change, creatively utilized by progressive monks, educators, reformers, environmentalists, medical doctors, researchers, activists, and peacebuilders. The experimental nature of a kind of sociopolitical and peace-oriented Dharma brought new followers to Buddhism in the West and revived Buddhist customs in the Asian lands of its birth and development. Traditionally inward and self-reflecting, Engaged Buddhism expanded Buddhist teaching to promote intergroup relations and societal structures that are inherently compassionate, just, and nonviolent. Its focus, embodied in the phrase *Peace Writ Large*, signifies a greater magnitude and more robust agenda for peace than the absence of war.

This chapter will focus on the emerging phenomenon of Engaged Buddhism East and West, looking at its traditional roots and contemporary branches and discerning its impact on peacefulness, justice, tolerance, human and environmental rights, and related sociopolitical concerns. It will explore the organizational leadership and participation in Engaged Buddhist processes, and what impact this movement has in both primarily Buddhist nations as well as in countries where Buddhists are a tiny minority and its practitioners may not have been born into Buddhist families.

Traditional Buddhism and Social Engagement

What is socially engaged Buddhism? For a religion that has traditionally focused on self-development and realization, its very designation indicates a dramatic departure. According to Buddhist scholar Joanna Macy, the term refers to the social application of Buddhist teachings that guide the practitioner into responsible and resilient relationship with the global community (Macy 2009). Chris Queen, who has edited two important volumes on Engaged Buddhism, observes that the form has developed "in the context of a global conversation on human rights, distributive justice, and social progress" (Queen 2000, 1). This application of Buddhist teachings to the resolution of communal and national problems is a recent innovation in the 2500-year-old history of Buddhism. Queen calls it "unprecedented and thus tantamount to a new chapter in the history of the tradition" (ibid., 1).

There are perhaps 400–500 million Buddhists in the world (Pew Research Center 2015). Most of them are not knowledgeable about Engaged Buddhism, yet mainly live in countries undergoing cataclysmic social, economic, and political change. Sallie King notes that contemporary Buddhist social activism was born out of "colonialism, foreign invasion, war, Westernization, oppression, social injustice, poverty, and discrimination" (Queen and King 1996, 401). In Buddhist countries, monks traditionally shared with monarchs the leadership roles in society. Over the centuries, foreign colonizers dethroned monarchs, became occupiers, imposed harsh economic and social conditions, and drove wedges within communities and between identity groups. As the facts of injustice and oppression by the demanding foreign occupiers became evident to the people of Asia, many turned to the ordained *sangha* (community of monks) as one of the few intact institutions capable of response and resistance. Engaged Buddhism became an active rejoinder to the very contemporary suffering and displacement of the people. Reacting to the ills of the modern world, campaigners for social development remained rooted in time-honored Buddhist philosophy and practice. Its leaders understood that harnessing the tenets of religion as a base for social engagement made the engagement accessible and believable to Buddhist adherents and offered them a path to survive the onslaughts of modernism. It endowed Buddhism with relevance to the social, economic, and political conditions that existed beyond the temple gates or the doors of the meditation hall.

Traditional Buddhism emphasizes individual liberation and awakening through undertaking a committed process of systemized meditation, which in traditional Asian Buddhism was possible for only a small minority of laypeople, the monks, and occasionally nuns. In the twentieth century, some monks, such as Aachan Chaa and Buddhadasa in Thailand and Mahasi Sayadaw and U Pandita in Burma, began training Asian and Western disciples in Buddhist disciplines. Some of the Westerners embarked on years of study with these Asian masters and brought the practice of meditation back to the West. At the same time, Suzuki Roshi, a brilliant Japanese meditation master, and others from Japan and Korea brought Zen practice to California and encouraged a generation of seekers to study in their Asian monasteries. Other Westerners gravitated to His Holiness the Dalai Lama and the practice of Tibetan Buddhism. The Karmapa, a high-level Tibetan teacher, came to the US because Buddhism was already present. Speaking through an interpreter, he said, "If there is a lake, the swans will go there" (Fields 1981, xiii).

Serious meditation is now practiced by millions of lay people in the Buddhist homelands of Asia and in the West. This interchange is a significant development in the history of Buddhism and is a movement of great power and promise. Great effort in meditation focuses and disciplines the mind, allowing the ever-present jumble of thoughts to quiet and concentration to increase. In this process of increasing stillness and reducing distraction, insight and awareness can arise. Through direct experience, the meditator can observe the fleeting nature of human experience, the interdependence of all events, and the rising and passing of every happiness and unhappiness. Traditional Buddhism promises a different kind of peacefulness from that of the street or the marketplace. It offers the potential of an inner peacefulness, a mind at rest and at ease, accepting without attachment each momentary encounter with life. Although internal peacefulness contributes to the wellbeing of others, that was not an explicit goal of the traditional practice, and there is no compelling evidence to suggest that the Buddha attempted or expected to change society.

> The primary goal of Buddhism is not a stable order or a just society but the discovery of genuine freedom (or awakening) by each person. It has never been asserted that the conditions of society are unimportant or unrelated to this more important goal, but it is crucial to stress the distinctions between what is primary and what is not.
>
> *(Smith in Queen and King 1996, 17)*

Socially engaged Buddhist monks and nuns differentiated themselves from traditional, monastic practices, not by rejecting the roots but by incorporating them into their newly developing practice of social responsibility. "*Sila*" (ethics) had been taught by the Buddha as essential to the pursuit of an enlightened life; traditionally, it was interpreted as a personal code of ethics. Engaged Buddhism expanded the understanding of *sila* to include standards of ethical behavior for society as a whole. This thinking came naturally to Western practitioners informed by religious traditions with long histories of social doctrines. As the number and sophistication of Western Buddhists grew, the influences on the growing Engaged Buddhist tradition began flowing back from West to East. Socially active lay Buddhists still practice meditation, ascribe to the essential teachings of the Buddhist canon, and regard the historical Buddha as the "awakened one." This new role for Buddhists is an activism that flows out of Buddhism, thus rooted in self-awareness and conscious of the external realities facing the human and natural world. It brings to engagement with life the very qualities cultivated by intense meditation practice, a balance of wisdom and compassion.

Buddhism in a Changing Asia

The role modern, socially engaged Buddhism has played in the independence movements of the various South Asian nations has varied profoundly and the impacts have often been mixed. Walpola Rahula (1907–1997), ordained early in the twentieth century as a Sri Lankan monk, became a scholar and author active in the transitional time of Sri Lanka's independence from the British Empire. He believed that an activist role for monks was contiguous with ancient traditions, noting that monks had always played a role in guiding their village communities in practical advice as well as ethics and moral behavior. Encouraging monks to engage in building the new nation, participate in social services, and develop their scholarly capacities was, in his understanding, within the bounds of monastic culture. While his focus was not on structural issues of war and peace, as a monk he vocally supported the independence movement and concerned himself with welfare for the lay public. Among Rahula's modern day successors in Sri Lanka is Dr. A.T. Ariyaratne, founder of the Sarvodaya movement, with its focus on village development, the sharing of labor, and the awakening of all. The growth of Buddhist nationalism and the action of members of the *sangha* supporting war against the Tamil population in the civil war mobilized Engaged Buddhists to oppose the manipulation of racist sentiments in the name of Buddhism. Some today are working to cool nationalist fervor among the *sangha* and encourage moderate Buddhists to engage in projects of social and political change.

Unlike Sri Lanka, its giant neighbor India, where Buddhism had first arisen, had by the colonial period become largely a Hindu and Muslim region. There might have been no Buddhist impact on the modern national history of India if not for the existence of Bhimrao Ramji Ambedkar (1891–1956). Arguably the most influential and controversial of the new breed of lay leaders in twentieth-century Buddhism, he was born a Hindu into a low caste, "untouchable" family at a time when there were firmly fixed boundaries of class and daunting obstacles to social mobility. It was also an India where the British Raj was under challenge by a growing movement for Indian independence, and, in the ferment of revolution, democratic change and demands for justice and the rights of man seemed possible and inevitable. It was a world in which a young dalit (a member of the lowest caste) might dream and come to reject the degradations and humiliations of low caste status as monumentally unjust and unnecessary.

Ambedkar had genius and ambition. He escaped India to seek and gain a first-class education in law in New York and London, and returned to India determined to abolish the caste system. The leaders of the Congress Party recognized his extraordinary legal abilities. He argued successfully with many of them that the caste system had no place in a free and democratic Indian nation, and in the new constitution that they drafted, a document that is still the basic law of India, there was no recognition of caste. However, the traditions of caste in this vast and conservative society have been very slow to change, even to the present, and in Ambedkar's day, beyond his liberal and enlightened friends in Congress, his challenges to the restrictions of Hindu-based caste were met with outrage, rejection, and violence.

Perceiving that Hinduism would never provide liberation from caste, much less justice and opportunity for his people, he saw that they could free themselves most easily by rejecting their identity as Hindus and adopting a new religion. Ambedkar undertook a vast and public study of the world's religions with a goal of finding the most satisfactory faith to which the dalits might convert. He proposed four criteria for a satisfactory religion. "Such a faith must foster morality, accord with scientific reason; offer liberty, equality, and fraternity; and not sanctify or ennoble poverty" (Queen and King 1996, 47). He reasoned that Buddhism best fit these criteria and felt that it could best provide a spiritual and cultural vehicle for advancing the freedom and dignity of the untouchable classes. His analysis instigated a mass conversion unprecedented in Buddhist history. In 1956, Ambedkar and his wife converted to Buddhism, witnessed by several hundred thousand members of untouchable castes. The next day, about half a million former low-caste Hindus followed their example.

Then and now, Ambedkar remains a controversial figure. His critics claim that his stripped-down Buddhism, void of adherence to Buddhist texts, doctrine, rituals, and the practice of meditation, fails to teach its converts the way to inner peace, compassion, and wisdom. But for Engaged Buddhism, his fiery resistance to oppression, his commitment to social, economic, and political liberation, and his vision of the possibility of advancing human society, offered a formidable challenge. In the name of Buddhism, he sought justice and dignity for millions of oppressed people. How could Buddhists committed to human dignity and social uplift fail to support this movement? According to Queen, who has studied the Ambedkar movement for many decades, "Ambedkar provided rich resources for a new hermeneutics of liberation, a new sense of identity and hope for millions of his low-caste followers in India, and a new conception of social activism for Engaged Buddhists of the coming generation" (Queen in Queen and King 1996, 67).

S.M. Goenka was born in Burma (Myanmar) to a high-caste Brahmin near the other end of the Indian caste hierarchy. With an ambition to return Buddhism to India, he studied for fourteen years with Burmese meditation master U Ba Khin, until his teacher authorized him to move to India to lead meditation retreats. A charismatic leader and skilled businessman, he established hundreds of meditation centers in India and around the world. He taught a pure form of Vipassana (Insight) meditation, with slight reference to the trappings of cultural and religious Buddhism. His movement was strictly for the purpose of mind training, expanding this liberating practice from the monastery to the lay community. He promoted no political, economic, or social agenda, though a strong case can be made that the best way to serve society is to help people attain higher consciousness. For Buddhists who struggle with the balance of social action and individual development, Goenka and Ambedkar represent different approaches to awakening and social uplift. Each has had a far-reaching impact on contemporary Buddhism.

A king whose power was absolute ruled Burma until the British overthrew the monarchy in the mid-nineteenth century. In this profoundly Buddhist country, the ordained *sangha* was very large. The monks had been generously provided for by the king and were expected in reciprocity to uphold the monarchy and provide education and social services for the populace. During the more than one hundred years of British occupation, with its imposition of foreign norms and a secular curriculum, the *sangha* held on because of the deep faith and symbiotic relationship between the population and the monks. Independence came at the end of World War II, after the Japanese were expelled and the British, under pressure from the growing self-determination movement led by General Aung San, withdrew from the country. A turbulent period of democratic rule was ended by a military coup in 1962 that killed Aung San, and the country fell under a long, dark period of brutal dictatorship that is only now beginning to ease.

During these years of oppression, the ordained *sangha* related to the military dictatorship as it related to the kings of previous centuries, accepting government largesse and supporting the government in return. Many brave monks, however, were on the front lines of the 1988 resistance against the military, and in 2008, very large numbers of monks left the monasteries to march in the streets in their Saffron Revolution, demanding an end to military rule. Some outspoken monks now openly support Aung San Su Kyi and her National League for Democracy, and engage with lay Buddhist colleagues and international donors in progressive social development and the establishment of civil society organizations. Most monks remain politically conservative, many cooperating in a campaign to alienate and persecute the small Muslim minority. At the same time, the *sangha* continues to produce influential and non-political meditation teachers who provide rigorous, high quality traditional meditation training to thousands of foreign and native seekers through large and organized meditation centers throughout the country.

Thailand was never colonized and is still ruled by a king. Traditionally, as in Burma, the King supports the Buddhist *sangha* and the *sangha* supports the king, leads rituals and meditation retreats, and serves the laity through the temples. Young boys ordain for a few months once in their lifetimes during a rains retreat, and some eventually ordain for their lifetime. Thais use their temples actively for personal prayers and worship, support the monks by donating daily alms, and identify deeply with Buddhist culture and traditions. Most are neither politically engaged nor adept at meditation. However, there have been extraordinary Engaged Buddhist monks, most especially Buddhadassa, and remarkable activists, most prominently Sulak Sivaraksa, who founded the International Network of Engaged Buddhists, discussed later in this chapter. A subgroup of monks is part of a noteworthy Buddhist environmental resistance movement that will also be explored below.

In Japan, largely a secular country, less than 40% of the population identify themselves as Buddhists, and very few claim Shintoism. Although the temple is not central to the lives of most Japanese as it remains to a large portion of the populations of Southeast Asian Buddhist countries, much of the Japanese population worships ancestors, maintains shrines or altars, and depends on the priesthood for funeral services (Wikipedia, "Religion in Japan").

Japanese Buddhism has been exported successfully in the form of Zen, thanks to East-West exchanges of students and teachers such as Suzuki Roshi and popular writers like Alan Watts. Nichiren Buddhism is also active in Japan and the West, especially with Soka Gakkai, which boasts about eight million members, and Nipponzan Myohoji, a small but extremely engaged sect that has an impact far beyond its numbers. Both of these Nichiren sects engage in efforts for world peace and harmony, each in very different ways. Nipponzan Myohiji will be examined later in the section on Engaged Buddhist exemplars.

In each of these national settings we see Buddhism at work, focused as it has been for millennia on the purification of the mind. Profoundly insightful in human psychology and possessing highly refined techniques developed over the centuries for helping practitioners recognize and root out defilements, Buddhist teaching excels at the task of cultivating wise, compassionate, and peaceful individuals among those who work hard at the challenges of meditation. With its perceptive understanding of how unconscious mind-states can corrupt the best intentions, Buddhism offers awareness of one's attitudes and behaviors to Western Buddhist social change workers. They, in turn, have offered a gift to Asian Buddhism in the form of social concern and application of Dharma teachings to the affairs of state and community relations. The multiplication of dysfunctional social, economic, and political institutions and the compounding of human misery in the present time has caused an unavoidable and irresistible challenge to Asian and Western Buddhists to address the woes of the world in a systemic and conscious way.

Kenneth Kraft has noted, "the principles and some of the techniques of an engaged Buddhism have been latent in the tradition since the time of its founder" (Kraft 1988, xiii). In the present era, many Buddhists search for social applications of teachings that may have existed in pre-modern Asia and are relevant to their own contexts. Western Buddhists, coming from religious traditions where social ethics, activism, and egalitarianism are strong, have been quick to recognize and adopt these latent principles and techniques. This experimentation then returns to influence and reinforce Engaged Buddhist movements in the Asian homelands. The foundational teachings of Buddhism support and inspire social engagement, and those who both engage in activism and simultaneously devote themselves to the practice of meditation, although small in number, find themselves in positions of leadership and teaching East and West, shaping the next generation of

Buddhists and imbuing their societies with Buddhist-inspired ways and means of working toward peace and justice.

Foundational Teachings of Buddhism and Social Engagement

Buddhists from all persuasions and backgrounds understand that the development of wisdom requires a measure of stillness and equanimity. Those who study and practice the science of mind training believe that although we will never be wise enough to foresee all the repercussions and unintended consequences of our actions, skillful and compassionate responses are essential. The Buddha's grasp of interdependence, which could be akin to current systems thinking and describes the interrelationship of all parts of a society or institution, can guide the community organizer in social analysis. Buddhist disciplines of meditation and contemplation offer valuable experiences in awareness, interconnection, and impermanence through which to formulate sound interventions. The multiplication of calamities perpetrated by human behavior has created such a threatening momentum that blocking actions and fresh starts are required to save the habitable planet.

Although time and circumstance have amended and updated the foundational teachings of Buddhism, contemporary social activist Buddhists, living 2500 years after the life of the Buddha in many different contexts and countries, are guided by the same elemental teachings that the Buddha enunciated in the forests of India. Each of these core principles can be said to contribute to individual liberation and communal peace. First and foremost among the treasures of the canon are the insights of the Four Noble Truths and the moral guidance of the Eightfold Path.

The Buddha's primary insight, gained according to the stories by forty days of concentrated meditation, became known as the Four Noble Truths.

> These four truths are the truth of suffering, its cause, its end, and the path to that end. This teaching is the first turning of the Wheel of Dharma, a wheel of awakening that over the centuries would roll over much of Asia and eventually cross the great oceans to arrive in the West.
> *(Goldstein 2002, 24)*

The essence of these truths is that suffering is common to all sentient beings and that a path exists for the cessation of suffering, which is non-attachment or letting go. Craving, grasping, desiring, and clinging, whether to relationships, ideas, material goods, the past or the present, or even one's current state of health, creates suffering, because it is in the nature of reality that everything is ephemeral, impermanent, and in flux.

To aid in this seemingly impossible task of reducing attachments to oneself, significant others, and one's treasured objects, the Buddha offers a prescriptive guide of self-restraint and morality called the Noble Eightfold Path. In translation from Pali, each of the steps on the path begins with the word "right." Many English-speaking Dharma teachers now prefer to substitute "skillful" or "wholesome," as "right" contains judgment and polarity. The path includes right view, right aspiration, right speech, right action, right livelihood, right effort, right mindfulness, and right concentration. Each step focuses on non-harming, contributing to the wellbeing of others, paying attention, behaving appropriately, and living as much as possible without delusion. Taken as a whole, the Eightfold Path offers a comprehensive and challenging guide to ethical choices and honorable behaviors.

The Four Noble Truths and the Noble Eightfold Path impart a positive influence on the thoughts and actions of socially concerned Buddhists. Activists are often motivated by awareness of the harmful consequences of war and injustice, and unless they are mindful, can become righteous or divisive in expressing views, judgments, and opinions. In the best of circumstances, Engaged Buddhists following the Eightfold Path will develop wholesome communication patterns and skillful means, thus adding positively to the social good. The Eightfold Path helps remind those engaged in social change to choose livelihoods carefully, restrain from mindless consumerism, and remain vigilant about the consequences of their thoughts and actions. Right effort, mindfulness, and concentration, the final three qualities of the Eightfold Path, encourage consistent reflection on the insights gained through meditation practice. Reframed positively, the path encourages care, compassion, and kindness in all of one's interactions, contributing to peacefulness and serving as a barrier against aggression and violence.

The Buddhist texts make repeated references to what they describe as the Three Poisons or Three Afflictions, which are unwholesome mental factors that contaminate the mind and must be transformed.

> The Buddhist image of the Wheel of Life contains various realms of beings; at the center are three figures representing greed, hatred, and delusion. They chase each other around, generating endless suffering, perpetuating a false sense of self or ego. Liberation from attachment to this false self is the central goal in Buddhist practice.
>
> *(Kaza in Queen 2000, 167)*

To this writer, the "poisons" and their antidotes have particular salience in teaching peacebuilding, and are referred to frequently as a guide to understanding the deepest causes of violent conflict. These three mental poisons are known as greed, anger, and delusion, the latter also described as foolishness or ignorance.

Greed and anger are more accessible and will be discussed first. There is no escaping the fact that greed in one guise or another is rampant in the human mind. Greed takes many forms: greed for fame, recognition, control, wealth, love, possessions, experiences, power, comfort, sensual pleasures, and more. Greed can be for the protection, advantage, or aggrandizement of the self, or for one's identity group or one's nation, and it can easily disguise itself as, for example, patriotism or ethnic pride. It may appear in the form of desire, avarice, lust, and longing, often masked because of its negative connotations, but recognizable as "wanting mind." In the world of war and peace, greed for land, water, and other natural resources, for dominance, for victory over one's opponents, or in defense of one's position and prosperity, creates armed conflict and thus endless harm. For the sake of living a life freed from the trap of endless craving as well as for the pursuit of justice and the security of the collective future, mastering one's greedy impulses is a lifelong project for each human being.

Anger takes the form of hatred, prejudice, violence, resentment, envy, competition, aversion, repulsion, fanaticism, xenophobia, and other extremely toxic emotions. Such negative predispositions and defilements exist within the human mind. Identifying and taming these negative thought-forms requires introspection and mindfulness so that the poisons can be rooted out and replaced with compassionate service. In communal and international relations, the toxicity of religious, ethnic, racial, gender, and national prejudice and stereotypes create havoc, destroying individuals and nations. Daily news is filled with stories of women despised and rejected, races vilified, ethnics cast aside, religions disparaged, and nations obliterated. All of these crimes arise from hatred and greed in the mind, the consequences of which cause interconnected and overlapping cycles of wounds and wounding, violence and revenge. A disciplined and cultivated mind, on the lookout for hindrances, will refrain from toxic warrior behaviors, remaining focused on creating the conditions for peace.

Anger at political greed, oppression, gratuitous violence, armed conflict, and other harmful behaviors on the world stage also arise in the minds of activists and often catalyze motivation for oppositional action. Burmese meditation master U Pandita of Myanmar, shortly before his death at age 95, told this author in a private interview that such anger was the "near enemy" of compassion and a defilement that would taint subsequent behavior. "The traditional term 'near enemy' points to some spiritually unhelpful quality or experience that can be mistaken for a helpful quality or experience" (*Wild Mind*). U Pandita recommended that Engaged Buddhists take time to quiet the mind, discern and subdue the elements of anger, greed, and ignorance within it, and apply wisdom to any plan or activity. In that way, the action would be pure, untainted by even subtle manifestations of anger.

Various writers and translators have described the third poison as the mental factor of delusion, ignorance, or foolishness in the mind. Buddhist meditation teachers use the phrase "monkey mind" to describe the constant movement, fantastic variety, and incoherence of the fleeting thoughts that cascade through the mind from moment to moment. As even a limited exposure to meditation reveals, believing this jumble of unexamined thoughts to be reality is a form of ignorance. In the world of social relations, delusion includes not perceiving the truth of our interdependence and our need for each other. Delusion creates the experience of separation and fear, keeping us blind to the fundamental truth of our interrelatedness and the deep web that connects us. Because the mind is cluttered with fear, anger, greed, and self-concern, we are unable to discern and experience our own true nature or recognize what Venerable Thich Naht Hanh calls our "interbeing" (Hanh 1987, 87). A central task of peacemaking is to guide communities and policy makers in the discovery of our common humanity and our interdependence, a fact made ever more visible in the current age of planetary climate change and threats to overall human existence.

Antidotes to mental poisons exist. Buddhist teachers recommend the active practice of generosity as an antidote to greed, compassion and kindness as a response to anger, and wakefulness or awareness as an antidote to delusion. Our spiritual struggle, and our opportunity to contribute to a world of peace and justice, depends on our waking up and staying awake, free of delusion and open to the moment-by-moment unfolding of life.

> It is through the spiritual struggle to continually orient our lives toward respecting others and working for the broader good of all that we are able to transcend and transform these poisons. The poisons undermine our individual happiness, impede our relationships and hinder the unfolding of our unique creative potential. Their influence, however, goes beyond this. On a societal level they well forth from the inner lives of individuals and become the cause of conflict, oppression, environmental destruction and gross inequalities among people. One Buddhist text expresses it this way: "Because anger increases in intensity, armed strife occurs. Because greed increases in intensity, famine arises. Because foolishness increases in intensity, pestilence breaks out. And because these three calamities occur, earthly desires [delusions] grow more numerous and powerful than ever, and false views increasingly flourish."
>
> *(Soka Gakkai International 2005)*

The last illustration of the Buddhist canon to be explored in this chapter is called the Five Precepts. Sharing the same basic concerns for ethics and morality as the guidelines mentioned above, the precepts are a training base for strengthening mindfulness and wholesome conduct. According to the Buddha, progress toward wisdom cannot be made in the absence of *sila* (morality). Buddhist practitioners take precepts, also described as vows, at the start of meditation retreats and at other important moments. Serious Buddhists make mindfulness of the precepts a lifetime practice. The Five Precepts have been enlarged and augmented for Engaged Buddhism by such leaders as Thich Nhat Hanh from Vietnam and Sulak Sivaraksa from Thailand (Hanh 1987, 89–102; Sivaraksa 1992, 73–79).

The first precept, to refrain from killing, sets forth a prohibition against armed conflict and other forms of taking life. The vow reminds Buddhist practitioners to seek whatever means possible to protect life and to solve problems through nonviolent means. For some Engaged Buddhists, this precept may extend to actively opposing national defense budgets, the ideologies of war, weapons production, the death penalty, and the spread of violence in the media. The most life-affirming course of action can, in some situations, be agonizingly difficult to discern. At times, keeping the precept has required standing courageously against great provocation and threat. Buddhists are not exempt from wrestling with the challenges of when, for example, taking a life appears to protect many other lives. "Through accepting this precept," Sivaraksa writes, "we recognize our relationship to all life and realize that harming any living creature harms oneself" (ibid, 72).

Stated simply, precept number two prohibits stealing or refraining from taking what is not ours. The social implications of this vow are profound and require the exercise of discernment, for theft is ubiquitous and often hidden in our societies. The precept can be applied widely to such issues as protecting resource extractions, restricting the plunder that accompanies neo-colonialism, advocating for appropriate development models, supporting equal distribution of the goods and services needed for life, and correcting the injustices of the capitalist economic order. The lens of the second precept can sometimes provide a refreshingly clear view of a complicated economic issue. The heart of this precept encourages a daily personal cultivation of generosity as part of living a spiritual life. The Buddha was said to have commented, "If you knew what I know about the power of giving, you would not let a single meal pass without sharing it in some way" (Goldstein and Kornfield 1987, 8).

The third precept, to refrain from false speech, guides practitioners to speak respectfully and constructively, to avoid gossip and discord, and to be aware of the energy and motivation behind one's words. In this age of the Internet and mass media, ever greater harms arise from destructive speech. Interfaith encounters and dialogue processes advocated by Engaged Buddhists follow this precept by using careful speech to build bridges of understanding across differences and refraining from negative characterizations about others. "Spiritual practice reveals the emptiness of any stereotyped enemy and the presence of the same violent and greedy tendencies in oneself" (Sivaraksa 1992, 77). Remaining mindful of this vow is an essential asset for those who would be peacemakers.

The fourth and fifth precepts relate to very personal harmful behaviors regarding the misuse of sexuality and intoxicants. The fourth is stated as refraining from sexual misconduct and the fifth to restrain from heedless use of intoxicants. Hanh emphasizes such admonitions as "do not lose yourself in dispersion" and "do not mistreat your body" (Hanh 1987, 94, 99). Fourth precept concerns for Engaged Buddhists may include examining global male dominance, exploitation of women and children, and support for issues of inclusion based on gender identity. For the fifth precept, a mind clouded by alcohol and drugs functions poorly, often leaving destruction in its wake. "In Buddhism, a clear mind is a precious gem" (Sivaraksa 1992, 78).

Human behavior lags behind human ideals and vows. Buddhist or not, socially active or not, humans are works in progress, striving to improve and struggling with the demons of greed, anger, and delusions that haunt the human condition. Spiritual teachings, amended to suit current sensibilities and norms, serve as ethical maps for seekers and social change implementers. Activists can become lost in the compelling passions of their actions and benefit from the reflective nature of Buddhist practice with its focus on equanimity. The quality of consciousness that one brings to the tasks of peacemaking impacts its outcomes. Buddhist teachings balance the two wings of compassion and wisdom. Used consciously and magnified with an eye toward social change, compassion and wisdom stabilize and steer the peacemaker, who brings those qualities to the wounded world. Exemplary Engaged Buddhist leaders, whose own wings fly on wisdom and compassion, point the way.

Exemplars of Engaged Buddhism

In the current era, the most visible Buddhist in the world is likely His Holiness the Dalai Lama. As the spiritual and formerly also political leader of the Tibetan people, he models active concern and engagement for the welfare and wellbeing not only of the Tibetans, but also on behalf of all people. He advocates ceaselessly for the freedom and liberation of Tibetans inside occupied Tibet, and for decades has held to a strict commitment to nonviolence as the only means to obtain that liberation. Despite pressure from young Tibetans in exile frustrated with the lack of progress and despairing for the future of their country, the Dalai Lama holds firmly to the previously discussed first precept of not killing or causing another to kill. Understanding the relationship between means and ends, he believes that violence begets further violence and will not lead to a peaceful and just solution for Tibet.

The Dalai Lama is engaged in worldwide speaking and teaching, reforming Tibetan practices to conform to the modern world, hosting seminars on brain science, technology, medicine, and other knowledge pursuits, participating in interfaith activities for the sake of interreligious harmony, and using his compassion and wisdom as a wise elder, mentor, advocate, humanist, and spiritual teacher. A winner of the 1989 Nobel Peace Prize, he has unexpectedly become a popular iconic figure, a true model of internal and social peace.

In recent years, the Dalai Lama, who has been a monk for more than seventy years, has searched for a means to circumvent the divisions that have sharpened globally in the name of religious identity. His hope is that human beings can transcend sectarianism and instead follow a shared ethics based on universal humanitarian principles. He titled a 2011 book *Beyond Religion: Ethics for a Whole World*, in which he discusses his search for a secular ethics that appeals to all, whether religiously identified and not, that neither contradicts nor depends on any particular religion. He speaks of two pillars of secular ethics:

Both of these can be easily grasped on the basis of our common experience as humans and our common sense, and both are supported by findings of contemporary research, particularly in such fields as psychology, neuroscience, and the clinical sciences. The first principle is the recognition of our shared humanity and our shared aspiration to happiness and the avoidance of suffering; the second is the understating of interdependence as a key feature of human reality, including our biological reality as social animals. . . . Together, I believe, they constitute an adequate basis for establishing ethical awareness and the cultivation of inner values. It is through such values that we gain a sense of connection with others, and it is by moving beyond narrow self-interest that we find meaning, purpose, and satisfaction in life.

(His Holiness the Dalai Lama 2011, 19)

Another monk and exile from his country, mentioned above, Venerable Thich Nhat Hanh, has been an outstanding spokesperson of peace from the Buddhist tradition. Originally from Vietnam, but long a political exile in France, he was thrust into activism as a young monk in the tragic years of the US war in Vietnam. Credited with coining the phrase "Engaged Buddhism," he has been one of its leading figures for fifty years. Thich Nhat Hanh explains that Engaged Buddhist practice occurs on the meditation cushion, in the home, on the streets, and in the halls of power, each form reinforcing and edifying the other. Like the Dalai Lama, his peacemaking is worldwide; going forth to teach and preach from his base community of Plum Village in Southern France to many countries, his light and sensitivity has attracted thousands of followers. Referencing the Three Poisons and the pain of violence and hatred, he notes, "our enemy is our anger, greed, fanaticism, and discrimination against people" (Hunt-Perry and Fine in Queen 2000, 38).

During the years of war in the 1960s and 1970s, Thich Nhat Hanh traveled throughout the United States, seeking a ceasefire and winning the affection of many Americans in anguish about the war who were touched by his depth, gentle presence, stirring poetry and prose, and message of nonviolence. On tour through the US Fellowship of Reconciliation, he connected with important activists of the time, including poet, priest, and activist Daniel Berrigan and Dr. Martin Luther King, Jr. Dr. King was, in fact, so drawn to Thich Nhat Hanh's message of humanity and his interweaving of spirituality and activism that he nominated him for the Nobel Peace Prize.

Through his travels, Thich Nhat Hanh recognized beneath the prosperity, there are "roots of violence, loneliness, materialism, and sorrow in Western society" (Hunt-Perry and Fine in Queen 2000, 61). Most remarkably, for years he has offered meditation retreats to Vietnam veterans, helping former soldiers who fought in a war that destroyed his country and who have lived with the suffering of trauma ever since. Leading these retreats demonstrates a profound example of forgiveness, reconciliation, and moral courage, visible for others to emulate as a unique path to peace. Now an elder, felled by a stroke but apparently still very much present in Plum Village, this beloved master instructs new generations of practitioners with the power of his presence and his radiant peace.

Thich Nhat Hanh's Engaged Buddhism, as well as the writing and anti-war activities of Aitkin Roshi, an American Zen teacher, inspired the formation of the US Buddhist Peace Fellowship (BPF) in 1978. A number of religiously identified peace fellowships had existed for decades under the auspicious of the pacifist ecumenical organization US Fellowship of Reconciliation. Based in California and welcoming Buddhists from a wide variety of backgrounds and practices, BPF quickly became a focal point for those members of the lay *sangha* with an activist bent. Most were Westerners in the first generation of exploring Buddhism in the US; not born into Buddhist families, they were free of cultural restrictions and began to shape Buddhism toward protest and engagement. When Thich Naht Hanh returned to the US in 1983, after years of absence during the war against Vietnam, he went on tour with BPF, and through attraction to his "vision, pragmatism, and compassion," the organization grew in size and stature (Simmer-Brown in Queen 2000, 76). BPF's foundational principles of peace and environmental, feminist, and social justice concerns have remained, and the leaders of the current generation have appropriately added current concerns with racism, economic injustice, heterosexism, prisons, labor, immigration, and oppression (Buddhist Peace Fellowship). Each of these issues is approached in the Buddhist way, identifying interdependence, the co-arising of multiple and systemic forms of harm, the expression of compassion, and the fundamental commitment to a world that refrains from personal and structural violence and protects all beings.

Awareness of our rapidly deteriorating environment and the impact of threats to life in the nuclear age have loomed large on the BPF agenda since its formation, led primarily by scholar and Buddhist teacher Joanna Macy. Macy is a proponent of systems thinking, which studies the interrelationship and flow of complex ideas and problems so as to serve the entire system and avoid unintended consequences. She considers ecosystems, for example, as complex wholes, where an intervention in one part of the system, such as deforestation, has disastrous consequences for all the other interdependent aspects of the system, such as water reserves, erosion, animal shelter, and human usage of forest products. Macy has devised compelling workshops based on systems thinking that attract large numbers to grieve the losses from environmental destruction and commit to sound and compassionate policies and behaviors on behalf of the global commons. She has also created workshops to overcome the despair of nuclearism and encourage empowering anti-nuclear responses. The basis of her workshops and her accompanying books, especially *Coming Back to Life* and *Active Hope*, is the Buddhist insight into the interdependence of all phenomena and the co-arising of mutually dependent systems. Called *paticca samuppad* in Pali, this is an ancient Buddhist teaching applied by Macy to contemporary problems (Macy 2009–2012).

Thich Nhat Hanh expressed this concept of the interaction of causes and conditions succinctly as "this is like this, because that is like that" (Thich Nhat Hanh 1998).

> When the Buddha taught, he was said to turn the Wheel of the Dharma. Indeed, his central doctrine is like a wheel, for through it he taught the dependent co-arising of all things, how they continually change and condition each other in interconnections as real as the spokes in a wheel. . . . The recognition of our essential nonseparateness from the world, beyond the shaky walls erected of our fear and greed, is a Dharma gift occurring in every generation. . . . Along with the destructive, even suicidal nature of many of our public policies, social and intellectual developments are converging now to bring into bold relief the Buddha's teaching of dependent co-arising—and the wheel of the Dharma turns again.
> *(Engaged Buddhism 2009–2012)*

One organization that has taken seriously the destruction of the forests and the web of unintended consequences is the International Network of Engaged Buddhists (INEB), founded by the remarkable Sulak Sivaraksa in Bangkok in 1989. INEB assembles Buddhist activists from Asia and the West, mounts conferences, develops workshops for monks and supporters, and inspires a movement of progressive Buddhists who advocate for equality, environment, and ethics in their own *sanghas*, home countries, and beyond. In Buddhist countries that have been closed to the outside world for decades, such as Myanmar, INEB plays a role in educating and empowering marginalized monks and social organizers eager to promote change. A new phenomenon in the Asian Buddhist world, where Buddhists have been divided over the centuries by history and sectarianism, INEB exerts a moral challenge to make Buddhism relevant to the current contexts of oppression and destruction of culture and nature. Although modest in size, INEB's inclusiveness brings together Buddhists from East Asian countries such as Japan and China, South Asian Indian Ambedkarites and Sri Lankans, and Southeast Asian Thais and Burmese, each with its own very different culture, economy, religious expressions, and social norms. Common ground includes balancing tradition with modernism in society and *sangha*, advancing liberation, encouraging ethical practices, and protecting life in all its forms and varieties.

Sulak Sivaraksa, a Buddhist scholar, author, keen social critic, and expansive activist, challenges structural injustice and exploitation in all its forms. He has been imprisoned for criticizing the king, a crime in Thailand, which has brought him measures of fame and blame. According to one of his biographers, Donald Swearer, "Sulak's fame as a social critic, intellectual gadfly, and activist has made him a controversial figure, especially in Thailand" (Swearer in Queen 1996, 196). Sulak has developed cherished friendships and accolades through worldwide travels as a spokesperson for Engaged Buddhism, environmental protection, alternatives to capitalism and consumerism, and appropriately scaled development. He has supported dissenting monks from Thailand and abroad, nudging Buddhism toward partnering to renew society and refresh outdated beliefs and practices within the *sangha*.

A visionary and a maverick, Sulak Sivaraksa has won the Right Livelihood Award, considered a people's alternative to the Nobel Peace Prize, for which he had been nominated in 1994. His nomination noted

> Sulak has all his life been a courageous and articulate voice for peace, human rights, and social justice. Rooted deeply in his Buddhist faith ... he has helped to form a community of persons dedicated to nonviolence in a region torn by violence and war.
> *(Swearer in Queen 1996, 198)*

As founder and guide, Sulak and INEB are linked; he inspires and leads the organization, which in turn offers him a platform to influence Engaged Buddhists East and West with his analysis of society and his remedies for reform and rejuvenation. Engaged Buddhism would be far less visible, resonant, and collegial without Sulak's passions and total commitment to a Buddhist renewal. One innovative approach to protect the environment, the ordaining of trees, arose through his and INEB's outreach and encouragement of social responsibility in Thailand.

Susan Darlington documented this unusual effort at environmental preservation by monks in *The Ordination of a Tree: The Thai Buddhist Environmental Movement* (2012). An issue in Thailand is the destruction of the forests, clear-cut to satisfy business and government financial interests but utterly destructive to rural Thais who depend on the forests for animals, birds, foraged food, fuel, clean water, and their protective spirits. Protests and advocacy campaigns failed to stop the deforestation. Local monks, whose lives are intertwined with the villagers, conceived of the image of making a tree holy so that loggers would not cut it down. Wrapping a piece of saffron clothing around a tree symbolizes the reverence offered to monks; a woodcutter would respect an "ordained" tree much as he would refrain from harming a monk. The movement, so visible and visceral, took hold, and eventually monks and villagers ordained entire perimeters of forests scheduled for clearcutting, which indeed stopped the woodcutters in their tracks. Darlington's book outlines the historical precedents, rituals, trajectory of the movement, and future direction of this innovative approach to forest preservation.

> In Thailand, Buddhism is a lived religion, one that responds to ever-changing circumstances and a variety of agendas. How it is interpreted and acted upon impacts not only how people perceive the world and their place within it, but their social responsibilities as well. Ordaining a tree is a radical, provocative and controversial act that challenges people to take responsibility—for themselves, their society and the natural environment.
> *(Darlington 2012, 1)*

In neighboring Burma, political circumstances have offered far less freedom and access to the wider world than in Thailand. Overtaken by a military coup in 1962, the Burmese have endured fifty-plus years of dictatorship and its attendant hardships. Monks have an activist history in Burma, also known as Myanmar, but expressing their solidarity with the struggling population resulted in severe punishment. Nonetheless, in 2007 the monks rose up in what became known as the Saffron Revolution, taking to the streets for days of demonstrations and demands for freedom. In Myanmar and other Southeast Asian countries, each monk carries an alms bowl that is filled daily by the laity, demonstrating the interdependent reciprocal relationship between monks and ordinary citizens, one receiving food and the other receiving all-important merit for offering food. During the demonstration days, monks turned over their alms bowls, indicating their refusal to receive food from the junta, denying them the possibility of attaining merit. The demonstrations grew by the day, monks and laity walking together, nonviolently protesting military rule.

> On 22 September around two thousand monks marched through Yangon and ten thousand through Mandalay, with other demonstrations in five townships across Myanmar. Those marching through the capital chanted the "Myitta Thote" (the Buddha's words on loving kindness) marching through a barricade on the street in front of Nobel Peace Prize laureate Aung San Suu Kyi, still under house arrest.... As of 22 September 2007, the Buddhist monks were reported to have withdrawn spiritual services from all military personnel in a symbolic move that was seen as very powerful in such a deeply religious country as Burma. The military rulers seemed at a loss as to how to deal with the demonstrations by the monks, as using violence against monks would incense and enrage the people of Burma even further, almost certainly prompting massive civil unrest and perhaps violence ... On 24 September eyewitnesses reported between 30,000 and 100,000 people demonstrating in Yangon.... The marches occurred simultaneously in at least 25 cities across Myanmar, with columns of monks stretching up to 1-kilometre.
>
> *("Saffron Revolution: September 22 Escalation")*

The Saffron Revolution demonstrates the power available in the monastic community, especially in alliance with the citizens of Burma, to lead efforts that might liberate the country from oppression and destruction. Unsuccessful in 2007, the repercussions of this rebellion contributed to the eventual weakening of the junta, which now shares power with Aung San Suu Kyi and her party, the National League for Democracy.

A Japanese peace movement led by a small Nichiren sect, Nipponzan Myohoji, will close this sampling of exemplary Engaged Buddhist leaders and organizations. Founded by Nichidatsu Fujii in 1945, he devoted this new Buddhist sect to the abolition of nuclear weapons, appropriate not only for a Japanese but poignantly for one whose sixtieth birthday fell on August 6, 1945, forever remembered as Hiroshima Day. "A monk since 1916, a disciple of the thirteenth-century prophet Nichiren, and a Japanese Buddhist with a profound tie to Mahatma Gandhi, Fujii held an unwavering commitment to nonviolence and peace" (Green in Queen 2000, 128). Fujii's band of monks, concentrated in Japan but spread around the world, participate in movements for peace and justice, attend demonstrations against war and tyranny, organize lengthy peace walks, and erect Peace Pagodas, or *stupas*, wherever they live as a way to purify the land and build resistance communities. Their Buddhist practice involves chanting a mantra while beating a hand drum, as well as reciting *sutras* (Buddhist texts). Unlike the Southeast Asian Buddhists or the Zen practitioners in Japan, there is no silent meditation, but for the monks and nuns of Nipponzan Myohoji, their drumming and chanting provides meditative concentration.

This author has known a number of monks and nuns ordained in this tradition through the coincidence (or perhaps twist of fate) of residing near their first Peace Pagoda and community in the US. For thirty-plus years, this author has connected with, and been inspired by, the monks and nuns of this order, for whom every moment of life is engagement and opportunity to serve, to practice peace, to become peaceful. Kato Shonin, the head monk of the order in the US, affirms that

> Life itself is engagement and we do not need to separate into engaged or not engaged Buddhism. The Buddha's teaching is not a tool or an ornament, but exists to bring peace to the world. We follow the teaching because it leads to peace.
>
> *(Green in Queen 2000, 154)*

This most politically active Buddhist sect, typically humble and always generous, can be counted on as participants in the peace movement, contributing their nonviolent commitments and high-minded values to whatever issues of justice or environmental preservation present themselves, and inspiring citizen activists in Japan and the West to eschew violence and build peaceful societies.

Shadows and Challenges

Nations with majority Buddhist populations do not rank as the most peaceful in the world. In fact, the Global Peace Index rates only Bhutan in its list of the twenty most peaceful countries in the world (Global Peace Index 2016). Sadly, Buddhists are not exempt from greed, anger, and delusion, resulting in their spawning warriors, demagogues, fierce nationalists, rapacious capitalists, and unjust societal structures. Cambodia, an almost all Buddhist country, collapsed into an auto-genocide led by the Khmer Rouge in 1975 that killed two million of their fellow citizens. Sri Lankan majority Sinhalese Buddhists led a twenty-five-year civil war against their Tamil, non-Buddhist minority. The Burmese Buddhist military staged a coup in 1962 that gave them total control over the country, which they brought to ruination in a fifty-year regime. Currently, factions of Burmese Buddhist monks engage in Islamophobic hate campaigns against their under-10-percent Muslim population. Japanese, including Buddhists, fought and committed war crimes in World War II.

Engaged Buddhism generally exists as a positive force in the creation of just and harmonious communities and nations. Most of them today oppose war and there is little support for just war theory among Engaged Buddhists. However, they represent a tiny fraction of the world's Buddhist population and exert only modest influence in their societies. The violence and sectarianism in Buddhist countries represents the struggle of all human beings to align the ethical teachings of their religion with the delusions of the mind, a fundamental ignorance that results in separation, fear, and self-protection. Buddhists, like all beings, are in an ongoing process of development and awareness, not yet prepared to live the truth of this Buddhist teaching from the Dhammapada (Byrom 1976, 3–4):

> We are what we think.
> All that we are arises with our thoughts.
> With our thoughts we make the world.
> Speak or act with an impure mind
> And trouble will follow you
> As the wheel follows the ox that draws the cart.
>
> In this world
> Hate never yet dispelled hate.
> Only love dispels hate.
> This is the law,
> Ancient and inexhaustible.

References

Buddhist Peace Fellowship: Cultivating Compassionate Action. 1978. "Welcome to BPF." www.bpf.org

Byrom, Thomas. 1976. *The Dhammapada: The Sayings of the Buddha*. New York: Vintage Books.

Darlington, Susan. 2012. *The Ordination of a Tree: The Thai Buddhist Environmental Movement*. Albany, NY: State University of New York Press.

Eppsteiner, Fred, ed. 1988. *The Path of Compassion: Writings on Socially Engaged Buddhism*. Berkeley, CA: Parallax Press.

Fields, Rick. 1981. *How the Swans Came to the Lake: A Narrative History of Buddhism in America*. Boston, MA: Shambhala Publications.

Global Peace Index. 2016. http://economicsandpeace.org/wp-content/uploads/2016/06/GPI-2016-Report_2.pdf

Goldstein, Joseph. 2002. *One Dharma: The Emerging Buddhist Wisdom*. New York: Harper Collins.

Goldstein, Joseph and Jack Kornfield. 1987. *Seeking the Heart of Wisdom: The Path of Insight Meditation*. Boston, MA: Shambhala Publications.

Hanh, Thich Nhat. 1987. *Being Peace*. Berkeley, CA: Parallax Press.

Hanh, Thich Nhat Hanh. 1998. "The Sutras on Dependent Co-Arising and Great Emptiness," *Dharma Talk*, March 19. http://www.buddhist-canon.com/PLAIN/TNHSUT-

His Holiness the Dalai Lama. 2011. *Beyond Religion: Ethics for a Whole World*. New York: Houghton Mifflin Harcourt Publishing Company.

Macy, Joanna. 2009. "Joanna Macy and Her Work." www.joannamacy.net

Macy, Joanna. 2009–2012. Engaged Buddhism. "Dependent Co-Arising." joannamacy.net

Pew Research Center. 2015. "Buddhists and Buddhism." www.pewresearchcenter.org

Queen, Christopher, ed. 2000. *Engaged Buddhism in the West*. Somerville, MA: Wisdom Publications.

Queen, Christopher and Sallie King, eds. 1996. *Engaged Buddhism: Buddhist Liberation Movements in Asia*. Albany, NY: State University of New York Press.

Sivaraksa, Sulak. 1992. *Seeds of Peace: A Buddhist Vision for Renewing Society*. Berkeley, CA: Parallax Press.

Soka Gakkai International, Buddhism in Action. October 2005. "Three Poisons—the Source of the Problem." SGI Quarterly. www.sgi.org

Vision of Humanity: Global Peace Index. 2016. "Global Rankings." www.visionofhumanity.org

Wikipedia. "Religion in Japan." https://en.wikipedia.org/wiki/Religion_in_Japan

Wikipedia. "Saffron Revolution: September 22 Escalation." https://en.wikipedia.org/wiki/Saffron_Revolution

Wild Mind Buddhist Meditation. "The Near Enemy of Even-minded Love." www.wildmind.org/tag/near-enemy

4
ASPECTS OF SOCIAL ENGAGEMENT WITHIN THE SOUTHEAST ASIAN BUDDHIST WORLD

Jordan Baskerville and Somboon Chungprampree

One of the central features of the Buddha's teachings is the spirit of non-violence. In a number of the earliest recorded Buddhist discourses, the Buddha preaches non-harming and non-violence, and the peaceful resolution to potentially volatile conflicts (see Appendix). The Buddha did not teach violence as a means of solving problems. It is therefore quite difficult for Buddhists to justify violence through scriptural means, and peace and peacebuilding should thus be a logical outcome for Buddhists. In this chapter, two of the leading Buddhist peacebuilders, Sulak Sivaraksa and Maha Ghosananda, are briefly examined, followed by a discussion of Asia-based peacebuilding initiatives that the International Network of Engaged Buddhists (INEB) have introduced.

The Buddha's adherence to non-violence rests on the basis of his quest, solution and teachings on overcoming suffering through the cultivation of ethics, wisdom and compassion. According to the life story of the Buddha, he became disillusioned with the inevitable suffering that comes with birth as a sentient being. Faced with these realities, he embarked on a quest to permanently overcome suffering and achieve the deepest form of happiness and contentment. After experimenting with a number of different spiritual paths that were in vogue at the time, the Buddha came to a realization of the path of the Middle Way—a path devoid of extremes such as starvation and sensory deprivation on the one hand and extreme sensory indulgence on the other. This Middle Way path, combined with deep concentration and insight into the nature of mind and reality, brought about a profound realization and shift in the Buddha—an event known as the Buddha's enlightenment—that is said to have revealed and uprooted the causes of suffering.

Within the Buddha's realizations that came with his experience of enlightenment, it is reported that he came to see the truth of karma—that actions have repercussions, both positive and negative. One of the primary ways of generating negative karma, that is, karma that will produce suffering for oneself and others, is partaking in violent actions of body, speech and mind. Partly as a result of this realization came the first of five ethical precepts for Buddhists: the precept of abstaining from harming living beings. This and the other four precepts—to abstain from false speech, theft, sexual misconduct and intoxicants—are known in Pāli as *pañcasīlāni* and are found throughout the various traditions of Buddhism. The five precepts are relevant for both lay and monastic Buddhists and are central to the Buddha's teaching on proper conduct and avoiding suffering. These precepts represent one of the important religiously inspired ethical bases for understanding the following peace-makers and initiatives in Southeast Asia.

Buddhist Peace Building: Sulak Sivaraksa

Sulak Sivaraksa was born in 1933 in Thonburi, across the Chao Praya River from Siam's capital, Bangkok. During his youth, he ordained as a novice at his family's temple, *Wat Thongnopphakhun*, in Khlong San, Thonburi. Sulak found he had a natural interest in learning about people with belief systems different from his own. He cites a long-standing interest in books "on comparative religion ... that respected other religion and rites" and an admirable (but critical) respect for other religious traditions (Sivaraksa 1998, 25). This early interest would translate in later life to a number of interreligious dialogues and work aimed at peacebuilding between Sulak and other religious leaders. He went to study philosophy, politics and law in England—spending a total of eight years there before returning to Thailand in 1962.

Sulak's shift towards social and political activism was prompted in part by the Vietnam War. He credits the Quaker group known as the American Friends Service Committee with first raising his awareness about the issues, immense suffering and related costs of the devastating nearby war. Despite his government's support of the conflict, the empathic illumination prompted by meetings with the Quaker group incited Sulak to commit to taking a stand against the war in Vietnam. The meeting with the Quakers would prove to have lasting effects in Sulak's life—in part by influencing his activism and inspiring him to speak out against violence and injustice. Sulak writes that he has been

> very attracted by the Quaker notions of the sacredness of a human being and nonviolence. I found the Quakers more articulate than Buddhists on the need to question and resist the powers of the state, to question the status quo; Buddhists have been coexisting with the state for too long.
> *(Rothberg 1993, 121–128)*

Following the meeting with the Quakers, he started to write about other political issues that reflected a gradual shift away from often-conservative, establishment-enforcing opinions to offering Buddhist-inspired, iconoclastic takes on contemporary situations in numerous books, talks and in in his influential journal, *The Social Science Review.*

A nominee for the Nobel Peace Prize, and 1995 winner of the Right Livelihood Award, Sulak has spent much of his life campaigning and organizing for a more just, peaceful world. He has also created a number of organizations that aim to bring people together for various goals, including peacebuilding, interfaith dialogue, alternative education and sustainable development. In contrast to classical Thai formulations of Buddhist theory and practice, Sulak turns his focus largely toward the external and societal causes of suffering (*dukkha*), and on a highly active approach to dealing with and alleviating those causes, primarily through education, activism, organizing, ethics and meditation. At the same time, he devotes some of his intellectual effort toward more classical Buddhist foci on internal causes of suffering and their alleviation. Sulak offers a vision of a reinvented Buddhism that he believes actively addresses the most pressing existential problems facing Thailand and the world: inequality, environmental destruction, exploitation, consumerism and warfare. Moreover, he attempts to theorize and practice a Buddhism that is relevant for a modern world in the face of perceived failure to do so by the Thai Buddhist *sangha* establishment.

In 1989, inspired by the Buddhist Peace Fellowship in America, Sulak, Pracha Hutanuwatr and others founded the International Network of Engaged Buddhists (INEB). The initial group consisted of a few members looking to connect and support socially aware Buddhists in Asia and western countries. In subsequent years, the small group would grow to a large network of practitioners across the globe. The network started as a NGO-type organization helping a Buddhist tribal group in Bangladesh and forming a "jungle university" close to the Burmese border that provided free education for students and minority groups fleeing the oppression in Burma following the uprising of 1988. Moreover, the group trained Sri Lankan and Cambodian monks in conflict resolution strategies and, with the help of prominent, influential members such as H.H. The Dalai Lama and Vietnamese monk, author and activist Thich Nhat Hanh, has grown to include branches in more than thirty-five countries. The numerous organizations Sulak has founded and is involved with—including the Spirit in Education Movement, INEB Institute and the Wongsanit Ashram, among others—are vehicles designed to preserve and transmit his message of the need for Buddhist-based social engagement and change.

Maha Ghosananda

Another significant figure in Southeast Asian Buddhist social engagement and peacebuilding is the late Cambodian monk, Venerable Maha Ghosananda. Nobel Peace prize nominee Ghosananda, called "the Gandhi of Cambodia" ("Preah Maha Ghosananda" 2017), was born in Takeo Province, Cambodia, where he took up the monastic life at age 8. He would go on to study in Phnom Penh, Battambang, and at Nalanda University in Bihar, India. In 1965, Ghoasanada studied meditation in southern Thailand until 1978 when he visited Cambodian refugees on the Thai-Cambodian border. At the camps, he offered hope, established temples and ordained monks. In 1988, Ghosananda was appointed head of the Cambodian sangha (*sanghreach*).

In 1992, he started one of a number of Dhammayietra, or peace walks, in order to bring hope to war-torn Cambodia. The first walk lasted sixteen days and covered approximately twenty-five miles. Somboon Chungprampree (current Secretariat of INEB) had the privilege of completing one of these peace walks in 1997 with Maha Ghosananda. During that time, the Khmer Rouge were still present in the area of western Cambodia, yet Dhammayietra participants were allowed in. The walk lasted nearly a month and included monks, nuns and laypeople from various countries. The Dhammayietra started in Battambang and ended along the Thai-Cambodian border. Walking would take place early in the dark hours of the morning and would commence before the temperature reached its zenith. The group would rest and Ghosananda would sometimes give Dharma talks. Participants would often stay for free in temples and schools. The route itself was dangerous as the countryside was, at that time, littered with landmines. At times, a bus would drive in front of the group and the marchers would have to walk in its tire tracks so as to be sure of avoiding any mines. On the route, participants would sometimes encounter weeping villagers. When asked why they were crying, they replied that they had not seen monks in twenty years because the Khmer Rouge had eliminated most of them.

At one point on the journey, an argument among some foreigners had erupted. Somboon remembers vividly Venerable Maha Ghosananda walking back to address the quarrelers. Referencing the *Tamonata Sutta*, he spoke of four kinds of people: "One in darkness who is headed for darkness, one in darkness who is headed for light, one in light who is headed for darkness, and one in light who is headed for light."[1] The arguing walkers heard this and quickly ended their quarrel. At another point during his third peace walk, two participants were killed in gunfire between Khmer Rouge soldiers and government forces. Following the deaths, Ghosanada stated, "this violence is indeed the reason we walk" ("Somdet Phra Maha Ghosananda" 2017). Maha Ghosanada brought Buddhist-inspired loving kindness (*metta*) into everyday life and provided optimism for many in Cambodia during a time of crisis, while simultaneously helping to restore the decimated Cambodian Buddhist sangha (see Maha Ghosananda 1991; Santidhammo Bhikkhu 2009). He died at the age of 93 in Northampton, Massachusetts.

The International Network of Engaged Buddhists (INEB)

The final case study in Southeast Asian peacebuilding efforts examined here is the Bangkok-based International Network of Engaged Buddhists (INEB). Buddhist values of compassion and non-violence play a central role in their initiatives and efforts (Baskerville 2016). Members of INEB value the Buddhist idea of the *kalyanamitra* or spiritual friends and focus on building long-term relationships with others, knowing that we can accomplish more when people work together. This model of friendship is not one of superficiality but reflects a deeper type of friendship where we are free to tell each other challenging things we may not want to hear but that are necessary. Members of INEB feel this is an important aspect of honoring the Buddhist precept of abstaining from false speech.

One of the recent efforts INEB has been involved with is the creation of the International Forum on Buddhist-Muslim relations. This initiative is aimed at building international, interreligious relationships that can help foster mutual understanding, mitigate conflict and work towards more collaboration in various arenas. Three summits have taken place so far. The first one, in 2006, arose from a need to address the ongoing conflict in Thailand's deep south and was held at Suan Dusit Rajabhat University in Bangkok. Thirty-five participants came from eight countries for the three-day summit. The second meeting, in 2013, was spurred by ongoing Muslim-Buddhist conflicts in Sri Lanka and Burma. Following the meeting, Buddhist and Muslim attendees released a joint pronouncement recognizing the need for peaceful solutions to these conflicts. The statement reads in part:

> If Buddhist and Muslim communities can overcome the challenges that confront them, there is tremendous potential for the growth and development of ideas and values that may help to transform the region. For Buddhist and Muslim philosophies embody gems of wisdom about the purpose of life, the position and role of the human being and her relationship with all other sentient beings and nature which could well liberate contemporary civilization from its multiple crises. The young in these communities in particular should be imbued with these profound ideas and values about life and its meaning.
>
> Our actions will include intrareligious and interreligious initiatives in education, advocacy, rapid reaction/solidarity visits/early warning/conflict prevention, constructive engagement with the government, strategic common action, and the effective use of media for positive messages. We will also engage in multi-stake holder partnerships with governments, inter-governmental bodies such as the association of South East Asian Nations (ASEAN), South Asian Association for Regional Cooperation (SAARC), the Organization of Islamic Cooperation (OIC), and the United Nations.[2]

In 2015, INEB co-sponsored a third summit with Buddhist and Muslim leaders in Yogyakarta, Indonesia. This meeting was designed to address common regional issues in Southeast Asia and to work collaboratively towards political solutions to them. Following the meeting, participants of the summit released a joint statement—translated into thirteen languages—designed to address some of these issues, while at the same time highlighting scriptural passages from both Islam and Buddhism that speak to the need for tolerance and peace. Part of the declaration reads:

> We, Buddhist and Muslim leaders, recognize that our followers have developed together a harmonious relationship, which has become the foundation for building peace and prosperity in many parts of the world. Buddhism and Islam share in their respective scriptures and other canonical texts the importance of holistic and positive peace, which encompasses the notions of inner peace, peace among humans, and peace with nature.
>
> We reaffirm that Islam and Buddhism are religions of mercy and compassion committed to justice for all of humankind. Both traditions respect the sacredness of life and inherent dignity of human existence, which is the foundation of all human rights without any distinction as to race, color, language, or religion. We reject the abuse of our religions in support of discrimination and violence. Buddhism and Islam have been misused by some for their own political purposes to fuel prejudice and stereotyping and to incite discrimination and violence. We categorically reject such abuse and pledge to counter extremist religious interpretations and actions with our authentic primary narratives of peace.[3]

Another enterprise INEB is currently involved with is the building of relationships with a wide range of other Buddhist groups, including some controversial ones such as those in Sri Lanka and Burma. The points of these activities are, similar to the Buddhist-Muslim initiative, designed to find common ground and foster friendships along the lines of the *kalyanamitra* ideal. Such efforts are also designed to help these groups to re-focus their energy and attention away from issues that are conflict-prone and into more constructive areas such as alternative education, consumer rights and sustainable development. By focusing on these areas of agreement, practitioners of differing traditions can develop relationships and engage in constructive collaborations that may lead to further areas of partnership across conflict lines.

The final peacebuilding project examined here is the INEB Institute. A long-time vision of Sulak Sivaraksa's, the INEB Institute is a recent, alternative education initiative held under the auspices of the International Network of Engaged Buddhists. The Institute's mission incudes:

> Promote understanding, cooperation, and networking among inter-Buddhist and inter-religious social action groups; act as an information resource related to areas of social concern; facilitate conferences, education and training, based on Buddhist values and practices that support and strengthen socially active individuals and groups.

("About" 2017)

The INEB Institute offers a three-month English for Engaged Social Service program that is "designed to foster English language for peace and justice that is grounded in Buddhist thought and practice."[4] Despite the emphasis on aspects of Buddhism, the program is open to all who wish to improve their English language skills while deepening their understanding of structural violence and ways of overcoming it. So far, students have come from a number of countries from across Asia. In part, the program is a means of building interregional friendships and a venue for religious, linguistic and cultural exchange and eventual peacebuilding.

The INEB Institute also offers a six-month "Awakening Leadership Program" aimed at training a new generation of leaders in peacebuilding, deep ecology, conflict transformation and inner transformation. The program, led by former monk, author and co-founder of INEB Pracha Hutanuwatr, features a series of modules that can be taken together or individually. The program is designed around Buddhist values but, like the English program, is open to all. The Awakening Leadership Program is focused on the following approaches to learning:

Contemplative: Meditation, mindfulness practice and time in silence are integrated into the learning experience. Right mindfulness is the most important key factor for awakening.

Participative: Participants and facilitators co-create the body of knowledge together. This includes sharing of authority in the learning community that we create during this course. Power sharing means empowerment; empowerment here means self-empowerment.

Reflective: Rigorous thinking and reflecting both individually and collectively on issues and experiences is a key part of the learning process. We emphasize learning how to unlearn and relearn as it is a critical component of being successfully socially active.[5]

For more information on the INEB Institute, see: http://inebinstitute.org/.

Conclusion

Seen together, each of these individuals and programs represent an important, coordinated effort within the Buddhist world of Southeast Asia and beyond, leading towards a more just, peaceful and sustainable world. With the existential crises of climate change, inequality and violence spread across the globe, more initiatives that seek to foster non-violence and positive social change are urgently needed. In particular, interreligious dialogue and cooperation are key to maintaining any hope of solving contemporary global challenges. It is our hope that the above-discussed individuals and initiatives can serve as a starting point for further action and engagement.

APPENDIX

The Buddha taught on a number of occasions about the importance of nonviolence and compassion for sentient beings. For example, in the *Sutta Nipata* (149–150), the Buddha says:

> Just as a mother would protect her only child at the risk of her own life, even so, cultivate a boundless heart toward all beings. Let your thoughts of boundless love pervade the world. Let your love flow outward through the universe, to its height, its depth, its broad extent, a limitless love, without hatred or envy.[6]

In the *Dhammapada* (129, 130, 131), one of the most well-known and important sets of the Buddha's teachings, he proclaims:

> All tremble at violence; all fear death. Putting oneself in the place of another, one should not kill nor cause another to kill.
> All tremble at violence; life is dear to all. Putting oneself in the place of another, one should not kill nor cause another to kill.
> One who while himself seeking happiness, oppresses with violence other beings who also desire happiness will not attain happiness hereafter.[7]

Another verse (256–257) states:

> Whoever settles a matter by violence is not just. The wise calmly considers what is right and what is wrong. Whoever guides others by a procedure that is nonviolent and fair is said to be a guardian of truth, wise and just.[8]

Again, the Buddha, in the *Dhammapada* (142) stresses non-violence when he says:

> Even though he be well attired, yet if he is poised, calm, controlled and established in the holy life, having set aside violence towards all beings—he, truly, is a holy man, a renunciate, a monk.[9]

The prohibition of non-violence pertains not just to physical violence, but to violent speech as well. On this, the Buddha (*Dhammapada*, 133) taught:
Do not speak harshly to anybody; those who are spoken to will answer thee in the same way. Angry speech is painful, blows for blows will touch thee.[10]

Notes

1 Full text of the Sutta available at: http://www.accesstoinsight.org/tipitaka/an/an04/an04.085.than.html
2 Full statement available at: www.inebnetwork.org/images/stories/Text_seedofpeace/Vol.29%20No.3%20Sept.-Dec.%202556%20(2013).pdf
3 Full statement available at: http://inebnetwork.org/images/stories/Text_seedofpeace/SEEDS%20OF%20PEACE_V31_no2.pdf
4 Baskerville, Jordan. "Opening of the INEB Institute," Seeds of Peace 32: 2 (May–August 2016): 26.
5 "Awakening Leadership Training," accessed July 1st, http://inebinstitute.org/blt/.
6 Buddha. "Dhammapada," Access to Insight, trans. Thanissaro Bhikkhu, accessed June 15, 2017. www.accesstoinsight.org/tipitaka/kn/dhp/index.html.
7 Ñanamoli Thera, trans. "The Practice of Loving-Kindness (Metta)As Taught by the Buddha in the Pali Canon," Access to Insight, accessed July 1, 2017. www.accesstoinsight.org/lib/authors/nanamoli/wheel007.html.
8 Buddha. "Dhammapada," Access to Insight, trans. Thanissaro Bhikkhu, accessed June 15, 2017. www.accesstoinsight.org/tipitaka/kn/dhp/index.html.
9 Buddha. "Dhammapada," Access to Insight, trans. Thanissaro Bhikkhu, accessed June 15, 2017. www.accesstoinsight.org/tipitaka/kn/dhp/index.html.
10 Buddha. "Dhammapada," Access to Insight, trans. Thanissaro Bhikkhu, accessed June 15, 2017. www.accesstoinsight.org/tipitaka/kn/dhp/index.html.

References

"About," INEB Institute, accessed June 25, 2017, http://inebinstitute.org/the-origin/.
"Awakening Leadership Training," accessed July 1, http://inebinstitute.org/blt/.
Baskerville, Jordan. "Opening of the INEB Institute," *Seeds of Peace* 32: 2 (May–August 2016): 26.
Bhikkhu, Santidhammo. *Maha Ghosananda: The Buddha of the Battlefield*. Nonthaburi, Thailand: S. R. Printing, 2009.
Buddha. "*Dhammapada*," *Access to Insight*, trans. Thanissaro Bhikkhu, accessed June 15, 2017. www.accesstoinsight.org/tipitaka/kn/dhp/index.html.
Ghosananda, Maha. *Step by Step: Meditations on Wisdom and Compassion*. Berkeley, CA: Parallax Press, 1991.
Ñanamoli Thera, trans. "The Practice of Loving-Kindness (Metta)As Taught by the Buddha in the Pali Canon," *Access to Insight*, accessed July 1, 2017. www.accesstoinsight.org/lib/authors/nanamoli/wheel007.html.

"Preah Maha Ghosananda," *Economist.com*, accessed July 5, 2017. www.economist.com/node/8881498.

Rothberg, Donald. "A Thai Perspective on Socially Engaged Buddhism: A Conversation With Sulak Sivaraksa," *ReVision* (1993): 121–128.

Sivaraksa, Sulak. *Loyalty Demands Dissent: Autobiography of an Engaged Buddhist*. Berkeley, CA: Parallax Press, 1998.

"Somdet Phra Maha Ghosananda," *Buddhanet*, accessed July 5, 2017. www.buddhanet.net/masters/maha-gosanada.htm.

Thanissaro Bhikkhu, trans. *Tamonata Sutta: Darkness. Access to Insight*. accessed July 21, 2017. https://www.accesstoinsight.org/tipitaka/an/an04/an04.085.than.html

PART II
The Jewish Tradition

5

WAR AND PEACE

Intertwining Threads in the Jewish Tradition

Rabbi Tirzah Firestone, PhD

Introduction

The Jewish tradition is far from monolithic. Within the compass of Jewish scripture and evolving thought, one finds the advocacy of both war-making and peacemaking, slaying and healing. At times such contradictory texts even run side-by-side. What do we make of this seeming double standard? And what guidance can we derive from it for our era?

In this chapter I will examine the Jewish tradition for its approaches to war, pointing out stories of retribution, injunctions to conquer and annihilate, and the moral imperative to kill for the sake of self-preservation. Side by side with these, I will investigate the Jewish principle that life must be saved at all cost, the injunction against murder, and the understanding that every human being is a sacred representation of *imago Dei*. I will also show the intertwining values of justice and peace made famous by the Hebrew prophets and the rabbinic value placed upon proactive peacemaking.

I will then study the tension of these apparent opposites in the light of two more forces, the first one mythical and the second historical. The national identity of chosenness stems from early Hebrew scripture and to this day holds enormous weight in the collective Jewish self-definition. The second is the traumatic impact of extreme persecution over centuries. I will elucidate how the identity of chosenness side by side with the fact of protracted Jewish historical trauma both influence the Jewish balance between war and peace on the world stage.

Finally, a third voice may also be heard in the tradition: one that urges the necessary discernment by which to stop, listen, and distinguish the requirements of the moment and one's responsibility to it. This too stems from Hebrew Scripture, and is called the *kol demama daka*, the delicate voice of silence, by which the

Living God may be heard. It is in this quiet discernment that the value for life, its preservation, and the call for taking the most appropriate and humane action resound with transcendent force.

A Rich Tapestry

To begin, an image: Each of our ancient traditions, like a rich bolt of woven fabric, rolls down to us through time, a veritable stream of cloth that has been crafted across generations. Throughout the ages, countless hands have made their own additions, each contribution holding to its own truest vision and capacity.

Imagine the tapestry of your own lineage before you now, sparkling with threads of prophetic gold, tiny translucent pearls of clarity, flecks of pith and wit peppered here and there. And then there are the dark parts, which over time were also swept into the weave: the remains of war, drops of blood, and scatterings of dust, small twigs, and human tears, the shells of small animals that happened to crawl into its path, all parts included. Multiple fibers and threads, colors and textures. The luminous and high-minded as well as the dark and self-serving; all braided together, yet still one fabric.

The long life of Judaism is like this: a gorgeous confusion of high and low, color and gloom, threads that are luminous and subtly woven next to fibers as coarse as rope. Stitches that are brilliant with universal altruism and those that are thick with pragmatism and self-protection. To describe the particular strands of war and pacifism in Judaism, one must tease out various and disparate threads that live side by side.

Judaism has been in the making for roughly 4,000 years and is far from monolithic. (The latter is most certainly true of all the traditions we are undertaking to discuss in this volume.) As I consider the two themes of war and pacifism in Judaism, I will draw from the Hebrew Bible and rabbinic literature, both of which lie at the core of the mythopoeic identity of the Jewish people. I invite the reader to join me in examining these illustrations from Judaism's long history as early precedents that form the many voices of the evolving Jewish ethos.

Nekamah: Retribution and Vengeance

We open our study with a look at a rare yet important theme in the Jewish cultural tapestry, that of retributive war. From Genesis, the wrathful faces of Simeon and Levi come to the fore: the sons of Jacob who entered the city of Shechem (today's Nablus) to kill all the men within its gates. Why did they do it? To avenge the rape of their sister Dinah at the hands of the city's prince (Gen. 34).

Although Dinah was never again mentioned in the written text, her dishonor was apparently too much for her brothers. They made a deceitful pact with the city's elders, prerequisite for the prince to marry their sister: Every male in the city would need to be circumcised. A war of ambush ensued as the men lay ailing.

Jacob's other sons joined Simeon and Levi in seizing the women and children and plundering the town.

Along the same thread of vengeance, we find Moses, the leader and prophet of the newly branded nation as he orders a special campaign *latet nikmat Adonai al Midian*: "to wreak the Lord's vengeance on Midian" (Numb. 31:3). This order included making war on the dynasty's five kings, with the injunction to kill every male and burn down their towns and encampments.

The oddity is that not long before this command, Moses had personally taken refuge with the Midianites in his flight from the Pharaoh (Ex. 2:13–15). While in Midian, he was mentored by the great Midianite Sheikh named Jethro. Moses had married Jethro's daughter named Tzippora, and with her sired two sons. After the miraculous exodus from Egypt, the famed Midianite called upon his son-in-law, Moses. Together in the Sinai desert the two men worshipped, ate, and discussed the perils of leadership. Moses gratefully received Jethro's wise instruction to alleviate his burden by delegating leaders and judges. Their relationship was to the end respectful and loving (Ex. 18, throughout).

How then did Moses command a war on Jethro and Tzippora's people? Was it Moses the man, or the tradition's legendary redaction that angrily chastises the military commanders for sparing Midian's females and children? In the text, Moses tells the martial leaders: "Go back and slay every male child and woman! Spare only the virgin girls" (Num. 31:15–18). One wonders: If indeed this was a later redaction (for there is no archeological evidence of such a genocide), who earned political benefit with this militant stance?

Before putting down the thread of retribution, it is noteworthy to mention that one of God's faces in the Hebrew Bible (which, by the way, I have named: The Elder Testament, rather than the Old Testament) is *El Nekamot*, a vengeful God. (The full line from the psalm reads: O Lord God, to whom vengeance belongs; O God o vengeance, shine forth. You judge the earth and render the arrogant their reward (Psalm 94:1).)

Here God as spiritual exemplar is envisioned as the one who gives retribution to the arrogant. But who are the arrogant? Indeed, when humans put on the mask of God, rendering judgment and righting the world's balance, danger is afoot.

Cherem: Conquest and Extermination

In Deuteronomy 20 we see a picture of the new Israelite nation ready to enter the Promised Land of Canaan. But this is not a land without a people. Seven tribes already inhabit this land of milk and honey. Before crossing the River Jordan, the Israelites are given God's command:

> When you come near a city to fight against it, then proclaim peace to it. And it shall be, if it gives you answer of peace and opens to you, then it shall be that all the people that are found in it shall be tributaries to you, and they

shall serve you. And if it will make no peace with you, but will make war against you, then you shall besiege it.

(Deut. 20:10–12)

This injunction encompasses the outlying settlements. As for the peoples who dwell within the land that God has given the Israelites as an inheritance, the order is uncompromising: "*Hacharem Tacharimem!* You shall utterly destroy anything that breathes" (Deut. 20:16). The command to devastate the six cultures inhabiting the Promised Land—the Hittites, Amorites, Canaanites, Perizzites, Hivites, and Jebusites—is uncompromising.

The root of the term *hacharem tacharim* is ch-r-m, which, according to Brown- Driver- Briggs (1907),[1] originally meant a *devoted thing*, that is, a thing that is set apart. (Similarly, a king's female *herem* derives from the same etymological root.) *Cherem*, then, denotes a thing or people delimited or demarcated by God.

In the Elder Testament, specifically in the books of Deuteronomy, Joshua, and Judges, the peoples singled out for *cherem* were ones who were understood to spiritually imperil the religious life of the new nation, and hence represented a danger to the latter's survival. The Israelites were commanded to kill them out so "that they teach you not to do after all their abominations, which they have done to their gods; so should you sin against the Lord your God" (Deut. 20:18). It was understood that to secure the "purity of the land," so to speak, and rid it of plurality and divisiveness, the indigenous tribes and their cultures needed to be destroyed.

This central commandment of *hacharem tacharimem* echoes with complexity in our era. It bespeaks not a brotherhood/sisterhood of humanity but one of Divine election. It is a sweeping, impersonal license that is predicated upon a self-identity of chosenness. This license, according to Ra'anan Boustan, is "a thoroughly violent commandment" that "in modern terms would be characterized as genocide" (2009, 3–5).

Another critical example of the term *herem* appears in the Book of Samuel. A look at this ancient story reveals a fateful scene that reverberates through Jewish history to our era. Here, Saul, the first king of the Israelite tribes, is following God's command *hacharamtam*, to utterly destroy a seventh local tribe, the Amalekites. God has told him: "Strike . . . and completely destroy all that they have, and spare them not; but slay both man and woman, infant and suckling, ox, and sheep, camel and ass" (Sam I. 15:3).

Saul does indeed destroy the Amalekite people by the sword. But for some unknown reason, he has spared their king, Agag. He has also kept the best of the sheep and cattle, the fat calves and lambs for himself and his men.

For this omission, Saul is harshly rebuked by God's emissary, Prophet Samuel, who reminds him of God's command to "completely destroy" the Amalekites. In the end, Samuel does the deed. He finishes off the Amalekite king and puts an end to every living creature in the Amalekite camp. But it is too late. Because he has not followed God's order scrupulously, Saul ultimately loses his throne and dies a tortured man.

It is at this moment that Amalek is singled out as the archetypal enemy of the ancient Israelites. Why such special notoriety? It was the Amalekites who attacked the beleaguered Hebrews when they emerged from Egypt, weary and defenseless. Because of their show of ruthlessness to the vulnerable, the Amalekites acquired the mythical identity of evil enemy that must be destroyed at all costs.

King Saul's fateful error—most likely greed and self-interest rather than compassion—of failing to destroy every last Amalekite presented the mythical opening for everlasting evil that is understood to plague the Jewish people to this day. In every generation, the teaching goes, Amalek calls for the Jews' demise. Haman the Persian, Hitler the German, Ahmadinejad the Iranian, and all those who have publicly called for Jewish genocide are deemed to hail from the Amalekite nation, which were not once and for all obliterated by King Saul. Amalek is the mythical symbol then of thorough wickedness, which is worthy of erasure but continuously defies capture.

Alas, today we see this archetypal name being bandied about with flippancy. As in many parts of the world, religious zealotry is alive and well in Israel today. One example is in East Jerusalem where the ancient theme of Amalek has come to life again. There dozens of Jewish youngsters recently arose at night to bang on doors in the Muslim Quarter of Jerusalem's Old City, calling out: "Destroy the seed of Amalek! The Temple will be rebuilt, the (Omar) Mosque will be burned" (Kashti, 2014, July 7)!

That Jewish children are tagging Muslims as Amalek, the archetypal foe of the Jewish people, is a leap that only adults could make, a conceptual misappropriation from scripture with combustible ramifications. To call another ethnic group by this name denoting evil condemns them to a dehumanization worthy of erasure. Fortunately, there are other voices in Israel today that would counterbalance such choleric passions.

Milchemet Mitzvah: A Commanded or Obligatory War

Nowhere in Jewish scripture do we find the term Holy War. However, there is a term that the early rabbis discussed liberally throughout the Mishnah, the first major work of Rabbinic literature. This term is *Milchemet Mitzvah*,[2] a war that is commanded and, therefore, obligatory. It might be argued that a commanded war and a holy war amount to one and the same thing. Within ancient Jewish law, there are two kinds of *Milchemet Mitzvah*, obligatory wars: The first is a war of conquest such as those we have touched upon, in which the new Israelite nation was commanded to route out the seven nations in their midst. The second category is a war fought for self-defense. Let us now examine this latter category, as it is extremely germane to our day.

La'amod al Naphsham: Self-Defense

A central theme within Jewish history relating to pacifism and warriorship is that of self-defense or self-preservation. Because the early Hebrew tribes and the Jewish people who stemmed from them were so often a persecuted minority, self-preservation has been of crucial concern. It is not strange then to find that within the Jewish tradition self-defense is not only a right but a positive moral duty. As scholar David Kopel (2017, 16) states:

> The law which God gave to the Israelites required use of deadly force in self-defense and defense of others. Deadly force was allowed in circumstances in which there was strong, but not incontrovertible, evidence that a criminal aggressor had murderous intent.

We see this principle vividly illustrated in a scripture dating back to the third century BCE. The Scroll of Esther is read in Jewish communities around the world each year at the spring celebration of Purim. Here we have a story of palace intrigue centered around a plot to kill all the Jews of Persia.

The genocide was thwarted by Queen Esther, the beautiful Jewess who bravely risks her life to save her people. Instead of being victims, the Jews are granted an edict to kill "all the people who wanted to kill them." Esther's husband, the Persian king Ahashverosh, allows the Jews to "fight for their lives . . . to destroy, to slay, and to annihilate any armed force that might attack them, along with their women and children" (Est. 8:11). In the end, the Jews *"nikhalu v'amod al naphsham"* gathered together and fought for their lives, disposing of their enemies numbering 75,000 (Est. 9:16). Among them were men, women, and children.

This brutal ending to an otherwise theatrical tale is understood by many as metaphorical. How could such a passive underdog nation defend itself in such a vigorous and unsparing way? Ironically, in the midst of a spring carnival-like holiday when Jews masquerade and act in all manner of silliness, violence has shown up throughout history.[3]

Biblical texts on the topic of self-defense demonstrate that the Torah explicitly exonerates personal and family self-defense resulting in death against criminal attack. For one often-cited example, the Book of Exodus absolves a homeowner who kills a burglar at night: "If a thief be found breaking up, and be smitten that he die, there shall be no blood shed for him" (Ex. 22:1). The Modern Language Bible renders the verse: "When a burglar is caught breaking in, and is fatally beaten, there shall be no charge of manslaughter."

Since ancient homes were made of clay walls, a burglar might have entered by tunneling through or beneath a wall. The traditional Hebrew translation refers to a thief who is found "while tunneling." And it was understood that a burglar who breaks in and enters is likely to kill.

Why are these antiquated texts so important? They are important and still cited because they serve as the floorboards, so to speak, for today's adjudications. This and other ancient verses are the very foundation upon which present day policies are made by the Jewish governance in the State of Israel, which bases its laws upon Jewish legal scriptures.

Under Mosaic Law, when a nocturnal burglar was killed in the act, no misdemeanor was assigned to the act. This means that the burglar's relatives had no right of restitution against the homeowner who killed their kin. The discussion surrounding the laws of self-defense stemming from Exodus 22 has been the subject of extensive commentary by a long line of rabbinic scholars. Whereas various scholars glean slightly different lessons about self-defense from the next two verses (Ex. 22:2–3), all rabbinic sources agree with the core principle that self-defense is permissible in all cases of necessity.

Perhaps the greatest legal scholar of the Jewish tradition was Rabbi Moshe ben Maimon, also known as Maimonides or "Rambam" (1153–1204). Rambam understood that the rationale for killing the burglar was the presumption of danger. Specifically, the rationale was explained that "[the burglar] was thought to enter with an intention to murder someone." In his fourteen-volume Mishnah Torah (2010), Maimonides elaborated on the law regarding self-defense against burglars in this way:

> When a person breaks into [a home]—whether at night or during the day—license is granted to kill him. Therefore if either the homeowner or another person kills him, they are not liable . . . If it is clear to the houseowner that the thief [who breaks in] will not kill him and instead is only seeking financial gain, it is forbidden to kill [the thief].
>
> *(Vol. 4: 73–74)*

Intricate attention to the thief's motives is applied not only by Maimonides but also by generations of Jewish legal commentators who follow. All are unanimous. If it is clear to the homeowner that the thief will not kill him but seeks only financial gain, it is forbidden to kill the thief. Mosaic Law did not allow one to kill a thief merely to protect physical property. Nor did it allow killing in other cases in which the crime victim could be sure that he or she was not in physical danger. But Jewish law does permit killing for the defense of self and others. In fact, it is not only permitted, but considered obligatory to kill in order to prevent murder.

Before laying down the thread of self-defense, one more much-quoted law from the Mishnah bears mentioning because it serves as a precedent permitting a pre-emptive strike against one's enemy. "*Im ba l'hargekha, hashkem l'hargo.* If someone comes to kill you, rise up and kill him (first)" (Mishna Sanhedrin, Chapter 8:72a). Jewish Law affirms this Talmudic principle by ruling: "If one sees that someone is pursuing him with the intention to kill him, he is permitted to defend himself and take the life of the one who is pursuing him" (Ganzfried, 2010, 125: 1).

All of these ancient biblical and rabbinic laws provide the rudiments for contemporary legal rulings about self-defense and even proactive war-making in the State of Israel. It is here that one finds the crux of justification for pre-emptive strikes against Israel's neighbors and what has been claimed to be disproportionate force in battle, such as Israel's reputedly aggressive strikes in Gaza, or the demolitions of the homes of Palestinian terrorists' families.

At this point the reader may well be asking: What about the Sixth Commandment, which states: *Thou Shalt Not Kill* (Ex. 20:13)? Scholars might answer that apart from the most famous King James translation, the original text says something other than what we might think.

In Hebrew, the Ten Commandments, also known as the Decalogue, are to the point and pithy. The sixth of the commandments is a mere two words: *Lo tirzach*, normally translated as "Thou shalt not kill." The etymological root of *tirzach* (r-z-ch) is murder. The Jewish Publication Society commentary on Exodus explains that this Hebrew verb "applies only to illegal killing and, unlike other verbs for the taking of life, is never used in the administration of justice or for killing in war" (Sarna, 1991, 113, n. 13). Thus, the sixth commandment is telling us that a Jew is required to abstain from killing an innocent person. In other words: "Do not murder."

Pikuach Nephesh: *Saving a Life*

Self-defense in Jewish law leads us to a gold thread, an arching principle in the ethos of Judaism known as *pikuach nephesh*, the saving of life.[4] Here we have a central tenet in Judaism, which states, in effect, that the preservation of human life overrides virtually all other religious considerations. In fact, every Jewish law can and should be broken in order to save a life, except in the case of three extreme situations in which the following are forced: the defamation of God's name, murder, and incest (BT Sanhedrin: 74a, b).

Pikuach nephesh leads us to the finely twined threads that promulgate peace and pacifism in the Judaic tradition. Closely related is the central tenet in Judaism known as *b'tselem Elohim*, also known as *imago Dei*: Human beings are created in the Divine image, hence all life, but in particular human life, is unalterably precious.

The notion that humans are created in the Divine image stems from yet another famous biblical story, that of Noah and the great flood. You may remember that after the colossal deluge, Noah sent a dove out of the ark to investigate the vestiges of the world. The mythic bird returns to the ark with an olive branch signaling hope, and Noah and his family are finally able to climb out of the battered ark. In the aftermath of massive global devastation, they find life once again emerging upon the earth.

Under the rainbow of renewed hope, the Creator makes a covenant with the survivors of the flood to never again destroy life on earth in this way. God asks the survivors to adopt seven basic laws. Here we have the first legal code of the Judeo-Christian tradition. Long before Moses, Mosaic Law, or the Torah, there were the *sheva mitzvoth Bnei Noach*, "the Noahide Laws," given by God as a universal law for all of humanity. Among these seven rules, God forbade murder and required the death penalty in all murder cases, saying: "Whoever sheds a human's blood, by man shall his blood be shed; *for in the image of God did God make humans*" (Gen. 9:6).

B'tselem Elohim: *In the Image of God* (Imago Dei)

The idea of *imago Dei* certainly merits its own roundtable! It has been called the bone and marrow of Judeo-Christian civilization and arguably provides the foundation for human rights and social justice within Western civilization. Simply put, the concept explains why human life is sacred and must be guarded. Because we are made in God's image, all humans, regardless of their origins or ethnicity, their gender or creed, their class or caste, share equal and inherent dignity.

In the Jerusalem Talmud, Rabbi Ben Azzai, noted scholar of the first century, put it this way: Because every human being was created in the image of G-d, each person must be treated with the honor and respect befitting one who has absolute value (JT: Tractate Nedarim 9:4a). How might this treatment be assured? Throughout Judaism we find the intertwining threads of human dignity, justice, and peace. As the Talmudic sage Rabbi Shimon ben Gamaliel used to say: "The world depends on three things: On justice, on truth, and on peace" (Mishnah Avot 1:18).

Here our discussion begs an introduction to the fiery Hebrew prophets who came long after Joshua, Samuel, and the Judges whom we have previously mentioned. I am speaking of later prophets such as Amos, Hosea, Jeremiah, and Isaiah II, who provided the moral backbone of the Hebrew tradition for thousands of years.[5] They exhorted their people to fight for justice and defend the human dignity of every person, regardless of lineage, gender, or class. Justice was their path to peace.

It is important to emphasize that the prophetic call to care for the marginalized and less privileged within society went (and still goes) hand in glove with exhortations for peace. *Shalom Shalom, v'eyn Shalom!* Peace, Peace, yet there is no peace! cried the prophet Jeremiah (6:14). He and his compatriots knew that declaring peace without acts of justice was a superficial balm, that peace cannot exist without justice, fairness, and equality.

Following this thread of the Jewish tapestry into the modern era, we find numerous modern contributions: Jews who heard the prophetic call at the turn of the twentieth century to organize and lead American labor unions. Jewish labor workers—both male and female—had an outsized influence on the creation of protective labor laws, industrial safety standards, livable wages, and a humane workweek. The same urgent call rallied hundreds of Jewish civil rights workers, legal aids activists, and Freedom Riders to the southern United States in the 1960s to further the civil rights movement.

Jews who had suffered unrelenting persecution for centuries as a minority in Christian Europe naturally empathized and understood the cry of the oppressed in America. During the civil rights era, the renowned theologian Rabbi Abraham Joshua Heschel wrote: "There is no other people in the world so absolutely committed to the sanctity of human rights and equality of all men [than the Jewish people]." He continued: "Our history is the most emphatic testimony that injustice to some men spells doom of all men" (1964, 14–15).

For those who are invested in these core Jewish principles, there lies an uncomfortable tension between Heschel's noble statements and the events currently transpiring in the world of Jewish affairs. I am speaking of the tension between Jewish values and actions, spiritual commitments and political ideology. We will address this tension shortly.

Bakesh Shalom v' Rodfehu: *Seeking Peace and Pursuing It*

Permeating our Jewish tapestry are the delicate strands relating to peace and peacemaking. These are prominent among the teachings of the rabbis beginning in the first century before the Common Era. One of the most important proponents of peace in Jewish history was Rabbi Hillel the Elder (37 BCE to 4 CE).

Hillel, who lived during Herod's rule, was himself considered the quintessential peacemaker. A poor immigrant from Babylonia, Hillel came to Israel with only the clothes on his back and began his Jewish studies at age 40. Often employing Aaron, brother of Moses, as the exemplar of peace, Hillel invoked him in a famous teaching tale.

When two men had quarreled with one another, Aaron would go and sit down with one and say to him: "My son, mark what your friend is crying! He beats his breast and tears his clothing, saying, 'Woe unto me! What have I done? How shall I lift my eyes to look at my friend? I am so ashamed, for it is I who have treated him badly.'"

Aaron would sit with the man until his anger had drained away, and then he would go and sit with the second friend, and say the same things he had said to the first. In this way, Aaron sowed seeds of peace between the two erstwhile friends. When the two finally met up with each other their hearts were already tenderized. They embraced and kissed one another in total peace.

Records show that Rabbi Hillel himself embodied all of Aaron's reputed qualities. One of the rabbi's most documented traits—and perhaps the mark of a peaceful person—was that of patience. The Talmud is full of stories about the contests that Hillel's mischievous students would create to see who could make their old teacher lose his temper, who might succeed in rupturing his peaceful aura. They would go to him at the most annoying hour, when the Sabbath was about to begin, or when he was on his way to the bathhouse, bringing him the most far-flung questions just to taunt him and test his nerve. But Hillel never lost his patience; at least, it was not recorded if he did. He was indeed a lover of peace, and he pursued it.

In another famous tale from the Babylonian Talmud, Hillel the Elder was asked by a cynical Roman guard to teach him the entire Torah while standing on one foot. The rabbi promptly balanced himself on one leg and replied: "That which is hateful to you, do not do to another. That is the whole Torah. All the rest is commentary. Now go and study" (Tractate Shabbat: 31a).

One commentator from the sixteenth century, Rabbi Shmuel Ozedah of Tsfat, commented on Hillel's teachings in his commentary on Mishnah Avot, saying: "Everyone likes to see themselves as lovers of peace. Even when we are full of strife and conflict, we do not see any fault in ourselves. That is why Hillel gave clear guidelines." R. Ozedah continued:

> To be a lover of peace means one who embraces peace within oneself and within one's home. To be a pursuer of peace means that we actively go from place to place bringing peace to others and making peace between people, husband and wife, community and community. But first we need to love peace within ourselves, so much so that we are drawn to literally go and bring peace between others.
>
> *(Roth, 2014)*

The Jewish mystics, also known as Kabbalists, understood that achieving peace is one of the delicate mysteries of the universe. The word for peace in Hebrew—*Shalom*—they taught, is one of God's mystical names. The term itself is composed of Hebrew letters that signify the comingling of the two elements of fire and water. Implied in this ancient letter arrangement is the understanding that peace is a marriage of opposites and cannot be had by means of overpowering or manipulating another to our way of seeing. Peace is had through the respectful and symmetrical co-existence of disparate entities.

For the Jewish mystic, the spirit of peace and harmony is the sign of God's presence. Peace is requisite for the Divine Presence (also known as the Shechinah) to abide between family members, business partners, and within the community's halls. As we saw in the teachings of Hillel the Elder, *shalom bayit*, the peace of home, family, and community, was so important that it could at times override absolute truth telling.

The Kabbalists teach that we can learn the intrinsic value of peace from none other than God. In Genesis, when God tells Sarah she will soon give birth to a son, she expresses disbelief, saying: "After I have waxed old shall I have pleasure, my husband being old also?" But when God speaks to Abraham, he says: "Why did Sarah laugh and say, 'Will I really have a child, now that I am old?'" (Gen. 18:12–13). The rabbis note that God omitted Sarah's mention of Abraham's age for a reason: out of concern for *shalom bayit* (Midrash Raba 65:2).

For the Jewish mystics and rationalists alike, it is axiomatic that when peace reigns between Jews, all goes well for them. But the opposite is also true. When Jews undermine, compete, or fight with one another, no matter how learned or ritually observant they are, they are easily conquered. Perhaps the most important rabbinic statement about peace comes from the great medieval legalist Rabbi Shmuel Eideles, known as the Maharsha (1555–1631), who declared that any Jewish law that does not lead to peace and harmony must be questioned for its veracity.[6]

For centuries, Jewish spiritual leaders have maintained that peacemaking coupled with justice and the abiding belief in the dignity of all beings bears overarching importance on the Jewish path, and the more actively undertaken, the better. By contrast, war and violence have an irrevocable impact on our lives and in the world. A classic Jewish teaching, the Mekhilta of Rabbi Ishmael, teaches: "There may be a mighty hero in a country, but once the arrow leaves his hand he is unable to make it come back" (Lauterbach, 2004, 190). Once we resort to war, we unleash a myriad of consequences that we can neither control nor reverse.

Before concluding this section, it must be stated clearly that although peacemaking is a supreme value in Judaism, pacifism is not a Jewish tradition. As renowned scholar Rabbi Maurice Lamm stated in his famous essay on pacifism and conscientious objection in the Jewish tradition: "It must be affirmed that Judaism rejected total pacifism, but that it believed strongly in pragmatic pacifism as a higher morally more noteworthy religious position" (1978, 221).

Complexities

By now we have seen that the long, rich fabric of Jewish tradition is composed of seemingly opposing values that intertwine like threads on a loom. Peacemaking within and beyond the community, and warriorship for both preservation and conquest, are dual and parallel standards. Each carry their own scriptural weight, historical precedence, and, some might say, Divine mandate.

Which value will be emphasized and energized as the twenty-first century unfolds? The answer depends entirely upon the era, the situational politics, and the governing leadership of the Jewish community. But before we lay down our many-textured tapestry, two other factors bear mentioning, for they too have a bearing on the outcome. Let's examine them briefly.

The Problem of Chosenness

Intrinsic to Jewish identity is the notion of being chosen or set apart. At the very inception of Jewish nationhood, just after the Hebrew tribes were liberated from Egyptian bondage, God called them: "My own treasure from among all peoples . . . a kingdom of priests and a holy nation" (Exodus 19:5–6). Soon afterwards Moses declares: "You are a nation set apart[7] for God your God who chose you to be His special people from all the nations on the face of the earth" (Deut. 7:6).

But as history has borne out, where preferential blessings are so steeply stacked, trouble lurks. Jewish chosenness has elicited anything but reverence and goodwill from the many "unchosen" on the face of the earth. In the context of the world stage upon which the Hebrew Bible played itself out, we see that Jewish distinction incited anything but social privilege. Much to the contrary, the oppositional impulse from the Jews' neighbors and hosts—the desire to convert, banish, and destroy—has been almost ubiquitous throughout Jewish history.

Of course, being God's favorite is not an exclusively Jewish claim. In fact, each of the three monotheistic religions assert their own unique argument for Divine election.[8] Further, the tendency to see one's own tribe as the most special was the topic of prolific study by developmental psychologist Erik Erikson in groups around the world. Erikson termed the concept for the tendency of groups to self-define as its own special species as *pseudo-speciation*. According to Erikson, when the core of any collective identity centers around its pseudo-speciation, oppression and violence are bound to play a part in that people's history (1966, 606).

Jewish history has certainly borne this out. Israeli journalist and political analyst Gideon Levy sees the doctrine of chosenness in contemporary Israeli society as the linchpin to growing cycles of violence there. "No principle in Israel society is more destructive, or more dangerous than this principle. Nor, unfortunately, more common," he writes. Levy is referring to the ancient Jewish self-identity of the chosen people, in Hebrew called *am nivchar*. "When [chosenness] is a fundamental principle," Levy predicted, "the next torching is only a matter of time" (2015, Aug. 2).

But Jews know the distinction of otherness. They have lived as the stranger, the unwelcome guest, and the scapegoat for centuries. Embedded in the fabric of the Jewish culture is a leitmotif found no less than 36 times in the Hebrew Bible pertaining to the other, the stranger. One of these iterations reads: "Do not oppress a stranger for you know the heart of a stranger, for you yourselves were once strangers" (Ex. 22:21).

Another leitmotif is that of the prophet Isaiah, whose declaration brings forth a different reading of chosenness altogether, one that challenges the Israelites to care for each other, to be "a light to all peoples, a beacon for the nations, to open eyes that are blind, to bring captives out of prison, out of the dungeons where they lie in darkness" (Is. 42:6–7).

Employing these radical texts, Jewish chosenness might be seen as a reclamation of the prophetic voice that described the Jewish tribe's potential to shine a light for the world. This new yet very ancient narrative puts the Jews' long history of persecution into the service of the central tenets of Judaism: to love and care for the other.

Jewish Historical Trauma

Hand in hand with Jewish chosenness and alterity is the impact of Jewish oppression and scapegoating. After 2,000 years of diaspora life, the Jewish people's struggle for survival culminated in a return to their biblical homeland, known today as the State of Israel. In its Declaration of Independence, the founders of Israel promised sanctuary to any Jew in need of a home. In the face of Jewish history, the reality and the urgency of a "Jewish homeland" is charged with profound emotional meaning for Jews the world over.

Since the state's founding in 1948, Diaspora Jews and their spiritual leaders around the world have enthusiastically supported the governing bodies of the State of Israel, even as the overall direction of the state moves decisively towards increasing security, military buildup, and war.

Israel's hyper-muscular stance must be seen within the larger context of Jewish history. For just as individuals carry the residue of trauma in the aftermath of extreme injury, so too do groups and entire ethnicities. Characteristic symptoms such as hypervigilance, reactivity, and an unyielding sense of unsafety in the world may be found in both. In the case of the Jews and the establishment of a state just three years after the end of World War II, a heightened level of self-defense should be seen in light of the savage atrocities that Jews endured at the hands of the Nazis.

It surely does not help that the part of the world in which Israel finds herself tends towards instability and truculence. Many of the surrounding Arab countries and militia organizations issue steady streams of hostile fiats and hate-filled schemes for Israel's downfall. Given the deeply inculcated wounds Jews incurred not only in the Holocaust but during centuries of anti-Semitic persecutions around the world, it is no surprise that Israel, a state comprised of Jewish refugees from Shanghai to Poland, has self-defense on her mind.

Nevertheless, the god of security stands in sharp contrast to the powerful legacy of the Hebrew prophets. The tensions at play rumble loudly as Israel's military occupation in the Palestinian territories reaches into its sixth decade. And while the state may have succeeded in winning a measure of short-term security for its citizens, the moral price has been exponentially high. In the process of subjugating another people, the self-definition of a tribe that holds precious the values of equality, justice, and democracy has been seriously eroded. In plain sight, yet still unconscious to many Jews who are preoccupied with the fight for security, is the handing-off of the archetypal roles of victim and scapegoat to another people. As the poet W. H. Auden wrote presciently in 1939: "Those to whom evil is done/ Do evil in return" (1940).

I would suggest that the very real struggle for security waged by Israel and felt by Jews around the world is intensified by the Jewish people's unhealed wounds. The sequelae of Jewish trauma—found in behaviors like rapid-fire reactivity and disproportionately strong military measures—in turn exacerbate the already serious nature of Israel's objective situation in a region flagrantly hostile toward her. The result is a tragic downward cycle of violence.

Instead of drawing upon Jewish cultural tropes of aggression, conquest, and nationalism to back its military choices, other themes of the Jewish tradition might be called upon at this time. These include the potent teachings of the Hebrew prophets, the principles of dialogue and third party assistance, and the foundational Jewish tenet that all humans are created *b'tselem Elohim*, in the Divine image.

Kol Demama Daka: *The Delicate Voice of Silence*

Central to our exploration of peacemaking and warriorship in Judaism are the psychological themes of self-perception and identity. How a people envision themselves vis-à-vis the world and its nations is all-important to our study, helping us to understand the choices it makes to either energize or ignore the various strands of its complex legacy. Clearly, the dual identities of Jewish chosenness and victimization resulting in historical trauma both influence the Jewish balance between war and peace on the world stage today.

It is important to remember that the position of the Jewish people in the world is now radically different than ever before in its history. Jews have risen from the ashes of the Nazi genocide with new power in the realms of statecraft, military, and finance. For the first time in 2,000 years, the State of Israel provides a refuge for Jews everywhere. Its burgeoning presence stands as a breathtaking reminder of the vicissitudes of history and the miraculous capacity of the human spirit to rebirth itself after near destruction. Even while anti-Semitism still exists and rears its ghastly head, so too many of the world's superpowers now rally with unprecedented support of the Jewish people.

But this does not mean that all is well. As we have seen, the legacy of alterity, otherness, is a fickle coin. Flipping from the side of specialness and superiority to that of the hated scapegoat and victim creates a template for further violence, especially in a state that wields enormous world power.

Perhaps we can look to one last teaching, a strand of the Jewish tapestry that is hardly seen due to its profound subtlety. The more prominent threads of Jewish tradition teach the keeping of the commandments given in an explosion of consciousness at Mount Sinai where God speaks in thunder and lightning and a mountain in flames.

But on the other end of the spectrum is the teaching, no less authentic or powerful, of Elijah the Prophet at the end of his career. Elijah was running for his life from the heavy-handed regime of the day. Depressed and beleaguered, he hid in a cave on the very mountain where the Mosaic revelation had occurred generations earlier. There he falls asleep and is wakened by an angelic voice.

Elijah emerges from his cave to encounter the Living God. But this time the Divine voice speaks not in thunder, nor in the earthquake, nor in the fire of history, but in *kol demama daka*, the delicate voice of silence (I Kgs. 19:9–13). Elijah must listen deeply for the instruction that is being given to him at that moment in time, different than all others.

So it is with us. At this moment in history we must listen carefully for the nuanced instruction befitting our day. This requires stilling the noise within and around us so that we can hear the delicate voice of silence calling to us now, instructing us how to go forward.

Perhaps it is in calm silence that we can discover how to respect all of the rich and beautiful fibers of history, the accrued wisdom of centuries. With quiet listening and great discernment, we can assess the perils of our day and the unprecedented facts on the ground. Attuning ourselves in this way may help us glean what we need most from our multi-textured religious traditions today: to remember the miraculous gift of life itself, so that we can preserve it for generations to come, and live wisely on this earth.

Notes

1 BDB, s.v. "חרם"
2 For example, see Jerusalem Talmud, Tractate Sotah 88:23a and Babylonian Talmud, Tractate Sotah 44b.
3 One contemporary example is the murderous figure, Baruch Goldstein, who committed a massacre on Purim in 1994 at the Tomb of the Patriarchs in Hebron, killing 29 Palestinian Muslims at prayer and wounding another 125. For more on Purim and the violence that this holiday has spawned through history, see Elliot Horowitz, (2006). *Reckless rites: Purim and the legacy of Jewish violence: Jews, Christians, and Muslims from the ancient to the modern world.* Princeton University Press: Princeton, NJ.
4 The overarching rule of *pikuach nephesh* stems from Lev. 18:5, which states, "You shall therefore keep my statutes and my rules; if a person does them, he shall live by them: I am the LORD." The rabbis add: "*That he shall live by them*, and not that he shall die by them" (Babylonian Talmud, Yoma 85b).
5 The latter Hebrew prophets exhorted the people to care for the marginalized, act kindly, and practice justice. One example found in Jeremiah 22:3 encapsulates this message: "This is what the Lord says: Do what is just and right. Rescue from the hand of the oppressor the one who has been robbed. Do no wrong or violence to the foreigner, the fatherless or the widow, and do not shed innocent blood in this place." These directives are found elsewhere in Hebrew Scripture, too, as in Proverbs 31:9, which counsels: "Speak up, judge righteously, champion the poor and the needy."
6 Rabbi Shmuel Eliezer Edeles (MaHaRSHA stands for Morenu Harav Shmuel Adel's—Our Teacher Rabbi Samuel Adel's). His famous commentary on the Talmud is entitled *Hidushei MaHaRSHA* ("New Explanations by the MaHaRSHA.") In this saying, he is commenting on Babylonian Talmud Tractate Yevamot, on the verse: "The Torah's ways are ways of pleasantness and all its paths are peace" (Prov. 3:17).
7 The word used is *kadosh*, from the Hebrew root KDSh. In its original sense, *kadosh* means singled out. Though it is normally translated as holy or consecrated, the word denotes the characteristic of being set apart, just as the Sabbath day is *kadosh*, set apart from all the days of the week, thereby making it holy.
8 For more on the topic of Divine election in monotheistic cultures, see Dr. Reuven Firestone, 2008.

References

Auden, W. H. (1940). *Another time.* New York: Random House.
Boustan, R. S. (2009). *Violence, scripture, and textual practice in early Judaism and Christianity.* Leiden: Brill.

Brown, F., Driver, S. R., and Briggs, C. A. (1907). *A Hebrew and English lexicon of the Old Testament*. Oxford: Clarendon.
Erikson, E. (1966). Ontogeny of ritualization. In *Psychoanalysis: A general psychology*, R. M. Lowenstein, L. M. Newman, M. Schur, and A. J. Solnit (Eds.). New York: International Universities Press, p. 606.
Firestone, R. (2008). *Who are the real Chosen People? The meaning of chosenness in Judaism, Christianity, and Islam*. Woodstock, VT: Skylight Paths Publishing.
Ganzfried, S. (2010). *Kitzur Shulchan Orech: Choshen Mishpat*. Lakewood, NJ: Moznaim.
Heschel, A. J. (1964, Winter). The plight of Russian Jews. *United Synagogue Review*.
Horowitz, E. (2006). *Reckless rites: Purim and the legacy of Jewish violence: Jews, Christians, and Muslims from the ancient to the modern world*. Princeton, NJ: Princeton University Press.
Kashti, O. (2014, July 7). Is it too late to clean Israel's education system of its racism? *Haaretz*.
Kopel, D. B. (2017). *The morality of self-defense and military action: The Judeo-Christian tradition*. Santa Barbara, CA: ABC-CLIO.
Lamm, M. (1978). After the war—Another look at Pacifism and Conscientious objection. In *Contemporary Jewish ethics*, M. M. Kellner (Ed.). New York: Sanhedrin Press, pp. 221–238.
Lauterbach, J. Z. (2004). *Mekhilta de-Rabbi Ishmael*, Vol. 4, Philadelphia, PA: Jewish Publication Society.
Levy, G. (2015, August 2). All Israelis are guilty of setting a Palestinian family on fire. *Haaretz*.
Maimonides, M., and Touger, E. (2010). *Mishneh Torah*, Vol. 4. Lakewood, NJ: Moznaim.
Roth, D. (2014). *The Rodef Shalom: From text to history to global network, Jerusalem*, Pardes Center for Judaism and Conflict Resolution. Retrieved from http://pcjcr.pardes.org/wp-content/uploads/2014/03/Being-a-Rodef-Shalom-From-Text-to-Global-Network.pdf
Sarna, N. M. (1991). *The JPS Torah commentary: Exodus*. Philadelphia, PA: Jewish Publication Society.

6

JEWISH, ISRAELI, AND ZIONIST TRADITIONS OF WAR AND PEACE

Paul Scham

Introduction

Both the trajectory and the current reality of the Jewish warrior and pacific tradition are in many ways unique and, I would contend, must be understood in a different framework than those of other religions and nations because of at least four major distinctions. The first is that, unlike all other major religions, Jewish traditions concerning war and peace were almost solely theoretical for over 1800 years, ever since the defeat of the Bar Kochba rebellion by the Roman army in 135 C.E. that marked the end of Jewish national existence until modern times. During this extended period, Judaism was not the dominant tradition anywhere except within subordinate local jurisdictions (Biale 1986), with the possible exception of semi-legendary eras such as that of the Khazars.[1] Laws of war and limitations on violence in warfare that had been adumbrated in the Torah and in other sacred writings and commentaries were preserved, studied, and expanded on during this period, often with an emphasis on when self-defense was allowed or warranted. Though other matters involving war were written on, they had little or no relationship to actual experience, much less as policy guides, until the very end of the nineteenth century (cf. Solomon 2006). During this period, Jews were notable for their aversion to war and violence, often accepting martyrdom instead of forced conversion (even if the conversion opportunity were presented).[2] Unquestionably, a desire to change this passive image and reality was one of the major spurs to the Zionist movement—and certainly affected its willingness to employ violence.

The second major distinction is that Judaism has been, from its inception until today, a tribal religion, in which peoplehood and religion are largely inseparable. It has never been possible to be religiously Jewish without being a member of the Jewish people (however defined). This national aspect of Judaism has become more salient—and various inherent contradictions have emerged—since large-scale exposure to the modern world and the rise of Zionism in the late nineteenth and twentieth centuries. One of the best descriptions of Zionism is that it originally sought to reframe Judaism in national instead of religious terms. That attempt had a variety of consequences, including both the establishment of the State of Israel and the paradoxical fact that the bond between Jewish religion and peoplehood has been considerably strengthened, especially in the last half century.

The third distinction, related to the second, is that Judaism, in the realm of war and peace, is today inextricably bound to the political fortunes of one state—Israel. While many states have special and strong relationships with a particular religion—Armenia, Greece, Iran, Russia, Pakistan, Saudi Arabia, for example—Israel's relationship with Judaism is unique in numerous ways. Thus, although half the Jews in the world live outside Israel, including rabbis, theologians, philosophers, and others who have delved deeply into the questions of the nature of the relationship between Diaspora Jews and the "Jewish State"; since 1948—and much more so since 1967—Jewish ideas of war and peace are today relevant only to Israel, at least in practice. Though an understanding of how Jewish ideas developed over three millennia is important in itself, an analysis of Judaism's present-day role with regard to war and peace must focus primarily on how they applied to Palestine (until 1948) and, subsequently, the State of Israel. A corollary to that is that any explication of these ideas must be understood in the context of Israel's unique political and security context—and thus this chapter will draw from politics and history at least as much as from theology.

The fourth distinction is the role of the Holocaust during World War II. The theological literature concerning it is considerable but not directly relevant to the subject at hand. However, the fact that Israel was founded just three years after the end of the Holocaust, which had succeeded in exterminating one-third of the world's Jews within a few years, had a decisive influence on the mentality of the new state. I will argue that this influence has in important respects—perhaps counter-intuitively—increased in the last 70 years and very much affected how Jews regard war and peace, politically and theologically.

Judaism in Modern Times

The second half of the nineteenth century was a decisive turning point in Jewish history when Eastern European Jews, perhaps 90% of the world's Jewish population at that time, were first confronted by modernity to a massive degree, leading to mass emigration from Europe, both secularization and the growth of extreme religiosity, conversion in some instances, assimilation, and the rise of various ideologies, among a number of other consequences. For the first time, large numbers of Jews joined western armies (see Penslar 2015; Solomon 2006) and thus dealt in practical terms with issues of war and peace. However, the existence of thousands of years of Jewish reflection on those subjects was virtually irrelevant to them, because they were serving in western armies and necessarily working within a different set of laws and traditions, i.e., western and Christian. See Solomon (2006) for a discussion regarding how Jews and their rabbinical authorities regarded the obligation of serving in war as a price of citizenship and emancipation. While Jewish scholars have certainly participated in the international discussion of war and peace—and many have employed insights from Jewish tradition—this again is not the subject of this chapter.

One fairly small aspect of the modernization, ideologization, and secularization process among Jews in the late nineteenth century was Zionism, the ideology that maintained that Jews were primarily a nation, and should "normalize" themselves as such preferably, though not necessarily, in their historic homeland, the Land of Israel, generally known then as Palestine, names that will be used interchangeably in this chapter. While approximately two million Jews left Eastern Europe for western countries between 1881 and the outbreak of World War I, only about 50,000 went to Palestine, and many soon left. Those who stayed in that period were mainly young, secular but with traditional backgrounds, inclined towards socialism, and determined to upend the nature of Jewish life by exposure to life on the land instead of study, and productivity rather than what they often called parasitism, i.e., commerce and other traditional Jewish occupations. All of them probably knew that Arabs and Muslims already lived there, but that was not a concern; they were coming for self-liberation and genuinely could not imagine themselves as conquerors or oppressors.

Despite these expectations, the new arrivals to the *Yishuv* (the pre-state Jewish settlement in Palestine) quickly found a need to deal with organized violence to some degree as participants, not simply as victims, which had been the overwhelming Jewish experience since the second century C.E. This was mostly in the context of protecting themselves against Bedouin raids, or from dispossessed tenants who had been evicted from land they had bought. After World War I and the beginnings of the British Mandate (1922–1948), early protective associations such as *Hashomer* (The Watchman, organized 1908) were amalgamated into the *Haganah* (Defense) organization (founded 1920), alternately supplementing, competing, and fighting with the British mandatory army and police forces.

The Haganah grew rapidly in response to the Arab-Jewish conflicts, after the first major Jewish-Muslim violence in 1920 and 1921, and especially during the major disturbances of 1929 and 1936–1939. The "Wailing Wall Riots" of 1929 were a major wake-up call to Zionists, who had hitherto largely ignored Palestinian Arab opposition to their project.[3] The extended fighting during the Palestinian Revolt of 1936–1939 led to the development of the Haganah as a significant, if illegal and irregular, force, providing the first military experience for future Israeli generals such as Moshe Dayan, Yigal Allon, and Yitzhak Rabin (Shapira 1999). Military doctrine was developed based on these experiences, and soldiers schooled in it became the nucleus of the Israeli Army, officially constituted on

May 14, 1948, when Israel was established as a state by virtue of UN General Assembly Resolution 181.

The new state immediately drafted all able-bodied men and most women, including those fresh off the boat from "Displaced Persons" camps in the wake of the Holocaust. What Israelis call their War of Independence and Palestinians refer to as the *Nakba* (catastrophe) lasted until the end of 1948, with the Jewish state almost completely victorious. Approximately 700,000 Palestinians became refugees and were prevented from returning to their homes, from which they had fled during the fighting.[4] Israel became, and to a considerable degree has remained, a nation under arms, with (largely) universal conscription of Jewish citizens (men and women) and portions of some Arab and Muslim groups (primarily Druze, Circassian, and Bedouin, and a recent emphasis on attracting Christian Palestinians).

It cannot be over-emphasized that serving in the army has been *the* major rite of passage for (Jewish) Israelis at age 18 ever since independence, especially, but not solely, for boys, and thus a major warrior tradition quickly took root and has flourished. Most Israelis have generally regarded each of its wars and military operations as existential (at least partly a legacy of the Holocaust) and most Jewish Israelis feel themselves and their state uniquely vulnerable, even as it has unquestionably been the most powerful regional power since at least 1967.

Though Israel was established as the Jewish State (or State of the Jews),[5] the warrior traditions developed before and in the decades immediately after independence had little to do with Judaism or Jewish tradition, for several reasons:

- Early Zionism was overwhelmingly a secular movement, and the few "Religious Zionists" (also known as "National Religious" or "Modern Orthodox") did not have a leading role until after 1967. Religious Zionists have always served in the military, in contrast to the "ultra-Orthodox" (*Haredim*), who won a blanket exemption partly because of their (then) small numbers in the post-Holocaust period. The Haredim were and are the primary repositories of Jewish traditional law, but have actively resisted developing either a warrior or pacifist body of law and tradition since the establishment of the state, largely because of their exemption from and aversion to the military. This may be changing somewhat in recent decades under the twin pressures of popular insistence that Haredim (now about 8% of the Jewish population) also shoulder the burden of service, and the development of a "National Haredi" (*hardal*) ideology.
- The National Religious (Heb. *dati le'umi*) were, until after 1967, largely liberal-minded and more interested in building up a civil religious infrastructure, leaving military leadership to the secular majority. More knowledgeable than their secular compatriots of Jewish law and tradition, they were also more uncomfortable with the cult of the military that quickly developed, though they served. Few became career officers and Jewish tradition was rarely

applied to current military issues, though Jewish traditions of nonviolence and peace were occasionally invoked, generally unsuccessfully, by those arguing for more dovish policies.

This situation began to reverse rapidly after the Six Day (June) War of 1967, in which Israel conquered the West Bank and East Jerusalem from Jordan, Gaza and the Sinai Peninsula from Egypt, and the Golan Heights from Syria. In the 1970s, a new generation of Israeli-born National Religious youth spearheaded building new settlements for Jews in the newly conquered territories. Some had by then developed a theology that incorporated Zionism into traditional Judaism, positing that the seemingly miraculous success of the 1967 war was unmistakably a harbinger of the longed-for messianic redemption, and that Zionist settlement of and Jewish sovereignty over the "Whole Land of Israel" (*Eretz Yisrael ha'shlaimah*) was an essential prerequisite for the Messiah to arrive. For believers, this was a powerful inducement to settle the land.

Religious Zionism became particularly influential, ideologically and politically, after 1977, when the rightist Likud party, under Prime Minister Menachem Begin, first came into power. Previous governments, led by the center-left Labor Party, were ambivalent about what to do with the territory conquered in 1967, hoping to trade part or even most of it for peace with the surrounding Arab countries.[6] The Likud, a conservative, nationalist, and secular party but with considerable respect for Jewish tradition (unlike their Labor rivals), along with the strong support of religious Zionism and its vanguard organization, *Gush Emunim* (Bloc of the Faithful), began building settlements in large numbers, especially in the West Bank, the historic homeland of the Jewish people in ancient times. From approximately 4000 West Bank settlers in 1977, there were over 100,000 by 1992, when Labor, under Yitzhak Rabin, was able to form a narrow center-left coalition government for the first time in 15 years. Today there are almost 400,000 Jewish settlers in the West Bank, not counting over 200,000 more in East Jerusalem, which was Jordanian or no-man's-land until 1967 (Sprinzak 1991; Taub 2010; Hirschhorn 2017; Shafir 2017).

By the 1990s, the Israeli ethos and society had changed immensely from what it had been before 1967. The country was far richer and more powerful and had become both more arrogant and more insecure, desiring peace and simultaneously afraid of it. A jagged chasm cleaving Israeli society between the overwhelmingly secular Left and the largely religious Right had grown to significant proportions, and has continued to expand since then. In the 1990s this developed into a full-scale *Kulturkampf*, with the fate of the West Bank, East Jerusalem, and Gaza—and the 3 million Palestinian Arabs living in them[7]—as the primary bone of contention. The political Right believes passionately, on both ideological and security grounds, that Israel must hold on to the territories. The religious Right, its smaller but highly visible vanguard, saw its dream of messianic redemption crumbling in the Oslo Peace Process, initiated by Prime Minister Rabin in 1993. It was clear to both supporters and opponents of the process that Oslo's logical culmination would be a Palestinian state in the West Bank, the heartland of Jewish history and religion (as well as in Gaza, which is far less theologically and historically important—and Israeli troops and settlers were evacuated from it in 2005).

The Left saw the situation in completely different terms. For it, Israel's occupation of this land containing millions of Palestinians was a corrupting, immoral enterprise, from which Israel had to extract itself as soon as possible, for its own sake as well as that of the Palestinians. This perception accelerated with the outbreak in December 1987 of the (First) *Intifada* (Arabic: "shaking off"), in which Palestinians in the territories, hitherto largely quiescent, rebelled against the occupation.

The conflict was by now defined more frequently in religious terms on both sides, with the increasing "religicization" of Israel and Islamicization of Palestine, concurrently with the rest of the Muslim world. For example, the Islamist/nationalist organization Hamas was established at the beginning of the Intifada as the Palestinian branch of the Muslim Brotherhood.

With the signing of the "Declaration of Principles" between Israel and the PLO on the White House lawn on September 13, 1993, the stage was set for a continuing and worsening rupture within Judaism and Israel on fundamental issues of peace and war, very much tied to the history and theology of Judaism and the Jewish people. While the Labor-led government moved towards partition of the land, the Right did all it could to alert the majority of Israelis to the danger they perceived to both the State of Israel and the Jewish people represented by the peace process. The culmination of this internecine conflict was the assassination of Prime Minister Rabin on November 4, 1995 by a rightwing religious Jew, who frankly proclaimed that he had done it to stop the peace process in the name of Judaism. Whether or not peace would have come had Rabin survived, the Oslo Process collapsed at the Camp David summit in 2000 and in the violence and suicide bombings of the Second Intifada (2000–2005).

By now there had developed—and continues to flower—a new Jewish ethic of the warrior and the pacifist. The National Religious portion of the population, having elaborated a theology justifying the conquest and settlement of the Land of Israel despite the opposition of its Arab inhabitants, now supplemented it with a theology of violence. Reversing their former, somewhat distant attitude towards the military, young National Religious Jews now attend religious military academies in large numbers to simultaneously prepare for their army service and to study Jewish law. Within the last 20 years, a disproportionate number of career officers are now National Religious. Rabbis have developed an overarching ethic justifying violence in the name of retaining the Land of Israel for the Jewish people, and a number of fringe, but still very visible, ideologies explaining, and even glorifying, violence against Arabs and Muslims. For example, some rabbis proclaimed that the commandment "Thou shalt not kill" pertained only to not killing Jews. Racist sayings, rare or at least kept under wraps in secular Jewish contexts, were heard widely, such as the decree (from one rabbi) that it was forbidden to rent an apartment to a non-Jew.

Of course, there were forces determinedly opposed to these tendencies. These tended to be secular and universalistic, but there were (and are) small but determined groups of leftwing religious Jews who proclaim the peaceful and nonviolent traditions of Judaism, and take an active part in interfaith and ecumenical activities. Interestingly, a disproportionate number of them were—and are—American (and some British) immigrants to Israel, or their children. Paradoxically, a greater and even more disproportionate number of the rightwing and religious settlers and their political leaders are likewise American immigrants or their children (Hirschhorn 2017). In the 1920s and 1930s, the philosopher Martin Buber and the first President of the Hebrew University, Rabbi Judah Magnes, were part of a small group of intellectuals called *Brit Shalom* (Covenant of Peace) that used Jewish tradition to argue for a binational state that respected Palestinian aspirations. Later, they helped form Ihud, a small political grouping that took that (extremely unpopular) position when the UN partition resolution was being debated in 1947.

This long historical introduction is essential for understanding the current vitriolic debate within Judaism, pitting the warrior and pacific traditions against each other. I do not use the word "pacifist" because there is little of such a tradition in Judaism, though there is a very strong tradition of peace and nonviolence.[8] However, based largely on biblical texts, especially in the Torah and Book of Joshua, there is likewise a strong warrior tradition that has been revived and amplified, especially since 1967, based on conquering the Land of Israel from the non-Jews who had inhabited it (e.g., Canaanites and Philistines, and later defending it from others, such as the Greeks and the Romans). The parallels with current situations are easy to make and amplify, with Palestinians often identified as Amalekites or Ishmaelites, biblical enemies of the Israelites.

I will briefly summarize the pre-Zionist attitudes towards war and peace but concentrate on the issues created by the emergence of Zionism and Israel as a major force in Jewish life in the first half of the twentieth century. It should be emphasized that the importance of the classic sacred Jewish texts to Jewish life and behavior was generally agreed on by Jewish opinion and community leaders until a period that began in the late nineteenth century and continued until the Holocaust, when the majority of the remaining traditionally Orthodox Jews were annihilated. This is the period when the rise of modernity largely left the traditional texts to the minority of Jews who still maintained religious traditions, while majority modernists, i.e., most Conservative, Reform, Reconstructionist[9] and unaffiliated, were increasingly unfamiliar with and not even interested in the traditions except when it suited them. This is the current situation, with most liberal and secular Jews largely ignorant of and uninterested in Jewish texts and traditions, while religious Jews study them avidly and use them as guides to current life issues, very much including war and peace.

Relevant Sources of Jewish Tradition

The primary text of Judaism is the Torah (the "Five Books of Moses"), every word of which is considered divinely written and therefore unalterable and inarguable. In practice, though, the Torah is understood almost completely through its commentaries, of which the most important is the Talmud (completed c. 525 C.E.). Hundreds, if not thousands, of later commentators expounded in turn on those texts, and modern ("rabbinic") Judaism is based primarily on their interpretations.

The remaining 19 books of the Hebrew Bible (most of which are shared, with some variation, with Christianity) are considered inspired by God, but attributed to human authorship. Thus, they are less authoritative than the Torah itself or interpretations based on it, but are significant authorities in themselves as well, and are also understood through their later commentaries. Of course, admirable figures in the Bible, and especially God's commandments, are considered guides to life. Like any rich tradition, all the Jewish sources are full of both admonitions for peace and stories of war. Both are absolutely integral to the received Jewish tradition. Between the earliest books and the latest (i.e., current) commentaries, they represent the varying ethos of almost 3000 years and innumerable different societies. One could say that, in general, war and extermination are sometimes considered necessary, but peace is extolled and preferred. There are few traditional texts that glorify war, though its necessity and ubiquity are explicitly and implicitly recognized. Wryly, in that context, it should be noted that only two of the books of the Bible (Ruth and the Song of Songs) lack any warlike episodes, the former portraying a peaceful and pastoral society and the latter a paean to erotic love set in a cosmopolitan and urban royal court.

It is utterly impossible, beyond these vague preferences, to summarize the attitudes towards violence even in the books of the Bible, let alone in the commentaries. They include several explicit commands of extermination (the Amalekites and many of the Canaanites) as well as innumerable wars. The Book of Joshua, which mainly relates the conquest of the Land of Israel after the Exodus, recounts some grisly massacres, which are explicated by later commentators but not generally considered relevant to actual contemporary behavior until the last few decades. All of these examples, however, have been utilized by modern Religious Zionist commentators and political leaders in the last half century to justify expulsion or even (so far, only in theory) extermination, based on analogizing the Palestinians to ancient peoples.

Robert Eisen (2011) discusses the tension between two major themes in the Bible and the commentaries: namely, the particular and the universal. On the one hand, the Bible clearly imparts moral and religious lessons meant for mankind as a whole.[10] On the other, it focuses mainly on the patriarch Abraham and his descendants, i.e., the Jewish people. Moreover, despite some ambiguous aspects, it frequently implicitly, or even explicitly, applauds some fairly bloodthirsty episodes, and even codifies them into commandments. Nevertheless, in general,

Rabbinic tradition is assumed to be nonviolent even by those who criticize it (Eisen 2011, 70).

Judaism as generally practiced for at least the last 1500 years is "rabbinic Judaism," i.e., interpreted through its commentators, the rabbis, who were both scholars and communal leaders.

> Most commentators in the field of Jewish ethics believe that rabbinic Judaism has a strong commitment to a peaceful ethic—much more so than the Bible ... The rabbis, instead of glorifying military heroism, exalt piety, devotion to God, and Torah study.
>
> *(Eisen 2011, 69)*

However, it should be noted that there was virtually no time after 135 C.E. that Jews had any option to engage in war. The last two episodes of war in Palestine (67–70 and 132–135 C.E.) had ended disastrously. Nevertheless, rabbis did write on commandments such as the extermination of the Amalekites, even though they had disappeared, even if they had ever existed. They also developed the criteria of "obligatory" and "discretionary" wars. The former were generally considered banned after the biblical period by most commentators until the last half century. There may be a trace of that in the Israeli insistence that all its wars until the First Lebanon War in 1982 were *ein bre'ira* (literally "no choice"; i.e., Israel had no choice but to fight). It is a phrase that has seemingly disappeared from the Israeli lexicon since then.

It should be noted that the traditional Jewish attitude towards the lengthy Jewish condition of exile and, frequently, persecution, was that they were a punishment by God for the sins of the Jewish people in their own land. The approach assumed that eventually God would relent and allow (or lead) his people back to their ancient home. However, it was rarely, if ever, imagined that it would be human volition that would spark the return. This was the reasoning behind the original almost universal Orthodox rejection of Zionism, with some significant exceptions mentioned below (see the discussions in Eisen 2011, 84, and Inbari 2017).

In general, it would be correct to generalize that rabbinic Judaism's disdainful attitude towards violence reflected an ethic of nonviolence or, perhaps more cynically, a recognition of Jewish powerlessness (Eisen 2011, 104).

Peace, War, and Modern Zionism

The Bible, Talmud, and later commentaries together constitute the most important traditional sources, studied by Jewish scholars for centuries but, without a land to defend or an army to command, the precepts regarding war and peace (as well as other institutions such as the Temple in Jerusalem) were merely theoretical. However, this changed over a period of about 80 years, beginning about 1900 with the advent of Zionism. As noted, Orthodox Judaism and especially the fairly new institution of "ultra-Orthodox" (*Haredi*) Judaism were largely opposed to

Zionism, as well as most other manifestations of modernity. However, Zionism was accepted—even embraced—by a few Orthodox rabbis. Religious Zionism's founder and most important early leader and theologian was Rav (Rabbi) Avraham Yitzhak HaCohen Kook (1865–1935), who moved to Palestine from Russia in 1904 and became the first Ashkenazi Chief Rabbi of the Land of Israel in 1921. His son, Rabbi Zvi Yehudah Kook (1891–1982), developed his father's largely mystical ideas in a strongly nationalistic direction and was, in certain respects, an equally important figure in his own right but in a very different context.

Rabbi A.Y. Kook (the elder) regarded Zionism as a divinely inspired movement, i.e., it was the long-promised Divine redemption. However, he had to deal with the important caveat that most Zionists, who were devoutly secular, had absolutely no idea that they were engaged in bringing the Messiah (cf. Kook 1997). He insisted that settlement of the land must be carried on peacefully, and Solomon contends that his thought on war and peace is "represented in Israel today by the religious peace movements" (2006, 62–63). A follower of his, Rabbi Moshe Amiel, Chief Rabbi of Tel Aviv in the 1930s, went further and contended that the commandment "'Thou shalt not kill' applied irrespective of whether the victim was Arab or Jew, and was the basis of Jewish ethics" (Solomon 2006, 63).

Rabbi A.Y. Kook died in 1935, before Arab-Jewish violence had spiraled out of control. His son, however, lived through the Palestinian Revolt of 1936–1939, the war of 1948, and the division of the Land. He discerned God's hand in the spectacular (seemingly miraculous) Israeli victory in 1967 that gave the modern state of Israel full control of its ancient patrimony—and he became the rabbinical authority for those National Religious (youth especially) who construed it as God's proof to the Jewish people that now was the time to redeem the land, by force if necessary. He was the chief religious authority for the vanguard organization Gush Emunim (the Bloc of the Faithful), which led the settler movement against all obstacles, especially Israeli governments before 1977, which were ambivalent regarding the West Bank. His rabbinical rulings construed the *mitzvah* (commandment) for Jews to settle the entire biblical Land of Israel as the most important of all Jewish religious laws, a novel interpretation that served to justify virtually any action carried out to accomplish it.

Rabbi Zvi Yehudah's ideology was largely adopted by significant parts of Religious Zionist movement, including the National Religious Party (which had been dovish before 1967). It has now transformed into the "Jewish Home" Party led by the charismatic Naftali Bennett, which advocates Israeli annexation of the West Bank. However, this has by no means been the extreme of religious Jewish interpretation. Thus, it is ironic that in Israel today, both the small Jewish peace movements (discussed below) and the much larger religious Zionist settler movement take their inspirations from the Rabbis Kook, father and son, respectively.

As noted, Israeli military doctrine developed in reaction to the Yishuv's, and then Israel's, political, diplomatic, and military circumstances, with little or no attention to the laws and commentaries that were central to Jewish tradition over the previous 3000 years. An important element of Zionism was that it was intended to transform the circumstances of the Jewish people, i.e., to "normalize" it. Another was to become the "subject" rather than the "object" of history. A number of early Zionists had particular disdain for what they considered the humiliating passivity of Jews during 2000 years of Diaspora. They saw themselves as the first generation to leave the ghetto and traditional Judaism—and they were determined not to allow such a tradition of passivity to become dominant in the new society they were building in Palestine. Some, for example, imitated the Bedouin, wearing cartridge bandoliers and riding Arabian horses.

A series of violent episodes in 1920, 1921, 1929, and 1936–1939 made it progressively clearer that the Arab inhabitants of the land regarded the increasing Jewish population as determined to dispossess them, and that they would oppose it with force. Thus, as the Jewish population swelled from fewer than 200,000 in 1930 to more than double that by the beginning of World War II due to Jews fleeing growing anti-semitism in Europe, the Yishuv became increasingly a mobilized and even militarized society. Thirty thousand Palestinian Jews received military training from the British during the War, and the Yishuv prepared for a war with the Arabs that they knew would follow the end of the World War. Although about 1% of the new state's population died in the 1948 war, Israel was the unambiguous victor.

The role of the memory of the Holocaust must be noted as well. For about 20 years it was little talked about in Israel, but it served as an omnipresent reminder of what Jewish powerlessness could lead to. There was—and continues to be—an implicit identification of Israel's enemies with anti-semites, from the Bible through the Nazis. This is both a religious and national process; religious as well as historical tropes have been used to delineate it.

What has changed since the 1970s is that this perception has become increasingly tied to religious Judaism of the National Religious kind—and is also becoming part of the Haredi worldview, which has elements of both anti-nationalism and extreme nationalism as well (Inbari 2017), though they are seemingly contradictory. Three generations of Holocaust education has, for many Israelis, conflated the Nazis with the Palestinians. Even an ideological dove like Israel's well-known Foreign Minister, Abba Eban (1915–2002), is perhaps best remembered among Israelis for his description of the 1967 borders (aka the "Green Line") as "Auschwitz borders."

Another arena in which Israeli opinion has drastically changed since 1967 is with regard to the Temple Mount/Haram al-Sharif. This has always been a national symbol as well as a religious site for Jews—hence the name Zionism (taken from the name of a hill next to the Mount) for the Jewish national movement. While 100 years ago, as Palestinian nationalism was first developing, the Haram al-Sharif was purely a religious site, in the last 50 years it has become a national site for Palestinians as well as a rallying cry for the world's Muslims.

There is now a nearly universal Muslim denial of any Jewish connection to the Haram/Temple Mount, including the two ancient Jewish Temples. This denial is well-known among Israelis and only strengthens their own connection to it, making the site that much more of a tinderbox (see Cohen 2017). Thus, the Second Intifada (2000–2004) is generally known as the al-Aksa Intifada, and the mini ('Stabbing') Intifada that began in 2014 and continued sporadically for several years, was primarily nourished by a general Palestinian belief that Israel was intent on changing the *status quo* on the Mount. It nearly reached a point of religious war in July 2017 before Israel uncharacteristically capitulated to Muslim demands and removed metal detectors and cameras it had installed on the Haram in the wake of an attack (Scham 2017).

The Israeli Prime Minister since 2009, Benjamin Netanyahu, is an old-fashioned secular nationalist, who almost certainly recognizes the dangers of attempting to change the site's *status quo*. However, many of his supporters, including at least one party in his governing coalition (The Jewish Home), views the conflict in explicitly ethno-religious terms. Though for hundreds of years Jewish religious law forbade Jews to go up to the Temple Mount, this interpretation is now changing; the idea of instituting Jewish prayer on the Mount, or even rebuilding the Temple, has in less than 20 years moved from the furthest fringes of Jewish religious thinking to become almost mainstream (Mescheloff 2017; Inbari 2017).

Another strand of recent extremist Jewish thought is represented by the followers of the assassinated Rabbi Meir Kahane (1932–1990). His theology was based on a notion of theological retaliation by God and the Jewish people against the "nations" (Heb: *goyim*) who had persecuted the Jewish people (Afterman 2015). Unlike the mainstream National Religious, who religiously venerate the State of Israel as the "first flowering of our redemption,"[11] Kahane's overtly racist message is based on violence and utter exclusivity. It is fringe, but has penetrated some of the younger elements of the National Religious movement.

One other religious strand that should be noted is that led by the late Rabbi Menachem Froman (1945–2013). He was the rabbi of the settlement of Tekoah in the West Bank, but unlike most settlers, who avoid and sometimes harass their Arab neighbors, he met with them, made friends with them, and expounded a philosophy of two peoples—one land, i.e. the Land of Israel/Palestine as indivisible and belonging to both peoples. His movement has been disdained by both the (overwhelmingly secular) mainstream Israeli peace movement as well as by his fellow settlers, who mostly embrace the traditional Zionist view that only the Jewish people has a genuine historical, religious, and mystical connection to the Land. Rabbi Froman's movement has attracted somewhat more attention and support in recent years, partly because it is increasingly difficult to envision a large-scale evacuation of Jewish settlers from the West Bank—and also because of some attraction to it by otherwise hardline Muslim religious figures, including some reputedly affiliated to Hamas. It also has some connection to some junior members of Knesset like Yehuda Glick, who welcomes Muslim as well as Jewish prayer on the Temple Mount/Haram al-Sharif (Fischer 2017).

Tomer Persico is a scholar at the Hartman Institute in Jerusalem, one of the few liberal modern Orthodox institutions in Israel. His theory (2017) is that Orthodoxy in Israel is rapidly changing from its 2000-year emphasis on Halachah (i.e., Jewish law) in a messianic direction. Ironically, this amounts to swerving away from the Kookian (both father and son) emphasis on the importance of creating and living in a Jewish state (or state of the Jews), which itself is an element of eventual (not imminent) redemption. He connects this directly to the new prominence, in the last two decades, of the Temple Mount itself, and the rapidly growing, seemingly serious discussion in religious circles about rebuilding the Temple. This is inherently apocalyptic for both political and religious reasons. Politically, because upending the *status quo* and erecting a Third Temple, whether or not it involves destruction of the Muslim holy places already there, would almost certainly destroy any chance of Israel living in peace with its neighbors and likely spark an overtly religious war. Religiously, it clearly implies that a Jewish state is solely a means to a Divine end.

It is not that Persico or most others believe this will be a dominant political trend. Nevertheless, it calls into question the future ability of significant elements of the religious public to participate in conventional politics, let alone be a force for peace. As he warns, "this wave of ethnonationalism centered on the Temple Mount that is now sweeping through Israeli society poses a great test for secular Israeli democracy" (Persico 2017, 119).

The Jewish Pacific Tradition Today

Like the warrior tradition, the modern Israeli pacific tradition began as a political movement. Unlike the warrior tradition, its adherents today remain overwhelmingly secular. In fact, being visibly observant is generally considered an almost foolproof symbol of one's views on war and peace. Secular people are not necessarily dovish, but there is a perception that religious people are in favor of settlements, the Greater Land of Israel, and a hard line towards Palestinians.

As noted, this has many of the aspects of a *Kulturkampf*. It is an interesting and important question why the Left has largely foregone the long and honorable Jewish tradition of peace while the Right has created a largely new tradition of war and violence, but basing them on their knowledge of and respect for Jewish tradition and Halachah.

Again, the reasons are sociological, historical, and political, and have very little to do with theology. There are interesting contrasts with other religions, however; while many Christians and Buddhists use Christianity or Buddhism respectively as the basis for their pacific orientation, the ratio of religious Jews to secular Jews in the Israeli peace movement is much lower by any estimation. Arguably, Judaism is much more comparable to Islam in this phenomenon.

Reasons for the lack of observant Jews and religious Jews in the Israeli peace movements include the following:

- While the Left is usually (though not always) more pacific and more secular than the Right, Zionism, as explained earlier, developed directly as a reaction to religious Judaism, and early Zionists rejected religious Judaism. They themselves were often the products of a religious education, but their children and grandchildren were not. That tradition, whether for actual descendants of early Zionists or not, is the basis for most of the mainstream peace organizations in Israel. Those which are not mainstream tend to be further Left and even more anti-religious.
- "Left" and "Right" in Israel are determined overwhelmingly by security, not economic considerations. The anti-religious attitude is an integral part of a worldview that is peace-oriented, as opposed to a more traditional worldview that is more nationalistic, more hawkish, and more religious. Thus, among the religious peacemakers, it is notable that a large majority are immigrants from the US (or the UK to a lesser extent) or their children. American Judaism is far less coercive than the Israeli model, and its adherents are far more liberal. Most America Jews identify with the more liberal denominations, while the approximately 10% who are Orthodox in the US overwhelmingly identify with Israeli/Jewish religious nationalism.
- Previously, I mentioned the Ashkenazi/Mizrachi cleavage, which is part of this dichotomy and a central element of the *Kulturkampf*. Mizrachim tend to be more religious in a more relaxed manner; Ashkenazim tend either to be secular or else Haredi or Religious Zionist. Mizrachim identify more with the religious parties, including attitudes against Arabs, which means being more hawkish. There is a Mizrachi peace movement, but it is even smaller than the mainly Ashkenazi religious peace movement.

Naomi Chazan, a retired Hebrew University Professor and former Member of Knesset, sees the Israeli peace camp as divided into two sets of groups after the Oslo Peace process fell apart in 2000. To the Left are more radical groups that emphasize activism in opposing the Occupation, including B'tselem, the Committee Against House Demolitions, and others, including one religious group, Rabbis for Human Rights (discussed below) (Chazan 2013, 274). The more moderate group of organizations includes the well-known Peace Now (Shalom Achshav), as well as the Geneva Initiative, the Council for Peace and Security (composed of several thousand high-ranking former military and security officers), and several more. It is notable that in Chazan's article, she only mentions Rabbis for Human Rights and Oz v'Shalom/Netivot Shalom one time each, in listing smaller peace groups.

The Jewish Religious Peace Movement

For reason discussed above, religious Judaism, despite its strong emphasis on peace and nonviolence through the centuries of Diaspora, has had, at best, a slight presence in the political/religious Israeli peace-oriented discourse. It is largely represented by two formerly separate organizations known as Oz v'Shalom/Netivot Shalom (Strength and Peace/Paths of Peace), founded in 1977 and 1982, respectively. For a while this tendency was represented by a political party, Meimad, led by Rabbi Michael Melchior, who was in the Knesset from 1999 to 2009 but was primarily affiliated with other liberal parties for most of that time. There is also a largely American group, Rabbis for Human Rights, which recently changed its name to *T'ruah* (representing the sound of the Shofar), that frequently joins demonstrations against house demolitions or other such official acts. As noted above, the adherents of the religious peace camp are very disproportionately American immigrants to Israel or their children, although the vast majority of religious American immigrants in Israel are firmly (and also disproportionately) in the National Religious camp. Numerous meetings have been held between peace-oriented rabbis and Muslim and Christian Palestinians, but little has emerged from them, except a literature emphasizing the inextricable connection between religion and peace (see, e.g., Gopin 2002).

Rabbi Marc Gopin is one of the best-known academic theoreticians of Jewish religious peacemaking. He is simultaneously an American academic and a liberal conflict resolution activist, and was also trained as an Orthodox rabbi. He regards the split in Israel between secular cultural and political elites, on the one hand, and religious authorities and their religious population, on the other, as integral to the inability of the State of Israel to make peace with its primarily Muslim adversaries. Taking the category of forgiveness as an example, he shows how it is understood very differently in different cultures, both secular and religious (2002, 108–129). In other words, estrangement by the secular liberal elites (who in Israel are often peace-oriented) from religious Judaism and its practitioners results in devaluing religion in general as inherently anachronistic and oppressive, as well as destroying the possibility of uniting Israelis behind a pacific policy, because the elites are not trusted by the large part of the Israeli population that does take religious Judaism seriously. His book is largely a critique of those Israeli secular elites for whom religious Judaism—and those who practice it—are both a closed book. He contends that this distrust on both sides, given Judaism's importance in Israeli society, necessarily renders a simply secular peace process, which is the only one envisioned in decades of negotiations, probably destined to fail unless the distrust is remedied. Religion is thus certainly a significant part of the problem, but also an essential part of the solution. Gopin believes that acceptance of the "Other" within Israel is possible, and a necessary prelude to accepting the external "Other."

A somewhat similar insight comes from Eva Ilouz, an Israeli academic and public intellectual. She, unlike most of her colleagues, is of Mizrachi background; her parents left Morocco in the great wave of Moroccan Jewish emigration in the 1950s and 1960s and moved to France, while she herself moved to Israel as an adult. She, formerly observant and always politically liberal, also indicts the secular Israeli elite, of which she is a recognized part, for having embraced in their atheistic (formerly socialist) Zionism a spurious universalism which was alien to the half of their own population that is Mizrachi and, at least spiritually, very Jewish-oriented. She also criticizes David Ben-Gurion, the very secular founder and first leader of the state, for having legally accepted the religious definition of Judaism, thus giving religious authorities a fundamental power over Israeli civil society and assuring the perpetuation of their control. She, unlike Gopin, is pessimistic that either side, the rightwing-oriented Mizrachi masses or the liberal, pro-peace secular elite, can ever reconcile sufficiently to make peace with their Arab neighbors (Ilouz 2017).

It should be noted that the analyses above refer primarily to Orthodox Judaism, the only branch of Judaism officially recognized in Israel. There are several hundred Reform, Conservative, and Reconstructionist rabbis and congregations in Israel, but they are often denigrated as an "American import." The Orthodox and ultra-Orthodox political parties have considerable political power, while the liberal denominations have virtually none. It should be noted that most of the liberal denominations identify to varying degrees with the "peace camp," but not necessarily from a religious or theological point of view, nor does peace seem to be their priority. It is notable that liberal American religious Jewish organizations were far more upset by the government's decision to cancel an arrangement for non-Orthodox prayer arrangements at Jerusalem's Western Wall (the Kotel) than they have ever been by the Israeli government's actions against Palestinians (see, e.g., Hod 2017).

Conclusions

It is both sad and ironic that the current effective connection between religious Judaism and peace is, at best, tenuous. It is ironic because for most of recorded history Judaism was, both in practice and theologically, probably the major religion least oriented towards violence and most oriented towards peace. This chapter has attempted to briefly explain how the national aspect of Judaism, largely in eclipse for 2000 years of Diaspora, has re-emerged with a vengeance in a manner that could not have been imagined less than 100 years ago, and largely reversed the Jewish theology of war and peace since 1967.

Perhaps it can serve as a particularly severe warning against the role of religion in politics. While religious parties are by no means inherently radical (the Christian Democratic movement in Europe comes readily to mind), many others have followed an illiberal and intolerant path. When inadvertently mixed with class and ethnic prejudice and discrimination, religion, as demonstrated above, too often assumes a particularly belligerent and intolerant aspect. An effective antidote has yet to be discovered.

Notes

1 The Khazars were a Turkic tribe that reputedly adopted Judaism and ruled an empire on the southwestern Russian steppe between the seventh and ninth centuries C.E. Historians differ as to whether their adoption of Judaism was real or legendary.

2 E.g., at the time of the notable massacres by crusaders in Mainz, Worms, Spiers, and other communities in 1096; at the massacre in York in 1190; and many other cases. Jewish self-defense was often notable for its absence until the late nineteenth century. The desire to reverse this perception and reality of passivity was a major impetus for the Zionist movement and its willingness to use violence.
3 One of the few who took it seriously was Yitzhak Epstein, who wrote an article in 1903 saying how Zionists treated the Palestinian Arabs was the "hidden question," but he was largely ignored. See Dowty (2001).
4 This is a major issue for peacemakers as well as historians, as Palestinians maintain the expulsion was planned and coordinated (cf. Pappe 2006), while the traditional Israeli view maintains Palestinians were told by their leaders to leave. Most Israeli historians in the last generation have accepted that most Palestinians left because of a combination of expulsion and fear.
5 See Theodor Herzl, *Der Judenstaat*, first published in 1988, which can be understood in either or both senses. The major tensions between these two very different implied conceptions of what role Judaism should play in the State of Israel remain today.
6 Some have construed this continued ambivalence as covert support by the Labor leadership. See, e.g., Gorenberg (2000), Zertal and Eldar (2007), and Raz (2012),
7 See Raz (2012), who shows that Israel wanted the "dowry" (i.e., the land) but not the "bride" (the people living on it).
8 Solomon states flatly that "there is no clear tradition of pacifism in Judaism" but goes on to list "an impressive array of Jewish pacifists" (2006, 60).
9 Non-Orthodox Judaism has scholars who are knowledgeable about the traditional texts, but very few non-Orthodox laypeople regularly study or have more than, at most, a superficial knowledge of those texts and the bases of Jewish tradition.
10 Instances can be multiplied almost indefinitely but take, for example, the seven "Noahide laws," which Jewish tradition holds are incumbent on all human beings. These are juxtaposed against the 613 commandments for Jews that are stipulated in Halachah.
11 A phrase from the official prayer for the State of Israel, composed by the Chief Rabbinate.

References

Afterman, Adam and Gedaliah Afterman. 2015. "Meir Kahane and Contemporary Jewish Theology of Revenge." *Soundings: An Interdisciplinary Journal*, vol. 98: 2. Pp. 192–217.

Biale, David. 1986. *Power and Powerlessness in Jewish History*. New York: Knopf.

Chazan, Naomi. 2013. "Israeli Peace Movements." Pp. 267–277, in the *Routledge Handbook on the Israeli-Palestinian Conflict*. Joel Peters and David Newman, eds. New York: Routledge.

Cohen, Hillel. 2017. "The Temple Mount/al-Aqsa in Zionist and Palestinian National Consciousness: A Comparative View." *Israel Studies Review*, vol. 32: 1. Pp. 1–19.

Dowty, Alan. 2001. "A Question That Outweighs All Others": Yitzhak Epstein and Zionist Recognition of the Arab Issue." *Israel Studies*, vol. 6: 1. Pp. 34–54.

Eisen, Robert. 2011. *The Peace and Violence of Judaism: From the Bible to Modern Zionism.* New York: Oxford University Press.

Fischer, Shlomo. 2017. "From Yehuda Etzion to Yehuda Glick: From Redemptive Revolution to Human Rights on the Temple Mount." *Israel Studies Review*, vol. 32: 1. Pp. 67–87.

Gopin, Marc. 2002. *Holy War, Holy Peace: How Religion Can Bring Peace to the Middle East.* New York: Oxford University Press.

Gorenberg, Gershom. 2000. *The End of Days: Fundamentalism and the Struggle for the Temple Mount.* New York: The Free Press.

Herzl, Theodor. 1988 [1896]. *The Jewish State [Der Judenstaat]*. New York: Dover Publications.
Hirschhorn, Sara. 2017. *City on a Hilltop: American Jews & the Israeli Settler Movement*. Cambridge, MA: Harvard University Press.
Hod, Rami. 2017. "Why American Jews Need to Lose All Faith in Israel's Government." *Ha'aretz*. July 11, 2017. www.haaretz.com/opinion/.premium-1.800600.
Ilouz, Eva. 2017. "From the Paradox of Liberation to the Demise of Liberal Elites." Pp. 49–64, in *The Great Regression*. Heinrich Geiselberger, ed. Malden, MA: Polity Press.
Inbari. Mordechai. 2017. "Uzi Meshulam's 'Mishkan Ohalim' Affair and the Influence of Radical Ultra-Orthodox Ideology." *Israel Studies Review*, vol. 32: 2.
Kook, Avraham. 1997. *War and Peace: The Teachings of HaRav Avraham Yitzhak HaCohen Kook*. David Samson and Tzvi Fishman, eds. Jerusalem: Torat Eretz Yisrael Publications.
Mescheloff, Shifra. 2017. "The Temple Mount in the Teachings of Rabbi Shlomo Goren." *Israel Studies Review* vol. 32: 1. Pp. 88–103.
Pappe, Ilan. 2006. *The Ethnic Cleansing of Palestine*. Oxford: One World Press.
Penslar, Derek. 2015. *Jews and the Military: A History*. Princeton, NJ: Princeton University Press.
Persico, Tomer. 2017 "The End Point of Zionism: Ethnocentrism and the Temple Mount." *Israel Studies Review*, vol. 32: 1. Pp. 104–122.
Raz, Avi. 2012. *The Bride and the Dowry: Israel, Jordan, and the Palestinians in the Aftermath of the June 1967 War*. New Haven, CT: Yale University Press.
Scham, Paul. 2017. "The Palestinians Won the 2017 Battle for Temple Mount: That's Good for Israel." *Ha'aretz*. August 2, 2017. www.haaretz.com/opinion/.premium-1.804553.
Shafir, Gershon. 2017. *A Half Century of Occupation: Israel, Palestine, and the World's Most Intractable Conflict*. Oakland: University of California Press.
Shapira, Anita. 1999. *Land and Power: The Zionist Resort to Force, 1881–1948*. Stanford: Stanford University Press.
Solomon, Norman. 2006. "The Ethics of War in Judaism." Pp. 39–80, in *The Ethics of War in Asian Civilizations*. Torkel Brekke, ed. New York: Routledge.
Sprinzak, Ehud. 1991. *The Ascendance of Israel's Radical Right*. New York: Oxford University Press.
Taub, Gadi. 2010. *The Settlers: And the Struggle Over the Meaning of Zionism*. New Haven, CT: Yale University Press.
Zertal, Idith and Akiva Eldar. 2007. *Lords of the Land: The War Over Israel's Settlements in the Occupied territories, 1967–2007*. New York: Nation Books.

7

"PURITY OF ARMS"

Educating Ethical Warriors in the Israeli Army

Noam Zion

Introduction

In the face of military attack, where sustained efforts at compromise or arbitration by peaceful means have not been successful, and the defense of human life and of the autonomous pursuit of one's particular way of collective life necessitate the use of organized violence, a state and an army are means to sacred ends of self-defense. Martin Buber makes this point in response to Mahatma Gandhi's letters urging German Jews under the Nazi regime to resort to nonviolent protest:

> I cannot help withstanding evil when I see that it is about to destroy the good. I am forced to withstand the evil in the world, just as I withstand the evil within myself. I can only strive not to have to do so by force. I do not want force. But if there is no other way of preventing the evil destroying the good, I trust I shall use force and give myself up into God's hands.
>
> *(Buber, 2005, 125)*

But Buber insists a nation minimize its use of violence as much as possible:

> It is indeed true that there can be no life without injustice . . . But the human aspect of life begins the moment we say to ourselves: we shall do no more injustice to others than we are forced to do in order to exist.
>
> *(Buber, 2005, 247)*

National states in conflict, however, have their own dangerous dynamic leading them to maximize violence, glorify in conquest, and identify whatever it does for survival and for growth as absolutely just. Nations then move easily from defensive nationalism to xenophobic, glory-seeking nationalism. In modern Hebrew, an important terminological difference distinguishes between immoral and moral nationalism—*leumanut* (pathological nationalism) as opposed to *leumiut* (normative democratic national self-determination). Armies also have a tendency to educate their soldiers with us versus them thinking, good versus evil polarization, and dehumanization of the enemy. The military means of self-defense are then glorified (i.e. militarism) and violence becomes an end rather than a means. For Buber and for the Israeli novelist Amos Oz, military activity is a necessary evil entailing virtues such as self-sacrifice, comradeship, and courage, but in danger of leading to vengeance, hate, and indiscriminate abuse of power.

In a world of warfare, what the contemporary religious Zionist theologian David Hartman calls "an unredeemed world," the ethical ideal is to teach soldiers that their calling is to minimize violence and make it morally discriminate in operation. Non-militaristic virtue education in the army, where most of Israel's young leaders and citizens of the state are educated under near universal compulsory conscription, requires developing a warrior ethos that teaches compassion rather than vengeance, discipline yet resistance to immoral orders, and deliberation over ethical dilemmas rather than raging aggressiveness. Instead of condemning all nationalism as fascist and all military tradition as militarism, the educational path of "the middle way," as Buber names it, is to reshape those powerful traditions, so they minimize violence and its glorification and maximize the promotion of human life and dignity extended as far as possible to the enemy.

The Israeli Army Education and Training Division has developed a fascinating study kit to teach ethics in war based on the basic value of human dignity and human life. The IDF Study Kit is called **Purity of Arms,** a unique Israeli term translating "*Tohar HaNeshek*." This value is one of ten basic values set out in **The Spirit of the Israel Defense Forces,** the official code of ethics of the Israeli Army (1994, revised 2001). The army calls it the identity card of the IDF. Chief of Staff Gabi Ashkenazi called it "the compass and the conscience of the IDF" (Israeli Defense Force Study Guide on the Spirit of the IDF, 2007). Composed by high ranking army officers in the division of education and by Israeli professors of philosophy and law, its purpose is to define the **mission statement** of the army as a professional organization. In the 1990s, when the IDF reformulated its mission as a value-motivated organization, the IDF had just completed fighting the first Intifada (1987). Its moral standards needed to be revisited after the nature of its warfare changed from army-to-army battles in nonurban terrain (1956, 1967, 1973) to army-to-substate guerilla and terrorist organizations in urbanized areas.[1] Our task is to survey the moral arguments and educational approaches employed (or ignored) in the Spirit of IDF Code, in the Purity of Arms Study Guide, and in the official Letters to the Soldier from Chief Education Officers or the Chief of Staff before large military operations in civilian areas (or, for example, in 1982 before entry into Lebanon). Special emphasis will be placed on the appeal to national and religious values.

The urgency and relevance of Purity of Arms to military goals and challenges today are manifest in the combat situations of many Western armies engaged in asymmetrical wars characteristic of the post-World War Two era (Vietnam, Afghanistan, former Yugoslavia, Iraq, Syria, Israel/Palestine). How does an army fight in ways that are both effective and moral, while battling irregular forces in civilian spaces? Often soldiers and low-ranking officers must make their own decisions, both tactical and ethical, in small-force skirmishes with guerillas and terrorists within urban settings and heavily populated rural areas. Distinguishing noncombatant civilians and armed combatants is a matter of life or death for the soldier as well as the civilian. Therefore, armies have a responsibility to help their military personnel develop moral judgment appropriate for functioning effectively both militarily and morally in liminal situations.

What is the form of ethical education appropriate in military training? Armies may draw on many models, such as philosophical axioms (like Kant); rule-based obedience; deliberation about ethical dilemmas (like case-based casuistic rabbinic law); development of practical judgment to apply universal principles to concrete situations (like Aristotle; see Schon 1983); virtue education to shape moral habits and character (like Aristotle, Maimonides); utilitarian ethics (like Bentham); and appeals to an honor code based on one's national, religious, and humanistic cultural identity. These categories can be applied fruitfully to an analysis of the educational study unit of the Israeli army designed to enlist the allegiance of its soldiers to its moral code, The Spirit of the IDF (Israel Defense Forces).

What is the content of military ethics? While ethics in the tradition of Kant claims universality, the ethics of a national army is often justified in terms of the values that a particular society represents (such as democracy, fairness, freedom, human dignity, equality, national honor, loyalty to the homeland, solidarity of a people, etc.). Today Israel, as a Jewish democratic state by its own definition, seeks to educate its soldiers to ethics in war by appealing to Jewish sources, both religiously and nationally Jewish, as well as Western ethics and law. In the IDF, this is the educational task of officers, not chaplains. Therefore, examining the educational curriculum of the IDF constitutes a rare laboratory for the intersection of religious, national and humanitarian ethics, and law in real-life situations.

Historical Background: The Birth of the Israeli Military Tradition of Purity of Arms

In Israel, in the face of indiscriminate terror against civilians during the Arab Revolt against the British Mandate (1936–1939), Zionist thinkers, like Berl Katznelson, developed an amorphous standard of moral warfare called "purity of arms" (a religious neologism).[2] This Zionist doctrine called on Jewish soldiers of the pre-state national militias (in 1939) and later its state army (in 1948) never to direct violence at enemy civilians not involved in combat, even if the enemy militias targeted Jewish and, later, Israeli civilians. That doctrine was controversial at the time, but with the establishment of Israel, the IDF adopted the doctrine of purity of arms and now teaches the original doctrine of purity of arms, integrating it with new international Western legal doctrines, such as minimizing collateral damage, and with select biblical and rabbinic traditions. The combination reflects the commitment of Israel to an identity as a Jewish democratic state.

The updated version of the Spirit of IDF, its Code of Honor (2001), was developed in the wake of quelling Palestinian uprisings in the occupied West Bank and Gaza (from 1987) and widespread suicide bombings in Israeli buses, restaurants, and youth nightclubs (from 2000). It aims to teach Israeli soldiers that they are expected not just to avoid harm (injustice) to enemy civilians, but also to do good, which entails risking their lives to minimize danger to enemy civilians by taking positive action. The IDF study guide makes the distinction between the demands of international law and the higher demand of the Spirit of the IDF honor code:

> What does the IDF principle of purity of arms add to the principle of limitation that prohibits targeting noncombatants and POWs? Not only does the code say "IDF soldiers will not use their weapons and force to harm human beings who are not combatants or prisoners of war," but also soldiers of the IDF will **do all in their power to prevent harming** their lives, bodies, dignity and property ... "To prevent harm," not just "to refrain from harming."
>
> *(IDF Study Guide: Purity of Arms)*

While the doctrine of purity of arms forms part of the Israeli consensus, the appropriate application of such unusually high ethical demands is controversial, since terrorist enemy forces do not distinguish civilian and military targets.

Research Categories

Our project is to analyze the Israeli Training Manual for teaching Purity of Arms and the Spirit of the IDF in terms of its ethical, religious, and nationalist ethos and its educational strategy and tactics. What is the image of the ethical warrior or soldier, and how does one educate towards that ideal? We will pursue this conceptual analysis of a written document under the following rubrics: ethical problematics on an asymmetrical battlefield; moral content and message; mode of ethics; self-corrective values and mechanisms when performance does not meet the standards; the presentation of self and other to the soldiers; and the varied sources of authority and wisdom invoked.

(1) Ethical Problematics

The military and hence moral challenges of the Israeli army in maintaining purity of arms are exacerbated when fighting an asymmetrical war against terrorist militias that, in the name of religious and nationalist ideologies, promote indiscriminate killing of civilians with a principled disregard for Western conventions of war. These terrorist combatants function within a generally politically supportive enemy alien population that is often indistinguishable from combatants. At times these enemy civilians join the combatants, hide them, and even participate in mob attacks on lone Israeli civilians who stray into their communities. In this chapter, as in the IDF study guide, there is no attempt to judge the grievance of the Palestinians or Lebanese Hezbollah combatants. As in all treatments of ethics *in* war, as distinct from ethics *of* war, the question of just cause for going to war should not influence how the war ought to be conducted (Merriam and Schmitt, 2015). This distinction is carefully emphasized in the IDF study guide.

Moshe Halbertal, a professor of law who was involved with updating the IDF Code of Ethics (2001), observes that in asymmetrical wars, more combat takes place in very small units in individual skirmishes than in big operations controlled directly by the high command. Hence, moral guidance in war must percolate to the lowest levels of army, officers, and rank and file:

> **In this new kind of micro-war, every soldier is a kind of commanding officer, a full moral and strategic agent. Every soldier must decide whether the individual standing before him in jeans and sneakers is a combatant or not.** What sorts of risks must a soldier assume in order to avoid killing civilians while targeting a seeming combatant? The challenge is to make these rules part of the inner world of each soldier.
>
> *(Halbertal, 2009)*

The IDF study guide begins by acknowledging that moral restraint and moral decision-making are particularly difficult in combat.

> The basic value of human dignity . . . has special significance in the army because of the danger of harming human life and the danger of the misuse of power and authority over our comrades and over those who stand opposite us—the civilian population and the enemy combatants.

Empathy for the challenges of the soldiers is the starting point of the education process, followed by analysis of these difficulties. Then solutions are offered and appeals are made to commit to a higher code of honor that represents the soldier's ideal identity.

The Challenge of the Evil Impulse: A Holy Camp

The study unit begins with a biblical law requiring that a Jewish army maintain purity in its camp.

> When you go out to war against your enemies, you shall keep yourselves from anything evil. If one of you becomes unclean because of a nocturnal emission, he shall go outside the camp; he shall not come back into the camp.... Since the LORD, your God, journeys along in the midst of your camp to deliver you and to give your enemies over to you, your camp must be holy, so that he does not see anything indecent in your midst and turn away from you.
>
> *(Deut. 23:10–11, 15)*

The choice of these verses is dictated by the modern Israeli term "purity of arms," which was coined in 1939 by a secular socialist Zionist in order to create a modernized biblical notion of ethical sanctity. In the original context, purity refers to ritual purity, but the study unit follows the moral reinterpretation of military purity offered by the thirteenth-century commentator **Nahmanides**:

> The Torah is warning of a time when sin is rampant. The well-known custom of military forces going to war is that they eat all abominable things, rob and plunder, and are not ashamed even of lewdness and all vileness. **The fairest of men by nature comes to be possessed of cruelty and fury when the army advances against the enemy**. Therefore, the Torah warned, *When your camp goes forth against your enemies, keep yourself far from every evil thing* (Deut. 23:10).
>
> *(Cited in IDF Study Guide Kit on Purity of Arms)*

Nahmanides warns that normally moral men are suddenly subject to evil urges in war situations when they are far from social supervision. This anarchic tendency is exacerbated when encountering enemies to whom one feels no moral obligation and from whom one expects to no quarter if one is defeated. The fighting spirit is inflamed, and it expresses itself in an irrational fury and an immoral cruelty that seem inseparable from the task of fighting itself.

Israeli soldiers, recalling their military experience in the Six Day War (1967), spoke of the way war makes animalistic urges rise to the surface, even among idealistic kibbutzniks:

> Avinoam: Definitely! **Like all other living creatures, we have primitive animal instincts which in daily life we firmly repress. They're kept at bay and held in check by a thousand and one different influences**—our surroundings, society, education, values and morality ... But it's just in those very moments when these instincts come to the fore that **we are capable of overcoming them**. That's to say, it's only then that we really face up to them. In normal everyday life there's no such opportunity.
>
> *(Shapira, 1971, 67–68; 178–179, 190–191)*

Similarly, the study guide cites the ideal moral character described by the Rabbis in the language of the ideal warrior: "Who is the *gibor* (hero)? The one who conquers his own *yetzer* (impulse)" (Avot 4:1).

To raise the consciousness of the soldiers to the tendency to disregard one's usual norms in wartime, the IDF study guide brings the following incident and the military judge's response. In the First Intifada (wide-spread civilian rioting against Israeli occupation beginning 1987) on August 22, 1988, a unit in Gaza was faced with a very violent civilian uprising. Many soldiers were bombarded with heavy stones by teenagers. Soldiers were sent in hot pursuit of two teenagers now hiding in their own apartment. The father of one of the rock throwers physically opposed the entry into the room where his oldest son was hiding.

> After the rock thrower was arrested and the situation was under military control, however, four soldiers continued to beat the father Al-Shami Hani Ben Dib for twenty minutes. Only then were he and his son sent to army holding area where a military doctor checked the injured father only cursorily ... Many hours later the father was found dead.
>
> *(IDF Study Guide: Purity of Arms)*

The doctor and four soldiers were convicted of manslaughter. The judge lamented:

> From the beginning of the trial we have been very disturbed by a hard question and that has become more and more disturbing as we have gotten to know the soldiers involved. How could soldiers, from such an elite unit who received a good education, have behaved so brutally? How could they shed the ethical heritage their parents and their teachers taught them and undergo such a metamorphosis so as to be able to beat someone to death with murderous blows?
>
> *(IDF Study Guide: Purity of Arms)*

The army teaches that the presence of power over those who are vulnerable, in liminal situations, without normal mechanisms of repression, brings out impulses that may lead to inhuman treatment of POWs and sometimes enemy civilians. But the assumption of Nahmanides, of the Israeli soldier Avinoam, and of the IDF study guide is that Israeli soldiers can master those evil impulses, especially if they understand them. In a famous letter to the soldiers in the Lebanese War, Nehemia Degania, the Chief Education Officer in 1982, wrote: "**Moral principles lie at the root of our Jewish tradition. Even in war, it is appropriate that relationship of human to human should be humane—not like that of a wolf.**"

The IDF study guide on Purity of Arms raises an interesting case study for analysis, in which a Palestinian teenager at a check point in the West Bank regularly curses out a soldier who is checking his identity card. "Tell me," says the soldier, "what should I do? Am I made out of wood?" The study guide initiates a discussion about how soldiers feel when their honor as human beings and as IDF soldiers is impugned. Then it asks: "Would a violent response to the curse be considered disproportionate abuse of power?" In the message that the soldiers are supposed to derive, the study guide states: "Moral dilemmas that arise while executing one's mission may only be decided based on operational considerations. Inappropriate considerations are the desire to teach the population a lesson, or to express feelings of hate, anger and so forth." While the IDF's educational method encourages the surfacing of angry feelings and opens the normative question about abuse of power, the official message is that such feelings must be mastered as both Jewish moral duty and an obligation to professionalism.

(2) Moral Content

The IDF study guide defines its message unequivocally, though its educational method encourages discussion and surfacing of objections and challenges to that authoritative position. A singular principle of morality applies to all human beings, whether Israeli or noncombatant enemy civilians—human dignity and human life: "The Spirit of IDF derives directly from the value of Human Dignity. It is the highest moral value and it is supposed to guide IDF soldiers in their activities." Surprisingly, an army, whose purpose is to kill and whose ethos is a willingness to risk one's life to perform one's mission, defines the highest value as human life.

Safety rather than dare-devil risks are praised.[3] Yet it is not only the life of one's comrades that must be saved, but also the lives and the honor of enemy civilians.

> **Purity of Arms**—The IDF servicemen and women will use their weapons and force only for the purpose of their mission, only to the necessary extent and will maintain their humanity even during combat. IDF soldiers will not use their weapons and force **to harm human beings** who are not combatants or prisoners of war, and will do all in their power to prevent harming their lives, bodies, dignity and property.
>
> *(Spirit of IDF Code)*

According to Dr. Shlomit Harosh, who works on defining and teaching ethics in war with army officers, average Israeli soldiers take for granted the validity of the commandment *You shall not murder*; therefore, they want to distinguish their killing in self-defense from murder, which is reprehensible. Hence, they see no necessary contradiction between honoring the value of human life and killing enemy combatants in order to prevent the enemy from killing soldiers and civilians.

The study guide specifies those Jewish values it commends as the basis of the Spirit of the IDF and thus reinforces many of the universal values it promotes as a Jewish national legacy as well:

> The tradition of the Jewish people embodies central values of love of one's fellow, recognition of human dignity, preservation of the image of God in human beings, love of the people and the land, responsibility to the public, faith in the sanctity of life. But Jewish tradition is not pacifist and it recognizes the right to respond to those assaulting us in order to kill us and to preempt their aggression and kill the aggressor first.

Nevertheless, it limits the practice of self-defense and emphasizes that the enemy is also a human being, as it says, "When your enemy falls, do not rejoice; when he stumbles, do not be happy, lest God see that behavior and disapprove" (Proverbs 24:17) (cited in Spirit of IDF Code).

Let us explicate the original doctrine of purity of arms, then its formulation in the Spirit of the IDF, and finally its operationalization according to international law, all of which are briefly explicated in the IDF study guide.

Berl Katznelson's doctrine of Purity of Arms emerged from the background of a strident left/right debate among various wings of the Zionist movement. The pressing issue was how to respond to the Arab guerilla attacks (1936–1939) and to the British Mandate government and its military, which closed the ports of Israel to Jewish refugees fleeing Hitler (1939). During this period, Palestinian Arabs participated not only in an armed revolt against the British but in systematic terrorist attacks on Jewish civilians. The study guide quotes Katznelson's formulation of the policy of self-restraint (*havlaga*) in response to Arab terrorism against civilians:

> *Havlagah* means, our weapons will be pure. We learn the use of weapons, we carry weapons, we resist those who come to attack us, but **we do not want our weapons to be stained with blood of innocents** . . . *Havlagah* is both a political and a moral system, caused by our history and reality, our behavior and the conditions of our fight. If we were not **loyal to ourselves** and adopted a different strategy, we would have lost the fight a long time ago.

For Katznelson, the motivating force for this doctrine is loyalty to historic Jewish values as our true self, not only universal ethics qua human beings. The use of weapons is sacred because "we resist those who come to attack us" in order to preserve our own lives from guilty assailants. Since previously Jews for almost 2000 years did not learn to defend themselves from their attackers by constructing their own militia, learning the art of self-defense is a revolution in values that has sacred overtones. But it also harbors the danger of illegitimate use of weapons to kill innocents. Appealing to biblical authority, sacred purity, and Zionist calling, the terminology of purity of weapons is absorbed into the honor code of a modern Israeli army.

Going beyond Katznelson's original formulation and international law, which specify only a principle of limitation on intentionally harming civilians using IDF weapons, the IDF makes a unique demand, according to Moshe Halbertal, a professor of law and one of the framers of the IDF Code:

> The IDF code states that soldiers have to do their utmost to avoid the harming of civilians. This principle states that it is not enough not to intend to kill civilians while attacking legitimate targets. **A deliberate effort has to be made not to harm them** ... **In the deliberations** about the Israeli army's code of military conduct, a crucial question emerged in connection with the requirement that efforts be made to avoid harming civilians. For such efforts surely must include **the expectation that soldiers assume some risk to their own lives in order to avoid causing the deaths of civilians.** As far as I know, **such an expectation is not demanded in international law—but it is demanded in Israel's military code**, and this has always been its tradition.
>
> *(Halbertal, 2009)*

International Law: Operational and Legal Definitions

Seamlessly, the study unit moves to international law to concretize its Israeli ethical commitment to purity of arms, so that Israeli soldiers will not see this as the imposition of the international community on Israel's freedom to defend itself. UN and humanitarian law advocates are seen, often with justification, as hostile to Israel's right to defend itself. Halbertal claims that UN commissions interpret international laws designed to protect enemy civilians in a way that makes it impossible to fight terrorist attacks on Israeli civilians (Halbertal, 2009). The IDF study guide thus identifies recent provisos of international law (1977) with foundational Israeli Jewish military tradition, such that upholding international law can be understood as demonstrating "our loyalty to ourselves." Katznelson's purity of arms and moral restraint is glossed with international law:

> **Principle of Proportionality**: Use of force must be proportional to the mission. In this kind of warfare which has been forced upon us, the obligation to focus and limit our force is **not less important** than the obligation to exercise force. Use of force that is unnecessary to the mission is **a moral error and an error in execution of the mission.**

> **Principle of Limitation:** Some activities are prohibited **even if they appear appropriate to executing the mission.** The distinction between combatants and noncombatants is the most basic limitation that we must maintain.
> *(IDF Study Guide: Purity of Arms; editor's emphasis)*

Further, the 1977 protocol (LOAC) requires the military **to warn the civilian population of attacks** that may affect them, when the circumstances so permit. That is also an ancient rabbinic military law:

> We are commanded that when we besiege a city, we must leave one of the sides unbesieged, so that if they want to flee, there will be an escape route, because through this **we learn to act mercifully even towards enemies in time of war.**
> And this law has another benefit: that we should open for them an opening to escape and then they won't resist us as strongly. As it is said, "And they made war on Midian as the Lord commanded Moses"... This is a mitzvah for all generations in all "permitted wars."
> *(Nahmanides, Comments and Supplements to Maimonides' Book of Mitzvot, Additional Positive Mitzvah #5, thirteenth-century Spain)*

The rabbinic law that a fourth side of the siege must be left open for civilians to flee is embodied today in the practice of giving a warning to enemy civilians before a military operation is launched in an asymmetrical war where the enemy combatants are located among the enemy civilians. In 2008, the Israeli army chose to warn civilians in Gaza of an impending attack by dropping leaflets in Arabic, calling their cell phones, and hitting the roofs with a dummy blast before blowing up the whole apartment building from which combatants were shooting (Halbertal, 2009).

While Nahmanides argued that allowing civilians and combatants to escape a siege had a utilitarian advantage, in the Gaza War, which was aimed at killing terrorists, that was not the case. The military cost of warnings in Gaza meant that many combatants could escape, the assault was delayed, and the advantage of surprise and forward momentum was lost. In the meantime, the enemy could continue shelling the Israeli army, which could not return effective fire until the warnings were issued.

(3) Mode of Ethics

The techniques of moral education employed by the IDF study guide and Spirit of IDF are varied: A. Rule-based obedience; B. Deliberative model; C. Virtue (character) education and conquering one's evil impulse; D. Utilitarian ethics; E. Professional ethics; F. Honor code.

A. Rule-based Obedience

As we saw earlier, the study guide presents binding rules as authoritative, such as the principle of limitation on targeting civilians directly. That is an example of **rule-based obedience**. But, surprisingly, the Israeli army also teaches soldiers when *not* to obey their officers and when to exercise independent moral reasoning:

> **Discipline**—IDF soldiers will be meticulous in giving **only lawful orders, and shall refrain from obeying blatantly illegal orders**.
> *(Spirit of IDF Code)*

As every soldier knows, at times some officers in the Israeli defense forces have issued blatantly illegal—that is, immoral, inhuman—orders. In Kfar Kaseem, when policing a curfew in an Israeli Arab village during the Sinai War in 1956, some officers ordered their men to shoot to kill innocent and peaceful citizens who had unintentionally violated the curfew. A few men obeyed, and 53 civilians were murdered. Officers and rank and file men were tried and convicted. The judge, Judge Benjamin Halevy, who was later a judge at the trial of Adolf Eichmann, established a precedent still taught and observed: "The distinguishing mark of a manifestly illegal order is that above such an order should fly, like a black flag, a warning saying: 'Prohibited!'" [4] The IDF explanation of the principle of discipline explicitly mentions the "massacre in Kfar Kaseem" and the judge's harsh condemnation of that scandalous behavior. Then it explains very precisely that armies need discipline, but "regarding orders that are manifestly immoral and illegal, soldiers are obligated to refuse the order. If the soldier obeys such a command, then the soldier will be punished" (IDF Study Guide: Purity of Arms).

To drive home this lesson about purity of arms, the study guide focuses on a harsh violation of purity of arms in a case study from Hebron. A Palestinian teenager was thrown off an army truck and died; the study guide makes it clear this behavior was not only immoral but illegal, and the perpetrators were punished.

B. Deliberative Model of Ethical Education

While in Kfar Kaseem, the morally and legally valid behavior of a soldier was clear; this is not the case when facing an enemy combatant in asymmetrical war. Soldiers are commanded to fight, so they must employ their weapons, one way or another, to achieve their military ends, and that too is moral action. Their problem is to figure out, in the fog of war, how to use discretion in applying these amorphous guidelines, while avoiding being killed or defeated. The fine distinctions of international lawyers are not available to combatants, nor do they have the peace of mind to think each event through. From an educational perspective, if a soldier thinks ethical rules are irrelevant to military reality and hence are utopian, then he will ignore them. Therefore, the Spirit of the IDF acknowledges the moral ambiguity of ethics in war:

> The value of purity of weapons is **not a simple one-sided instruction about how to behave but rather a value that requires deliberation and discretion in order to be put into practice in army activities**. Purity of weapons characterizes the IDF as a professional army **employing judgment especially in situations of difficult combat. The reality in the field is complex.**
>
> The fight to eradicate terror against Israeli citizens takes place in the heart of a civilian population such that innocent people may be injured. Our task is to carry out the missions in light of the purity of weapons and to minimize injury to innocent civilians **as much as possible.**
>
> (IDF Study Guide: Purity of Arms)

As Aristotle teaches, moral judgment is a matter of more or less on a spectrum. It is a practical art, not a deductive science derived from clear axioms by deductive logic. Therefore, soldiers must be sensitized and trained to use their own judgment in the field. The moral ideal for combatants in the military is not literalist obedience, but deliberative conversation. The fallen soldier Alex Singer reflects on that moral ideal of deliberation in writing to a friend about the Israeli army:

> July 15, 1986 [Officer School]
>
> **All around me are guys arguing about moral dilemmas in battle**. (Literally arguing! We just had a formal discussion on the subject and they've continued long since the discussion ended.) On the one hand, war appears to be the most immoral of human activity, as the goal of both sides always involves killing. But, I know from my very limited experience, **the spectrum of morality in war is very broad, and even the most horrible things can be done immorally or morally**.... Israelis ... spend years learning how to kill, but also discussing and thinking about the moral side of every step they take.
>
> Don't worry. Love, Alex
(Singer, 2015, 213)

For Aristotle, the moral calculus of deliberation is the search of the golden mean, such as reckless audacity and cowardly reticence, while in rabbinic thought the deliberation is between conflicting values, such as caring for one's own well-being and risking one's life for the well-being of others. As the founder of rabbinic Judaism, Hillel formulated the dilemma: "If I am not for myself, who will be for me? But if I am only for myself, what kind of person am I?" (Avot 1:14). The value of saving human life when applied to the question of targeting terrorist in Gaza leaves the soldier in quandary. How does one choose between the military objective of saving Israeli civilian lives under bombardment by Hamas, who shoot from civilian neighborhoods in Gaza, and the moral obligation to minimize death to enemy civilians? Similarly, an officer must weigh his moral duty to protect his comrades' lives and the risk to enemy civilians near Hamas batteries within a civilian building. Thus the axiom of the 1977 Geneva protocol about targeting fails to solve dilemmas that must be subject to moral deliberation in the field.

Deliberative ethics is a situational ethics, not a rule-bound one. No absolute balance can be found. For Buber, no exact instructions can be predetermined independent of the particular person, the unique moment, and the idiosyncratic situation in which the soldier decides and acts:

> The "line of demarcation" is an individual compass indicating the right direction to take in every situation, "the shifting meeting point in an ongoing clash of two total commitments": to absolute morality and to the group for which, as a statesman, one bears responsibility. Because every historical situation is new, one cannot rely on established precedent to set a more distinct boundary between the two conflicting obligations. The line must be redrawn anew in each situation. The critical choice for Buber is not between politics and morality but "how far to go." To what extent, in a given situation, can we serve both God and our group?"
> *(Luz, 2003, 170–171)*

Even after making a moral decision, the soldier cannot know with a high level of certainty and comprehensiveness what the outcome of his decision will be in reality. Therefore, the IDF study guide emphasizes the need of each soldier to confront "conflicts of values, dilemmas, and especially complex questions. Military events and operations will present clashes between different values or within the same value. Such situations will require judgments about the relative weight of various values." Therefore, the study guide offers many case studies for moral deliberation and explicitly teaches officers this mode of ethical thinking. When two IDF values, such as purity of arms and tenacity to achieve victory, conflict, then one may either prefer one value over the other or try to embody both values in part in the same operation. The bottom-line message of these discussions is:

> The parameters for the proper use of force vary from one mission to the next. In light of the local conditions, the officer has the responsibility to determine what is necessary force—**as long as the decision was made after confronting the dilemma in the light of the Spirit of the IDF.**

C. Virtue (Character) Education: The Code of Honor and Conquering Your Evil Impulses

Rule-bound obedience and deliberative ethics focus on determining what is the right action within a given situation. Generally, the ethical decision is caught on the horns of a value conflict and a gap between what the ideal demands and what military reality permits. By contrast, virtue education, also characteristic of Aristotelian and Maimonidean ethics, seeks to shape a moral character. That moral personality is a prime end of the IDF study unit for both the individual and the collective—the IDF and the society of Israel. As we noted earlier, the IDF unit opens with an acknowledgment that war can bring out the worst in people. I would assert that military service and war are also capable of bringing out the best—comradeship, solidarity, altruism, sacrifice of the self for the collective, developing courage, leadership, and responsibility—beyond anything civilian life can engender for the average citizen. Those values are the subject of the Spirit of IDF as much as sensitivity to human dignity and value of human life.

The virtues celebrated by the Spirit of the IDF are: courage, self-sacrifice, tenacity, fraternity, and devotion to their comrades. Embodying these virtues is an honor code of an elite army that takes pride in those values. Each soldier is to see him/herself as a representative of this guild of excellence—the IDF. Soldiers, but especially officers, are expected to be "meritorious role models." Demanding more of themselves, they usually lead the way in combat action with the cry "after me!" The same model is expected in humane behavior: "The IDF servicemen and women . . . will maintain **their humanity** (*tzelem enoshi*) even during combat."

Here "humanity" refers not to the human dignity of each person as an absolute value, but to the humanity of the soldier who is to remain—despite the emotions and chaos of war—on a higher moral plane. While we often say, "I am only human," meaning "I am flawed. Don't expect too much of me," the IDF wants its soldiers to say, "I am humane!," which demands more sensitivity to the other. The Hebrew term chosen for humane is unusual—*tzelem enoshi*. *Tzelem* is the biblical term for the image of God, the basis of the absolute and equal value of each human being. But *enoshi* means mortal, sensitive to vulnerability, and hence humane.

The IDF study unit cites a letter written by a soldier disturbed by a **lack of sensitivity** to the civilians under Israeli occupation by soldiers stationed there. He complains, with moral pathos, about a unit in Samaria (the northern district of the West Bank under the Palestinian Authority). The soldiers were going into an Arab town to identify stolen Israeli cars (an epidemic phenomenon). The visiting officer saw soldiers smash into the side mirror of an Arab car unintentionally, yet none of the officers made any attempt to apologize or compensate the owner. Nor did they tell the rank and file soldiers to be more careful next time. The reason for this insensitivity was not, he argued, dark passions like vengeance or hate or lack of agreement with IDF norms about respecting civilian property. Instead, the soldiers shrugged and spoke of being burned out by their long, tiring service in Samaria. It was apathy that the officer excoriated as an unacceptable excuse for such laxity. He urged soldiers to show the moral courage to make comments whenever they see abuse of the weak and not to acquiesce to such infractions on the grounds of fatigue. That same theme is raised elsewhere in the IDF study guide as an unacceptable but frequent rationalization for acts of moral insensitivity to the civilian population under occupation.

D. Utilitarian Ethics

Alongside rule-based, deliberative, and virtue ethics, one would expect to find in an eclectic educational unit on purity of arms an appeal to utilitarian reasons for maintaining purity of arms. Idealism integrated with realism ought to have strong appeal to the soldier concerned with effectiveness in pursuing his mission as much as he is motivated by an honor code reflecting higher aspirations. Yet such utilitarian arguments are downplayed in the IDF study unit, except when explaining the indirect damage caused by abusing enemy civilians. Harming the civilian population when unnecessary for carrying out a military mission is forbidden for moral, value, and legal reasons. It also damages the moral fortitude of the IDF and its soldiers in three ways:

a. Harming the soldier himself. The soldier may adopt negative norms as a citizen in the State of Israel.
b. Harming the web of life within the unit. Violent norms and moral insensitivity have negative effects on the unit.
c. Harming the interests of the State of Israel. How one carries out a mission on a **tactical** level has an effect on the level of military **strategy**, government policy, and international relations. Tactics influence **the image of the State of Israel among the international media** (IDF Study Unit on Purity of Arms).

All the pragmatic arguments speak to utility for the self—the soldier, his unit, and his state, not to the injury to the civilian. But before offering these pragmatic considerations, the study guide explicitly prohibits such behavior morally and legally. Harming another human being is not being reduced to considerations of self-interest, but another layer of justification is being added eclectically. The conceptual point is that morality is not, as Kant would argue, indifferent to consequences and that moral behavior need not be altruistic. Rather, as Aristotle would argue, ethics contributes to general happiness and welfare. Presupposing the principles of Aristotelian and Maimonidean character education, the study guide explains that bad behavior is habit-forming and norm-generating. Those habits of relating to the other spread to the relationship to one's own society, and that will negatively affect its functioning: "There is a danger that these values will become normative in the army unit and afterward spill over into life as a citizen."

In the third utilitarian argument, the rationale is not moral but instrumental. As a soldier who is expected to perform military operations in service of the interests of the government and the state, the combatant must understand how tactics relates to strategy and how military norms affect political goal. Whatever the combatant's moral judgment on the treatment of enemy civilians, and whatever he thinks about the unfair treatment of Israel in the foreign press, his duty to the army's strategy and his self-interest as a citizen require him to act judiciously when faced with an enemy civilian.

E. Professional Ethics

Not only is the Israeli soldier called upon to be true to morality and to Jewish values, but also to professional standards. In the Spirit of the IDF we find many values of professionalism: "striving continuously **to perfect their personal and collective achievements**"; "**successfully complete all that is required of them**"; "conduct themselves with courage **in the face of all dangers and obstacles**"; "**they will carry out their duties** at all times with initiative, involvement and diligence."

What, you may ask, has professional excellence to do with Purity of Arms?

First, purity of arms is defined as a goal of the military mission in and of itself, not just as a constraint on how to get the job done. The study guide makes this explicit in the principle of proportionality: "Employing force that is unnecessary to the performance of the mission is a moral error that constitutes an operational error." In a case study of how to arrest a suspected terrorist in his apartment within a seven-floor civilian apartment building, the message is that "the mission is not only to arrest the suspect but also to avoid harming those who are innocent and therefore one must aspire to execute the mission by observing all its aspects."

Several army educators have explained to me that discipline and responsibility are the first countermeasures to releasing evil impulses—vengeance, cruelty, and abuse of power. Further, efficient and professional military operations involve gathering intelligence, evaluating outcomes, identifying military targets, and debriefing honestly. The soldier must take upon himself the responsibility for his actions and their consequences. All of those processes are necessary to make informed judgments about the principle of proportionality—the relative military advantage compared to collateral damage. Indiscriminate use of weapons causes the most civilian casualties, so the more discriminating and self-controlled the professional soldier the less unintended and unnecessary harm will be caused.

While the appeal to moral sensitivity for enemy civilians may not motivate many soldiers and may seem irrelevant to their task, the appeal to be professional precisely because it seems morally neutral has a stronger claim for many soldiers. The IDF seeks to combine the two kinds of ethics—professional and moral—by making them inseparable aspects of the same training. To be professional is to follow the rules and to suppress anarchic impulses and indiscriminate use of firepower.

F. Honor Code

The Spirit of the IDF is an honor code characteristic of an ancient warrior guild. Many modern ethicists have regarded honor as an amoral if not immoral category, and lamented the wars fought for defending honor. But today there is a revival of the appeal to honor as one motivation for ethical treatment of others, especially within a modern army.[5] The philosopher of ethics in war, Daniel Demetriou, has argued persuasively that armies today still appeal to a code of honor, with strict rules defining honorable and dishonorable behavior. Only one who lives up to higher standards, under difficult conditions, earns a positive social standing.

While the Spirit of the IDF does not appeal to honor explicitly, it does implicitly, when speaking of the army's higher mission and the soldiers' need to be its "representative." By implication, soldiers who violate the code bring shame on themselves, their unit, and the whole army, which has committed itself to behave unconditionally according to its basic values.

For example, soldiers who mistreat civilians tarnish the image of humanity in themselves. Hence the IDF Code insists: "he will maintain his humanity [literally, his human image] even in combat." Unlike the unconditional right to respect as a human being by virtue of being created in the image of God, one's humanity in relating to others can be maintained or lost. For example, a warrior must fight fairly, by the rules of honor, and engage in combat with a worthy opponent, not someone unarmed, a child, a woman, or an elderly man. Therefore, Demetriou argues that an honor code reinforces the moral demand that even enemy civilians be protected:

> Honor does an excellent job of encouraging honorable treatment of noncombatants—indeed, it may be that honor ethics provides the best justifications for distinguishing between a fighting soldier, on the one hand, and a civilian working in a munitions plant, on the other.
> *(Demetriou, 2013)*

An honorable soldier will not resort to the cowardly, dishonorable tactics of a terrorist who hides behind a mosque or a woman's skirt and uses superior firepower indiscriminately on civilians. Thus, an Israeli is expected to maintain a higher standard than a terrorist foe who flouts international conventions of war.

An honor code rejects the principle of reciprocity or conventional consent that holds that if your enemy violates the Geneva conventions, for example, then the soldier is exempt from obeying them. But for the warrior ethos, one maintains one's standards unilaterally. Often the term integrity is used to describe this same desire for respect and honor or self-respect.

> The man of honor . . . is true to himself . . . A man must judge for himself what is right, what is wrong . . . The man of honor . . . is true to himself . . . He clings to what he knows is right with all his strength.
> *(United States Military Code of Honor of Corps of Cadets at West Point in 2002, cited in Robinson, 2007, 262)*

So too integrity is the virtue of sticking to one's principles, moral or otherwise, in the face of temptation. Integrity in the IDF is staying true to our intrinsic humanity. Therefore, the Israeli soldier as a representative of the IDF merits his good standing in both his professional fighting abilities, such as tenacity, courage, and skill, and preserving his/her humanity by fighting, according to civilized rules, with combatants only.

(4) Self-Corrective Mechanisms

Earlier we quoted Moshe Halbertal who spoke of the moral and educational challenge of fighting an asymmetrical war:

> **In this new kind of micro-war [asymmetrical war], every soldier is a kind of commanding officer, a full moral and strategic agent. Every soldier must decide whether the individual standing before him in jeans and sneakers is a combatant or not** ... The challenge is to make these rules part of the inner world of each soldier, and this takes more than just formulating the norms and the rules properly.
>
> *(Halbertal, 2009)*

While prosecution is necessary for war crimes and disciplinary action is important for less serious violations of the IDF code, the criminalization of the normal practice of combat by putting average soldiers on trial in international tribunals is not the best educational policy. It is unfair to hold soldiers in the fog of war to judicial standards of some humanitarian ideal that does not take into account real battle conditions. Internal military discipline is generally more effective than exceptional cases of criminal prosecution in reshaping an army's moral practices in the field. Halbertal has said that a disciplined army that is good at its military tasks is least likely to violate the moral norms, because such behavior usually detracts from operational effectiveness. Many human rights violations emerge where military discipline is poorly enforced.

The development of the IDF Code or Spirit of IDF was one response to the educational challenge. Each soldier not only learns the code, but also carries it at all times. But the primary agents of moral and military education in the IDF are the actual norms of behavior manifest in the personal conduct of officers and in the collective opinion of comrades. Therefore, officers, first, and rank and file soldiers, second, must be persuaded that these guidelines are practical and important to their superiors. The IDF study guide was written for lower rank officers and NCOs.

Two educational techniques are employed to help officers engage their soldiers in thinking about moral dilemmas in the army. First, the officers identify the kind of emotional, moral, and operational challenges that they and their soldiers feel when asked to obey the strictures of purity of arms in the field. This technique enables officers to explore the reservations their soldiers may have about obeying the army's policies about purity of arms. For example, officers are given these guidelines for discussing Purity of Arms:

You must make an open discussion possible, so soldiers can ask questions, express feelings, opinions and fears ... Ask the soldiers to give example of incidents in which the value of purity of arms was respected or ignored. How did the soldiers and the officers react in those incidents? What factors make it difficult to maintain the value of purity of arms in the field?

The second educational technique is the well-known army practice of debriefing after every operation so as to draw lessons as to how to improve mission effectiveness for the next operation. For honest debriefing and self-criticism, the most important basic values in the Spirit of the IDF are responsibility and credibility, which obligate the soldier to tell the truth and take account of one's actions in retrospect. A soldier must be "**prepared to bear responsibility** for their conduct" and able "to present things **objectively, completely and precisely**, in planning, performing and reporting."

This method of self-critical debriefing and constructive criticism for drawing practical lessons from imperfectly executed missions is applied by the study unit to the moral and legal flaws in military operations. The effectiveness of officers' moral supervision of their soldiers is analyzed around case studies of previous failings. For example, the beating of Palestinians at a check point in 2004 is discussed and then suggestions for preventing similar violations are solicited.

The debriefing and constructive self-examination of flawed operations is deeply rooted in Jewish religious culture, where it is called *heshbon hanefesh*, soul-searching moral accounting. While taking moral stock, confessing, and seeking to repent are part of daily prayer, these are executed more extensively once a year on the Yom Kippur, the Day of Atonement. Here the same traditional religious practice is implicit in the IDF practices of moral self-examination regarding purity of arms, though it is also reinforced by the military tradition of the IDF to improve the effectiveness of other aspects of its performance through critical debriefing.

(5) Self and Other

In contemporary ethics, especially under the influence of Emanuel Levinas, the most important test of ethics is the relationship to the other. Killing the other is the most grievous form of dehumanization. The dialectical definition of the communal self by negation of the other is considered most problematic, because it is inherently non-egalitarian. In addition, universalist ethics in the Kantian tradition seeks to disregard the particularity of self or of the other as an ethical desideratum. Rather, Kantians insist on the common humanity of all human beings as fellow rational and autonomous human beings. Thus, the distinction between enemy civilians and one's own countrymen is rejected. Even the notion that an army medic should treat a wounded comrade in arms before treating a more seriously injured enemy soldier is condemned as immoral.

But historically, military solidarity, fighting spirit, and sense of mission have been shaped by the nation's differentiated identity and by us/them, self/other dynamics of war. In times of war, armies in general are designed to fight the other that threatens one's own historic territory, one's own political autonomy, one's type of regime, and one's cultural self-determination. The IDF Code mandates explicitly the task of protecting one's own citizens, land, and state, but it does not characterize the other—the enemies—by their ethnic, religious, or national identity. Rather, the hostile others are defined by their aggression against Israeli daily life and, in the case of terrorists, by their indiscriminate murder of civilians and their lack of concern for their own civilian casualties, though not by their ideology (for example, radical Islam or Palestinian nationalism).

The IDF study guide pays almost no attention to the enemy as Israel's other and whose otherness defines Israel's selfness. This educational choice is remarkable for several reasons. First, the IDF is self-consciously the army of a particular people with a unique identity that is proudly differentiated from other peoples and cultures. Further, Israel has been involved, since its birth, in an existential life and death struggle with others who regard Israel as having no right to exist. Those enemies have strong identities of their own defined by their opposition to Israel's existence, even though those identities have changed their focus over time (Nasser's Pan Arabism and Anti-Colonialism, Palestinian nationalism, Pan Islamist ideology and Sunni ISIS jihad).

Second, Israeli soldiers are taught much about the history of their land, the Holocaust, and Jewish tradition. In a Jewish discourse, contemporary enemies are often compared to ancient enemies. Thus, the Nazis, Khomeini, and Hamas have been equated with Amalek, the biblical symbol of a people or today an ideology of radical evil committed to the destruction of Israel, of all Jews anywhere, and of humane values.

Third, as Daniel Demetriou observes, the emphasis on just-war theory in Western countries permits the justification of war only if the other side initiated immoral or illegal aggression. Humanitarian wars, such as the war against ISIS, also entail characterization of the enemy as evil. Therefore, the us/them, self/other distinction is reinforced today, just as it was in World War One and especially in World War Two against the Nazis. But such black and white moral language may encourage soldiers to disregard the humanity of the enemy POW whose army and country are described as acting unjustly and inhumanely, Demetriou argues (Demetriou, 2013, 309).

Instead of projecting a self/other identity formation on the soldiers, the implicit strategy of the IDF study unit is to avoid generalizing about their enemy and instead to build a consensus around how one relates to enemy civilians simply as human beings, even if they belong to and identify with a hostile national or religious community. Only in a few instances is self/other language invoked. For example, on June 11, 1982, a letter from Nehemia Degania, the Chief Education Officer, was issued to every soldier during the Lebanon incursion against the

Palestinian Liberation Organization headed by Yasser Arafat. The letter argues that IDF soldiers must maintain a **higher standard of distinction between civilian and combatant** than the enemy, whom he calls "cruel," does. His letter is called "The Moral Image of the Israeli Soldier":

> The IDF fought this time a particularly cruel enemy who often used terror against defenseless civilians. However **the IDF is forbidden to use the same standards as our enemy. Our uniqueness and our strength lie in preserving the image of humanity.**

The point of the favorable comparison of Israeli moral restraint is not to condemn the other or to congratulate the Jewish community on its higher morality and make it complacent about criticism. Rather, it is designed to urge restraint by soldiers who might otherwise argue that "we in IDF are justified to treat them the same way they treat us."

In official army speeches and study guides, the language of hate and vengeance has been removed from the IDF's rationale for fighting its enemies. Rather, those feelings have been identified as emotional weakness, understandable after fellow soldiers have been killed by the enemy, but not acknowledged as a justification for indiscriminate violence against enemy civilians identified with the enemy combatants who have inflicted such losses on the IDF. Instead, the study guide invokes Jewish tradition: "If your enemy falls, do not celebrate; if he falls, let not your heart rejoice" (Prov. 24:17). It would be naïve to assume that Jewish and Israeli culture have no place for joy at the downfall of an enemy, but the attempt to identify and control feelings of vengeance is central to the ethical education of this IDF study unit.

(6) Sources of Authority and Wisdom

The study unit appeals to a soldier's moral commitment, not to personal preferences (as does the values clarification approach to ethics). Moral authority derives primarily from the communal cultural resources that shape Israeli group identity: the Israeli regime as Jewish and democratic; Jewish national values through the ages; universal moral principles; and the Western tradition of international law with which most IDF soldiers identify. Most Israelis feel they belong more within the family of Western democratic states, especially America and Western Europe, than the Middle East.

A list of the sources of law invoked at the conclusion of the study guide reinforces the thesis that Israeli, Jewish, and Western identities, in that order, shape the logic of persuasion to gain the allegiance of soldiers to purity of arms:

> The obligation of the State of Israel to basic moral values and human rights is formulated in the **Declaration of Independence** [1948].[6] . . .

It expresses the credo of the state ... as a democratic state founded on law. [The legal basis of these values is] the **[Israeli] Basic Law of Human Dignity and Freedom** [1992].[7] The IDF is the army of a democratic Jewish state and as such it is subject to the State's laws.

[The roots of the moral standards in war are found in the Jewish tradition, even though those moral standards have evolved since the time of the **Bible:** "When you go to war against your enemy, avoid all evil" (Deut. 23:10).

Events in world history that undergird recognition of human rights and the duty to defend them: Magna Carta (1215); ... Declaration of Rights of Man and of the Citizen (1789); ... Geneva Conventions on humanitarian issues in war (1949); ... UN Universal Declaration of Human Rights (UDHR, 1948), which derived from the powerful reaction to the events of World War Two.

(IDF Study Guide: Purity of Arms)

Summary and Conclusions

The IDF curriculum on Purity of Arms presents the soldier, not with an order, but with a moral challenge to live up to a higher standard of honor. Recognizing that war is barbaric, and a source of moral impurity, the soldier is reminded in the language of the rabbis that a human being has the capacity to master the evil impulses released in wartime. Instead, the Torah insists that the military camp ought to be a place of the Divine presence represented by the Ark of the Ten Commandments in its midst. Moral impurity is a great threat, but observing purity of arms, as Katznelson called it, is the way to maintain our integrity and elevate the use of arms to a sacred calling of self-defense.

Ethics in war is not just about observing the law—a low standard. The IDF sets a high bar as befits an honor code like purity of arms. The task of the IDF curriculum is to persuade its soldiers to adopt a code of unilateral self-restraint in the face of the indiscriminate terror of its enemy. The terrorist enemy unscrupulously endangers its own civilians and abuses international protections for ambulances and mosques to transfer munitions and hide its combatants, while all the time assaulting Israeli soldiers and civilians. An ethics of moral reciprocity and a Hobbesian contractual ethics constructed on rational self-interest and mutual consent cannot justify self-restraint against such an opponent. Only a higher ethics of integrity can keep the Israeli soldier true to his own values in such a cruel and cynical world.

The IDF guide to the Spirit of the IDF explains to the soldier the difference between a legal code and an educational code of values. The former establishes a low bar for legal behavior, and its violators are transgressors of the law. The latter sets the high bar of excellence towards which a soldier should aspire and which they should strive to emulate, to teach others and to use when judging oneself.

The low bar stipulates only what is forbidden, while the high bar includes positive acts. That said, the Spirit of IDF is binding even on soldiers who do not consent to its values or their application. Officers and their soldiers are taught that a violation of the principle of defense of human life and dignity and of the code of purity of arms is punishable by military disciple and at times by criminal courts. In court ruling, the judges have referred to the Spirit of the IDF as legally binding.

Although it teaches the laws about targeting enemy civilians and makes clear that their violation is punishable in a democratic society, the educational goal of the study kit is not primarily to criminalize soldiers for their infractions or for their dark feelings of vengeance after losing a comrade in arms to the enemy. Rather, the point is to develop moral sensitivity, to appeal the one's better angels and higher aspirations, and to engage officers in preemptive thinking about how to prevent such violations.

The struggle against a cruel ideological enemy, whose goal is the destruction of the state of Israel and sometimes the genocide of all Jews, often leads soldiers to dehumanize the enemy and to generalize about his whole community. But the IDF educational approach rejects the demonization of the enemy and carefully avoids generalizing from the nature of the terrorist enemy combatant to those enemy civilians (Palestinians, Arabs, or Muslims) whom the terrorists claim to represent and who are subject to virulent anti-Israel ideological indoctrination. Instead, in some of the guide's case studies, thoughtful and nuanced analyses of the causes of the Palestinian Intifada are presented to soldiers before they are asked to discuss violations of purity of arms by soldiers ordered to quell the Intifada. Thus, Palestinians are presented in this unit as rational actors in a national political struggle, not as wicked, irrational, religiously crazed anti-Semitic enemies.

The primary ethical value of the study unit of IDF on Purity of Arms is human dignity, both as a universal philosophical concept and as a cultural value associated with the soldier's group identity (Jewish, Western, and Israeli). The IDF study guide appeals to an eclectic basket of reasons and layers of identities to achieve greater motivation and greater consensus within a pluralist, democratic army. The study guide speaks of Israeli and Jewish national values, but never of explicitly rabbinic *halakhic* (legal warrants for purity of arms). Why? Increasingly Orthodox religious soldiers have felt conflicted between their loyalty to Israeli law and to rabbinic law as interpreted by some rightwing nationalist rabbis. Therefore, the IDF study guide has circumvented the question of the relative allegiance to Israeli and rabbinic law by appealing only to Jewish national values, not to religious laws, even though they freely quote rabbinic sources as nonbinding sources of Jewish wisdom about IDF ethics.

Ethics in practice are understood not as absolute values, not even when speaking of human life and dignity. Both international laws (even with their operational guidelines) and the Spirit of IDF code (even with its protocols for opening fire) necessarily leave soldiers with difficult ethical and operational dilemmas to decide on their own in the field. Great ambiguity is an unavoidable aspect of warfare, not only because of the fog of war, but because incommensurable values are often in conflict, such as the moral duty to minimize risk to enemy civilians as much as possible, to protect one's own country's civilians and national security by neutralizing the enemy attack as quickly as possible, and to maximize force protection so as to save the lives and combat capabilities of one's comrades in arms. Minimizing collateral damage and enemy civilian deaths is not the only moral responsibility of soldier or even the first priority, which is most probably defending one's own country. Balancing these competing values during battle is never easy.

The purpose of the IDF study guide is to teach soldiers "a common value language for the whole army" by which one judges oneself and educates others. "The Spirit of the IDF is supposed to help sharpen the conflict and facilitate decisions in practice." The Spirit of the IDF, while patriotic, appears to us to avoid the fanaticism of militarism and chauvinist nationalism. It seems congenial to the values and concerns of two great Israeli intellectuals who were always worried that the army and the state would corrupt the Jewish people. While strong supporters of military self-defense, both the philosopher Martin Buber and the novelist Amos Oz help us see how to frame the ideal place of the army in Israeli and Western society. Buber's position can be summarized as follows:

> A core commitment to the preservation of humanity—our own and that of our enemies—means that we do not shy away from protecting ourselves, our civilians, and our values, but that **when we fight, we do so not with bombast and arrogance, but with fear and trembling.** We never delight in the opportunity to fight, and we work to ensure that our soldiers' conduct in war lives up to the highest possible standards of moral decency. The fact that a nation may have a legitimate need to fight does not justify recklessness.
>
> *(Luz, 2003, 170–171)*

Amos Oz reiterates that position eloquently and explains why war and even nationalism are necessary evils that should not be embraced as virtues, but merely as necessary means in an unredeemed world:

> I think that the nation-state is a tool, an instrument, that is necessary for a return to Zion, but I am not enamored of this instrument.... I would be more than happy to live in a world composed of dozens of civilizations, each developing in accordance with its own internal rhythm, all cross-pollinating one another, without any one emerging as a nation-state: no flag, no emblem, no passport, no anthem. No nothing. Only spiritual civilizations tied somehow to their lands, without the tools of statehood and without the instruments of war ... [But] for me [after] the murder of Europe's Jews by Hitler ... I am forced to take it upon myself to play the "game of nations," with all the tools of statehood, even though it causes me to feel....

> To play the game with an emblem, and a flag and a passport and an army, and even war, provided that such war is an absolute existential necessity. I accept those rules of the game because existence without the tools of statehood is a matter of moral danger, but I accept them only up to this point. To take pride in these tools of statehood? To worship these toys? To crow about them? Not I. If we must maintain these tools, including the instruments of death, it must be not only without glee but with wisdom as well . . . and with caution.
>
> *(Amos Oz, Acceptance Speech for Goethe Prize, City of Frankfurt, 2005, reprinted in Oz, 1983, 130)*

While the Israeli army does promote patriotism through giving awards to brave soldiers and through staging multiple ceremonies, relatively speaking, the IDF and Israeli society is surprisingly reserved about engaging in **military fanfare**. But after the Six Day War victory in 1967, glorification of the military reached its highest peak in Israeli history. In protest, a bold critique of Israeli paeans to dead heroes, "A Song for Peace," was composed and performed by the Nahal IDF Army Band in 1969. The lyrics attribute to dead soldiers a strident call to replace ritual memorials with the bringing of peace:

> Lift your eyes with hope, not through the rifle sights. Sing a song for love, And not for wars. Don't say the day will come, bring the day, because it is not a dream. Within all the city's squares, cheer only for peace.[8]

This protest song was written within the army and is sung in army medleys, as well as at peace rallies. On the night Prime Minister Yitzhak Rabin was assassinated in 1995 at a massive peace rally in Tel Aviv, he too sang that song at the rally. After his death, his personal copy of the song was found folded in his pocket and soaked with his own blood.

Notes

1 IDF in Lebanon fought with the PLO, 1982; Intifada with Palestinians in Gaza and West Bank, 1987, 2000; Gaza with Hamas and Lebanese operations Hezbollah, 2006, 2008, 2015
2 Anita Shapira, Berl, Am Oved, Tel Aviv, 1980, pp. 588–589
3 "William Ian Miller rightly says, honour systems have 'a built-in bias towards rashness to avoid insinuations of fearfulness or cowardice' (The Mystery of Courage, Harvard University Press, 2002: 163)." Cited in Paul Robinson, "Magnanimity and Integrity as Military Virtues," *Journal of Military Ethics*, 6:4, 265)
4 Leora Y. Bilsky, Transformative Justice: Israeli Identity on Trial (Law, Meaning, and Violence), University of Michigan Press, 2004, pp 169–197, 310-324.
5 Kwame Anthony Appiah, *The Honor Code: How Moral Revolutions Happen*, 2010, 18.
6 Israeli Declaration of Independence (1948): "The State of Israel will foster the development of the country for the benefit of all its inhabitants; it will be based on freedom, justice and peace as envisaged by the prophets of Israel; it will ensure complete equality

of social and political rights to all its inhabitants irrespective of religion, race or sex; it will guarantee freedom of religion, conscience, language, education and culture; it will safeguard the Holy Places of all religions; and it will be faithful to the principles of the Charter of the United Nations." http://stateofisrael.com/declaration/

7 Israeli Knesset, The Basic Law of Human Dignity and Freedom (1992) http://www.knesset.gov.il/laws/special/eng/basic3_eng.htm

1. The purpose of this Basic Law is to protect human dignity and liberty, in order to establish in a Basic Law the values of the State of Israel as a Jewish and democratic state.
2. There shall be no violation of the life, body or dignity of any person as such.
3. There shall be no violation of the property of a person.
4. All persons are entitled to protection of their life, body and dignity.
5. There shall be no deprivation or restriction of the liberty of a person by imprisonment, arrest, extradition or otherwise.

8 "A Song for Peace" by the Israel Defence Force, Nahal Army Band / Jacob Rotblit and Yair Rosenblum (1969). See Regev, Motti; Seroussi, Edwin (2004). Popular Music and National Culture in Israel. Berkeley: University of California Press. p. 106.

References

Appiah, Kwame Anthony, *The Honor Code: How Moral Revolutions Happen*, New York: W.W. Norton, 2010.

Buber, Martin, *A Land of Two Peoples*, edited by Paul R. Mendes-Flohr, Chicago: University of Chicago Press, 2005.

Demetriou, Daniel, *Honor for Intro*, private paper published. http://philpapers.org/rec/DEMHFI, 2014. www.academic.edu

Demetriou, Daniel, "Honor War Theory: Romance or Reality?" *Philosophical Papers*, November 2013.

Halbertal, Moshe, "The Goldstone Illusion: What the U.N. Report Gets Wrong About Gaza—and War," *The New Republic*, November 6, 2009.

Israeli Declaration of Independence, 1948. http://stateofisrael.com/declaration/

Israeli Knesset, *The Basic Law of Human Dignity and Freedom*, 1992. http://www.knesset.gov.il/laws/special/eng/basic3_eng.htm

Israeli Defense Force, *The Spirit of the IDF*, 2001. http://www.jewishvirtuallibrary.org/ruach-tzahal-idf-code-of-ethics

Israeli Defense Force, *IDF Study Guide on Spirit of IDF* (*Ruakh Tzahal*, Hebrew) by Moshe Halbertal, Avi Sagi, Daniel Statman, Yaacov Kastel, and Shaul Smilanksy, 2007.

Israeli Defense Force, *IDF Study Guide Kit on Purity of Arms* (*Tohar HaNeshek*, Hebrew), by officers Anat Harel, Olga Sarikh, Nurit Kutik, Limor Hovizlich, and Shira Rodberg, approximately 2007.

Israeli Defense Force, IDF Letter of Nehemia Degania, the Chief Education Officer to all Soldiers, War for the Peace of the Galilee in Lebanon, June 11, 1982.

Luz, Ehud, *Wrestling With an Angel: Power, Morality, and Jewish Identity*, New Haven: Yale University Press, 2003.

Merriam, John J., and Schmitt, Michael N. "Israeli Targeting: A Legal Appraisal," *Naval College Review*, Autumn 2015, 68: 4.

Oz, Amos, *In the Land of Israel*, Orlando: Am Oved, Hebrew, Harcourt Brace, 1983.

Robinson, Paul, "Magnanimity and Integrity as Military Virtues," *Journal of Military Ethics*, 6: 4, 2007, citing United States Military Code of Honor of Corps of Cadets at West Point, 2002.

Schon, Donald, *The Reflective Practitioner: How Professionals Think in Action*, New York: Basic Books, 1983.
Shapira, Avraham Near, ed., *The Seventh Day: Soldiers Talk about the Six-Day War*, Hunter, NY: Scribners, 1971.
Singer, Alex, *Building A Life*, Jerusalem: Gefen Publishing, 2015.

PART III
The Christian Tradition

8

PEACE AND WAR IN CHRISTIAN THOUGHT

A Partisan Guide

Nigel Biggar

Introduction

Christianity has generated two conflicting traditions of thought about the morality of the use of physically violent, perhaps lethal, force. On the one hand, the pacifist tradition considers any use of such force in any circumstances whatsoever to be immoral. On the other hand, the alternative, 'just war' tradition thinks that force can be used morally—and indeed, that its use can be morally obliged—under certain conditions. Insofar as both points of view claim to be Christian, they are bound to justify themselves in terms of the New Testament, which is the basic moral authority in Christian churches.

In Section I of this essay, therefore, I present the most thorough, systematic, and sophisticated pacifist reading of the New Testament that has been offered to date—namely, that made by Richard Hays (1996) in *The Moral Vision of the New Testament*. In the following section I offer my own 'just war' critique of Hays' interpretation. Section III proceeds to address, briefly, the historical question of Christian attitudes to military service during the first three centuries of the Christian Church. Section IV summarizes the views of St Augustine, which have been seminal for subsequent Christian 'just war' thinking. Section V describes the Scholastic development of Augustinian thought, particularly its constraint of 'holy war' by the moral norms of 'just war'. The penultimate section presents the two sets of criteria for 'just war' in their most elaborate, contemporary form. Finally, the Conclusion summarizes what Christian pacifists and just war proponents share in common and where the main points of difference between them lie.

I. The New Testament: Richard Hays' Pacifist Reading[1]

Widely showered with superlatives by biblical scholars on its first publication in 1996,[2] and rated a 'classic' and a 'masterpiece' in 2006[3] and 2007,[4] *The Moral Vision* devotes its fourteenth chapter to arguing that the New Testament forbids the use of violence under all circumstances, even when the defence of justice seems to require it.

Hays' pacifist argument about the New Testament's view of violence opens, predictably, with the Sermon on the Mount in the Gospel of Matthew (chapters 5–7). This he sees as Jesus' "basic training on the life of discipleship", his "programmatic disclosure of the kingdom of God and of the life to which the community of disciples is called", and "a definitive charter for the life of the new covenant community". While not taking the form of "a comprehensive new legal code", this 'charter' "suggests by way of a few examples the character of this new community". And what is this character? *Inter alia*, one in which "anger is overcome through reconciliation (5:21–26), . . . retaliation is renounced (5:38–42), and enemy-love replaces hate (5:43–48)" (ibid., 321). In sum, "the transcendence of violence through loving the enemy is the most salient feature of this new model *polis*" (ibid., 322).

Lest it be supposed that this vision of a non-violent Christian community is confined to the Sermon on the Mount, Hays proceeds to argue that it finds confirmation in Matthew's "overall portrayal of Jesus". In the temptation narrative (4:1–11), for example, Jesus renounces the option of "wielding power" over the kingdoms of the world, and (following Yoder), his deflection of the temptation to refuse the cup of suffering amounts to a renunciation of the resort to armed resistance (ibid., 322).

Hays' next move is to tackle "various ingenious interpretations that mitigate the normative claim of this text [Matthew 5:38–48]" (ibid., 320). Among these are interpretations holding that the only violence prohibited is that in self-defence (and that violence in defence of third parties is implicitly permitted). Against these, Hays invokes the "larger paradigm of Jesus' own conduct in Matthew's Gospel", which "indicates a deliberate renunciation of violence as an instrument of God's will" (ibid., 323). He substantiates this by appeal to the temptation narrative, where Jesus "does not seek to defend the interests of the poor and oppressed in Palestine by organizing armed resistance against the Romans or against the privileged Jewish collaborators with Roman authority". He also appeals to the narrative of Jesus' arrest, where the disciple who draws his sword in defence of his master receives a severe dominical rebuke (Matthew 26:47–52). This he takes to be "an explicit refutation" of the justifiability of the use of violence in defence of a third party (ibid., 324).

A second set of interpretations that Hays seeks to discredit are those that would limit the meaning of the prohibitions of violence in terms of their social and political context. One of these readings is offered by Robert Guelich (1982), who argues that the scope of Matthew 5:39a ("But I say to you, Do not resist one who is evil") should be limited to a courtroom context, specifying its meaning as an injunction against seeking judicial redress against a false accuser. Hays concedes that one of the illustrative injunctions in Matthew 5:38–48 does have a specifically judicial meaning (v. 40: "and if anyone would sue you and take your coat, let him have your cloak as well"), but he denies that the others (e.g., v. 39b: "But if one strikes you on the right cheek, turn to him the other also") can be confined to a forensic context. He points out that Guelich himself admits that verses 41 and 42 ("and if any one forces you to go one mile, go with him two miles. Give to him who begs from you, and do not refuse him who would borrow from you") cannot be so constrained (Hays 1996). Hays' case here seems cogent.

Another restrictive interpretation that Hays seeks to discredit is Richard Horsley's. Horsley argues that in the original historical setting, the 'enemies' whom Jesus exhorted his disciples to love (Matthew 5:44) referred only to 'personal enemies'—other members of small Palestinian villages who found themselves competing against one another for scarce economic resources—rather than foreign or military ones; and that Jesus' primary concern was to get the peasants to stop squabbling with each other so as to cooperate for mutual economic benefit (Horsley 1987, 255–273). Hays' first counter-argument is that such a reading commands no lexicographical support: the Greek word *echthroi* in Matthew 5:44, translated as 'enemies', is a generic term and is often used in biblical Greek of national or military enemies, not just of personal or local ones. His second point is that nothing in the Gospel of Matthew suggests such a precisely local social situation, and that Horsley himself acknowledges that the Matthaean context actually requires the more general interpretation of enemies as "outsiders and persecutors" (Hays 1996, 328). However, Hays' main complaint is methodological, namely that Horsley makes normative his reconstruction of the history *behind* the text, and uses it to trump the intended meaning of the Matthaean text itself. On the contrary, according to Hays, "the canonical narrative context governs the normative theological use of the text; the historical reconstruction remains speculative" (ibid., 324; cp., 328).

After his defence of a pacifist reading of the Gospel of Matthew, Hays proceeds to the synthetic task of showing that the non-violent stance of this Gospel is echoed throughout the canonical New Testament as a whole. The Gospels, he finds, are unanimous in portraying Jesus as a Messiah who subverts all prior expectations by assuming the vocation of suffering "rather than conquering Israel's enemies" (ibid., 329). The Acts of the Apostles present the martyr Stephen, praying for the forgiveness of his enemies (Acts 7:60), as the model of a Christian response to violence. In his epistles, Paul presents God himself as responding to his enemies, not by killing them, but by seeking reconciliation through the "self giving" of His Son (ibid., 330) And while Paul writes that the governing authority bears the sword to execute God's wrath (Romans 13:4), that, according to Hays, is not the role of believers. Those who are members of the one body in Christ (12:5) are never to take vengeance (12:19); they are to bless their persecutors and minister to their enemies, returning good for evil. Likewise, the Epistle to the Hebrews and the Catholic Epistles offer "a consistent portrayal of the community as called to suffer without anger or retaliation" (ibid., 331). Finally, the Revelation to John

> seeks to inculcate in its readers precisely the same character qualities that we have seen extolled through the rest of the New Testament canon: faithful

endurance in suffering, trust in God's eschatological vindication of his people, and a response to adversity modeled on the paradigm of "the Lamb who was slaughtered".

(ibid., 332)

The concluding move that Hays makes in his synthetic argument is to deal with certain particular texts that "seem to stand in tension with the central witness of the New Testament concerning violence" (ibid., 332). Prominent among these are the passages where soldiers make an appearance. In Luke 3:14–15, John the Baptist does not exhort them to abandon their profession, but merely to pursue it honestly without exploiting the civilian population. In Matthew 8:5–13 and Luke 7:1–10, Jesus marvels at the faith of the centurion whose servant he has healed, but raises no questions about his military profession. In Mark 15:39, it is a centurion at the foot of the cross who is the first human character in the Gospel to recognize Jesus as the Son of God. And in Acts 10:1–11:18, the centurion Cornelius, described as "an upright and God-fearing man", converts to the Christian faith, but there is no indication that this is supposed to involve his renunciation of military service. Hays' response to these awkward texts is to argue that they have a particular literary role, that is, "to dramatize the power of the Word of God to reach even the unlikeliest people". In Luke 3:12–13, for example, soldiers appear alongside tax collectors as examples of how John's preaching reached even the most "unsavory characters" (ibid., 335). Moreover, when measured against "a synthetic statement of the New Testament's witness", the examples of individual "good soldiers" in the New Testament "weigh negligibly": in the light of the vocation of the Christian community to the work of reconciliation and to suffer in the face of great injustice, "the place of the soldier within the church can only be seen as anomalous" (ibid., 337).

After the synthetic operation comes the hermeneutical or interpretative one. Now that we have before us *an* account of *the* view of violence that the New Testament takes, how should we respond to it? According to Hays, first of all, we should note that testimony against violence is to be found in all four normative modes—rules, principles, paradigms, and symbolic world. What this means is that the evidence that the New Testament sets its face against any justification for the use of violence "accumulates overwhelmingly" (ibid., 340). Therefore, given the primacy of the New Testament among ethical authorities, Christian ethics has no option but to jettison the tradition of just war thinking (ibid., 297, 341)

One classic objection to this is that since

> the Sermon on the Mount was addressed to a marginal community outside the circle of power, its teachings cannot be directly applied in a context where Christians hold positions of power and influence, or where they constitute the majority in a democratic political order.

However, while this position reckons very seriously with "the historical fact" that the political context for Christian ethics has changed dramatically from the time of the New Testament writers, "an equally serious case can be made that, on balance, history teaches that violence simply begets violence" (ibid., 342).

II. The New Testament: A 'Just War' Critique of Hays' Pacifist Reading

The Soldier Narratives: The Thin End of the Wedge

I begin my critique at the point where may be found, according to Hays, "the one possible legitimate basis for arguing that Christian discipleship does not necessarily preclude the exercise of violence in defence of social order or justice": the narratives about soldiers (ibid., 335–336). As he sees it, however, the basis is "fragile" (ibid., 340), since these passages are intended to play a particular literary role, namely, to illustrate the dramatically generous capaciousness of Jesus' version of the kingdom of God—its capacity to embrace even 'sinners' such as tax collectors and soldiers.

As I see it, four problems attend this interpretation. First, to say that soldiers are presented as notorious sinners is not yet to identify what their sin consists of. If one is going to assume—as Hays does—that the sin of soldiers is that of *being a soldier*, then presumably one should also assume that the sin of tax-collectors is that of *collecting taxes*. Zacchaeus' story, however, makes it clear that his sin was fraud (Luke 19:8). Similarly, according to the only place in the New Testament where military sin is actually spelt out, it comprises robbery by violence and false accusation, and discontent over wages (Luke 3:12–14). Yes indeed, this is only John the Baptist's view; but it is one that neither Jesus nor any of the evangelists seem to have felt the need to improve upon.

Similarly, second, the centurion's acknowledgement of the crucified Jesus as Son of God in Mark (15:39) and Matthew (27:54) is certainly dramatic, but not because it comes from the lips of a sinner-as-sword-wielder, but rather because it comes from a sinner-as-gentile. In Luke (23:47), the centurion's testimony serves to confirm Pilate's earlier judgement of Jesus' innocence (Luke 23:14, 22). The drama here issues from that fact that these gentiles perceived what the chief priests and scribes of 'God's people' could not.

Third, the centurion at Capernaum (Matthew 8:5–13; Luke 7:1–10) and the centurion Cornelius (Acts 10:1–11:18) are not presented to the reader as 'sinners' (except insofar as they were gentiles). In the case of the former, the elders of the Jews commend him to Jesus as "one who is worthy to have you do this [i.e., heal his slave] for him, for he loves our nation" (Luke 7:3–4). After meeting him, Jesus himself comments,

> Truly, I tell you, not even in Israel have I found such faith. I tell you, many will come from east and west and sit at table with Abraham, Isaac, and Jacob in the kingdom of heaven, while the sons of the kingdom will be thrown into the outer darkness.
>
> *(Matthew 8:10b)*

Similarly, Cornelius is introduced as "a devout man who feared God . . ., gave alms liberally to the people, and prayed constantly to God"; his servants introduce him to Peter as "an upright and God-fearing man, who is well spoken of by the whole Jewish nation" (Acts 10:2, 22); and the upshot of their encounter is that Peter exclaims, "Truly I perceive that God shows no partiality, but in every nation anyone who fears him and does what is right is acceptable to him" (Acts 10:34). Note: in both cases the drama depends on the status of these soldiers *as gentiles* and consists in the fact that Jesus and Peter transcend Jewish law by not treating them as "unclean" (Acts 10:28).

Fourth, sinners who become Christian disciples are invariably portrayed by the New Testament as renouncing their sinful practices;[5] and Hays himself notes that, whereas the Acts of the Apostles takes care to mention that the Ephesian magicians who became 'believers' publicly burned their magic books (Acts 19:18–20), it makes no suggestion whatsoever that the God-fearing Cornelius was moved to surrender his military profession (Acts 10:1–11:18; ibid., 335). Likewise, Hays could also have mentioned that whereas the Gospel of Luke makes a point of showing that a tax collector's salvation involves the public mending of his extortionate ways (Luke 19:1–10), on no occasion does it suggest that a soldier's salvation involves the renunciation of military service as such. If the New Testament understood Jesus to mean non-violence simply, and regarded participation in the military profession as intrinsically sinful, then *surely* its authors would have taken care to tell us that soldiers who became Christian disciples renounced military service? That they do not amounts to a silence that speaks volumes.

The awkward presence in the text of soldiers who are neither rebuked for their profession, nor repent of it, makes the stance of the New Testament canon toward the use of violent force far less "unambiguous" (ibid., 341) and the grounds for arguing that Christian discipleship could include it far more robust than Hays supposes. His response to this awkwardness is to claim that it "weigh[s] negligibly" in a synthetic statement of the New Testament's witness (ibid., 337). What he means by this is that the New Testament is so predominantly in favour of non-violence that these soldier stories may be discounted. The fact that they *need* to be discounted at all, of course, implies that, notwithstanding his attempt to tame them, Hays recognizes that they continue to carry non-pacifist significance. More important, his synthesis (which is already interpretation) takes it for granted that absolute 'non-violence' best captures what the New Testament is centrally and predominantly against. I shall argue later that this assumption is wrong; and that Hays is incorrect to assume that love for one's enemies and a commitment to reconciliation necessarily rules out the use of (sometimes lethal) force. Rather than brush the awkward finger aside, therefore, I will let it guide us toward a non-pacifist reading of the New Testament, which does better justice to *all* of the relevant material.

Romans 13: On Not Importing the 'Anabaptist Distinction'

If we take our cue from the soldier narratives and suppose that the New Testament does not regard military service as incompatible with Christian discipleship, then we may infer that it has no objection *in principle* to the publicly authorized use of lethal force. This implication finds explicit corroboration in St Paul's Epistle to the Romans, when he writes that "[he who is in governing authority] does not bear the sword in vain; he is the servant of God to execute his wrath on the wrongdoer" (13:4).

It is true that Paul also enjoins members of the body of Christ not to avenge themselves but to leave vengeance to the wrath of God (12:19). Instead, they should minister to their enemies (12:20), repaying no one evil for evil (12:17). Hays reads this along classic Anabaptist lines: the governing authority's use of force to punish the wicked is ordained by God, but "that is not the role of believers".[6] That role is to bear witness to an alternative society so completely governed by God as to lack need for the sword. This distinction of roles, however, is not coherent. If such a 'peaceable kingdom' were currently practicable *as an alternative* to the 'coercive kingdom', then presumably God would have ordained the former *instead of* the latter. I say 'presumably', because a benevolent God would not ordain unnecessary coercion. Since, however, God has ordained it, he evidently thinks it necessary. The implication is that, under the current spiritually and morally ambiguous conditions of this secular age, the 'peaceable kingdom' cannot be alternative; it can only be parasitic. This puts pacifist believers in the intellectually incoherent position of contradicting in principle what they depend upon in practice, and in the morally inconsistent position of keeping their own hands clean only because others are required to get theirs dirty.

Instead of this incoherent view, one might regard the non-coercive, entirely God-governed society not as a current alternative to one where the public use of force is ordained, but rather as its ideal goal. Thus, the pacific ideal would so function as to qualify and discipline the current use of force, which ultimately intends it. Rather than produce two distinct classes of people—those who use the sword, and those who point to peace—it would produce one class only—those who struggle to use the sword pacifically. This, however, would bring us not to pacifism, but to the doctrine of just war.

Whether the Anabaptist distinction is coherent is one issue; whether it makes best sense of St Paul is another. Hays' interpretation gathers its exegetical force from the fact that what the governing authority is instituted by God to do—namely, to execute God's wrath on the wrongdoer (13:4b: "he [who is in authority] is the servant of God to execute his wrath on the wrongdoer" [Θεου γαρ διακονος εστιν, εκδικος εις οργην τω το κακον πράσσοντι])—is precisely what the Christians at Rome are forbidden to do (12.19: "Beloved, never avenge yourselves, but leave it to the wrath of God; for it is written, 'Vengeance is mine, I will repay, says the Lord'" [μη εαυτους εκδικουντες, αγαπητοι, αλλα δοτε τοπον τη οργη. γεγραπται γαρ, Εμοι εκδικησις, εγω ανταποδωσω, λεγει Κυριος]). This need not be read, however, as asserting a general distinction between the calling of Christians and the calling of publicly authorized sword-users—and given the incoherence of such a distinction, it *should* not be so read. Rather, it should be understood as an answer to the ad hoc question of whether or not Christians should respond to their persecutors—be they pagan Romans, Jews, or other (Gentile or Jewish) Christians—by avenging themselves, taking the law into their own hands, and so making themselves into a threat to public order.[7] As J. D. G. Dunn, writes:

> the growing and increasingly desperate activity of the Zealots in Palestine was warning enough of how an oppressed people or persecuted minority might turn to acts of revenge . . . (the fire of Rome and Nero's persecution of the Christians were to follow in less than ten years).
>
> *(Dunn 1988, 749)*

Paul's response to the temptation facing the Roman Christians was that rather than yield to it, they should bear injustice patiently and charitably—"Be patient in tribulation" (12:12), "Bless those who persecute you" (12:14)—trusting the public authorities to fulfil their Divine commission. We may not take this to imply that Paul held all private use of violent force in defence or promotion of justice to be forbidden to Christians. We may only infer that Paul considered public order to be a sufficiently precious good that Christians should bear some injustice—and try to turn it to good—rather than conjure up an anarchy of private vendettas and provoke the brutality of public repression.

As we read it so far, then, the New Testament does not object in principle to the publicly authorized use of violence. As for its private use, we may say at least that St Paul had very strong reservations. The remedying of injustice is the proper, divinely instituted task of public authorities; and even where the authorities fail to complete their task—as they are bound to from time to time—private (Christian) persons should bear some injustice and respond to it constructively rather than take the law into their own hands and risk all the grave attendant evils of resultant anarchy.

Jesus' Repudiation of Religious Nationalist Revolt

St Paul's concern about the evils of private violence finds a strong echo in Jesus' teaching and practice. According to Hays, Jesus and the Gospels repudiate the use of violence, not just in self-defence, but also in defence of justice. As witness he calls the temptation narrative in the Gospel of Matthew (4:1–11), where Jesus refuses "to defend the interests of the poor and oppressed in Palestine by organizing armed resistance against the Romans or against the privileged Jewish collaborators with Roman authority" (Hays 1996, 324). He also appeals to the narrative of Jesus' arrest in the Garden of Gethsemane, where a disciple draws his sword in defence of his master, but Jesus, perceiving the same temptation, rebukes him (Matthew 26:47–52).[8] This Hays takes to be "an explicit refutation" of the justifiability of the use of violence in defence of a third party (ibid., 324). Here as elsewhere, however, he generalizes beyond the evidence. The option historically available to Jesus was not an abstract 'violence in defence of third parties against injustice', but specifically private violence motivated by a conviction that Israel is *the* divinely chosen nation and by a corresponding hatred of her gentile imperial masters.

This is controversial. Not every New Testament scholar sees in Jesus' hinterland the option of violent religious nationalism (although Hays himself evidently does).[9] Richard Horsley has argued that, excepting "the terrorism of the Sicarii directed against their own high priests", Jewish resistance to Roman rule during Jesus' lifetime was "fundamentally non-violent" (Horsley 1987, 117). *Pace* those interpreters who see the 'Zealots' as a continuous movement or party straddling the first seven decades of the first century AD and make of them "a convenient foil over against which to portray Jesus of Nazareth as a sober prophet of a pacific love of one's enemies", Horsley holds that they did not come into existence until the winter of 66–67 AD (ibid., x–xi). Against this it is reasonable to argue that the absence from Jesus' context of the 'Zealots' as a definite party need not be taken to mean the absence of militant nationalism *tout court*. That had erupted in 4 BC and it was to erupt again in 66 AD. While it is possible that the failure of the earlier revolt had completely discredited violent nationalism during the intervening period—and so during Jesus' lifetime—it is *prima facie* unlikely. While crushed revolts may confirm some—typically the middle-aged, married, and propertied— in their conviction that armed resistance is futile and counter-productive, they tend to provide others—typically gangs of young bachelors—with heroes, an activist ideal, and a lust for revenge.[10] What is more, even if Horsley is correct in claiming that the violence of the Sicarii was directed only at "their own high priests", the rule of this religious elite can hardly be considered something entirely separate from Roman hegemony.

What the temptation and Gethsemane narratives permit us to say, then, is only that Jesus declined to participate in violence that was not publicly authorized and that was inspired by religious nationalism. Why he should have done so, the text does not make explicit. We know, however, that in Jesus' view the boundaries of the kingdom of God were defined less by ethno-national identity than by faith—that is the implied significance of his response to the centurion at Capernaum (Matthew 8:5–13 and Luke 7:1–10).[11] Moreover, according to both the apostle Peter (in Acts 10 and 11) and the apostle Paul, this was a main defining feature of the religious tradition emanating from their Lord. It seems, therefore, that Jesus had strong theological reason to distance himself from religious nationalism.

On Being Discriminate About 'Violence'

Beyond these reservations about its private, unauthorized use, especially as that is inspired by religious nationalism, does the New Testament manifest any more general concerns about violence? Of course it does. As Hays (1996, 321, 322) points out, it forbids anger, hatred, and retaliation—and the violence that issues from them. However, we should not assume—as Hays does—that anger is all of one piece or that all violence is immorally angry, hateful, and retaliatory. It is not.

To begin with, an important distinction may be made with regard to anger. On the one hand, there is the anger that is both appropriate and proportionate. It is appropriate because it is the human emotion by which we take injustice seriously, recognizing it for the evil it is and setting ourselves against it; and it is proportionate because it is tempered by a loving intention to seek reconciliation. On the other hand, there is the anger that, driven by rage and indignation, intemperately answers injustice with injustice. This distinction between two kinds of anger may be made, and the Anglican moral philosopher, Joseph Butler, made it.[12] But, as Butler pointed out, so does the New Testament. St Paul, for example, implicitly distinguishes a moral kind of anger from a sinful one, when he exhorts Christians at Ephesus, "Be angry, but do not sin; do not let the sun go down on your anger" (Ephesians 4:26). This moral anger is characterized both by a certain candour and by a certain fraternal restraint in telling the critical truth (Ephesians 4:25: "let everyone speak the truth with his neighbor, for we are members one of another"). If we proceed to review Jesus' own conduct and teaching in the light of this distinction, then we notice that Jesus himself evidently thought that fierce anger was an appropriate response to the oppressiveness of Pharisaic religion:

> But woe to you, scribes and Pharisees, hypocrites! ... Woe to you, scribes and Pharisees, hypocrites! ... Woe to you, blind guides ... You blind fools! ... You blind men! ... Woe to you, scribes and Pharisees, hypocrites! ... You blind guides. . .! Woe to you, scribes and Pharisees, hypocrites! ... You blind Pharisee! ... Woe to you, scribes and Pharisees, hypocrites! ... Woe to you, scribes and Pharisees, hypocrites! ... You serpents, you brood of vipers, how are you to escape being sentenced to hell?
>
> *(Matthew 23 passim)*

Further, we notice that the anger that Jesus prohibits in the Sermon on the Mount is of a specifically insulting kind: "But I say to you that everyone who is angry with his brother shall be liable to judgement; whoever *insults* his brother shall be liable to the council" (Matthew 5:22—my emphasis). The New Testament itself, therefore, implies that anger is not all of one piece: sometimes it can be appropriate or proportionate, sometimes it can withhold itself from insult, and sometimes it can be restrained by an awareness of fraternity in the midst of hostility. We may infer, then, that the New Testament forbids violence motivated by anger that is disproportionate, contemptuous, and issues from hatred.

What about violence that is retaliatory? The answer hangs on what is meant by 'retaliation'. In one sense, any hostile response to injustice is retaliatory, a form of payback—not excluding Jesus' tirades against the Pharisees or his overturning of the moneychangers' tables in the Temple. Presumably that is not what the New Testament forbids. In a more colloquial sense, 'retaliation' also connotes a touchy, vengeful reaction that lacks control by any sense of proportion or of moral duty. In such retaliation one hits back instinctively, no matter how trivial the injury; and even if one's retaliation is designed to deter and not merely to inflict suffering, it defends the self without any (fraternal) regard for what one owes the aggressor. In this light, it is noteworthy that none of the injuries with which Jesus illustrates his prohibition of retaliation are very serious ones. If we should understand being struck on the right cheek (Matthew 5:39) by the back of someone's left hand as a calculated insult,[13] then that is merely an offence against dignity, and relatively trivial; and as a purely physical injury being struck on one's cheek hardly rates highly. Losing one's coat to an extortionate creditor (Matthew 5:40) and being coerced into carrying military equipment for a mile (Matthew 5:41) are more serious forms of oppression, but still less than grave ones. What the text allows us to say, then, is that the Sermon on the Mount urges Christians not to respond instinctively and vengefully to tolerable injuries to oneself. In this sense, Jesus' disciples are indeed to relinquish the "tit-for-tat ethic of the *lex talionis*" (Hays 1996, 326). Clearly, there is here a definite bias away from the knee-jerk returning of evil for evil, and toward more forbearing, generous, and conciliatory responses. Nevertheless, the text does not allow us to infer—as Hays does—an absolute prohibition of any violent response to injury. It does not forbid a violent response that is not motivated by touchy self-regard or vengeful anger, allows fraternity to govern hostility, observes the moral claims of the aggressor, aspires to achieve a just reconciliation, and *therefore* attests the fact of a grave injustice and opposes it. As we should distinguish between appropriate anger and immoderate anger, so we should distinguish between, on the one hand, retaliation governed by a certain care for the aggressor and a desire for genuine peace, and on the other hand, retaliation that is driven by a self-regarding indignation. Or, to put the matter more succinctly, we should distinguish between retaliation that is directed by love and that which is not.

Notwithstanding this, it might be protested that loving retaliation cannot be violent, and *a fortiori* it cannot be lethally violent. According to Hays, the practice of loving enemies is, *pace* Augustine and Reinhold Niebuhr, "incompatible with killing them" (ibid., 329). This is not so, however. I might intentionally kill an aggressor, not at all because I hate him, nor because I reckon his life worth less than anyone else's, nor because I want him dead, but because, tragically, I know of no other way to prevent him from perpetrating a serious injury on an innocent neighbour. My intentional killing is loving, therefore, in two respects: first, its overriding aim is to protect the innocent from serious harm; and second, it acknowledges the aggressor's equal dignity, it wishes him no evil, and it would gladly spare him if it could.

One of my main complaints against Richard Hays' pacifist reading of the New Testament is that it generalizes too much and distinguishes too little. The New Testament does forbid certain kinds of violence: that which is disproportionate because motivated by contemptuous or hateful or vengeful anger; that which retaliates in response to trivial or tolerable personal injury; that which lacks public authorization; and that which is inspired by religious nationalism. But its prohibition of violence is specific, not absolute. Therefore, it is not accurate to summarize the New Testament's position in terms of a commitment to 'non-violence' *simpliciter*.

The Christian's Vocation: Not to Suffer-in-General

The specification or delimitation of the violence forbidden by the New Testament implies a corresponding delimitation of the patient suffering that it recommends as morally normative for Christian life and ethics. We should demur from saying, as Hays does, that all four evangelists present Jesus' choice of messianic career, epitomized in the symbol of the cross, as involving "the vocation of suffering" rather than conquering Israel's enemies (ibid., 329); and that the Epistle to the Hebrews and the Catholic Epistles prescribe the suffering of violence as the pattern of Christian life.[14] To talk of 'the vocation of suffering' is to make the negative practice of suffering in general the central and defining feature of Jesus' life and teaching. However, Jesus' vocation would be better—because more fully and more positively—characterized as that of wooing sinners and enemies and gentiles into a generous, compassionate, if not undemanding, kingdom of God. Such a vocation did entail the abjuring of hatred, unloving anger and retaliation, knee-jerk recourse to private violence in self-defence, and religious nationalism. And it therefore entailed a patient endurance of the *correlative* suffering. But suffering is not the first thing to say about the character or pattern of Christian life, and *suffering-in-general* should not be said about it at all.[15]

Paul's Theology of the Atonement: Why It Includes Killing

The final element of Hays' interpretation of the New Testament with which we take issue is his reading of St Paul's theology of the Atonement in the Epistle to the Romans. This, too, falls prey to lack of moral analysis. As Hays presents it, Paul infers from the death of Christ that God deals with his enemies, not by killing them, but by seeking peace through "self-giving" or "self-emptying service"; and that those whose lives are reshaped in Christ must treat their enemies likewise (Hays 1996, 330). In textual substantiation of this interpretation, Hays quotes Romans 5:8–10:

> But God shows his love for us in that while we were yet sinners Christ died for us. Since, therefore, we are now justified by his blood, much more shall we be saved by him from the wrath of God. For if while we were enemies we were reconciled to God by the death of his Son, much more now that we are reconciled, shall we be saved by his life.

This clearly affirms that God regards sinners with love, that he has taken gracious initiative toward sparing them his wrath by being reconciled with them, and that this initiative has expressed itself in the death of his Son, Jesus Christ. What ethical implications may Christians draw from this theology? Certainly, that they should respond with love to those who do them wrong, that they should therefore desire reconciliation above punishment (or wrath), and that this predominant desire should express itself in the taking of appropriate initiatives. Can we go further and, with Hays, infer an absolute prohibition of the use of lethal force? I think not. While the text clearly implies that God wants to save sinners from his wrath and that those who are 'in Christ' shall be saved, it does not imply that salvation will embrace all the rest. It follows that if (with Hays) we take death to be the effect of Divine wrath on sinners, then, notwithstanding God's active desire that they should be saved, he nevertheless ends up 'killing' those who do not participate 'in Christ'.

Paul's talk here of being 'justified' or 'acquitted' (δικαιωθέντες) and being saved from God's 'wrath' (τῆς ὀργῆς)—the execution of which, he later tells us, is the task of governing authorities (Romans 13:4)—makes metaphorical use of the administration of criminal justice. God is being likened to a civil magistrate, and his wrath to the execution of capital punishment. The notion that God 'kills' sinners as a magistrate authorizes the capital penalty is, of course, one to which many contemporary Christians strongly object. The reasons for their objection bear reflection. The first carries little weight: namely, the fact that in Western societies—or at least among their liberal elites—capital punishment is widely assumed to be a pre-modern, 'medieval' barbarity. There is ground for this view, of course, in the (to us) shocking and brutal readiness with which regimes in previous centuries meted out the death penalty for (to us) trivial crimes. On the other hand, there is ample room for twenty-first-century Western liberals to become more mindful of the extent to which they enjoy the luxury of historically unprecedented public order and social peace; of the horrors and terrors into which a society can very quickly plunge when that order breaks down; and of the immense difficulty of hauling that society back into a condition of civilization. There is an argument—and to my mind it is a good one—that the infliction of capital punishment may be warranted *in extremis*, when a society cannot afford other effective means of containing violent crime.[16] The death penalty is always severe and terrible; but it need not be gratuitously cruel.

A second objection assumes that anyone authorizing the death penalty must be motivated by a sadistic or vengeful ill will and *wants* to see the criminal or sinner dead. But this need not be so. The condemning judge might have no such desire. What he might desire is the safety of innocent citizens; and if this could be secured by any means other than the tragic death of the criminal, he would gladly choose it. But because there is no alternative, he reluctantly accepts the death of the criminal as an unavoidable and proportionate side-effect of ensuring public security.

A third reason for declining to think of God killing sinners as magistrates kill capital criminals is that human magistrates are warranted in so doing by the exigencies of history, whereas almighty God is presumably not subject to these. The rationale for capital punishment that I have articulated above is that it might be the only effective way for a society to contain grave violence: that is, it might be warranted *in extremis socialibus*.[17] While it might be justified, the death penalty is nevertheless tragic. It involves causing at least two evils—the cutting off of the possibility of a criminal human being's (earthly) repentance and reformation and reconciliation, as well as his physical death. Were there an alternative way of securing innocent neighbours against the threat of violence, the execution of the criminal would not be justified; but sometimes history constrains us into a tragic set of circumstances where we cannot do our primary duty to our innocent neighbours without bringing grave evil (albeit justifiably) upon the heads of those who threaten them. Presumably in his dealings with sinners and their moral and spiritual wrongdoing, almighty God is never so constrained.

On the contrary, he might be. Whatever the radically different conditions of the Next World, the ultimate well-being of creation will require the eradication of sin and the threat it poses; and if some sinners should persist in cordial commitment to their sin, then the ultimate well-being of creation would require their destruction too. It might prove to be the case that God's love is sufficiently powerful to woo every last sinner away from their sin—that his Yes will exhaust all our Noes. But with Karl Barth, we can only hope and pray so; we cannot know so for sure.[18] And it has to be said that, in the face of some notorious cases of persistent and atrocious wickedness, repentance looks most unlikely.[19] As the dignity of free will makes possible the voluntary growth of human beings into virtuous maturity, so it necessarily also makes possible the voluntary degeneration of human beings into terminal corruption. We must entertain the possibility, then, that the ultimate salvation of creation will require the permanent removal of some sinners along with the sin to which they are inextricably attached; and unless we can conceive of a form of permanent removal short of final destruction, then we must entertain the possibility that ultimate death will be the destiny of some sinners.

It is true, of course, that St Paul's use of the terms of criminal justice to talk about God's dealing with sinners is metaphorical, and that there might be other ways of talking that have certain advantages over this one. Paul Fiddes (1989, 91–93), for example, recommends that we think of the ultimate death of sinners in naturalistic, rather than judicial, terms: as the natural, automatic consequence of persistent spiritual alienation from God, rather than the result of an act that God decides to perform. This has the advantage of making clear that the immediate responsibility for a sinner's death belongs to the sinner. However, insofar as it is designed to dissociate God from all responsibility for the death of sinners, it both fails and misleads. It fails because God, having deliberately created the world as it is, remains indirectly responsible for death being the natural end of intractable sinners. Therefore, the ultimate death of sinners remains the result of a deliberate decision of God, by which God presumably still stands.

This naturalistic conception of the death of sinners also misleads in that it assumes that if God is (at all) responsible for the death of sinners, then he must be culpable. But God's responsibility here is not that of one who malevolently *wants* the sinner dead (which would be morally culpable). Rather, it is the responsibility of one who, for the sake of the possibility of the voluntary growth of virtuous persons into human fulfilment, is willing to risk the possibility of the voluntary degeneration of vicious persons to the point of ultimate death—and is ready to accept its realization.[20]

Whither has this extended discussion brought us? How does it help us to answer the question of whether Richard Hays is correct to claim that St Paul's theology of the Atonement conceives of God responding to sinners by serving rather than killing them; and that therefore Christians are forbidden to kill their enemies? First, Paul does not say that all sinners will escape God's 'wrath'. Second, it is not inappropriate for Christians to think of God dealing with incorrigible sinners as magistrates deal *in extremis* with criminals who continue to pose a grave threat—since the authorization of the death penalty need not be malevolent or wanton; since its execution need not be cruel or barbarous; since the dignity of free will requires that sinners be allowed to become inextricably attached to their sin; since the ultimate fulfilment of creation requires the permanent removal of sin; and since in the case of incorrigible sinners this must amount to their death.

I conclude, then, that we should think of God as being prepared to respond to incorrigible sinners (should there be any) by authorizing their deaths, not at all because he wants them dead, but because he wants to secure the fulfilment of creation, and because he cannot have the latter without the former. In this sense we may say that God kills incorrigible sinners. And we may say so without in any way detracting from God's driving desire to save sinners from their sin, and from the costly, gracious initiatives that he has taken to do so. Accordingly, I think Hays mistaken to infer from St Paul's theology of the Atonement that Christians may never kill their enemies.

Taking Methodological Stock

I have tested Richard Hays' pacifist reading of the New Testament against what the text itself says. What I have taken the text to say has been determined by three factors. The first is what it consistently and significantly fails to say—namely, that soldiers should abandon their immoral profession. The second is a relevant feature of the social context of its main subject, Jesus—that is, the option of revolutionary violence inspired by religious nationalism. The third factor comprises the logical limits of what we may take the text strictly to imply—namely, that we may not infer an absolute prohibition of the use of lethal violence from the prohibition of vengeance, anger, hatred, and retaliation, or from the injunction of love for one's enemies, or from St Paul's theology of the Atonement. According to this interpretation of the text, we may say that the New Testament abjures vengeance, hatred, unloving anger and retaliation, knee-jerk recourse to private violence in self-defence, and violence inspired by religious nationalism. We may say that it enjoins whatever faithful suffering is involved by forbearance from these. We may say that, beyond the passive suffering of frustration, insult, and tolerable injustice, it also enjoins the active, generous, and enterprising desire for reconciliation. From this, however, it does not follow that the New Testament absolutely forbids the publicly authorized use of lethal violence by Christians, nor even their use of private violence *in extremis*. My concluding verdict, therefore, is that the New Testament does not bear Richard Hays' pacifist reading.

I am aware of three objections that this interpretation might attract. One objects to its use of argument from silence with regard to the soldiers who appear in the New Testament. An argument from what is *not* said is obviously weaker than an argument from what *is* said. Still, an argument from what is not said can have force. Some silences are simply empty and ambiguous, and they can be read in opposite ways with equal justification. Other silences, however, are loaded. Were the pacifist reading of the New Testament correct, there is strong reason to expect that soldiers whose faith was approved by Jesus or his disciples would be shown to distance themselves from their fundamentally incompatible profession. But they are not so shown. The New Testament's silence on this matter is, therefore, loud with significance. And when set within hearing of St Paul's affirmation of the public use of force in Romans 13, it becomes even louder.

A second objection to my interpretation might be that I distinguish too much, meaning either that I use moral distinctions that are spurious or that I import moral distinctions that are 'unbiblical'. One of these distinctions that many consider to be spurious is that between, on the one hand, a deliberate act that it is foreseen will likely or certainly cause an evil (such as death), where that evil effect is reluctantly accepted, and, on the other hand, a deliberate act that it is foreseen will likely or certainly cause an evil, where that evil is intended or wanted. Whether this doctrine of double effect is or is not spurious is the subject of longstanding controversy and it remains controversial. Those who think that it is spurious tend to be utilitarian philosophers; and I have explained elsewhere why I think that they are wrong.[21]

Another distinction that is held to be spurious is that between loving and hateful violence. Here it is assumed that violence is always driven by hatred. But that assumption is empirically false, for it is widely recognized that soldiers in battle are usually motivated by loyalty to their comrades and by fear of shame, rather than by hatred for the enemy. Moreover, there is also the phenomenon of soldiers regarding and treating their enemies with a certain 'amiability'.[22]

As for the charge that I use moral distinctions that are 'unbiblical', that is either untrue or beside the point. The distinction between what is permitted public officials and what is permitted private subjects or citizens is implied in Romans 12–13, where Paul makes plain that only the governing authorities may mediate the wrath of God on wrongdoers. And the distinction between anger that is sinful and anger that is not is implied in Ephesians 4:6. However, whether or not a moral distinction is actually to be found, explicitly or implicitly, in the Bible is not important. One does not have to hold as true *only* what the Bible states or implies, in order to regard it as authoritative. I am not aware that the Bible states or uses the doctrine of double effect; but I still have good reason to think it valid. And even if the Bible does not distinguish between murder and manslaughter, we would, I suggest, still have good reason to do so. Obviously, it would be problematic for a Christian theologian to espouse things that the Bible unequivocally denies. But 'non-biblical' distinctions are not necessarily 'anti-biblical'. They might be, of course, but that remains to be shown.

This brings us to a third possible objection. When I say that there is 'good reason' to hold something that the Bible does not affirm, what kind of good reason am I talking about? I am talking about reasons furnished by human experience of the world and reflection upon it. The idea that the moral quality of an act depends not primarily on its good or evil effects, but upon the intention or circumspection of the agent is, in my view, correct. It is not one, however, that I am aware of having first learned from the Bible. As for the idea that soldiers might not be motivated by hatred, I am aware that it came to me from military witnesses belonging to the twentieth and twenty-first centuries. Some might find it suspect that I presume to take these fruits of experience into my reading of the New Testament. My own view is that there is no such thing as pure interpretation or even pure exegesis. It is surely a truism that no exegete or interpreter comes to the text as a *tabula rasa*. Richard Hays agrees. He acknowledges that experience is involved in interpretation (Hays 1996, 209), and that the hermeneutical, synthetic, and descriptive tasks "inevitably interpenetrate and overlap" (ibid., 199). He appears, however, to think of experience in curiously narrow, religious terms; and he confines its primary role to that of confirming the truth of the teaching of Scripture. As an example, he cites the experience of God's love confirming that eschatological hope is not futile (ibid., p. 297). I think, however, that a far wider range of human experience of the world that God has created should come into play. I also think that one of its main roles should be to help determine the meaning of Scripture, and not merely to confirm its truth. I agree with Hays that we cannot take the apparent deliverances of experience at face value. These can deceive, and we must test them. I also agree that the data of experience must find their place "within the world narrated by the New Testament witnesses" (ibid., 296). Therefore, if what the text clearly, recurrently, and predominantly says simply will not wear the moral distinctions and empirical data that I bring to it, then as a Christian ethicist I must reconsider and perhaps abandon them. But if the text will wear them, then I may infer that its meaning includes them. At it happens, Hays himself brings more empirical data—and brings it more deeply—into his exegetical and synthetic work than he himself recognizes. It seems to me that the reason why he reads Jesus' death on the cross as meaning the absolute repudiation of all violence everywhere is that he has imported empirical assumptions about anger and violence as necessarily vengeful and malevolent. I do not complain at all about the importation. I merely dissent from the assumptions.

Conclusion

In spite of these three objections, then, I persist in judging that the New Testament does not bear Richard Hays' pacifist reading. What is more, I think that Hays is wrong to claim that "it is not possible to use the just war tradition as a hermeneutical device for illuminating the New Testament" (ibid., 341). It is not only possible, but preferable, for the doctrine of just war can make better sense than pacifism of all that the New Testament text does and does not say. On the one hand, of course, this doctrine does not prohibit the publicly legitimate use of violent force by police or soldiers. On the other hand, it insists that lethal violence may only ever be used with the intention of securing a just peace (or reconciliation). This intention is incompatible with motives such as unloving anger or vengeance or hatred. And it is all the more incompatible with a religious nationalist view of the enemy, which sees them as infidels to be ruthlessly destroyed by the righteous, rather than as one set of fellow-sinners whose evil actions must, alas, be curtailed by another set. Given the basic requirement of an intention of just peace, it follows that recourse to lethal violence cannot be justified unless its inevitable evils are made sufficiently proportionate by the serious prospect of actually ending grave and intolerable injustice. This implies that injustices that are less than grave should be suffered rather than used as a pretext for impatient violence; but it also implies that they should be suffered in a creative manner that extends compassion to the oppressor in the hope of wooing repentance and making peace. Just war doctrine encompasses, therefore, not only moments of the use of lethal violence that intend peace and are disciplined by it, but also moments of forbearance, suffering, and compassion.

III. Was the Christian Church Originally Pacifist?

It is often claimed that the Christian Church was overwhelmingly pacifist during the immediate post-Apostolic era, and that it only came to endorse the idea of 'just war' after its fall from original grace under the emperor Constantine in the early fourth century. This Constantinian 'fall' refers to the era following the

Edict of Milan of 313, when the Christian religion first became tolerated in the Roman empire and then, as it became established, was seduced and corrupted by the temptations of political power. In fact, there are several reasons to suppose that this story is more myth than history.

While it is true that many early Christians opposed service in the Roman army, the reason for their opposition was not always principled opposition to the use of force. As one of the leading modern theological proponents of Christian pacifism, John Howard Yoder, admits, the Christian refusal of violence in the Church's first two centuries was associated with a wider rejection of the culture of the Roman empire. The early Christians were "globally polarized" against all that Caesar and his empire meant, he tells us, because

> Caesar stood for polytheism and idolatry, . . . Caesar was sometimes honoured in a cultic way, . . . The life of the soldier involved regularly swearing oaths . . . Caesar's agents occasionally persecuted Christians, . . . Caesar's total lifestyle was immoral and blasphemous.
> *(Yoder 2009b, 48–49)*

(To this, Yoder could have added that Christian attitudes to military service were often coloured by their disgust at the general bloodthirstiness of Roman culture, as epitomized by the regular slaughter of animals and human beings for popular entertainment in the 'games'.[23])

That said, Yoder is correct to reject the argument that early Christians *only* rejected military service on account of its association with idolatry.[24] Judging by those views that have come down to us, early post-Apostolic opposition to Christian participation in the Roman army was not always grounded *simply* on its entailment of idolatry or on its association with a wantonly bloodthirsty culture. Tertullian, for one, can be found appealing directly to the teaching of Jesus as delivered by the Gospels. So, for example, he writes: "Shall it be held lawful to make an occupation of the sword, when the Lord proclaims that he who uses the sword shall perish by the sword?" (Tertullian 1869).

Nevertheless, David Hunter's 1992 survey of the relevant literature—deemed "even-handed" by the pacifist Richard Hays (2010, 190n.10)—judged that the old consensus that the earliest Christians were overwhelmingly pacifist is *passé*, and that a new consensus had arisen. This holds that the most vociferous opponents of military service (such as Tertullian) "based their objections on a variety of factors"; that at least from the end of the second century Christian opinion and practice on the matter was divided; that throughout the third century Christian support for military service grew (which is why Tertullian was provoked to write against it); and that Christian just war thinking "stand[s] in fundamental continuity with at least one strand of pre-Constantinian tradition" (Hunter 1992, 93). In his 2013 book, *Augustine on War and Military Service*, Phillip Wynn confirms Hunter's thesis (Wynn 2013).

IV. St Augustine, the Turn to Motive, and 'Just War'

Given the prominence of the themes of love and reconciliation in the originating events and foundational documents of Christianity, any attempt by Christians to justify the use of armed force is bound to operate within their terms. And in the Christian 'just war' tradition, this is what it does.

In the year 411 or 412, Augustine (354–430AD), who was then bishop of Hippo in what is now Tunisia, wrote a pastoral letter to a military tribune (or regimental commander), Flavius Marcellinus. Evidently, Marcellinus' Christian conscience was perplexed by his duty to use physical force. In responding, Augustine made a crucial interpretative move, in which he identified the moral wrongness of the use of force, not with the act's effects, but with its motive and intention: "For what is it 'not to return evil for evil' (Romans 12.17; I Thess. 5.15)", he asks rhetorically, "except to shrink from a passion for revenge . . .?" (Augustine 2001, Letter 138, p. 35, s.9).

Consistently, Augustine justifies armed coercion by appeal to Jesus' command that we should love our neighbours and especially our enemies. For example, he invokes this command in his letter to a second military tribune, Boniface, before proceeding shortly afterwards to discuss the propriety of a Christian serving as a soldier (ibid., Letter 189, p. 215, s.2; p. 216, s.4.) and to prescribe peace as the proper end of a just war (ibid., p. 217, s.6); and he does it again in another letter to Boniface, when enjoining "single-minded love" toward the enemy, even while treating them with "an unpleasant severity" (ibid., Letter 220, p. 222, s.8). But even when Augustine makes no overt reference to the dominical injunction, he affirms it implicitly by consistently describing just war as a benevolent response to injustice, which intends just peace. So in his letter to Marcellinus, after initially arguing that Christians should eschew the passion for revenge and intend to persuade the wrongdoer to repent and embrace peace (ibid., Letter 138, p. 35, s.9; p. 36, s.11), he then articulates what this implies: namely, that just war is waged out of a benevolent concern for the interests of the unjust enemy, punishing him "with a sort of kind harshness" (ibid., p. 38, s.14.). And in the *City of God*, he defines just war as a necessary response to injustice (Augustine 1972, Book XIX.7, p. 862), which intends just peace (ibid., XIX.12, p. 866).

Nevertheless, Augustine was acutely—and, I think, admirably—aware of the tragic dilemmas that 'secular' history presents us with, and of the morally ambiguous and dangerous compromises that it requires us to make in response. The word 'secular' here refers to the *saeculum* or age that runs between the token of the glorious transformation of the world, which is the Resurrection of Jesus from the dead, and its fulfilment. This is the age when human moral and political endeavours are fraught with tragic tension, aspiring to ideals that can only be realized partially, ambiguously, and fleetingly. In *The City of God*, Augustine offers an arresting judicial example of the tragic character of secular endeavour: the need perchance to torture someone who might be innocent, in order to find out the truth about a crime (ibid., XIX.6, pp. 859–861). And at one point in a letter to Paulinus of Nola in AD 408, he gives moving voice to the spiritual agony that the exercise of judicial office produces in the judge:

> On the subject of punishing and refraining from punishment, what am I to say? It is our desire that when we decide whether or not to punish people, in either case it should contribute wholly to their security. These are indeed deep and obscure matters: what limit ought to be set to punishment with regard to both the nature and extent of guilt, and also the strength of spirit the wrongdoers possess? What ought each one to suffer? ... What do we do when, as often happens, punishing someone will lead to his destruction, but leaving him unpunished will lead to someone else being destroyed? ... What trembling, what darkness! ... "Trembling and fear have come upon me and darkness has covered me, and I said, Who will give me wings like a dove's? Then I will fly away and be at rest". [Psalm 55 (54):5–8].
>
> (Augustine 2001, 23–24)

V. Scholasticism and the Distinction Between 'Just War' and 'Holy War'

Augustine never wrote a systematic treatise on war; his thoughts about the use of force are scattered throughout his later writings. It was not until after the emergence of Scholastic thought in the schools of Bologna and Paris in the late twelfth and early thirteenth centuries that these Augustinian fragments were gathered together and incorporated into a coherent theory of 'just war'—as, for famous example, by Thomas Aquinas ([1265–1274] 1920, IaIIae, q. 40) in his *Summa Theologiae*. In its rational, methodical, Scholastic form, Christian 'just war' thinking tamed the 'holy war' justifications of the earliest Crusades. Whereas these rested heavily on the authority of an alleged Divine command, mediated by the Pope, 'just war' reasoning appealed instead to moral norms prescribed by natural law and the law of nations. By the fifteenth and sixteenth centuries, the Popes (e.g., Eugenius IV in the 1430s on the Portuguese conquest of the Canary Islands, and Innocent IV in the 1500s on the conquest of the Indies) no longer gave a 'holy war' justification for the conquest of the Americas, but sought to justify it in normative terms as necessary to protect morally legitimate free trade or missionary activity. In other words, 'just war' reasoning had come to exercise a constraining effect upon the reasons for belligerency. Thus, in the sixteenth century Francisco de Vitoria contradicted the Conquistadors' claim that they were warranted in using force against the Caribbean natives to force the benefits of the Gospel upon them and to civilize them, arguing that war can only be justified by the need to stop egregious sins 'against nature' such as the practices of cannibalism and mass human sacrifice.

VI. 'Just War' Thinking Today

Stemming from Augustine in the early fifth century AD and developed by the Scholastics from the thirteenth to the seventeenth centuries, 'just war' thinking has now been elaborated into two sets of criteria, which subject the use of force to the constraints of moral norms. The first judges when going to war is justified (*ius ad bellum*):

(i) a just cause (a grave injustice);
(ii) a right intention (to rectify the grave injustice);
(iii) a last resort (all other, feasible, non-violent means exhausted);
(iv) legitimate authority;
(v) proportionality (the resort to war is apt to the political end); and
(vi) a reasonable prospect of success.

The second, shorter set of criteria governs the manner of waging war (*ius in bello*):

(vi) proportionality (minimum necessary force; means apt to military end); and
(vii) discrimination (no *intentional* killing of non-combatants).

VII. Conclusion

Christian just warriors agree with their pacifist *confrères* that vengeance is not a proper motive for fighting. They also recognize the terrible (non-moral) evils that war causes. That is why a just cause must comprise an injustice so grave as to warrant the risks, hazards, and costs of war; why war should only be launched as a last resort, all non-belligerent alternatives having been exhausted; why it should be an apt means to achieve a political end; why it should employ the minimum force necessary; and why it should not intend to kill non-combatants.

Unlike Christian pacifists, however, Christian proponents of 'just war' think that the use of force can be governed by the motive of love and by the intention of the end of a just peace. They locate the moral wrongness of force, not simply in the evil effects of the act, but primarily in the motives and intention of the agent. They think that love sometimes, tragically, obliges us to use force to stop one neighbour suffering grave injustice at the hands of another.

They also doubt that waging war is always more costly than avoiding it.

The phrase 'just war' can be misleading. It can connote the idea of a morally pure war. That is not what is meant, at least by Christians. In Christian thinking, a 'just war' can only ever be waged by one set of sinful creatures against another set, never by the simply righteous against the simply unrighteous. The purpose of just war can therefore never be to rid the world of the wicked, but only to stop and reverse particular instances of egregious wickedness. 'Just wars' are not morally pure wars; they are merely wars that are morally justified, *all things considered*.

Since they are waged by sinners, they will themselves invariably include elements of wrongdoing, from which just warriors will need to repent. Even when it is justified, war is still a tragic necessity, causing terrible evils, and replete with moral danger. "What trembling, what darkness! . . . 'Trembling and fear have come upon me and darkness has covered me, and I said, Who will give me wings like a dove's? Then I will fly away and be at rest'". But here in the *saeculum* wings are not to be had. Here, until the End of history, we must stay and shoulder the burdens of trying to do justice, even to the point of dirtying our hands in the use of physical force.

Notes

1. The first section of this essay comprises an expanded and revised version of Biggar (2009). The revision has been made in the light of Richard Hays (2010).
2. Among the pre-publication plaudits to be found on the back cover and opening page are these: "Hays's . . . book . . . has neither peer nor rival" (Leander Keck, Yale Divinity School); "Hays has pulled off, with a success for which I can think of no contemporary parallel, one of the most difficult tasks in theological and biblical writing today" (James Dunn, University of Durham); "[Hays's] description of the variegated ethical vision of the early church is state-of-the-art, and the application of that vision to contemporary issues is hermeneutically skillful" (George Lindbeck, Yale Divinity School); "A gem that sparkles on every page" (Graham Stanton, University of London); "an extraordinary accomplishment" (Allen Verhey, Hope College); "Hays's method and proposals will . . . prove a benchmark for future scholarship" (L. Gregory Jones); "a rare and fine book" (John Riches, University of Glasgow).
3. For example, by Swartley (2006, 439, 441): "Hays's *Moral Vision* is a classic for its penetrating, succinct exegesis of selected NT writings; his hermeneutical model. . .; and his perceptive treatment of five major voices in theological ethics, . . . Hays's treatments of Mark, Matthew, Luke-Acts, and John are incisive"; and by Morgan (2006, 48), who refers to "Hays's . . . subsequent masterpiece *The Moral Vision of the New Testament*."
4. In the first chapter of his own, alternative reading of New Testament ethics, Richard Burridge (2007, 14–15) writes of *The Moral Vision* that "it has quickly established itself as the classic treatment and has been widely appreciated."
5. In "Narrate and Embody", Hays offers the counterexample of the sinful woman who washes Jesus' feet in Luke 7:36–50. My response in the subsequent correspondence in *Studies in Christian Ethics*, 23/1 (February 2010) was this: "It's true that we're not told here explicitly that she formally renounced her former ways, like Zacchaeus. But on the assumption that the pronouncement of absolution, salvation, and reconciliation ("Your sins are forgiven . . . Your faith has saved you; go in peace") only makes sense as a response to repentance, albeit implicit (in her tears), the story implies that woman was not about to return to her sin".
6. Ibid., 331. The 1527 Schleitheim Confession, the classic statement of Anabaptist faith, puts the point thus in its sixth article: "The sword is ordained of God outside the perfection of Christ . . . [I]t is not appropriate for a Christian to serve as a magistrate" (in Leith 1973, 287, 289). Stanley Hauerwas (1988, 178) alludes to the Confession in taking up the same ecclesiological position: "The Christian does not deny that often the state does some good through its violence; the point is rather that the sword of the state is outside the 'perfection of Christ.'"
7. The exact nature of the historical situation of the Christian community in Rome, to which Paul's letter was addressed, is uncertain. Nevertheless, there is reason to suppose

that it had been involved in conflict with local Jews, and had also suffered strife between its own Jewish and gentile members, to the point of disturbing the civil peace. The Roman historian, Suetonius, reports that in 49 AD, about eight years before Paul sat down to write, the Jews living in Rome had been expelled by the emperor Claudius, because of rioting "instigated by Chrestus" (*The Lives of the Caesars*, "Claudius", s.25). Most scholars believe that this refers to civil disturbance caused by controversy among Roman Jews *about* Jesus and Christian claims for him.

8   Hays reads the disciple's offer of defence as another instance of the temptation that Jesus had earlier refused (ibid., 324): "the temptation that Jesus rejects in the wilderness and again at Gethsemane".

9   He says as much in his interpretation of Matthew's temptation narrative (see the immediately preceding paragraph). Among the good company in which this places him is Seán Freyne, the eminent historian of first-century Palestine. In Freyne's *Jesus: A Jewish Galilean: A New Reading of the Jesus Story* (2004), he writes that "Jesus refused to endorse the triumphant Zion ideology which viewed the nations as Israel's servants, and which was to provide a rallying call for some of Jesus' near-contemporaries in their struggle against Roman imperialism" (p. 135); "Jesus was not prepared to share the violent response to such conditions [of oppressive imperial rule], espoused by many Jews throughout the first century, which eventually plunged the nation into a disastrous revolt" (p. 149).

10 It is true that I am generalizing here on very particular ground—namely, the pattern of support for the I.R.A. evident in Co. Cork in the aftermath of the failed Easter Rising of 1916 (see Hart 1999). Still, I take it to be common sense that human beings who are old enough to have developed commitments to spouses and families and adequate livelihoods are likely to be less keen than herds of young unattached males to run the risks and unleash the unbiddable forces of violent revolution.

11 What is implied here is made quite explicit in Luke's story of the apostle Peter's encounter with Cornelius (Acts 10:34, 45).

12 Butler argues that anger or what he calls 'resentment' is a natural passion that may take either virtuous or vicious form according to circumstances (Butler 1953, 123).

13 This is David Daube's (1956, 260–263) interpretation in *The New Testament and Rabbinic Judaism* (London: Athlone, 1956), which Robert Guelich (1982, 222) follows but Hays does not (1996, 326).

14 Ibid., 331–332: "in Hebrews and the catholic Epistles we encounter a consistent portrayal of the community as called to suffer without anger or retaliation . . . [T]he author of I Peter holds up the suffering of Christ as a paradigm for Christian faithfulness". To his credit, Hays reports the qualifications that these texts make on the suffering to which Christians are called—the suffering *of Christ*, and suffering *without anger or retaliation*—as he reports the qualification that the Gospels make on the suffering to which Jesus himself was called—suffering *rather than the conquest of Israel's enemies*. His mistake, however, is that he does not notice the strict implication of these qualifications—namely, that they only require the enduring of some kinds of violence under certain circumstances, rather than all kinds of violence everywhere.

15 I have argued this point more fully in Biggar (2004, 49–55).

16 See Oliver O'Donovan 1977, 21–22. As my former colleague, Dr John Perry, pointed out to me, this is also the view of the Roman Catholic Church (Chapman, 1994, sections 2266–2267).

17 This, of course, is a non-Kantian rationale, for it is not the intrinsic nature of the criminal's crime alone that makes him worthy of the death penalty, but also the capacity of his society to contain violence. The consideration here is prudential, but it does not render our rationale consequentialist or utilitarian: the death penalty may only be inflicted on someone who has committed a crime by a public body that has a duty to protect

citizens from criminal violence. It may not be inflicted on an innocent by a public body that aspires to achieve the greatest happiness of the greatest number of people.
18 See, for example, Karl Barth, *Church Dogmatics* (1957, 417–418; Barth 1962, 477).
19 I write this with Andrzej Wajda's film, *Katyń* (2007)—about the meticulous murder in cold blood of 8,000 Polish officers by the Soviets in 1940—fresh in my mind. After my first viewing I exited the cinema with the overriding thought that there *must* be a hell for Stalin and his like. What it would mean for a Stalin to repent, I just cannot imagine. Nevertheless, I concede that God's imagination is greater than mine.
20 At this point some atheist philosophers might enter the objection that God (if we suppose that he exists) would have been culpably rash in risking the possibility of ultimate death for the sake of the possibility of virtuous growth. That might be. But, frankly, what human being has the competence to say so? Who among us can judge that the terrible annihilation of incorrigible sinners 'outweighs' the shining beauty of fulfilled humanity? (And is the ultimate bringing to nought of a Hitler or Stalin or Pol Pot really so terrible?) How do we begin to compare the relative 'weights' of annihilation and fulfilment? Who has the numbers and proportions of saved and damned to hand? It is not manifestly unreasonable to trust that a world in which some sinners might perish beyond hope is worth a world where other sinners might grow into glory. Nor is it unreasonable, therefore, to trust that God was not being culpably rash when he made it so.
21 Biggar (2004, ch. 3), "The Morality of Acts of Killing".
22 See, for example, Joanna Bourke, *An Intimate History of Killing: Face-to-Face Killing in Twentieth Century Warfare* (London: Basic, 2000 chapter 5, "Love and Hate", especially pp. 141–148. A reader of an earlier version of this chapter judged that my view of military motivation smacks of an armchair perspective. In case readers of the present version should think likewise, let me say that my armchair has afforded me the opportunity to read copious amounts of military history, which furnishes plenty of cases where soldiers have regarded their enemy with respect rather than hatred. I present some of them in Chapter Two. Moreover, on one occasion I managed to struggle out of my armchair to speak with a colonel in the Royal Marines, who confirmed my bookish view by testifying that military training with which he is familiar positively discourages 'hot' violence in favour of 'cool'. This is because violence that is motivated by intemperate anger or hatred lacks self-control, and therefore makes mistakes, jeopardizes plans, and endangers comrades. Violence that would be efficient and effective cannot afford such distractions. If you doubt it, ask a boxer.
23 See, for example, Athenagoras, *A Plea for the Christians*, XXXV: "But we, deeming that to see a man put to death is much the same as killing him, have abjured such spectacles", in *Ante-Nicene Fathers* (Roberts and Donaldson 1885, 147); and Lactantius, *The Divine Institutes*, VI.20: "And yet they call these sports in which human blood is shed. So far has the feeling of humanity departed from the men, that when they destroy the lives of men, they think that they are amusing themselves with sport" (Roberts and Donaldson 1886, 186).
24 Yoder, "The Pacifism of Pre-Constantinian Christianity" (2009, 45, 47n.2).

References

Athenagoras the Athenian. "A Plea for the Christians." Accessed July 29, 2017. www.newadvent.org/fathers/0205.htm.
Augustine. *City of God*. Translated by Henry Bettenson. London: Penguin, 1972.
Augustine. *Political Writings*. Edited by E. M. Atkins and R. J. Dodaro. 1st ed. Cambridge; New York: Cambridge University Press, 2001.

Barth, Karl. *The Doctrine of God.* Edited by G. W. Bromiley and T. F. Torrance. Translated by T. H. L. Parker and J. L. M. Haire. Vol. II. London: Bloomsbury T & T Clark, 1957.
Barth, Karl. *The Doctrine of Reconciliation.* Edited by T. F. Torrance. Translated by G. W. Bromiley. 1st ed. London: Bloomsbury T & T Clark, 1962.
Biggar, Nigel. *Aiming to Kill: The Ethics of Suicide and Euthanasia.* London: Darton, Longman, and Todd, 2004.
Biggar, Nigel. "Specify and Distinguish! Interpreting the New Testament on 'Non-Violence.'" *Studies in Christian Ethics,* 22/2 (May 2009).
Bourke, Joanna. *An Intimate History of Killing: Face to Face Killing in Twentieth Century Warfare.* Revised ed. LaVergne, TN: Basic Books, 2000.
Burridge, Richard. *Imitating Jesus: An Inclusive Approach to New Testament Ethics.* Grand Rapids, MI: Eerdmans, 2007.
Butler, Joseph. "Upon Resentment." In *Fifteen Sermons,* ed. W. R. Matthews. London: G. Bell & Sons, 1953.
Chapman, Geoffrey. *Catechism of the Catholic Church.* London: Continuum International Publishing, 1994.
Daube, David. *The New Testament and Rabbinic Judaism.* London: Athlone, 1956.
Dunn, James D. G. *Word Biblical Commentary,* Vol. 38B, Romans 9–16. Waco, TX: Word Books, 1988.
Fiddes, Paul S. *Past Event and Present Salvation: The Christian Idea of Atonement.* Louisville, KY: Westminster John Knox Press, 1989.
Freyne, Sean. *Jesus, a Jewish Galilean: A New Reading of the Jesus Story.* London; New York: Bloomsbury T & T Clark, 2004.
Guelich, Robert A. *The Sermon on the Mount: A Foundation for Understanding.* Waco, TX: W Publishing Group, 1982.
Hart, Peter. *The I.R.A. and Its Enemies: Violence and Community in Cork, 1916–1923.* Oxford: Oxford University Press, 1999.
Hauerwas, Stanley. "Epilogue." In *Speak Up for Just War or Pacifism: A Critique of the United Methodist Bishops' Pastoral Letter in Defense of Creation,* ed. Paul Ramsey, 149–182. State College, PA: Penn State Press, 1988.
Hays, Richard B. *Moral Vision of the New Testament: A Contemporary Introduction to New Testament Ethics.* Edinburgh: T & T Clark, 1996.
Hays, Richard B. "Narrate and Embody! A Response to Nigel Biggar." *Studies in Christian Ethics,* 23/1 (February, 2010): 185–198.
Horsley, Richard. *Jesus and the Spiral of Violence: Popular Jewish Resistance in Roman Palestine.* San Francisco: Harper and Row, 1987.
Hunter, David G. "A Decade of Research on Early Christians and Military Service." *Religious Studies Review,* 18, no. 2 (1992): 87–94.
Leith, John, ed., *Creeds of the Churches: A Reader in Christian Doctrine from the Bible to the Present.* Rev. ed. Atlanta: John Knox, 1973.
Morgan, Robert. "New Testament." *The Oxford Handbook of Biblical Studies.* Oxford: Oxford University Press, 2006.O'Donovan, Oliver. *Measure for Measure: Justice in Punishment and the Sentence of Death: Grove Booklet on Ethics no. 19.* Bramcote: Grove Books, 1977.
Roberts, Alexander, and James Donaldson, eds. *Ante-Nicene Fathers,* Vol. 2: "Fathers of the Second Century: Hermes, Tatian, Athenagoras, Theophilus, and Clement of Alexandria." Rev. A. Cleveland Coxe. New York: Christian Literature Publishing Co., 1885.
Roberts, Alexander, and James Donaldson, eds. *Ante-Nicene Fathers,* Vol. 7: "Fathers of the Third and Fourth Centuries: Lactantius, Venantius, Asterius, Victorinus, Dionysius,

Apostolic Teaching and Constitutions, Homily, and Liturgies." Rev. A. Cleveland Coxe. New York: Christian Literature Publishing Co., 1886.

Swartley, Willard M. *Covenant of Peace: The Missing Peace in New Testament Theology and Ethics*. Grand Rapids, MI: Eerdmans, 2006.

Tertullian. "The Soldier's Chapelet." In *Ante-Nicene Christian Library: Translations of the Writings of the Fathers Down to A.D. 325, Volume 11: The Writings of Tertullian, Volume 1*, eds. Alexander Roberts and James Donaldson, Digitized by Google, 333–355. Edinburgh: T & T Clark, 1869. http://archive.org/details/AnteNiceneChristianLibraryV11.

Wajda, Andrzej (dir.). *Katyń*. 2007.

Wynn, Phillip. *Augustine on War and Military Service*. Minneapolis: Fortress Press, 2015.

Yoder, John Howard. *Christian Attitudes to War, Peace, and Revolution*. Edited by Theodore J. Koontz and Andy Alexis-Baker. Grand Rapids, MI: Brazos Press, 2009a.

Yoder, John Howard. *The War of the Lamb: The Ethics of Nonviolence and Peacemaking*. Grand Rapids, MI: Brazos Press, 2009b.

9

NONVIOLENCE

A Style of Politics for Peace[1]

Pope Francis

1. At the beginning of this New Year, I offer heartfelt wishes of peace to the world's peoples and nations, to heads of state and government, and to religious, civic and community leaders. I wish peace to every man, woman and child, and I pray that the image and likeness of God in each person will enable us to acknowledge one another as sacred gifts endowed with immense dignity. Especially in situations of conflict, let us respect this, our "deepest dignity" (Pope Francis 2013, 228), and make active nonviolence our way of life.

This is the fiftieth Message for the World Day of Peace. In the first, Blessed Pope Paul VI addressed all peoples, not simply Catholics, with utter clarity. "Peace is the only true direction of human progress—and not the tensions caused by ambitious nationalisms, nor conquests by violence, nor repressions which serve as mainstay for a false civil order". He warned of "the danger of believing that international controversies cannot be resolved by the ways of reason, that is, by negotiations founded on law, justice, and equity, but only by means of deterrent and murderous forces". Instead, citing the encyclical *Pacem in Terris* of his predecessor Saint John XXIII, he extolled "the sense and love of peace founded upon truth, justice, freedom and love" (Pope Paul VI, 1968). In the intervening fifty years, these words have lost none of their significance or urgency.

On this occasion, I would like to reflect on *nonviolence* as a style of politics for peace. I ask God to help all of us to cultivate nonviolence in our most personal thoughts and values. May charity and nonviolence govern how we treat each other as individuals, within society and in international life. When victims of violence are able to resist the temptation to retaliate, they become the most credible promoters of nonviolent peacemaking. In the most local and ordinary situations and in the international order, may nonviolence become the hallmark of our decisions, our relationships and our actions, and indeed of political life in all its forms.

A Broken World

2. While the last century knew the devastation of two deadly World Wars, the threat of nuclear war and a great number of other conflicts, today, sadly, we find ourselves engaged in a horrifying *world war fought piecemeal*. It is not easy to know if our world is presently more or less violent than in the past, or to know whether modern means of communications and greater mobility have made us more aware of violence, or, on the other hand, increasingly inured to it.

In any case, we know that this "piecemeal" violence, of different kinds and levels, causes great suffering: wars in different countries and continents; terrorism, organized crime and unforeseen acts of violence; the abuses suffered by migrants and victims of human trafficking; and the devastation of the environment. Where does this lead? Can violence achieve any goal of lasting value? Or does it merely lead to retaliation and a cycle of deadly conflicts that benefit only a few "warlords"?

Violence is not the cure for our broken world. Countering violence with violence leads at best to forced migrations and enormous suffering, because vast amounts of resources are diverted to military ends and away from the everyday needs of young people, families experiencing hardship, the elderly, the infirm and the great majority of people in our world. At worst, it can lead to the death, physical and spiritual, of many people, if not of all.

The Good News

3. Jesus himself lived in violent times. Yet he taught that the true battlefield, where violence and peace meet, is the human heart: for "it is from within, from the human heart, that evil intentions come" (*Mk* 7:21). But Christ's message in this regard offers a radically positive approach. He unfailingly preached God's unconditional love, which welcomes and forgives. He taught his disciples to love their enemies (cf. *Mt* 5:44) and to turn the other cheek (cf. *Mt* 5:39). When he stopped her accusers from stoning the woman caught in adultery (cf. *Jn* 8:1–11), and when, on the night before he died, he told Peter to put away his sword (cf. *Mt* 26:52), Jesus marked out the path of nonviolence. He walked that path to the very end, to the cross, whereby he became our peace and put an end to hostility (cf. *Eph* 2:14–16). Whoever accepts the Good News of Jesus is able to acknowledge the violence within and be healed by God's mercy, becoming in turn an instrument of reconciliation. In the words of Saint Francis of Assisi: "As you announce peace with your mouth, make sure that you have greater peace in your hearts" ("The Legend of the Three Companions").

To be true followers of Jesus today also includes embracing his teaching about nonviolence. As my predecessor Benedict XVI observed, that teaching "is realistic because it takes into account that in the world there is *too much* violence, *too much* injustice, and therefore that this situation cannot be overcome except by countering it with *more* love, with *more* goodness. This '*more*' comes from God" (Pope Benedict XVI 2007). He went on to stress that: "For Christians, nonviolence is not merely tactical behaviour but a person's way of being, the attitude of one who is *so convinced of God's love and power* that he or she is not afraid to tackle evil with the weapons of love and truth alone. Love of one's enemy constitutes the nucleus of the 'Christian revolution'" (ibid.). The Gospel command to *love your enemies* (cf. *Lk* 6:27) "is rightly considered the *magna carta* of Christian nonviolence. It does not consist in succumbing to evil . . ., but in responding to evil with good (cf. *Rom* 12:17–21), and thereby breaking the chain of injustice" (ibid.).

More Powerful Than Violence

4. Nonviolence is sometimes taken to mean surrender, lack of involvement and passivity, but this is not the case. When Mother Teresa received the Nobel Peace Prize in 1979, she clearly stated her own message of active nonviolence: "We in our family don't need bombs and guns, to destroy to bring peace—just get together, love one another . . . And we will be able to overcome all the evil that is in the world" (Mother Teresa 1979). For the force of arms is deceptive. "While weapons traffickers do their work, there are poor peacemakers who give their lives to help one person, then another and another and another"; for such peacemakers, Mother Teresa is "a symbol, an icon of our times" (Pope Francis 2015, 19 November). Last September, I had the great joy of proclaiming her a Saint. I praised her readiness to make herself available for everyone "through her welcome and defence of human life, those unborn and those abandoned and discarded . . . She bowed down before those who were spent, left to die on the side of the road, seeing in them their God-given dignity; she made her voice heard before the powers of this world, so that they might recognize their guilt for the crimes—the crimes!—of poverty they created" (Pope Francis 2016, 4 September). In response, her mission—and she stands for thousands, even millions of persons—was to reach out to the suffering, with generous dedication, touching and binding up every wounded body, healing every broken life.

The decisive and consistent practice of nonviolence has produced impressive results. The achievements of Mahatma Gandhi and Khan Abdul Ghaffar Khan in the liberation of India, and of Dr Martin Luther King, Jr, in combating racial discrimination will never be forgotten. Women in particular are often leaders of nonviolence, as for example, was Leymah Gbowee and the thousands of Liberian women who organized pray-ins and nonviolent protest that resulted in high-level peace talks to end the second civil war in Liberia.

Nor can we forget the eventful decade that ended with the fall of Communist regimes in Europe. The Christian communities made their own contribution by their insistent prayer and courageous action. Particularly influential were the ministry and teaching of Saint John Paul II. Reflecting on the events of 1989 in his 1991 encyclical *Centesimus Annus*, my predecessor highlighted the fact that momentous change in the lives of people, nations and states had come about "by means of peaceful protest, using only the weapons of truth and justice" (Saint John Paul II 1991). This peaceful political transition was made possible in part "by the non-violent commitment of people who, while always refusing to yield to the force of power, succeeded time after time in finding effective ways of bearing witness to the truth". Pope John Paul went on to say: "May people learn to fight for justice without violence, renouncing class struggle in their internal disputes and war in international ones" (ibid.).

The Church has been involved in nonviolent peacebuilding strategies in many countries, engaging even the most violent parties in efforts to build a just and lasting peace.

Such efforts on behalf of the victims of injustice and violence are not the legacy of the Catholic Church alone, but are typical of many religious traditions, for which "compassion and nonviolence are essential elements pointing to the way of life" (Pope Francis 2016, 3 November). I emphatically reaffirm that "no religion is terrorist" (Pope Francis 2016, 5 November). Violence profanes the name of God (Pope Francis 2016, 2 October). Let us never tire of repeating: "The name of God cannot be used to justify violence. Peace alone is holy. Peace alone is holy, not war" (Pope Francis 2016, 20 September)!

The Domestic Roots of a Politics of Nonviolence

5. If violence has its source in the human heart, then it is fundamental that nonviolence be practised before all else within families. This is part of that joy of love which I described last March in my Exhortation *Amoris Laetitia*, in the wake of two years of reflection by the Church on marriage and the family. The family is the indispensable crucible in which spouses, parents and children, brothers and sisters, learn to communicate and to show generous concern for one another, and in which frictions and even conflicts have to be resolved not by force but by dialogue, respect, concern for the good of the other, mercy and forgiveness (Cf. Pope Francis 2016, 19 March). From within families, the joy of love spills out into the world and radiates to the whole of society (cf. ibid., 133, 194, 234). An ethics of fraternity and peaceful coexistence between individuals and among peoples cannot be based on the logic of fear, violence and closed-mindedness, but on responsibility, respect and sincere dialogue. Hence, I plead for disarmament and for the prohibition and abolition of nuclear weapons: nuclear deterrence and the threat of mutual assured destruction are incapable of grounding such an ethics (Pope

Francis 2014, 7 December). I plead with equal urgency for an end to domestic violence and to the abuse of women and children.

The Jubilee of Mercy that ended in November encouraged each one of us to look deeply within and to allow God's mercy to enter there. The Jubilee taught us to realize how many and diverse are the individuals and social groups treated with indifference and subjected to injustice and violence. They too are part of our "family"; they too are our brothers and sisters. The politics of nonviolence have to begin in the home and then spread to the entire human family. "Saint Therese of Lisieux invites us to practise the little way of love, not to miss out on a kind word, a smile or any small gesture which sows peace and friendship. An integral ecology is also made up of simple daily gestures that break with the logic of violence, exploitation and selfishness" (Pope Francis 2015, 24 May).

My Invitation

6. Peacebuilding through active nonviolence is the natural and necessary complement to the Church's continuing efforts to limit the use of force by the application of moral norms; she does so by her participation in the work of international institutions and through the competent contribution made by so many Christians to the drafting of legislation at all levels. Jesus himself offers a "manual" for this strategy of peacemaking in the Sermon on the Mount. The eight Beatitudes (cf. *Mt* 5:3–10) provide a portrait of the person we could describe as blessed, good and authentic. Blessed are the meek, Jesus tells us, the merciful and the peacemakers, those who are pure in heart, and those who hunger and thirst for justice.

This is also a programme and a challenge for political and religious leaders, the heads of international institutions, and business and media executives: to apply the Beatitudes in the exercise of their respective responsibilities. It is a challenge to build up society, communities and businesses by acting as peacemakers. It is to show mercy by refusing to discard people, harm the environment or seek to win at any cost. To do so requires "the willingness to face conflict head on, to resolve it and to make it a link in the chain of a new process" (Pope Francis 2013, 227). To act in this way means to choose solidarity as a way of making history and building friendship in society. Active nonviolence is a way of showing that unity is truly more powerful and more fruitful than conflict. Everything in the world is inter-connected (Pope Francis 2016, 24 May, 16, 117, 138). Certainly differences can cause frictions. But let us face them constructively and violently, so that "tensions and oppositions can achieve a diversified and life-giving unity", preserving "what is valid and useful on both sides" (Pope Francis 2013, 228).

I pledge the assistance of the Church in every effort to build peace through active and creative nonviolence. On 1 January 2017, the new Dicastery for Promoting Integral Human Development will begin its work. It will help the Church to promote in an ever more effective way "the inestimable goods of justice, peace, and the care of creation" and concern for "migrants, those in need, the sick, the excluded and marginalized, the imprisoned and the unemployed, as well as victims of armed conflict, natural disasters, and all forms of slavery and torture" (Pope Francis 2016, 17 August). Every such response, however modest, helps to build a world free of violence, the first step towards justice and peace.

In Conclusion

7. As is traditional, I am signing this Message on 8 December, the Solemnity of the Immaculate Conception of the Blessed Virgin Mary. Mary is the Queen of Peace. At the birth of her Son, the angels gave glory to God and wished peace on earth to men and women of good will (cf. *Lk* 2:14). Let us pray for her guidance.

"All of us want peace. Many people build it day by day through small gestures and acts; many of them are suffering, yet patiently persevere in their efforts to be peacemakers" (Pope Francis 2014, 25 May). In 2017, may we dedicate ourselves prayerfully and actively to banishing violence from our hearts, words and deeds, and to becoming nonviolent people and to building nonviolent communities that care for our common home. "Nothing is impossible if we turn to God in prayer. Everyone can be an artisan of peace" (Pope Francis 2016, 20 September).

From the Vatican, 8 December 2016, **Franciscus**

Note

1 Message of His Holiness Pope Francis for the Celebration of the Fiftieth World Day of Peace, 1 January 2017. ©LIBRERIA EDITRICE VATICANA. Reprinted with permission.

References

"The Legend of the Three Companions," *Fonti Francescane*, No. 1469. https://PopeFran ciscantradition.org/PopeFrancis-of-assisi-early-documents/the-founder/the-legend-of-the-three-companions/1157-fa-ed-2-page-66

Mother Teresa, 1979, 11 December. *Nobel Lecture.* https://www.nobelprize.org/nobel_ prizes/peace/laureates/1979/teresa-lecture.html

Pope Benedict XVI, 2007, 18 February. *Angelus.* https://w2.vatican.va/content/benedict-xvi/en/angelus/2007/documents/hf_ben-xvi_ang_20070218.html

Pope Paul VI, 1968, 1 January. *Message for the First World Day of Peace.* http://w2.vatican. va/content/paul-vi/en/messages/peace/documents/hf_p-vi_mes_19671208_i-world-day-for-peace.html

Pope Francis, 2013, 24 November. "Apostolic Exhortation", *Evangelii Gaudium.* http:// w2.vatican.va/content/francesco/en/apost_exhortations/documents/papa-francesco_ esortazione-ap_20131124_evangelii-gaudium.html

Pope Francis, 2014, 25 May. "Regina Coeli", Bethlehem. https://w2.vatican.va/content/ francesco/en/angelus/2014/documents/papa-francesco_regina-coeli-terra-santa_2014 0525.html

Pope Francis, 2014, 7 December. "Message for the Conference on the Humanitarian Impact of Nuclear Weapons". https://w2.vatican.va/content/francesco/en/messages/pont-messages/2014/documents/papa-francesco_20141207_messaggio-conferenza-vienna-nucleare.html

Pope Francis, 2015, 19 November. "Meditation", *The Road of Peace*, Chapel of the *Domus Sanctae Marthae*. https://w2.vatican.va/content/francesco/en/cotidie/2015/documents/papa-francesco-cotidie_20151119_the-way-of-peace.html

Pope Francis, 2015, 24 May. "Encyclical *Laudato Si*". http://w2.vatican.va/content/francesco/en/encyclicals/documents/papa-francesco_20150524_enciclica-laudato-si.html

Pope Francis, 2016, 17 August. "Apostolic Letter", issued *Motu Proprio* instituting the Dicastery for Promoting Integral Human Development. https://w2.vatican.va/content/francesco/en/messages/peace/documents/papa-francesco_20161208_messaggio-l-giornata-mondiale-pace-2017.html#_ftnref23

Pope Francis, 2016, 4 September. "Homily for the Canonization of Mother Teresa of Calcutta". https://w2.vatican.va/content/francesco/en/homilies/2016/documents/papa-francesco_20160904_omelia-canonizzazione-madre-teresa.html

Pope Francis, 2016, 20 September. "Thirst for Peace: Faiths and Cultures in Dialogue" Address in Assisi. http://w2.vatican.va/content/francesco/en/speeches/2016/september/documents/papa-francesco_20160920_assisi-preghiera-pace.html

Pope Francis, 2016, 2 October. "Address at the Interreligious Meeting with the Sheikh of the Muslims of the Caucasus and Representatives of Different Religious Communities, Baku". https://w2.vatican.va/content/francesco/en/messages/peace/documents/papa-francesco_20161208_messaggio-l-giornata-mondiale-pace-2017.html#_ftn14

Pope Francis, 2016, 3 November. "Address to Representatives of Different Religions". https://w2.vatican.va/content/francesco/en/messages/peace/documents/papa-francesco_20161208_messaggio-l-giornata-mondiale-pace-2017.html#_ftn12

Pope Francis, 2016, 5 November. "Address to the Third World Meeting of Popular Movements". https://w2.vatican.va/content/francesco/en/messages/peace/documents/papa-francesco_20161208_messaggio-l-giornata-mondiale-pace-2017.html#_ftnref13

Pope Francis, 2016, 19 March. "Post-Synodal Apostolic Exhortation", *Amoris Laetitia*, 90–130. https://w2.vatican.va/content/dam/francesco/pdf/apost_exhortations/documents/papa-francesco_esortazione-ap_20160319_amoris-laetitia_en.pdf

Saint John Paul II, 1991. *Centesimus Annus*, No. 23. http://w2.vatican.va/content/john-paul-ii/en/encyclicals/documents/hf_jp-ii_enc_01051991_centesimus-annus.html

10

CHRISTIANITY AND ISLAM IN AN AGE OF TRANSITION

Violence or Healing?

Joseph A. Camilleri

In an era of pervasive turbulence, not to say existential crisis, it is well to ask what role religion is playing and might play in the future. Many seek to shed light on the sacred texts and their perspective on conflict generally and war in particular; others examine how this or that religion has intruded into this or that conflict; others still have explored the notion of 'religious violence' or the place of religion in the task of conflict resolution. But the questions we must grapple with are much deeper and the stakes much higher.

Situating Religion in the Global Context

The far-reaching impact of cultural, economic and political changes of the last hundred years is only now beginning to emerge. The two world wars, the Great Depression, the rise of fascism, the Holocaust, the advent of nuclear weapons, the ensuing Cold War and the dissolution of European empires, post-Cold War hegemonic ambitions and now international terrorism and the 'war on terror', involving a succession of great power military interventions, are part of a complex and still unfolding historical dynamic. The 'globalisation of insecurity' is one of its defining characteristics (Camilleri and Falk 2009, 446–457).

Weapon systems, alliances and ideologies with global reach, nuclear proliferation, the long list of collapsed, failed or failing states, the periodic reconfiguration of geopolitical boundaries and the deepening tensions 'between Islam and the West' have meant declining national control over physical space and increasing interpenetration of the national and international domains (Albert, Brock & Wolf, 2000). The sheer scale, speed and intensity of cross-border flows—flows of goods and services, technology, money, arms, pathogens, greenhouse gases, people, images and information—are giving rise to the internationalisation of conflict and a globalised dynamic that feeds and amplifies a deep sense of generalised insecurity. The sovereign national state remains the single most important actor with responsibilities in the field of security, but its sovereignty is steadily eroding, in practice if not in name, as its borders become increasingly porous. Multilateral treaties, conventions and institutions have been created to complement the problem-solving capacities of states, but they have not as yet yielded the desired results. Existing institutions, both national and international, seem unable to meet the challenges posed by the globalisation of insecurity. Expressed a little differently, the organisation of human affairs is suffering from a growing legitimation deficit.

What, then, is to be the role of religion in this period of profound transition? Can it assist humanity to diagnose its current ailments? Can it help to establish the normative foundations for a peaceful and ecologically sustainable world order? Can it generate the wisdom and energy needed to find constructive pathways across geopolitical fault lines that pit one major centre of power against another; economic fault lines that divide the North and South; identity fault lines that polarise states, ethnic and faith communities; and civilisational fault lines, most dramatically between the Orient and Occident?

The questions are all the more salient given the widely acknowledged resurgence of religion (Thomas 2005). Contrary to the expectations of secularisation theory, religious beliefs, rituals and institutions have not given way to a secular ethic. Nor is this resurgence confined to the upsurge of so-called fundamentalist movements, notably in the Muslim world. It encompasses the potent presence of Christianity in American public life, the revival of the Orthodox Church in Russia, the growth of both Catholic and Protestant churches in China, the rise of Evangelical or Charismatic Protestantism in Brazil, other parts of Latin America and the Philippines, and the rapid expansion of Buddhism in a number of Western countries. This global phenomenon cannot be so easily dismissed as the lingering expression of tradition and social irrationality soon to be swept aside by the onset of modernising influences. A recent study estimates that the number of atheists, agnostics and others who do not affiliate with any religion, though increasing in such countries as the United States and France, will decline as a proportion of the world's total population from 16.4% in 2010 to 13.2% in 2010 (Pew Research Center 2015).

Interpreting the Religious Domain

To observe religion's firm hold on the human imagination is one thing; to characterise its actual and potential impact on ethical discourse and practice and, specifically, on the handling of the current turbulence is quite another. The religious domain is difficult to interpret precisely because it is heterogeneous, multidimensional and variable over time. The sacred texts provide a crucial point of entry to the religious domain, but they do not fully capture it. Religion encompasses beliefs, a narrative about God and the universe, attitudes, emotions, experiences, rituals, ties that bind the community of believers and, importantly, a sense of the 'sacred' that makes places, persons, other creatures and objects worthy of empathy, respect and reverence. To make sense of the cognitive, relational, behavioural and ritualistic components of religion, we need both textual and contextual analysis. A study of the sacred texts, the teaching of prophets and the commentaries of widely acknowledged religious scholars and theologians can shed light on the moral principles and rules which are meant to govern the good life and establish a harmonious synthesis of the natural and supernatural worlds. However, they are likely to prove less than illuminating unless we also consider the influences of history, geography and culture on religious beliefs and the fabric of religious communities and institutions as well as the challenges posed by the current social and political conjuncture.

Though all the world's major religions merit careful consideration, no single paper can do justice to such a wide canvas. Even in confining its attention to Christianity and Islam, this paper can offer only a glimpse of what is a vast terrain. These two traditions readily suggest themselves by virtue of their global presence, with the world's Christians numbering some 2.17 billion and Muslims just under 1.6 billion. Together they accounted for 54.6% of the world's population in 2010. But considerations of scale aside, these two traditions are central to the current geopolitical landscape, a position they will continue to occupy indefinitely into the future. Christianity and Islam have had a long, complex and at times difficult relationship that has historically oscillated between dialogue and cooperation on the one hand and profound mistrust and hostility on the other. It is a relationship that continues to underpin a number of conflicts in the Middle East and, to a lesser extent, in Africa and Southeast Asia. More recently, it has emerged as central to Western Europe's self-understanding and its social cohesion and political identity.

The world's major religious traditions can be said to appeal to humanity's higher instincts and to privilege a conception of the cosmos that bestows meaning and purpose on human existence and takes the longer view on humanity's future. In the case of Christianity and Islam, the sacred texts point to a Divine order that is well intentioned towards human beings and working for their well-being as long as they themselves are willing to be faithful to the Divine will as revealed to them and not to upset it by perversion or rebellion. In this sense, both the Christian and Islamic faiths privilege an ethical order centred on such values as justice, mercy and compassion. Yet, when it comes to the organisation of human affairs generally and the role of coercive authority and violence in particular, the prescriptions offered in the Bible and the Qur'an respectively are often ambivalent and at times open to sharply competing interpretations. Several studies have drawn attention to the multiple ways that Christian theology, Islamic law and the history of both traditions have at times justified and at others condemned the use of violence (Johnson and Kelsay 1990). But seldom have they drawn out the implications of such ambiguity for the contemporary relevance of either tradition and its capacity to respond to the current human predicament.

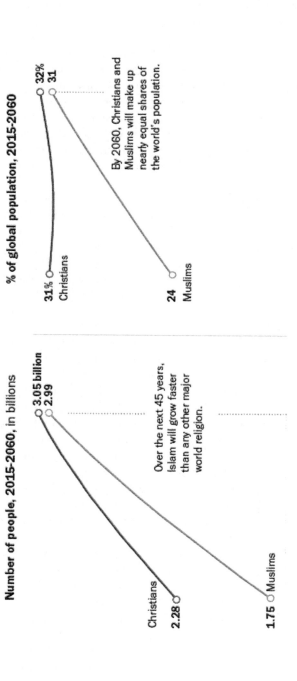

FIGURE 10.1 Projected Change in Global Christian and Muslim Populations, 2015–2060

Source: Pew Research Center, 'The Changing Global Religious Landscape', 5 April 2017 www.pewforum.org/2017/04/05/the-changing-global-religious-landscape/

The Christian Tradition

In the Western world and perhaps more widely Christian approaches to issues of war and peace are generally well known. Much of the Bible, including the Old Testament, portrays God as a loving, merciful and compassionate father who demands righteousness and justice, issues commandments that include a blanket prohibition on killing (Deuteronomy 5:6–21) and offers an eschatological vision of peace where 'the wolf shall dwell with the lamb, and the leopard shall lie down with the young goat, and the calf and the lion and the fattened calf together; and a little child shall lead them' (Isaiah 11:6). And with Jesus comes the Sermon on the Mount, which recognises the 'peacemakers' as 'children of God', and announces a new dispensation:

> And if anyone requires you to go one mile, go two miles with him . . . I say this to you, love your enemies and pray for those who persecute you; so that you may be children of your Father in heaven, for he causes his sun to rise on the bad as well as the good, and sends down rain to fall on the upright and the wicked alike.
>
> *(Matthew 5:1–45)*

Yet, violence is hardly absent from the biblical account. The brutal murder of Abel by his brother Cain is followed by God's protection of the murderer Cain. Seeing the wickedness of humankind, Yahweh regrets his decision to create the earth: 'I shall rid the surface of the earth of the human beings whom I created—human and animal, the creeping things and the birds of heaven—for I regret having made them' (Genesis 6:7). It is Yahweh who sends fire and brimstone upon Sodom and Gomorrah and whose blessing and guidance are decisive in the destruction of the Egyptian army in the Red Sea (Exodus 14:1–30). Similarly with the conquest of Canaan and the destruction of Jericho: 'They enforced the curse of destruction on everyone in the city: men and women, young and old, including the oxen, the sheep and the donkeys, slaughtering them all' (Joshua 6:21). Indeed, the whole biblical account is presented as a series of battles between good and evil, light and darkness, an account that finds its culmination in the Book of Revelation and the cosmic battle that sees the powers of evil conquered and wiped out by God and His angels. Whether this apocalyptic account refers to actual events or, most likely, is a symbolic representation of the ongoing struggle between good and evil, there is no denying the ferocity with which this struggle is depicted. Jesus himself is reported to have said that he came 'not to bring peace but a sword' (Matthew 10:34). When visiting the Temple in Jerusalem, we are told by all four evangelists, Jesus physically confronted the merchants and money lenders: 'Making a whip out of cord, he drove them all out of the Temple, sheep and cattle as well, scattered the money changers' coins, knocked their tables over'

(John 2:15). Paul, we should remember, counselled submission to civil authority, arguing that it derived from God.

> So anyone who disobeys an authority is rebelling against God's ordinance; and rebels must expect to receive the condemnation they deserve . . . it is not for nothing that the symbol of authority is the sword: it is there to serve God, too, as his avenger, to bring retribution to wrongdoers.
> *(Romans 13:4)*

Indeed, much of atonement theology, which seeks to explain the crucifixion, can be said to legitimise the use of violence, at least by implication. According to an early version of the atonement theory God allowed his son to be killed as a ransom payment to redeem humankind that had become the captive of Satan. God then triumphed over Satan by raising Jesus from the dead. A subsequent version, which continues to have currency, argues that human sin had offended God's honour and upset the Divine order. Jesus' death was necessary to satisfy God's honour and so restore the Divine order. These two versions of atonement doctrine suggest, in different ways, that 'satisfaction depends on a divinely sanctioned death as that which is necessary to satisfy the offended Divine entity, whether God or God's law or God's honor' (Weaver 2001).

In the light of the deeply embedded ambiguity of the biblical message, it is not surprising that Christians should have reached different conclusions about the meaning of violence in human affairs and the most appropriate ways of managing violence in both its personal and societal manifestations. Much has been made in this regard of the contrast in Christian discourse and practice between the nonviolent or pacifist tradition on the one hand and the just war doctrine on the other. In some respects, the pacifist/nonviolent reading of the life and teaching of Jesus is the more complex in part because it oscillates between a relatively passive shunning of physical violence (or pacifism) and an active resistance to evil (nonviolence), and in particular to injustice.

An added complication arises from the tendency to contrast the pacifism of the church of the first three centuries with the progressive acceptance of the use of force in what is often referred to as the post-Constantinian accommodation (Bainton 1960; Cadoux 1982). The contrast, however, appears to have been overstated. The pacific philosophy that supposedly guided the early church may be attributable less to a definitive or comprehensive commitment to nonviolence than to the widespread belief that the 'Reign of God' was at hand. As expectations of the second coming began to fade, Christians turned their attention to more immediate concerns. Adjusting to life under the empire led many to accept military service (Schaff 1962; Swift 1983; Childress 1984). The condemnation of war, it should be said, is relatively absent from the writings of the early church fathers. Clement of Alexandria (c.150–215) was perhaps the first to introduce key elements of what would become the just war doctrine. However, it was only with Ambrose (c.339–397) that we begin to see a fuller articulation of the concept. While preserving the Christian presumption against the use of violence, he is prepared to entertain the idea that war can be justly waged if it is to defend—not so much self as the wider community, so long as agreements are honoured and the defeated are treated with mercy. Ambrose went so far as to propose protection of religious orthodoxy as a possible justification for war.

The young Augustine (354–430) went further, arguing that it was just to persecute heretics in the interests of their own spiritual health and the safety of the state. He justified the use of force by the state to compel heretics and schismatics to rejoin the Church. Augustine's early view of war is especially remarkable when viewed with a modern lens:

> When war is undertaken in obedience to God, who would rebuke, or humble, or crush the pride of man, it must be allowed to be a righteous war; for even the wars which arise from human passion cannot harm the eternal well-being of God, nor even hurt His saints ... Since, therefore, a righteous man ... may do the duty belonging to his position in the State in fighting by the order of his sovereign ... how much more must the man be blameless who carries on war on the authority of God?
>
> *(Augustine 400, Book XXII)*

In later years Augustine's approach to war underwent considerable change. He no longer viewed killing by a soldier as simply the carrying out of a Divine command. Nor was he willing to give the conduct of the Roman emperor a moral blank cheque. Amidst the violence and chaos of a declining empire, he now viewed war as a tragic event in which the Christian, as the righteous citizen of the City of God, might need to participate. War, and the taking of human life, was the legacy of man's fallen nature (Augustine 1956). But to be just, war had to:

a) serve a just cause (e.g. defence from external invasion; defence of allies; punishment for a nation's wrongdoings; securing the return of what was wrongfully taken);
b) be well intentioned—seek to restore the peace; shun conquest or expansion; avoid actions likely to provoke a war;
c) be declared by a competent authority.

Moreover, the conduct of war itself had to accord with the principles of justice. The use of force had to be a proportional response to the wrong to be avenged. It had to discriminate between combatants and non-combatants, scrupulously observe treaties and show respect for the enemy. But in line with the primacy he accorded spiritual over temporal goods, Augustine saw temporal peace as at best an anomalous condition. It stood in stark contrast to the ultimate peace which was the preserve of the City of God and the inner peace which pilgrim citizens of the City of God could experience during their sojourn on earth (Lanagan 1984).

Augustine's theology of war and peace, we should note, gained relatively little traction in Eastern Christendom, and even in the West it would lie dormant for many centuries. The Crusades, a series of intermittent military campaigns sanctioned by various Popes in the Middle Ages from 1096 to 1487, though they may have been conceived as just, cannot be said to have involved a direct application of just war doctrine as formulated by Augustine and further developed by Aquinas. The crusades were more in tune with Gratian's Decretum (c.1148), which emphasised 'authority, a declaration of war, and the avenging of injuries' and argued that 'excommunicates could be killed without committing murder, knights had a moral duty to wage war against heretics, and bishops could command wars for Church purposes' (Duncan 2003). Crusaders were engaged in something more than mere defence against an unjust attack; they were fighting not only for the defence of Christianity against its enemies but also for God. The crusade was thus meant to have a salvific effect. As one historian has put it, the inner attitude of the crusader 'made his actions meritorious before God', and war against the Muslim enemy was all the more commendable in that it was waged on behalf of 'threatened fellow Christians' (Jaspert 2006, 16).

The conditions of the just war were subsequently refined. In the case of Aquinas, they were reduced to three conditions: first, war must be declared by a proper authority and not by private citizens or groups; second, it must be waged for a just cause; and third, there must be a rightful intention which boils down to the advancement of good and the avoidance of evil. It was Aquinas' intent that the use of the sword should be regulated by two interlinked principles: charity and prudence. Charity because the decision to use force must be animated by the intention to ensure the conditions for human flourishing, and prudence because when military activity is directed to the common good, it must proceed prudently, for to do otherwise would be to prejudice the common good (Hittinger 2000).

In the post-Medieval world, the just war doctrine would gain increasing currency both in its religious and secular renditions. However, notwithstanding its commendable underlying intent, its capacity to exercise an effective moral, let alone political, restraint on the frequency and intensity of war has been questioned with increasing severity. Its diminished appeal in a century marked by total war and weapons of mass destruction is hardly surprising. It is difficult to imagine a circumstance in which the use of nuclear weapons or any other military action likely to provoke their use can ever be deemed to be just. The lethality and long-term health and planetary effects of these weapons are inconsistent with any concept of proportionality or any distinction between defence and offence, combatant and non-combatant and even between friend and foe. The risk of uncontrollable escalation and the computerisation of strategic decision-making render the exercise of political, let alone moral, judgement virtually impossible.

Modern warfare has become effectively incompatible with Thomistic notions of charity and prudence.

Other considerations have also fuelled the critique of just war thinking. The post-1945 period, far from ushering in a new era of peace, has witnessed an endless succession of wars, some of extraordinary ferocity resulting in wholesale civilian casualties and unprecedented levels of forced displacement.[1] Most governments involved in these wars, including every Western government, have claimed both their cause and their conduct in war to be just. Yet, there is little evidence that the policy makers or war planners in Washington, London, Paris or Moscow that make these claims have actually engaged in a serious study of just war requirements and how they might apply to the various wars they are prosecuting. Nor have church leaders in most countries been prepared to question the legitimacy of these wars, and where they have their assessments have seldom been clearly, forcefully or persistently articulated. They have certainly not spelt out what the implications might be for the Christian political or military leader prosecuting an unjust war, let alone for the Christian soldier or the civilian engaged in a supporting role.

The most serious shortcoming of just war principles is their elusiveness. They don't easily translate into a coherent course of action for either the individual or the polity. The argument that violence may at times be necessary in order to resist evil (e.g. mass atrocity crimes) or achieve a positive good (e.g. national liberation) is not terribly helpful when determining the ethical status of military intervention in Afghanistan, Iraq, Libya or Syria. The perennial difficulty of determining whether war has been declared—or external intervention has been sought—by a competent authority is compounded by a rapidly evolving international system in which many states are described as 'weak,' 'failed', 'failing' or 'collapsed' states. Moreover, it is becoming less and less clear whether the decision to use force can still be regarded as the preserve of a state authority or whether it needs the express authorisation of the United Nations.

Against this backdrop of national and international disorder, the last few decades have seen a revival of Christian nonviolence in both theology and practice. Contemporary exponents of the tradition draw on the Gospel and the teachings of Jesus, his 'victory on the cross and resurrection and the intermittent witness of the Church' (Cornell 2015). They find inspiration not only in the words and deeds of the early church fathers (Justin Martyr, Tertullian and Origen), but in the witness of Francis of Assisi, the ministry of peacemaking that has persisted as a central element of Franciscan spirituality, the mysticism of the fourteenth-century preacher Meister Eckhart, the contribution of the peace churches from the seventeenth century to the present and contemporary advocates and practitioners, including Dorothy Day, Thomas Merton, Martin Luther King, and many outside the Christian tradition, notably Gandhi and Thích Nhất Hạnh. It should be said that the contemporary Christian contribution to non-violence, at least in the West, has been most clearly expressed in the politics of protest, whether in opposition to nuclear deterrence, to the Vietnam War and other military interventions, to apartheid and other forms of racial discrimination, or to human rights violations. Simply put, advocacy of non-violence has been far more articulate when diagnosing and resisting evil than when propounding an alternative to ailing institutions and faltering policies and practices.

In the light of the enormity of the challenge that defines the current period of transition, it is understandable that many have grown tired of what they perceive to be the sometimes sterile debate that pits the just war and nonviolent traditions against each other. In practice the gap separating the two may be less dramatic than is often imagined. A maximalist application of just war standards would rule out not just a future nuclear war but the vast majority of current armed conflicts. At the same time, given the pervasiveness of violence in the international system, continuing efforts have been made to restrict the occasions when states can legally resort to the unilateral use of force and to regulate the use of force on the battlefield. The adoption of the UN Charter, the considerable development of international humanitarian law and the establishment of the International Criminal Court attest to the importance of such efforts.

But many in the Christian world do not consider this to be enough, which explains why they have in recent decades stressed the need for more radical approaches to disarmament, peacemaking and peacebuilding. Within mainstream Catholicism, John XXIII's encyclical *Pacem in Terris* (1963), the Second Vatican Council (1962–1965) and in particular one of the four constitutions resulting from it, the Pastoral Constitution *The Church in the Modern World Gaudium Et Spes* (1965), may be considered landmark developments. The trend has continued with the release of several other encyclicals and papal pronouncements, most recently *Laudato Si'* (2015) by Pope Francis, and a great number of national statements, notably the 1983 pastoral letter of the US Catholic Conference of Bishops, *The Challenge of Peace*. A recent conference convened by the Pontifical Council for Justice and Peace and Pax Christi International called on the Catholic Church to:

- integrate Gospel nonviolence explicitly into the life, including the sacramental life, and work of the Church through dioceses, parishes, agencies, schools, universities, seminaries ...
- promote nonviolent practices and strategies (e.g., nonviolent resistance, restorative justice, trauma healing, unarmed civilian protection, conflict transformation, and peacebuilding ...
- initiate a global conversation on nonviolence within the Church, with people of other faiths, and with the larger world ...
- no longer use or teach 'just war theory'; continue advocating for the abolition of war ...
- ... challenge unjust world powers and to support and defend those ... whose work for peace and justice puts their lives at risk (Pax Christi International 2016).

This trend is mirrored in the stream of official statements issued by other Christian Churches and by the ecumenical movement. The World Council of Churches (WCC) has played a crucial role in this regard. Among its notable contributions have been the *World Conference on Church and Society* held in Geneva in 1966 in response to the challenges of a divided world in the Cold War era; the *Programme to Combat Racism* that brought the churches together in the struggle against the apartheid regime in South Africa: and the *Decade to Overcome Violence: Churches Seeking Reconciliation and Peace 2001–2010*. A later section will consider the potential of these pioneering developments and the still unresolved questions that Christian peacemaking will need to address in the coming decades.

The Islamic Tradition

When it comes to the politics of justice and peace, Islamic discourse and practice share a good many of the ambiguities we encounter in the Christian experience, except that in this case the contestation is, if anything, sharper and the questions to be addressed are even more complex.

When explicating the Islamic approach to the temporal order and specifically to issues of peace and war, care must be taken to distinguish between the sacred sources, specifically the Qur'an and the Sunnah (or the traditions of the Prophet Muhammad) and the large body of Islamic jurisprudence (or fiqh). These in turn have to be distinguished from the understanding and motives of the individual believer. The task of explication becomes especially difficult when the believer engages in violence and claims that he is acting in accordance with Islamic law (Shariah). As we have seen, the issue of religiously inspired violence is not peculiar to Islam, but there are aspects of the relationship between religion and violence that are specific to it.

Before proceeding any further, it may be helpful to digress for a moment to note that the rapidly expanding literature on the role of religion in contemporary national and international politics makes frequent reference to the notion of 'religious violence', though from vastly different perspectives. For some, though all religions have within them elements that justify and even encourage violence, most religious actors do not engage in violence or, if they do, they do not invoke religious belief to justify their violence. In other words, religious violence is generally marginal to the religious life (Juergensmeyer 2003). In this sense, contemporary Islamism—and the terrorist actions which it inspires—is said to occupy the margins of Islam in that it represents the response of a small minority which, in common with other religious actors that engage in violence, feels that the prevailing culture is indifferent or hostile to religious belief. Others argue that religion is inherently violent because all faiths are ultimately in competition with each other—they are all competing for a scarce commodity. Religion's hold on the human imagination is said to depend on access to transcendent goods which constitute the core of their identity and for which the believer is willing to kill and to die (Avalos 2005). Others still are altogether dismissive of the 'religious violence' frame of reference. They see Western history as having created a false dichotomy between the religious and secular domains in which religion comes to be seen as irrational, illiberal and violent. By definition, religion becomes normatively violent.

This latter interpretation is especially relevant because it has been a feature of the European imagination dating back to the Middle Ages to view Islam with fear and suspicion, and portray Islamic *jihad* as 'holy war', understood a commitment to spread Islam by the sword. The ethos of violence is said to lie at the core of Islam. The Islamic response to this highly negative portrayal has taken many forms, and given rise to many lines of argument.

While Islam entertains the use of force in certain circumstance, the weight of Islamic scholarship across the different jurisprudential schools portrays Islam as a religion deeply committed to justice and peace. As one writer puts it, the established position of Islam is that war is not the intent of Islam and that 'peace is the natural state in which God created man as well as other things' (Adeyemo 2013, 56). One of the main attributes of Allah is said to be 'peace' (*'al-Salaam*); the word Islam (*Islaam*) is derived from the same root as the word Peace (*Salaam*): S L M. Islam is understood as a call to service: service to Allah and through him to the whole of humanity. In this sense the metaphysical foundation of peace and peaceful co-existence lies in the unity of Allah's creation. For Islam prayer, *zakat*, fasting and the *Hajj* are different ways of expressing compassion and human solidarity. Respect for human life, a deep commitment to justice, mercy and the unity of the human family are values that permeate much of the Qur'an and the Prophet's message. A few examples will suffice:

> O you who believe! Stand out firmly for justice, as witnesses to Allah, even though it be against yourselves, or your parents, or your kin, be he rich or poor. Allah is a better protector to both (than you). So follow not the desires lest you may avoid justice.
>
> *(Qur'an 4:135)*

> O ye who believe! Be steadfast witnesses for Allah in equity, and let not hatred of any people seduce you that ye deal not justly. Deal justly, that is nearer to your duty. Observe your duty to Allah. Lo! Allah is informed of what ye do.
>
> *(Qur'an 5:8)*

> And if two factions of the believers fight, you should make peace between them. But if one of them continues to do wrong to the other, fight the transgressor until they return to Allah's command. If they then do so, then make a just peace between them for Allah loves the just ones.
>
> *(Qur'an 49:8)*

We believe in Allah, and the revelation given to us, and to Abraham, Ishmael, Isaac, Jacob, and the Tribes, and that given to Moses and Jesus, and that given to (all) Prophets from their Lord: We make no difference between one and another of them: and we are (all) *muslimuun* [surrendering to Allah's Will].

(Qur'an 2:136)

O people, your Lord is one and your father Adam is one. There is no virtue of an Arab over a foreigner nor a foreigner over an Arab, and neither white over black nor black over white, except through righteousness. Have I not delivered the message?

(The Prophet's Farewell Sermon, source: Musnad Ahmad 22978)

Side by side, however, with this all-embracing message is the distinction drawn between those who hear Allah's word and submit to His will and those who do not:

So if they believe in the like of that which you believe, then they are rightly guided, but if they turn away, then they are only in opposition. So Allah will suffice you against them. And He is the All-Hearer, the All-Knower.

(Qur'an 2:137)

Simply put, though Islam is a religion of peace, it must be prepared to oppose oppression:

And prepare against them whatever you are able of power and of steeds of war by which you may terrify the enemy of Allah and your enemy and others besides them whom you do not know [but] whom Allah knows. And whatever you spend in the cause of Allah will be fully repaid to you, and you will not be wronged.

(Qur'an 8:60)

The question arises: what are the guidelines for determining when and how it is right to resist, if necessary by the use of force?

To address this question, I begin by dwelling on the exposition of the Islamic law of war offered by Al-Dawoody. He is at pains to emphasise the failings of Western scholars (Khadouri 1955; Firestone 1999), especially when it comes to an understanding of *jihad*, and sharply distinguishes the outsider (Western) from the insider (Islamic) literature on the subject. He quotes approvingly the handful of Western scholars who have acknowledged that Western 'scholarship on Islamic normative tradition on war is considerably less well developed' (Johnson 1997, 21). His first step is to differentiate between the Prophet's preaching and fighting missions. Of the total of twenty-seven engagements (*ghazawāt*), Al-Dawoody identifies nine as having involved armed hostilities, and all of them, he concludes, were defensive in nature. They were conducted in response to the offensive attacks launched by the Quraysh and associated clans which saw the growing acceptance of the Prophet's leadership as a threat to their economy, power and prestige. The advent of Islam, we are reminded, occurred at a time when a state of war was the normal condition of relations between the various tribes in Arabia (Al-Dawoody 2011, 11–41).

Simply put, the argument is that the Prophet's leadership was faithful to the Qur'anic injunction which prohibits aggression, and permits recourse to war only as defence against aggression. The relevant Qur'anic texts, as set out in the Medinan revelations, are clear on this point:

> Permission to fight is given to those (i.e. believers against disbelievers), who are fighting them, (and) because they (believers) have been wronged, and surely, Allah is able to give them (believers) victory. Those who have been expelled from their homes unjustly only because they said: 'Our Lord is Allah.'—For had it not been that Allah checks one set of people by means of another, monasteries, churches, synagogues, and mosques, wherein the Name of Allah is mentioned, much would surely have been pulled down. Verily, Allah will help those who help His (Cause). Truly, Allah is All-Strong, All-Mighty.
>
> *(Qur'an 22:39–40)*

The kind of fighting that is permitted is given further clarification in this passage:

> And fight in the Way of Allah those who fight you, but transgress not the limits. Truly, Allah likes not the transgressors. And kill them wherever you find them, and turn them out from where they have turned you out. And Al-Fitnah [persecution] is worse than killing. And fight not with them at Al-Masjid-al-Haram (the sanctuary at Makkah), unless they (first) fight you there. But if they attack you, then kill them. Such is the recompense of the disbelievers. But if they cease, then Allah is Oft-Forgiving, Most Merciful. And fight them until there is no more Fitnah [persecution] and (all and every kind of) worship is for Allah (Alone). But if they cease, let there be no transgression except against Az-Zalimun (the polytheists, and wrong-doers, etc.) [often translated as the oppressors or wrongdoers]. The sacred month is for the sacred month, and for the prohibited things, there is the Law of Equality (Qisas). Then whoever transgresses the prohibition against you, you transgress likewise against him. And fear Allah, and know that Allah is with Al-Muttaqun (the pious—see V.2:2).
>
> *(Qur'an 2:190–194)*

These two passages may be said to provide the basis for what is permitted (defence against aggression and persecution) and prohibited (aggression) under Islam, but also an indication of the restraints that must be observed in war, including the principle of proportionality.

It is worth noting here that for Al-Dawoody, as for Taymiyyah, Abu Zahrah and other leading classical and contemporary scholars, unbelief (or *Kufr*) does not of itself provide a justification for war. It is only when Islam is confronted by the unbeliever's hostility and aggression that the intrinsic right to self-defence comes into play. Differently expressed, it is the unbeliever's use of force aimed at preventing the preaching of Islam which provides 'a justification for the recourse to war, that is, *jihad* in its limited sense' (Al-Dawoody 2013, 84). The point made repeatedly by Al-Dawoody and others is that the use of force is entertained only as a last resort and is but one element of the all-encompassing notion of *jihad*. It is a reaction to the wrongdoing of others, to the persecution of Islam, to Muslims being forced to renounce their religion. Contrary to the view shared by a good number of Western scholars—and, it should be said, some Islamic scholars—the alternative view of *jihad* rejects the idea of a permanent state of belligerence with non-believers and emphasises instead the concept of self-exertion. *Jihad* is said to refer primarily to effort or struggle, as much spiritual as material, whether in defence of one's home or as self-purification from evil desires (Abou El Fadl 2000).

If peace is the norm and war is to be considered a departure from the norm, an anomaly, even a disease, what constitutes for Islam the political context within which the use of force becomes permissible, perhaps necessary? The answer to this question, though contained fundamentally in the Qur'an and the Sunnah, is to be found in the reasoning of Islamic jurists (*fiqh*) who, attached to different schools of law, have sought from classical to modern times to extract from the primary sources of Islamic law the particular rules or guidelines that are to apply to contemporary practical situations. Al-Dawoody argues that the defensive character of *jihad* features in the work of several early classical jurists, and that though many of the rules of international law formulated during this period were based on the assumption of a state of war between Islamic and non-Islamic states, this assumption rested not on a reading of Islamic sources but on prevailing political realities. He concedes that another position, propounded by al-Shafi'i and some Hanbali jurists, requires Muslims to fight unbelievers if they refuse to accept Islam or submit to Muslim rule. However, he notes that this provision applies only to Arab polytheists, and that non-Arab polytheists and people of the book have the added option of paying *jizyah* (an annual tax) if they are to be spared. Moreover, al-Shafi'is interpretation, which rests on the theory that the Qur'anic texts 9:5 and 9:29 abrogate all other texts and relevant Hadiths, is said to be at odds on this point with the other major classical schools of jurisprudence and the mainstream of contemporary Islamic scholarship. These differences of interpretation are reflected in the way classical jurists conceptualised the division of the world into three spheres: *dar al-Islam* (house of Islam/house of peace), *dar al-Harb* (house of war) and *dar al-Sulh* (house of covenant or accommodation). However, the different ways in which these three spheres and their interrelationships were articulated are widely thought to have been a reflection of historical circumstances and to have lost whatever significance they may have once had.

As with Christian notions of just war, the Islamic conception is clearly subject to interpretation. Some issues remain contentious, while others are not directly or persuasively addressed. Even if one accepts the view that force may be used only for purposes of defence, we are still left with the perennial difficulty of distinguishing between offence and defence. What appears defensive to one side can easily appear aggressive to another. From this problematic distinction follow a set of other troublesome questions: Who is to be considered the aggressor in a given conflict—the one who attacks first or the one who threatens to attack first? What degree of threat is severe enough to warrant military retaliation? At what point can the military build-up by one side be justifiably interpreted by the other side as indicating aggressive intent? And, who has the authority to provide a definitive answer to these questions? These are the very questions that have plagued interstate relations in the modern period.

Given the vastness and complexity of the sacred texts (Qur'an and Hadiths), the use of one text in preference to another can easily lead to divergent and at times contradictory conclusions. Consensus at any given time may be difficult to detect even within the confines of the Sunni branch of Islam. Determining the detailed provisions of Islamic law generally and international law in particular becomes especially taxing when account is taken of three other complicating factors. The first has to do with the question of abrogation (*naskh*) whereby one Shariah ruling may be suspended in favour of another or altogether superseded by it. Abrogation applies almost exclusively to the Qur'an and the Sunnah, but is understood to be confined to the lifetime of the Prophet. Especially with regard to the Qur'an, there is disagreement both in principle and on the number of instances in which *naskh* occurred. A second difficulty facing modern Islamic jurisprudence stems from the actions of autocratic regimes in much of the Muslim world, which have found it expedient to exercise direct or indirect control over religious and scholarly institutions. The net effect has been to circumscribe the independence of religious scholarship, reducing it often to an instrument of government, thereby diminishing its standing in the Muslim community and creating a vacuum which marginal and at times extremist elements of dubious religious and intellectual competence have tried to fill. A third factor limiting the efficacy of Modern Islamic jurisprudence has been its inability to internalise the impact of globalisation on economic, cultural and political relationships within and between countries. Of particular relevance in this context is the emergence of sizeable and rapidly growing Muslim communities in much of the Western world and the transnational challenges to security which exceed the problem-solving capacities of national institutions and transcend the religious and ideological divisions of an earlier age.

It is nevertheless the case that a number of voices in both Muslim majority and Muslim minority countries have begun to articulate new ways in which

Islam can join the international conversation on the defining issues of the current period of transition. Some have drawn attention to Islam's past and future contribution to international law generally and to humanitarian law in particular (Ali and Rehman 2005). Especially relevant in this context are the rules of warfare developed by Islamic jurisprudence, including the various categories of protected persons (children, women, the elderly, the physically and mentally disabled and the sick) and the important distinction between combatants and enemy non-combatants (Cockayne 2002; Haruna, Bukar and Karoumi 2014; Bennounne 1994). Others, drawing on the Prophet's example, especially during the Meccan period, but also on Islamic scripture and religious teachings, have pointed to a rich reservoir of resources which can be brought to bear on the peaceful resolution of conflicts, including a range of mediation, peacemaking and consultative strategies and practices (Abu-Nimer 2001).

From Legalistic Prescription to Holistic Vision

As the preceding survey makes clear, both Christianity and Islam have had a chequered history when addressing the violence and injustice embedded in the social, legal and political structures of the day. The sacred texts speak of a loving, compassionate and merciful God, and love of God and love of neighbour are presented as the supreme requirement of faith. But, as we have seen, in matters of social and political organisation, the exercise of authority and decisions on war and peace, the texts are not entirely devoid of ambiguity. Though peace is the irreplaceable aspiration, violence is seen by many as an inescapable reality, which therefore permits—indeed, requires—the use of force in certain prescribed circumstances.

When it comes to practice, the following summary may be simplistic but not wholly inaccurate. Historically, a small minority of Christians and Muslims have pursued the cause of peace and justice in exemplary fashion, often at great personal cost, because they have understood this to be at the core of their faith as revealed to them by God and His prophets. Another small minority have directly promoted violence and injustice, either oblivious to the tenets of their faith or seeking justification through dubious claims that they were acting in the name of their religion or in obedience to God's will. Probably the majority of Christians and Muslims have been happy to follow the lead of their religious and political leaders without giving much thought to the spiritual and ethical implications, contenting themselves with a privatised or at least ritualised view of their faith.

If Christianity and Islam are to respond to the current human predicament by appealing to the deeper wisdom and nobler sentiments they each embody, religious praxis in both cases may need to shift its centre of gravity. This section of the chapter and the one that follows address respectively the two key dimensions of such a shift: vision and praxis.

While drawing inspiration from scripture and tradition, Christianity and Islam need to fashion a vision of the human future which points to the challenges ahead and to how believers are called upon to respond. Rather than focus on a legalistic analysis of the relative scriptural standing of just war versus non-violence or seek to frame a long list of commands and prohibitions, a more valuable exercise would be for Christianity and Islam to reflect on how their understanding of God can facilitate and guide this journey. If God has revealed himself first and foremost as a loving, compassionate and forgiving God, then it behoves these two Abrahamic faiths—religious leaders in conversation with the faithful—to think through in some depth how they propose to bring love, compassion and forgiveness to the centre of their ministry. As Ted Grimsrud puts it, if the Christian sees Jesus as revelatory of God, then he cannot see God's power as in any way 'a projection of human power politics' (Grimsrud 2003). Kaufman expresses the same insight, but in a more dramatic and positive formulation. He refers to Christ's appearance on earth as ushering in a new order of relationships, 'a living and significant moment and force in human affairs', so that men and women caught up in this vision

> now felt drawn to give themselves in work directed toward the transformation of our inhuman world—with its warring and self-destructive practices and institutions, selves and communities—into the 'kingdom of God', that is into those communities of love and peace and justice in which all could find their full integrity and self-respect.
>
> *(Kaufman 1995, 389)*

Similarly in Islam, leading thinkers have pointed to the process of intellectual and spiritual renewal as inextricably linked with *ijtihad* and 'the best tool or a quantum-phase transition to improve thinking patterns, reassess the present situation, push forth reform agendas and build up a forward-looking vision' (Altwaijri 2015, 14) Others have called for the re-interpretation of Islamic concepts:

> *Umma* is easily 'universalisable'. In a period of globalization where people are becoming citizens of the global village they are in reality members of the same community. Thus the *Umma* of Islam (*Ummat al-Islamiyya*) may be extended to the *Umma* of humankind (*Ummat al-Insaniyya*).
>
> *(Mozaffari 2002, 212)*

Several Islamic principles clearly have universal applicability, not least equality of human beings and rejection of racism. Islam's focus on justice (*'adala*) and the virtues of compassion (*sabr*) and solidarity (*ta'awun*) have particular resonance in a world system so lacking in these attributes. In the same vein, a number of Islamic scholars have called for a renewed focus on peacebuilding, tolerance, dialogue and patience, which they see as integral to the transformative power of Divine revelation, the Hadiths and the Islamic tradition (Abu-Nimer 2001, 229–232).

From Discourse to Practice

It is possible then for both Islam and Christianity to derive from their respective scriptures, narratives and scholarly traditions a coherent and compelling vision of human destiny attuned to the trials and tribulations of a globalising yet broken world. This should not be taken to mean that the task will be an easy one or in any way assured of success. In any case, articulating such a vision is but a necessary first step which will not of itself bear fruit unless it is accompanied by a second, equally important step. For the vision to command attention, it needs to be appropriated not just by a few sages, religious leaders or scholars, but by a substantial cross-section of believers. It has to animate a profound renewal of the religious experience of the community of believers and infuse the life of prayer and observance of other religious obligations, customs and practices. Simply put, it has to give content and meaning to the concrete conditions of everyday life.

The shift from the purely reflective and scholarly to the experiential dimensions of the renewed religious vision of the future must take into account a number of strategic considerations. Three merit particular attention: one is endogenous to the religion and refers to institutional and pedagogical practice; the other two are exogenous and concern relations with political authority on the one hand and with other faiths and intellectual movements on the other.

Religious institutions, even in the case of Islam which is more loosely organised and usually has a more decentralised clerical establishment, are critical to religion's role in society. They largely shape the manner in which the vision is articulated, propagated and experienced (Wilkinson 2012). The institutional infrastructure of religion includes the organisations, laws and decision-making processes which govern relations among believers. They wield authority in the interpretation of sacred texts, organisation of rites and rituals and application of the teachings of founders and prophets. They largely influence the pedagogical processes which transmit the religion from one generation to the next. The running of religious educational institutions (seminaries, monasteries, theological colleges, universities, schools, madrassas, study circles in churches and mosques, bookshops, libraries, websites) plays a vital role in shaping religious faithfulness (Oxford Encyclopedia of the Islamic World 2009; Thomas and Lamport 2015). The question here is the extent to which these institutions, through their ethos, curriculum and pedagogy, enable the community of believers to engage with the defining issues of social, economic and political life, and equip them to live harmoniously and creatively with each other, with people of other faiths and with the wider community generally. In the case of both Islam and Christianity, current pedagogical practice leaves a great deal to be desired.

This brings us to the external environment. People of faith do not live in isolation. They relate in one way or another to the political and economic norms and policies which shape the structure and distribution of authority, power, status and wealth locally, nationally and internationally. The question here is relatively simple, though the answer is inescapably complex: Are people of religious faith, as individuals and communities, able to influence such norms, policies and structures in ways which privilege the dignity of the human person, the satisfaction of basic human needs and the peaceful settlement of disputes?

Perhaps the single most powerful constraint bearing upon the religious ethic is the state itself, and the coercive apparatus on which it is based in both its internal and external conduct (Fox 2008, 12–31). The actual or threatened use of force has been a constant feature of the political landscape. In both industrial and developing states, political repression has been widespread, with ethnic and religious minorities often the victims of wholesale discrimination by states, whether by commission or omission.

As a general proposition, both Christianity and Islam have, for different reasons and in different ways, found it difficult to address the shortcomings of the modern state, to construct credible responses to the misuse of power and the attendant failure to integrate ethical principles into decision-making processes and institutions. How might we explain this widespread paucity of discursive and practical intervention? The operation of two deeply entrenched ideologies, each the antithesis of the other, provides a partial answer: the 'separation of church and state' on the one hand and the 'fusion of religion and state' on the other.

The first principle is often interpreted to mean that God and politics do not mix, that religion is essentially a private matter, and that personal spirituality cannot or should not inform one's role in the public sphere. Taken to its ultimate conclusion, this principle limits religion's capacity to inform collective decisions. It absolves religion from nurturing a social conscience, from articulating the ethical principles that can guide the affairs of state. The second principle is equally prejudicial because, by making religion and state virtually inseparable—at times by placing a religious or clerical class in charge of the state—religion is denied the capacity to evaluate the ethical propriety of state actions and institutional practices (Besier 2008). Paradoxically, both ideological premises have the same practical effect: they both clip the wings of the religious imagination, and substitute instead a stultifying isolationism in one case and a constricting pragmatism on the other. Religion is more likely to uphold ethical standards and be able to point the way to peace with justice if it intimately engages in the public sphere, contributing to the deliberations and decisions that vitally affect the human future. To remain true to its spiritual impulse, religion must be able to speak truth to power.

Another factor which has curtailed Islam's and Christianity's capacity to act as a persuasive advocate of humane and legitimate governance is the pronounced tendency of religious establishments to intervene in the political sphere in defence of self-interested objectives. The various causes which those in positions of authority often espouse with predictable vociferousness and at times intransigence generally fall into two categories: political pressure designed to protect and expand the physical infrastructure of religious establishments (not just places of worship but schools, hospitals and fundraising arrangements) on which depend their authority and prestige; and advocacy of certain rules and regulations which form part of personal morality, with particular reference to sexual relations. A third tendency straddling the two categories is the attempt of predominantly Christian or Islamic societies to acquire or maintain privileged positions vis-à-vis minority faiths, with respect to moral code, protection of physical assets and access to public funds, whether through outright grants, funding of religious educational and other institutions or tax exemptions. The net effect of such narrowly based advocacy is to blunt religion's capacity to be an effective voice on behalf of the 'other' and in defence of religious and cultural pluralism. The net effect is to tarnish religion's image and so feed a widespread perception that religious activism is no less self-interested or more far-sighted than other self-seeking pressure groups.

The World Council of Churches and the Holy See have made pronouncements on a range of international issues and have periodically supported with considerable energy and enthusiasm a number of international campaigns. Notable amongst these was the role played by the World Council of Churches in mobilising church support for the anti-apartheid struggles of the 1970s and 1980s, and specifically for the economic boycott of South Africa. Similarly, the Catholic Church greatly contributed to the effectiveness of the debt forgiveness campaign, with Pope John Paul II proclaiming the year 2000 as a 'Jubilee year' which explicitly identified debt forgiveness for poor countries as its primary economic goal. But these efforts have been sporadic, have often lacked the deeper analytical frame of reference needed to make sense of new developments and have generally failed to bridge the gap between enunciation of abstract principles and religious and educational practice. Though the mode of operation is markedly different, Islamic pronouncements (2004 Amman Message; 2007 open letter by Islamic leaders addressed to their Christian counterparts *A Common Word Between Us and You*) and the actions of the Organisation of Islamic Cooperation have been similarly constrained. As a general proposition, the major religious traditions remain, despite their universalist ethic, strangely insular. The exemplary wisdom and advocacy of such notable religious leaders as the former Archbishop of Canterbury Rowan Williams, Pope Francis, Patriarch Bartholomew (spiritual leader of the world's 300 million Orthodox Christians) or former president of Iran Mohamed Khatami seem somehow unable to percolate through deeply entrenched habits and bureaucracies.

The task ahead for both religious traditions is not to rehearse once more the scholastic or jurisprudential disputes of the past that pit just war and pacifist arguments against each other. The imperative for each of them is to articulate and operationalise an authentic and coherent response to humanity's current predicament. The Nonviolence and Just Peace conference convened by the Pontifical Council for Justice and Peace and several Catholic organisations in April 2016 is perhaps a harbinger of things to come. It affirmed active nonviolence as central to the Christian vision and message of Jesus, and hence to the life of the church, and to the long-term vocation of healing and reconciling both people and the planet.

These sentiments were echoed a few months later in Pope Francis's message for the celebration of the 50th World Day of Peace in 2017, *Nonviolence: A Style of Politics for Peace*. These are but the first tentative steps in what is likely to be a long and at times arduous journey from which both they and the world have much to gain. Their journey will be especially rewarding if they choose to travel together, periodically stopping along the way to listen to and learn from each other.

Note

1 UNHCR reported that the number of people forcibly displaced at the end of 2014 had risen to a staggering 59.5 million compared to 51.2 million a year earlier and 37.5 million a decade ago (UNHCR 2015).

References

Abou El Fadl, Khaled. (2000), 'The Use and Abuse of "Holy War"', *Ethics & International Affairs* (accessed at www.carnegiecouncil.org/publications/journal/14/review_essays/216.html).
Abu-Nimer, Mohammed. (2001), 'A Framework for Nonviolence and Peacebuilding in Islam', *Journal of Law and Religion*, 15(1–2), 217–265.
A Common Word between Us and You. (2009). [An open letter signed by 138 leading Muslim scholars representing every branch of Islam and dated 13 October 2007 was delivered to Christian leaders throughout the world]. Jordan: The Royal Aal Al-Bayt Institute for Islamic Thought.
Adeyemo, Lateef Kayode. (2013), 'The Primacy of Peace in the Teachings of Islam', *Ulum Islamiyah Journal*, 10(June), 53–80.
Albert, Mathias, Lothar Brock, and Klaus Dieter Wolf. (2000), *Civilizing World Politics: Society and Community Beyond the State*. Lanham: Rowman & Littlefield Publishers.
Al-Dawoody, Ahmet. (2011), *The Islamic Law of War Justifications and Regulations*. London: Palgrave Macmillan.
Ali, Shaheen Sardar and Javaid Rehman. (2005), 'The Concept of Jihad in Islamic International Law', *Journal of Conflict and Security Law*, 10(3), 321–343.
Altwajiri, Abdulaziz Othman. (2015), 'Towards a Renewal of Islamic Thought', *Islam Today*, 31, 13–34.
Amman Message. (2004), *Statement released by H. M. King Abdullah II bin Al-Hussein in Amman*, Jordan on 9 November 2004 (accessed at http://ammanmessage.com/the-amman-message-full/.
Augustine. (1956), '*City of God [De civitate Dei]*' Written between 413 and 426 and translated by Marcus Dods, in *The Nicene and Post-Nicene Fathers*, edited by Philip Schaff, First Series. Vol. II. Grand Rapids, MI: Eerdmans.
Augustine. (400), *Contra Faustum Manicheum* (accessed at http://gnosis.org/library/contf2.htm).
Avalos, Hector. (2005), *Fighting Words: The Origins of Religious Violence*. Amherst, NY: Prometheus Books.
Bainton, Rolland H. (1960), *Christian Attitudes toward War and Peace: A Historical Survey and Critical Re-Evaluation*. Nashville: Abingdon.
Benounne, K. (1994), 'As-Salamu 'Alaykum? Humanitarian Law in Islamic Jurisprudence', *Massachusetts Journal of IL*, 605–643.

Besier, Gerhard. (2008), *Religion, State and Society in the Transformations of the Twentieth Century: Modernization, Innovation and Decline*. Berlin: Lit Verlag.
Cadoux, C. John. (1982), *The Early Christian Attitude to War*. New York: Seabury Press.
Camilleri, Joseph A. and Jim Falk. (2009). *Worlds in Transition: Evolving Governance Across a Stressed Planet*. Cheltenham, UK: Edward Elgar.
Childress, James F. (1984), 'Moral Discourse About War in the Early Church', *The Journal of Religious Ethics*, 12(1), 2–18.
Cockayne, James. (2002), 'Islam and International Humanitarian Law: From a Clash to a Conversation Between Civilizations', *International Review of the Red Cross*, 84(847) (accessed at www.icrc.org/eng/resources/documents/misc/5fld2f.htm).
Cornell, Tom. (2015), 'The Future of Christian Nonviolence', *Plough Quarterly*, 5, Summer 2015 (accessed at www.plough.com/en/topics/justice/nonviolence/the-future-of-christian-nonviolence).
Duncan, Bruce. (2003), 'What the Just War Tradition Has to Offer Today', *Compass*, 38 (accessed at http://compassreview.org/winter03/7.html).
Firestone, Reuven. (1999), *Jihād: The Origin of Holy War in Islam*. New York: Oxford University Press.
Fox, Jonathan. (2008), *A World Survey of Religion and the State*. Cambridge: Cambridge University Press.
Grimsrud, Ted. (2003), 'Is God Nonviolent?' *The Conrad Grebel Review*, 21(1), 13–17.
Haruna, A. A., Laminu Bukar and Babagana Karoumi. (2014), 'War and Islamic Humanitarian Law: Appraising Warfare and Distinction as a Principle in Hostilities', *International Journal of Humanities and Social Science*, 4(5), 225–235.
Hittinger, John P. (2000), 'Roots of Order and Disorder: Aquinas and Augustine on War, Peace and Politics', Talk delivered at Thomistic Institute, July 20, 2000 (accessed at www3.nd.edu/~maritain/jmc/ti00/hitinger.htm).
Jaspert, Nikolas. (2006), *The Crusades*. Translated by Phyllis G. Jestice. London: Routledge.
Johnson, James Turner. (1997), *The Holy War Idea in Western and Islamic Traditions*. University Park, PA: Pennsylvania State University Press.
Johnson, James Turner and John Kelsay. (eds.) (1990), *Cross, Crescent, and Sword: The Justification and Limitation of War in Western and Islamic Tradition*. Westernport, CT: Greenwood Press.
Juergensmeyer, Mark. (2003), *Terror in the Mind of God: The Global Rise of Religious Violence*. Berkeley, CA: University of California Press.
Kaufman, Gordon D. (1995), *In the Face of Mystery: A Constructive Theology*. Cambridge, MA: Harvard University Press.
Khadduri, Majid. (1955), *War and Peace in the Law of Islam*. Baltimore, MD: Johns Hopkins Press.
Kurian, George Thomas and Mark A. Lamport. (2015), 'Introduction', in *Encyclopedia of Christian Education*, edited by G. T. Thomas and M. A. Lamport. 3 vols. Lanham, MD: Rowman & Littlefield.
Lanagan, John. (1984), 'The Elements of St. Augustine's Just War Theory', *The Journal of Religious Ethics*, 12(1), 19–38.
Mozzafari, Mehdi. (2002), *Globalization and Civilizations*. London: Routledge.
Oxford Encyclopedia of the Islamic World. (2009), edited by John Esposito. Oxford: Oxford University Press [section on 'Education] (accessed at www.oxfordislamicstudies.com/article/opr/t236/e0212#e0212-s3).
Pax Christi International. (2016), 'An Appeal to the Catholic Church to Re-Commit to the Centrality of Gospel Nonviolence', Conference on Nonviolence and Just Peace:

Contributing to the Catholic Understanding of and Commitment to Nonviolence, Rome, April 11–13, 2016 (accessed at www.paxchristi.net/sites/default/files/documents/appeal-to-catholic-church-to-recommit-to-nonviolence.pdf).

Pew Research Centre, *The Future of World Religions: Population Growth Projections, 2010–2050*, April 2, 2015 (accessed at www.pewforum.org/2015/04/02/religious-projections-2010-2050/).

Schaff, Philip. (1962), *History of the Christian Church*. Grand Rapids, MI: Eerdmans.

Swift, Louis J. (1983), *The Early Church Fathers on War and Military Service*. Wilmington, DE: Michael Glazier.

Thomas, Scott M. (2005), *The Global Resurgence of Religion and the Transformation of International Relations: The Struggle for the Soul of the Twenty-First Century*. New York: Palgrave Macmillan.

UNHCR. (2015), 'World at War: Global Trends, Forced Displacement in 2014' (accessed at http://unhcr.org/556725e69.html).

Weaver, J. Denny. (2001), *The Nonviolent Atonement*. Grand Rapids, MI: Eerdmans.

Wilkinson, Michael. (2012), 'The Institutionalization of Religion', in *Godly Love: Impediments and Possibilities*, edited by Matthew T. Lee and Amos Yong. Lanham, MD: Lexington Books.

PART IV
The Islamic Tradition

11

MAKING PEACE WITH ISLAM

The Muslim as Peacemaker

Afra Jalabi

> *Relate to them in truth the story of the two sons of Adam. They each presented an offering. It was accepted from one, but not from the other. Said he, "Be sure that I shall kill you." Said the other, "God accepts from those who repel wrong. If you raise your hand to kill me, I shall not raise my hand against you to kill you, for I fear the Lord of all worlds."*
>
> *(Quran: 5:27–28)*

The Buddha left the palace and never came back. He found another palace at the end of suffering. Having walked on a treacherous path, a special portal opened up out of the human condition. The eightfold path could carry the code for opening up the gate.

Moses left the palace but returned—not to rule but to ask Pharaoh to let his people go and to advise Pharaoh not to oppress the weak and needy. The tablets had the code for the portal.

Jesus found the palace within, another portal into the kingdom of God, whose gate is tight and whose path is also treacherous but is one which leads to life.

Muhammad was offered the palace in Mecca to stop his new calling but declined—yet he ended up becoming a ruler without a palace, and received the code in the Quran to the portal of kingdom in the world and in heaven.

Despite the different angles, the diverse metaphors and imagery, and dramatic plots, the religious and the political are always intertwined in our traditions. This tension is the common thread of our human history regardless of the various folds and diverse religious manifestations. At the root of each major religious tradition is a figure embarking upon a serious concerted effort to break through the human condition, to transcend it in ways that would create a different world. The Awakened one or the Prophet offers a new vision: instead of tyranny, justice; instead of suffering, salvation; and instead of violence and chaos, compassion and peace.

We have been creative on this planet in many ways, and excelled in creating new forms of truth claims within various modalities and paradigms, perhaps to conceal in some ways our equally excellent ways in crafting many forms of harm and methods of subjugating each other, not to mention the sophisticated weaponry that we are still developing. We have developed various forms of knowledge in our common human journey in the last several thousand years; religion has been part of our history and part of our imagination, and still shows signs of resourcefulness and potent forms of energy, even if it tends to blow up when mishandled or misplaced.

There has been experimentation as well in more recent history, in part as a direct reaction to religiously legitimated wrongs, doing away with religion and creating new visions of justice and peace. And just as with our religious traditions, these secular attempts offer a spectrum of inspirations and achievements as well as failures and, in many contexts, disastrous injustices.

Considering some of the serious challenges facing us today, whether political, economic or environmental, we need to ask ourselves whether we can find ways to stop doing harm to one another or upon our environment and natural habitat, and whether we can weather current challenges. Could we embark upon new possibilities, a new palace of cooperation, compassion, justice and peace—within and without? Given the creative and resourceful potential in our religious traditions, it behoves us to ask if religion could be part of the conversation on violence and nonviolence in this age, beyond the rhetorical debates about violence being the ultimate cause or the ultimate antidote. Could we utilize our accumulative experiences—religious, cultural and secular—to aid us in dealing with some of the challenges facing us in our current moment?

As a Muslim, I see myself as a member of the larger human tribe while also part of a smaller family. Being Muslim, Buddhist, Christian, Jewish or any other group means we can simultaneously respond to collective universal angst and yet also serve and contribute from our own particular position in our given communities. The mother in me thinks that if each family were thriving and contributing in unique ways, we would have a much richer, larger society. I welcome and feel open to all the criticisms coming towards Islam, some of them severe and vehement, as tools that provide a mirror to our cultural and religious conditioning. But I also see that our malaise as a larger human society is rather more common, and our problems when it comes to power and division and aggression are far more similar and common than we would like to admit.

Islam as Active Peacemaking

The term, *Islam,* is a word derived from the word *salam* (peace) in Arabic. But the word Islam, often mistranslated in English as "submission," could more accurately be translated as peace-activation, or peacemaking, since it is a verb noun referring to the active moving or spreading of peace. In contrast, the word for submission, in Arabic, is *Isstislam*, a verb noun that refers to a state of peacefulness that has been imposed externally. The term "Muslim," therefore, sounds different from "Musstaslim." The first is a reference to the active peacemaker, while the latter is a reference to the one who has been made peaceable—also a term used for the defeated in war terminology. The two forms of conjugating the word peace in the verb forms have different implications. In the first active form, agency is with the doer, while in the latter, agency is external. This difference, which may seem subtle at first, is significant. The difference in the place of active agency creates a whole other paradigm. Being actively peaceful is different from being subdued by or forced to give in to peacefulness as a result of external means, to an external agent, and hence, its implications also have to do with agency, freedom and initiative. To be Muslim, therefore, in the pure grammatical sense, is to be an active agent of peace and not a passively resigned one. In understanding this difference, we come to see why nonviolence could be seen and re-understood as a central teaching in the Quranic text and as being compatible with Muhammad's own conduct.

There is a need for a re-reading and re-interpreting certain terms that easily lend themselves to new readings. Peacefulness in Islam, in this understanding, is a positive action and not a state of defeat and resignation. It is not about remaining peaceful as long as there are peaceful conditions around us; it is about actively choosing peaceful ways of thought and action even when the conditions are compelling one to speak or behave otherwise.[1]

Since the word Islam means active peace, in a grammatical sense, it is also worth noting how Islam is used in this sense in the Quranic text. The word Islam is used in the Quranic text in two senses of the term: first, as an inclusive term, and second, in a more particular sense, as a label to refer to those who accepted the call of Muhammad inviting them to become Muslim. The word Islam is used in a generic manner in the Quran. It is the state of the universe and its sentient beings—for having aligned peacefully to the will of God. "To Him have become Muslim, all those in heavens and upon earth" (3:83). Islam is also used in the Quran to indicate the state of those who accepted peace and embraced the practice of peace, and as a result Islam as a term is used quite extensively throughout the Quranic text to refer to various figures, communities and other sentient beings. It is used, for example, to refer to the Apostles of Jesus when, at the Last Supper, they say to Jesus, "Witness that we are Muslims" (3:52). The Queen of Sheba accepts the Unity of the Divine in the message of Solomon and declares, "I have become Muslim with Solomon" (27:44). Islam is also used as a verb to describe the state of the Jewish Prophets guiding to peacefulness in the light of the Torah (5:44). Even the Jinn, non-physical beings, when they describe their ranks and spiritual conditions, declare that "some of us are Muslim, some are not, those who are not seeking the guidance of truth." (72:14).

The state of Islam in the Quranic ethos, when examining the verses that include the word Islam, we see that it is a term that is used to underscore an inclusive state, or field of being possible for all—with additional specific verses inviting us ALL to enter this peacefulness—into "Silm" (Peaceability). "All of you, who have faith, enter Peace and do not follow upon the steps of Satan, for he is your avowed enemy." (2:208). Reading these passages—and there are more of these references to both Islam as a universally peaceful way of being—we come to see that this peaceful, active surrender to truth and to the ways of compassion is not a state that could be claimed exclusively by one particular religion or group in the language of the Quran.

The Quranic voice does not limit itself to Arabs or Muslims (as in those following the teachings of Muhammad), but states repeatedly its appeal to all of humanity. Many verses on peace or justice start with the usual appeal: "Ya Ayuha al-Nas" ("O, people!").

In this chapter, I would like to present a framework that shows the possibilities for an organic Islamic hermeneutics of nonviolence—interpretations based on Islamic sources—with the aim of widening the horizons of the discussion of an Islamic pacifist approach. The Quran and Hadith or Sunnah (The Prophet's traditions and sayings) are two of the four sources of Sharia (Islamic jurisprudence). The other two are consensus and analogical reason. The Quran and Hadith traditions both provide ample resources for rich and varied resources for many aspects of life, including ones that deal with both violent and nonviolent alternatives. Islamic Law, referred to in Arabic as "fiqh," literally means deep comprehension. Sharia is not meant to be a fixed body of rules, but rather a dynamic and methodical way of responding to life's situations and conditions by understanding the laws of God within the self and without. This then provides ways of reading and re-interpreting the sources with the challenges of the present. Muhammad Iqbal, the Indian philosopher and poet, argues that the Quran introduces pushes us beyond "text" in its limited scriptural dimension to include the "reality" of self and the universe as sources of knowledge—that the "signs" of God are not limited to revelation but are references to that which are unfolding within self and the universe. For him, reality is the Divine logos constantly invoking comprehension requiring an appropriate response from us.[2]

Having understood the significance of the sources of Islamic tradition and Islamic law, one sees the possibilities for many re-interpretations and readings that could offer alternative feminist, environmentalist, egalitarian and pacifist readings that could still be compatible with the basic tenets of Islam. After all, this is exactly what the various schools did over the course of several centuries—read the sources and offered, through various scholars and schools, particular frameworks of values and prescriptions of actions that suited and responded to their needs and reflected the time and space in which they lived.

Given the rich and often repeated themes of nonviolent and pacifist material in both the Quran and Hadith, Islam as a religion lends itself easily to a nonviolent interpretation and framework. It is therefore not surprising that nonviolent figures or movements have surfaced throughout Islam's historical trajectory, as is also the case in other religious traditions. Encountering original

Islamic sources has the potential to inspire radical nonviolent responses as well as violent ones.

Twenty-First-Century Islam

The term Islam is used to refer to a religion practiced by over one billion people living across several continents, each of whom is a walking and living version of being Muslim. Each naturally adds a unique vibe to the large landscape we call Islam even if that landscape contains a huge spectrum of beliefs and practices.

But what I find somewhat ironic as a Muslim living in the twenty-first century, having grown up in a family committed to nonviolence, is to hear or see Islam singled out as a violent religion or one that promotes violence. This is seen in some of the mainstream media, and sadly sometimes in a subtler manner in some academic discussions—as if Islam were a monolith suspended in the air, capable of agency and paused in time. This is not how human beings experience religion in society or politics, let alone in their own lives. After all, humans are the agents who live, modify and exhibit religious behaviour. They are the agents. Nor is this the way religion unfolds across space and time. The way religion is lived and practiced is always contextual and varied in relation to space and time.

Discussions on religious violence with reference to Islam are usually undertaken without much consideration for the political and economic realities of Muslim societies or where there are majority Muslims populations. It is not that there are not Muslims doing violent things, but we need to discuss violence in a more open manner without limiting ourselves to reductionist and facile casualties. We live in a world that is still spinning to the dated momentum of a violent ethos, and Muslims are no exception. Muslims do not have a monopoly on violence in a world in which the highest forms of weapons of mass destruction are considered the greatest political markers and signs of the most significant technological achievements in today's sad global environment.

As is the case with every religious practice and belief, the spectrum within each faith community is the result of having been lived and carried across space and thus accumulating human experiences over time. Most significantly, however, is that most have been subject to interest, privilege and power dynamics. How much truth remains, I wonder sometimes, in the layers of dust and legacy that served dynasties, justified pillaging and the taking away of land and resources from others? If we have learned anything from history, we know that humans seem very savvy about creating spiritual and religious facades when it comes to conquests and acquisition. Religion, therefore, is easily one of the resources that fuels our desire for power. We cannot parse or think about our religious traditions without taking into consideration all the power dynamics and privileges that go into creating our spiritual tapestries and truth claims. Who stands to benefit? Who are the ones it elevates and, most importantly, at whose expense? These are questions that we do not like to examine when we are caught up in our spiritual, emotional reveries, but perhaps, given the commands of self-inquiry and warnings about the trappings of the worldly dimensions placed upon us in our religious teachings, they might be the lights that we need to shine into the darkness within, before we consider facing anything externally.

Where Is the Light?

For the purposes of this chapter, the focus is on some nonviolent possibilities that are often hidden in the trenches of our victorious religious histories and narratives. I also find it necessary to touch upon some difficult issues here, even if briefly.

To understand the relationship between religion and violence or nonviolence requires widening the horizon of our discussion beyond the usually narrow casualties.

We tend to exoticize others while redeeming our own cultural and religious practices. We clutch our traditions and fetishize them. We are too attached to our labels and identity markers, and look down at the "other" if she happens to differ from what we claim as the only version of truth—even when it is our own contingent and proverbial truth. And one of the oldest forms of attachment in the dark tunnel is the supremacy complex present in almost every religious community. The exclusive claims to truth are ways of concealing forms of "will to power," and they lead to and justify rejection of the "other." These underlying dynamics in religious discourses also conceal much of the light within these teachings. The rise of extremist sensibilities in religious communities around the globe in recent years highlights the levels of fear towards the other and, ironically, fear of self. Paradoxically, fear of the "other" reveals a crisis of the "self."

We are all guilty of this in our various religious communities. It is quite comical to see how common it is to deny our very commonness. We are the same in rejecting our sameness.

And yet there is light, despite the dark alleys of bygone eras and their dated ways. There is a code in every religious tradition for opening up new portals, new pathways to other possibilities—if only we look a bit more closely beneath the accumulated layers and scratch beyond the narratives told by the victors. What would the one who lost the battle say, the one who was defeated and killed and buried? What is the voice of defeat, and would we even hear it if it were to speak? Our religious traditions fell prey to the ethos of cultures of power and triumph.

By searching for new possibilities, we would find that all our religions, cultures and wisdom literature, without exception, offer new gates to peacefulness—new portals out of our present darkness. We would find ways to diagnose our obsessive love for force and power and see them as narrow and limiting tunnels, in which we not only do not hear one another but also deny one another.

And yet both the Abrahamic lineage, with its three major offspring, and the Buddhist path are about breaking free from attachment. They offer liberation from false beliefs. The iconoclast is not the one who breaks the possessions of others, but one who is a warrior willing to break his or her own attachments—whether they manifest as physical or conceptual idols. It feels like a cosmic joke to see how our religious traditions have become, in many contexts, webs of attachment and warehouses of piles of chipped idols.

All our religious traditions have displayed capacities for shocking cruelty and shocking compassion, revealing in the process how ideas and concepts are moulded in ways that reflect the human condition and its polarities and possibilities.

How would we respond to active peacemaking? How can we break free from the attachments that have got in the way?

I will attempt a modest and fairly limited answer within an Islamic framework. We could do this first by re-reading and reclaiming the paradigm of active peacefulness within Islamic textual treasures—in scripture, the Prophetic "Hadith" traditions and in later nonviolent values practices that arose throughout Islamic history—and second by dealing with the discrepancy between ideal and practice.

Understanding the universality of Islam as a state of peacefulness open and possible to all, and as the rightful inheritance to all of humanity, enables Muslims to widen our horizons of belonging and, as a result, appreciate the variety of "paths" leading to truth as stated by the Quran (29:69). Understanding identity at both universal and particular levels helps Muslims in affirming what the Quran demands of us—as having one Source for everything and hence in seeing our diversity as the multiple manifestations of the Oneness of the Divine. Seeing the One in the many.

The Malaise of Humanity

In the creation narrative in the Quran, this universality is demonstrated through the potentiality of the human condition: in the possibility of rising above our condition as well as in the possibility of succumbing to our common challenges and shadows. The creation story is the first narrative we encounter at the beginning of the Quranic text. The story of creation sets the scene for the entrance of humanity into existence—God announces to the angels the placement of a representative on earth. Humanity is presented as a singular unit, a Divine project to unfold upon earth. Yet, the angels, who never object, nor resist, question this decision. They seem panicked. They use two reasons to justify their concerns. Here is the passage from Surat Al Baqurah:[3]

وَإِذْ قَالَ رَبُّكَ لِلْمَلَائِكَةِ إِنِّي جَاعِلٌ فِي الأَرْضِ خَلِيفَةً قَالُواْ أَتَجْعَلُ فِيهَا مَن يُفْسِدُ فِيهَا وَيَسْفِكُ الدِّمَاء وَنَحْنُ نُسَبِّحُ بِحَمْدِكَ وَنُقَدِّسُ لَكَ قَالَ إِنِّي أَعْلَمُ مَا لاَ تَعْلَمُونَ.(البقرة:30)

Behold, your Lord said to the angels: "I shall create a 'khalipha' [vicegerent or divine representative] on earth." They said: "Will You place therein one who will cause corruption and shed blood?—whilst we do celebrate Your praises and glorify Your holy name?" He said: "I know what you know not."

(2:30)

"I know what you know not" is a significant answer. It has possibilities. The Divine voice does not respond directly. It does not give a yes or no answer to the angelic accusations. The Divine answer is rather pregnant with possibilities. It is beyond negation and affirmation. But also, the answer underscores the potential in humanity to rise beyond the accusations of corruption and blood-shedding. It is a promise of Divine knowing.

Our current existential dilemmas reflect well the two main angelic concerns about humanity: 1—Corruption; 2—Bloodshed.

Can humanity then rise to the status of Divine knowing and actualize Divine representation on earth beyond these two afflictions?

Corruption ("Fassad" in the Quranic passage) is used in other Quranic contexts to refer to various forms of tyranny, excesses, aggression, stealing, harming others, deceit and lying and committing injustice. Various classical and modern scholars, including al Tabari, considered "fassad" as a generic reference to oppression and injustice. The scholars located the meaning in connection to the modality of economic and political tyranny in the Quran—using intertextuality—since in various passages Pharaoh is presented as being among those who had committed "fassad."

With the creative narrative as one of the main opening scenes in the Quran, the forward trajectory is set. The text sets out the two underlying challenges to our collective malaise, and thus foreshadows the exit strategy of this model. The prophets in the Quran are presented as performing two functions: each prophet is both bashir and nadhir (bearer of promise and bearer of warning). The prophets are the ones raising alarm in their communities or to the ruling elites (as in the story of Moses to Pharaoh and his court) about what may come their way if they continue their injustices; they are also the ones bearing the promise to those who are willing to step out of these old ways of domination and injustice. The prophets lay the path of salvation out of our old dated modalities of coercion and conditioned slide towards physical violence. By symbolically compressing the problem from an external point of view, the passage highlights our existential dilemma as a collective community.

Another symbolic event shows the potential and possibility within humanity. The other narrative that raises a response to the angelic fears is the story of Adam's two sons. Their encounter carries within it the angelic accusations while also fulfilling the Divine knowing regarding the capacity of this new representative to break through the angelic predictions.

The encounter of Adam's two sons represents a creative departure from the paradigm of force and coercion. The story in the Quranic version relates the dialogue that takes place in this confrontation between the non-creative repetitive stance that has afflicted humanity and the creative nonviolent one:

وَاتْلُ عَلَيْهِمْ نَبَأَ ابْنَيْ آدَمَ بِالْحَقِّ إِذْ قَرَّبَا قُرْبَانًا فَتُقُبِّلَ مِنْ أَحَدِهِمَا وَلَمْ يُتَقَبَّلْ مِنَ الْآخَرِ قَالَ لَأَقْتُلَنَّكَ قَالَ إِنَّمَا يَتَقَبَّلُ اللَّهُ مِنَ الْمُتَّقِينَ. لَئِنْ بَسَطْتَ إِلَيَّ يَدَكَ لِتَقْتُلَنِي مَا أَنَا بِبَاسِطٍ يَدِيَ إِلَيْكَ لِأَقْتُلَكَ إِنِّي أَخَافُ اللَّهَ رَبَّ الْعَالَمِينَ. إِنِّي أُرِيدُ أَنْ تَبُوءَ بِإِثْمِي وَإِثْمِكَ فَتَكُونَ مِنْ أَصْحَابِ النَّارِ وَذَلِكَ جَزَاءُ الظَّالِمِينَ. فَطَوَّعَتْ

لَهُ نَفْسُهُ قَتْلَ أَخِيهِ فَقَتَلَهُ فَأَصْبَحَ مِنَ الْخَاسِرِينَ. فَبَعَثَ اللَّهُ غُرَابًا يَبْحَثُ فِي الْأَرْضِ لِيُرِيَهُ كَيْفَ يُوَارِي سَوْءَةَ أَخِيهِ قَالَ يَا وَيْلَتَى أَعَجَزْتُ أَنْ أَكُونَ مِثْلَ هَذَا الْغُرَابِ فَأُوَارِيَ سَوْءَةَ أَخِي فَأَصْبَحَ مِنَ النَّادِمِينَ. 27-31: المائدة

Relate to them in truth the story of the two sons of Adam. They each presented an offering. It was accepted from one, but not from the other. Said he, "Be sure that I shall kill you." Said the other, "God accepts from those who repel wrong. If you raise your hand to kill me, I shall not raise my hand against you to kill you, for I fear the Lord of all worlds."

(Quran 5:27–28)

His self justified for him the killing of his brother. He killed him. He then became among the losers. Then God sent a raven, who scratched the earth to show him how to hide the shame of his brother. "Woe unto me," he said, "Was I not even able to be as this raven, to hide the shame of [killing] my brother?" He then became among those who are filled with regret.

(Quran 5: 28–31)

We find within these verses two models: one who believes in spilling blood—exactly as the angels predicted humans would do—and killing as a solution, and one who refuses to kill even in self-defence. This narrative established a blueprint for both potentialities—an archetypal narrative about the human condition. It also hints at and points to the possibility of a completely other radical way of responding to violence. By zooming into the dialogues, the Quranic text provides something beyond the event of the first murder. The text provides the rationale through both the words and thoughts of the two—of the killer and of the killed. We see in this story the blueprint of a radical alternative to violence. When declining self-defence, Abel says, "I fear the Lord of all Worlds." It is as if Abel is saying to his brother: Death is inevitable, but killing is a choice. Therefore, I would rather die without having killed, because I will die anyway. It is here in this dialogue that the text provides an example in which the fear of killing is greater than the fear of dying.

In the encounter of the two brothers, the Quran offers the path of active and conscious peacefulness as a possible alternative to killing—being actively Muslim as a response to mindless threat and aggression. Active peacefulness is presented as the first exit strategy into a new possibility, and as a different mode of being in the world. The Quranic narrative of Adam's two sons leaves them anonymous—figures without names, unlike the more detailed narrative in the Book of Genesis and the story of Cain and Abel. And yet the Quran zooms into the moment before the crime and relates the dialogue. The Quranic version of the first crimes retrieves the scene and gives a microphone to the defeated—or who may seem defeated. But once we know what he said, the parameters of victory and defeat shift in the narrative. The remorse of his brother is understood in a new light. Battle is different from crime. By offering no resistance, it became a murder. Gandhi once said that what makes nonviolence powerful is the deep aversion in human beings to committing a crime, while seeing bravery and heroism in fighting. In the Quran, we do not know the name of Adam's first son, but we do know what he said before being murdered. He said:"I will not raise my hand to kill you for I fear the Lord of all Worlds." We know the voice of his conscience. Suddenly, what could have been defeat and loss is cast anew. Abel's voice in the Quran is the voice of all those who actively choose peacefulness even when threatened, those who decline self-defence. From the very scene of murder arises a new possibility, that of a new human being who refuses to kill even when threatened with death. This passage with its compact dialogue maps the malaise in the aggression of the loser and also the salvation of that he who is able to step out of the battle of reactive aggression and resistance. What may seem like non-resistance by the first son of Adam is an internally active and brave step up to a higher choice—the choice of doing no harm.

This story is one of the last revelations in the Quran, even though it is about the beginning of humanity—and textually is one of the early surahs in the Quran text. So, it is not a passage exclusive to the Meccan period. It is one of the final passages to contemplate and one that provides an ultimate modality by which to re-read the entire Quranic text. It lays before us the inclinations of both mindless aggression and radical peacefulness. It also carries within it the genetic code for the rest of Quranic narratives; the moral thrust rising throughout the text—the behaviours of the two brothers as the two distinct modes of action; the use of violence, threat and aggression by Pharaoh and others and the use of nonviolence and refusal to do harm by the prophets and the wise ones.

By having the prophets repel with compassion threats of violence and killing in other passages, the Quran provides this model of active peacefulness as the alternative path. This structure of domination and aggression in other narratives and the model of nonviolence in facing them is a repetitive moral spread throughout the Quranic text. We see this repeated in various contexts and narratives in the Quran, with the highlight being the archetypal encounter of Pharaoh and Moses; the problem of domination and violence and the prophetic response of transforming society through the power of the word and truth without coercion or aggression.

Active peacefulness—being consciously in the state of Islam—was the modus operandi for the early Muslim community in Mecca. This was maintained despite the oppression, persecution, torture and killing of some of the early converts. As Islam later spread into other parts of Arabia and Muhammad and his small community were asked by the residents of the city of Yathrib, who had become Muslim, to take residence among them and chose Muhammad as their political leader, a new political dimension was about to unfold. Islam in this phase moved to a city-state model with other regions and towns joining. The limited warfare was done in this context with priority and preference given tribal alliances, negotiations, truce and peace treaties (even when unfair to the Medina community). Muhammad gradually united Arabia under a centralized political system out of the chaotic tribal code predominant then.

Given these political developments, and with some examination of the events within the Quranic teachings, one could argue that violence from a Muslim perspective is not a tool to spread or prevent belief but is constrained within a political context that has do with civil order and rule of law. This is a lengthy discussion, but I mention it here briefly to show that the elements of warrior values in the Quranic text deal with limited use of violence in greatly restrained contexts and with specific conditions. In some ways, there are quite compatible parallels between the conditions and criteria that allow legitimate armed Jihad and the Christian just war doctrine. However, as we all know, and as I pointed out earlier, such criteria are always subject to interests and interpretations by various groups.

The political project of creating a peaceful Arabian peninsula under some centralized rule of law was different from building a religious spiritual community. It is important to delineate the roles Muhammad had as a spiritual religious teacher and a political leader who united the Arabian tribes under a centralized system of polity, governance and taxation—with many non-Muslim and Christian tribes joining this alliance. The preference for even unfair peace treaties at the height of his political and military power testify to Muhammad's larger political project that was underway.

The emphasis on ending tribal warfare and tribal killing caused by the honour code of revenge is evident in his famous last sermon. When the Prophet gave his last well-known address to the community, known as *Khubat al Wada'* ("The Farewell Sermon"), to the newly formed community in Mecca, he focused on two main themes. "Do NOT revert back, after I leave you, to the ways of ignorance (Jahiliyah) where you go back to denying truth and killing one another." He also pleaded with the community during the sermon to treat women well: "Your women have rights upon you." Then he said:

> O, people, your Lord is one and your father is one. You belong to Adam and Adam was from earth; the best among you is that he who could repel wrong (taquwa). No Arab has a degree above a foreigner (ajammi).[4]

Moreover, there are other Hadith traditions (sayings of the Prophet outside the Quranic text—and which are part of the canonized literature) that reflect a similar ethos of nonviolence and command non-resistance in contexts of conflict and aggression. Muhammad warned the new Muslims of times of chaos and disorder towards the end of his life. In some of the classic Hadith books one finds commands that go with the spirit of using non-resistance. The Prophet is reported to have said: "There shall be chaos (fitnah) and those lying flat are better than those sitting, those sitting are better than those standing, those standing are better than those walking, and those walking are better than those striving." The Prophet was then asked, "Ya Rasoulallah, what do you command me to do?" The Prophet said, "That he who has camels let him attend to his camels, and that he who has sheep let him attend to his sheep and that he who has land let him attend to his land!" He was asked again, "And that he who has none of this, what shall he do?" The

Prophet said, "Then let him take his sword and hit its edge on a rock, and let him then try to spare himself as much as he could."[5]

The prophetic method of social and political reform falls within this alternative modality in the Quran, in which humanity has the potential to rise beyond the angel's accusations—achieving God's will for this young species that has the Divine trust.

The Quranic text contains 5638 verses; only about 25 deal with combat with conditions and within specific contexts. Although we know that texts could not be best approached quantitatively and that hermeneutical issues are beyond numbers, it still gives us a view of the general overwhelming ambience of the Quranic tone. The structure of the story of the encounter of the two sons of Adam reflect an ethical modality in the encounter between the prophets and their people(s). The refusal to defend oneself becomes the prototype that delineates two modes of human responses in these narratives; the prophets who decline self-defence and the threat of violence and exile from their communities. The common repetitive underlying pattern in these passages indicate that non-resistance, or "repelling with that which is more beautiful" (41: 34) is rather the norm throughout the Quranic text and not the exception.

Nonviolence as the Creative Tool of the Prophets

The Prophet, be it Moses or Jesus or Saleh, stands in the face of the dominant culture by finding exit strategies—new tools to transcend the status quo—not just in standing for truth against those who object to them, but also in stepping out of the larger paradigm of coercion and violence.

Here we come to understand the injunctions of the Prophet better, his commands in line with the Quranic teachings. See how he uses the example of Adams's two sons to guide the community about violence and chaos. We also find other similar Hadiths echoing this nonviolent message by the Prophet. In a Hadith related by one of the young companions, Abu Moussa al Ash'arie, Muhammad said,

> In my hands stretching into time are periods of disorder (fitnas) like pieces of a dark night, a person of faith wakes up in faith, then loses faith as the night falls ... Those who sit still are better than those striving (moving in action). So, break your arrows and cut the threads of your arches, hit your swords upon rocks, and if anyone enters your home, then be like the best of Adam's two sons.[6]

The Prophets vs. Their Nations (or Tyrants)

This ethos of non-resistance runs in many narratives in the Quran. Here is a passage about the Prophet Noah when his people threaten him. He then responds with non-resistance, echoing the same ethos as in the discourse of Adam's first son:[7]

وَاتْلُ عَلَيْهِمْ نَبَأَ نُوحٍ إِذْ قَالَ لِقَوْمِهِ يَا قَوْمِ إِن كَانَ كَبُرَ عَلَيْكُم مَّقَامِي وَتَذْكِيرِي بِآيَاتِ اللّهِ فَعَلَى اللّهِ تَوَكَّلْتُ فَأَجْمِعُواْ أَمْرَكُمْ وَشُرَكَاءَكُمْ ثُمَّ لاَ يَكُنْ أَمْرُكُمْ عَلَيْكُمْ غُمَّةً ثُمَّ اقْضُواْ إِلَيَّ وَلاَ تُنظِرُونِ

فَإِن تَوَلَّيْتُمْ فَمَا سَأَلْتُكُم مِّنْ أَجْرٍ إِنْ أَجْرِيَ إِلاَّ عَلَى اللّهِ وَأُمِرْتُ أَنْ أَكُونَ مِنَ الْمُسْلِمِينَ

And relate to them the story of Noah—when he said to his people: "O my people, if my presence [among you] and my reminding you of God's signs are repugnant to you—then, I shall deliver myself to God. Summon up all you have [against me] and what you have decided amongst your allies; and once you have chosen your course of action, let no hesitation deflect you, and carry out against me and do not give me respite. If you turn away [from the message] I have asked no reward whatsoever of you; my reward rests with none but God, for I have been bidden to be among those who have surrendered themselves (to be a Muslim)."

(10:71–72)

These passages run through the Quran. There are many specific examples of particular prophets and their nations. But see how in this passage in Surah Ibrahim there is a collective prophetic model in the face of the collective human tendency. Read the following verses to see how the Quran sets out these modes of faith and action—trust in God and patience and non-resistance in the face of harm one the one hand, by several prophets, *and* trust in coercion, violence and exile in the face of new ideas on the part of their societies:

أَلَمْ يَأْتِكُمْ نَبَأُ الَّذِينَ مِن قَبْلِكُمْ قَوْمِ نُوحٍ وَعَادٍ وَثَمُودَ وَالَّذِينَ مِن بَعْدِهِمْ لاَ يَعْلَمُهُمْ إِلاَّ اللّهُ جَاءَتْهُمْ رُسُلُهُم بِالْبَيِّنَاتِ فَرَدُّواْ أَيْدِيَهُمْ فِي أَفْوَاهِهِمْ وَقَالُواْ إِنَّا كَفَرْنَا بِمَا أُرْسِلْتُم بِهِ وَإِنَّا لَفِي شَكٍّ مِّمَّا تَدْعُونَنَا إِلَيْهِ مُرِيبٍ

قَالَتْ رُسُلُهُمْ أَفِي اللّهِ شَكٌّ فَاطِرِ السَّمَاوَاتِ وَالأَرْضِ يَدْعُوكُمْ لِيَغْفِرَ لَكُم مِّن ذُنُوبِكُمْ وَيُؤَخِّرَكُمْ إِلَى أَجَلٍ مُّسَمًّى قَالُواْ إِنْ أَنتُمْ إِلاَّ بَشَرٌ مِّثْلُنَا تُرِيدُونَ أَن تَصُدُّونَا عَمَّا كَانَ يَعْبُدُ آبَاؤُنَا فَأْتُونَا بِسُلْطَانٍ مُّبِينٍ

قَالَتْ لَهُمْ رُسُلُهُمْ إِن نَّحْنُ إِلاَّ بَشَرٌ مِّثْلُكُمْ وَلَكِنَّ اللّهَ يَمُنُّ عَلَى مَن يَشَاءُ مِنْ عِبَادِهِ وَمَا كَانَ لَنَا أَن نَّأْتِيَكُم بِسُلْطَانٍ إِلاَّ بِإِذْنِ اللّهِ وَعَلَى اللّهِ فَلْيَتَوَكَّلِ الْمُؤْمِنُونَ

وَمَا لَنَا أَلاَّ نَتَوَكَّلَ عَلَى اللّهِ وَقَدْ هَدَانَا سُبُلَنَا وَلَنَصْبِرَنَّ عَلَى مَا آذَيْتُمُونَا وَعَلَى اللّهِ فَلْيَتَوَكَّلِ الْمُتَوَكِّلُونَ

وَقَالَ الَّذِينَ كَفَرُواْ لِرُسُلِهِمْ لَنُخْرِجَنَّكُم مِّنْ أَرْضِنَا أَوْ لَتَعُودُنَّ فِي مِلَّتِنَا فَأَوْحَى إِلَيْهِمْ رَبُّهُمْ لَنُهْلِكَنَّ الظَّالِمِينَ

وَلَنُسْكِنَنَّكُمُ الأَرْضَ مِن بَعْدِهِمْ ذَلِكَ لِمَنْ خَافَ مَقَامِي وَخَافَ وَعِيدِ

Have the stories of those before you never come to you—the people of Noah, and of A'ad and Thamud, and those who came after them, none knows them except God. There came upon them their messengers with evidence (clarity)—but they covered their mouths with their hands and said [to their messengers]: We reject (deny) that which you have been entrusted with; we are in grave doubt and suspicion about all that to which you are calling us. Said the messengers: "Can there be any doubt about God, the originator of the heavens and earth? It is He who calls upon you so that He may forgive you and grant you respite to a differed set term." But they replied [to the messengers]: "You are nothing but moral human beings like ourselves, and yet you want to turn us away from what our fathers worshipped. Provide us with a clear proof." The messengers then said to them: "True, we are nothing but mortal human beings like yourselves, but God bestows His blessings upon whomever He wills of his worshippers. And it is not within our power to provide you a proof unless it be by God's leave, and so it is in God that those of us of faith place their trust (rely upon God). And how could we not place our trusts in God, seeing that it is He who has guided us our ways. *We shall bear with patience whatever hurt you have done us.* Let those of faith place their trust in God (rely upon God). But those who denied the truth told their messengers: "We shall expel you from our land, or shall return to our ways." Whereupon their Lord revealed to them [to the messengers]: We shall destroy the unjust ones, and make you to dwell the earth after them. This is [my promise] to all those who stand in awe of my Presence and of my warning.

(14:9–14)

Active Peace in Modern Islam

Encounters with this material clearly have the potential to awaken radical nonviolence. It is, therefore, not surprising that Abdul Ghafar Khan, one of the leaders of the Pashtun tribes in some of the most difficult and complicated contexts in the twentieth century, was inspired by his faith to help form one of the most disciplined and organized nonviolent movements known in modern history in the rugged terrains of Khyber Pass.[8]

In our world, Gandhi is used as the iconic figure of nonviolent struggle in the modern era. However, if history were chronicled according to facts and events, there would be a Muslim figure alongside him equally central. The image of Gandhi as the leading figure in the nonviolent struggle of India would not be complete without his friend and partner Abdul Ghaffar Khan (known as Badshah Khan)—who had already been committed to nonviolence when he joined forces with Gandhi and other leaders. When explaining his commitment to nonviolence, Khan said he was not doing anything other than what Muhammad did all the time he was in Mecca. Having closely studied the Quran and Hadith tradition, Khan had scholarly aspirations at a young age, but due to family circumstance he could not pursue his such academic interests. Instead, he walked his understanding among his people, the Pashtun of the Khyber Pass, and taught them to be radical Muslims—radically nonviolent, radically compassionate. Khan ended up creating a living scholarship of active peace that is still breath-taking in its scope and depth of commitment. His three main principles were love, work and invincible faith (mahabat, amal, yaqeen). For him, faith was in trusting in the laws that govern the moral dimension, and hence having certainty about the power of compassion and living a life of service and no harm.[9]

Those encountering Khan's legacy for the first time may find his radical nonviolence surprising, especially because it had been specifically Islamically inspired. But it was precisely this commitment to being a devout, observant Muslim and a committed reader of the Quran and Prophetic path that inspired Khan to part ways with the tribal violence that plagued his region. He wanted to live as an authentic Muslim, walking the path of Muhammad. He was able to re-channel his tribe's code of honour, based on revenge and fighting prowess, to become an honour code constructed around the values of patient endurance and social service. Khan inspired his community to view strength and dignity not in taking revenge but in being faithful and withstanding difficulties, imprisonment and even being killed by the colonial British. Khan created a new code of honour—in service, faith and nonviolent action on the ground. His nonviolence was not a foreign paradigm imported from outside his cultural and religious worldview. It was his deep commitment to wanting to live a more Islamically authentic life that made him see beyond the confines of his immediate particular cultural context. He also had come to see that many of the tribal values were draining the Pashtun tribes in the rugged mountainous region of Khyber Pass. Khan first started his activism by focusing on opening schools and digging wells and latrines. In addition, in his community projects he was committed to making women's education and political engagement one of the community's priorities. This is another area in which he went against the grain of the strong patriarchal and macho values of the tribal code—seeing what he did, one could easily consider him a natural feminist. This is one of the radical and drastic differences from Gandhi, who was not as sensitive as Khan to gender inequalities and the significance of women's presence in any reform and liberation movement, particularly in nonviolent struggle. Khan insisted on recruiting women into his army of the Khudai Khidmatgar (Army of Servant of God) from the initial stages.

Khan did not frown upon the passion and authentic tribal values that motivated and fuelled his people. He instead redirected this passion for dignity and pride from a basis of violence and compulsive reactions to a basis of self-restraint and service—naturally requiring more patience and resilience. Instead of rejecting his people by reacting negatively to them or accepting the ways of his people by being pulled into tribal violence, Khan did something quite rare and unique. He transformed his culture by using the very source that caused violence as sources that inspired nonviolence. He offered a change in valence—the intensity of the code of honour was still there, but its direction was completely shifted.

The ability to transform his culture in positive ways is what makes Khan stand out as a unique leader and a model from which to study and learn. He represents what it means to be Muslim, to be an active and conscious peace-maker in extremely challenging conditions and circumstances. He was a leader who advanced the cause of his people through nonviolent means in one of the most war-honouring cultures, one which many regional and foreign powers utilized—unfortunately still to this day—to advance their interests. Khan showed his people, by example, that one does not stop being a warrior. He showed them that being a brave warrior can take various forms, including a new kind of warrior that might have seemed unfamiliar to them. He showed them how to be warriors of peace when he founded the first and only organized nonviolent army in human history.

Khan deserves more space given his outstanding legacy, but I briefly use his example here to show a modern model that relied on Islamic sources and which sprang organically from within a deeply religious and traditional Islamic milieu. Khan's great legacy is evidence that Muslim culture has deeply rooted, authentic nonviolent and pacifist values—quite present to those who are willing to think and look beyond orthodox, institutionalized religious discourse. Khan was not always a welcome figure among the clergy or spiritual Sufi masters given his commitment to land reform, gender equality and the willingness to courageously stand for the week and underprivileged, regardless of their religious affiliations.

What Khan created was a living theology—a new dynamic of Islamic faith and action that used the available resources in coming up with creative and ethical responses.

Khan's lived theology points to the possibilities for a more positive and proactive frame of action—paving an alternative paradigm in dealing with oppression and injustice that go beyond either the reactionary violent discourses or the resigned complacent apologetic ones. The challenge is in constructing a new theology of nonviolence as an authentic Islamic alternative to facing injustices and transforming one's conditions. The ethos of armed resistance unfortunately still plagues most of the liberation discourse in many developing societies—not just Islamic ones. Armed struggle and violent resistance have had long and enduring legacies and are seen as the path to freedom, when all the arms-dealing and world economic hierarchies work to cause further subjugation of these very struggles. Many societies in poorer, colonial and totalitarian contexts fall prey and are lured to armed struggle as a means of alleviating their conditions, at a tremendous cost in lives and resources, and with horrific outcomes.

However, given the rich and varied resources for nonviolent ethos, it is not surprising that the values of nonviolence have repeatedly arisen, even if somewhat limited or crushed. The fact that active peacefulness and commitment to nonviolent action on the ground in the face of injustice and oppression have surfaced in various forms across different eras or contexts in Muslim societies, regardless of scope or results, shows that alternative modes of resistance are available, even if not as easily accessible or as loud and mainstream as others. This commitment to nonviolence arose in several contexts in the Arab world in the past few years, more so in some contexts than others, in the Arab Spring that swept many countries from Tunisia to Yemen. And yet, sadly many of these fledgling and nascent nonviolent movements in these contexts were brutally crushed, and sometimes sidelined by louder and stronger movements within revolutionary discourses—especially in Syria, where arming was seen as a necessity in dealing the regime violence and brutality, including by many secularist voices. Sadly, Khan's movement was also crushed by the local Pakistani government after independence and partition.

When the Buddha Meets the Children of Abraham

All these challenges and the momentum of violent ethos give further significance to the concept of Jihad in Islam—which literally means exerting energy and effort in a focused and concerted manner in a specific direction. To go against the grain of our cultural programming—i.e., using force and reacting with aggression— requires tremendous effort, conscious redirecting of our energies and repeated practice. And this counter-consciousness is what is commonly present in all our traditions. It is the movement of energy in a different direction. We each have to create and construct our active, peaceful paths given the strong historical momentum of our violent cultures and the valorisation of the violent hero.

And although our faiths and wisdom traditions all have many transformative tools and teachings, they also are often hidden and marginalized, and remain abstract and conceptual in scriptural and ritualized art. In some ways they are the beautiful, somewhat irrelevant soundtrack to the main religious, often fundamentalist, discourse.

Sometimes, when I am praying at a mosque and the imam recites, during salat, passages in the Quran, and quite often in a melodic singing voice, with strong messages of radical forgiveness, radical compassion and radical nonviolence, I am surprised anew at the freshness and power of this direction, and yet leave wondering how we can hear these recitations pushing counter to our mainstream cultures without much impact. But then I remember that there are similar passages in the Torah and Gospel and in other religious literature, and these are heard without really being understood as radical philosophical maxims inviting us into a completely new paradigm. There is a fair amount of complacency and adaptation in all religious traditions with the ethos of power and divisiveness.

This is perhaps because in our collective human cultures we generally associate peacefulness with idleness, even if somewhat unconsciously, and violence with action. We conceive of peace as passive and of war as active. In Islamic teachings, emphasized in the Quran and Hadith, as I have been arguing in this chapter, this is where a paradigm shift could occur, where peace is placed within an active frame of consciousness and with a practical directive for action. This explains the added emphasis on active peace, in Islam, because we are and have been surrounded by the other paradigm of aggression and reaction. Islam, as active peacefulness, is therefore an invitation to a new paradigm of active and conscious action in a nonviolent manner. This is naturally connected to our trust in another source of power, where if we are capable of achieving a certain state of trust in the law of compassion, as Khan always taught, we could become conduits for this current of peacefulness, and see it manifest different kind of consequences.

This state of being consciously and actively peaceful is a state where we are alive, aligned and in tune with the universe—entering the field of peacefulness and compassion and achieving results based on the laws that govern this field. This implies that once we lose our old, dated trust in the power of coercion and aggression, then whatever we do would stem from an alternative paradigm. These are not esoteric claims, as Khan demonstrated to his community, who had ample access to some spiritual and mystical teachings but were entrapped in a violent paradigm. What Khan wanted to show his community was the efficacy of nonviolence—the tools for active peacefulness to resolve one's own situational difficulties. In one of his well-known quotes, he said to his community:

> I am going to give you such a weapon that the police and the army will not be able to stand against it. It is the weapon of the Prophet, but you are not aware of it. That weapon is patience and righteousness. No power on earth can stand against it.
>
> *(Easwaran 1999)*

It is important to find ways to turn these values into practical approaches and render them applicable at both the individual and communal levels; to push beyond idealistic aspirations towards an empirical understanding of peace—and hence have the chance to observe its different consequences in various contexts. The importance given in Buddhism to the experiential dimension is something that could enhance and complement our Abrahamic faiths. It was the Buddha who asked those around him to test his teachings in lived contexts. The Quranic text does the same, first by pairing faith with action and second by repeatedly asking us to observe and wait for the results and consequences, whether good or bad, in various narratives (11:121–122). Muhammad Iqbal, in discussing the shift to the experiential in Islam, found in the shift to more instances of inductive logic in the text argues that this shift, over the span of several centuries, helped Muslim scientists, culminating in works like those of Ibn al-Haithem and others, in setting the foundations for empiricism. But for him, this shift was not exclusive to natural phenomena. Iqbal discusses the Quranic verses that point to the signs of the "horizons" and within "ourselves" as directing us to understand both natural material phenomenon and the inner realms through empirical methodology. He quotes a poem by Rumi about the nature of reality in which a group of Sufis have a group of scholars knock on their door. We have a great deal of knowledge to impart to you, they say to them. But the Sufis inside reply, If you have books, we have many books, but [if] you bring footprints, please come inside. "The truth is that all search for knowledge is essentially a form of prayer," says Iqbal (2013, 91). "The scientific observer of Nature is a kind of mystic seeker in the act of prayer." This practical application of compassion is the real test for all of us who claim compassion but fall back on familiar patterns in actual life situations—individually and collectively. Do we have books and words on compassion, or do we bring footprints?

There is a narrative in the Quranic text about the failure of religion and the challenge in living our ideals beyond conceptual forms. It is a story that beautifully and humorously captures the shortcomings of our grand claims even, or especially, when we are making the highest religious claims. This gap in aligning our highest ideals to our real actions is metaphorically highlighted in the encounter of Moses with a wise teacher. For many Muslim scholars throughout the centuries, there has been an inclination to link the wise man to the figure of the Buddha. Moses, as one of the leading and central Prophets in the Quranic scripture, represents the ultimate prophetic figure. And yet he is summoned to encounter another dimension of knowledge—another reality, another ocean of possibilities. Moses represents religion at its most received form; he is the archetypal prophet holding the tablets—the Word of God made physically incarnate, and yet, in Surah al Kahf, he is commanded to go and learn from a wise teacher who has been endowed with "within-ly knowledge" (Al i'lm al-Ladduniey)—the "inner science." The mystic scholars in their teachings had given much attention to this particular story and the figure of the wise "servant of God" because it underscores the discrepancy between our ideal discursive levels and experientially lived journeys.

In the narrative, Moses accepts the command and arrives at the appointed place "at the meeting of the two oceans" (18:60). And the wise one, the Buddha, takes Moses on a journey. The only condition the Buddha demands of Moses is to have patience. He states to Moses, "You shall not be able to be patient with me. How shall you be patient with that around which you have no knowledge." Moses, however, confidently assures him of his patience: "You shall find me, God willing, patient and I shall not disobey any of your commands" (18:69).

Easier said than done!

Moses goes on the trip and at every turn and event he reacts, completely losing his patience, as certain things trigger him. After three mishaps, the Buddha then ends the journey and explains to Moses all that he did not understand—all the things around which he did not have knowledge. The narrative highlights the difference between what we promise verbally or think we know conceptually and the actual experience of living these values in our own lives. It is precisely this line drawn in the sand of life between the saying and the doing which the passage invites us to contemplate and observe—between the ideal and the experiential, between our grand claims and actual modest delivering. The Buddha figure in the story draws our attention to the difference between upholding conceptual values and the challenge of living them; between talking the talk and walking the walk at the meeting of the two oceans.

It does seem logical that the Buddha has been considered by some Muslim scholars as the wise teacher, the one to direct the children of Abraham to test out patience, to test drive it rather than simply preach it—the Buddha helping these

Abrahamic communities step from the tablets and scripture to interact with life and to see life as the living holy Writ demanding patience and compassion as it unfolds.

This meeting between Moses and the Buddha captures the core of our dilemma, especially in our idealized self-image(s). The story holds a mirror to the human condition. Our patience is as real as our doing patience and not as our claims of being patient. Peace is to the extent we are capable of living in this "beautiful patience" (rather than our uses of patience as a slogan and claim).

It is this walking of active patience instead of talking patience that leads to the end of suffering; our walking of active peace instead of talking peace that could end our dark age of war and the compiling of arms. This will not happen if we wait for peace to descend upon us. Peace is always available. But choosing active peacefulness means we choose to become consciously and actively peaceful, and to challenge the killing brother so deeply programmed within, like Khan did when he transformed his community's values and creatively challenged both colonial British brutality and Pashtun violence through active peacefulness.

We have both possibilities, being afraid and falling into mindless rage and reaction, or stepping above all this and freeing ourselves from the old programs to connect to a higher frame of reference—where harming another is scarier than dying. We all come for brief visits and our departure is certain; yet our choices during our brief stay are in that narrow space of freedom in which we could take alternative paths. Choosing to be actively Muslim, consciously peaceful and compassionate, means we respond to God by finding creative ways out of harm and actively and willingly choose to enter Peace.

This Peace has many paths, and they all are capable of ushering us into the palace where there is no fear or grief, where the end of war is no longer a dream but a real possibility, where love is not a word but a verb.

Notes

1 For a more detailed discussion of the meaning of Islam and of being Muslim, with clarifications regarding the grammatical differences in translating Islam in an active positive sense or as a passive state, read Nevin Reda (2012), "The 'Good' Muslim, 'Bad' Muslim, Puzzle? The Assertion of Muslim Women's Identity in the Sharia Debates in Canada," in *Debating Sharia: Islam, Gender Politics, and Family Law Arbitration*, ed. Anna Korteweg and Jennifer Selby. University of Toronto Press, 2012, p. 243.
2 Mohammad Iqbal discusses of the sources of knowledge beyond scripture and revelation, and the dynamic and open discourse of the Quran in relation to both self and the universe, in his well-known classic, *The Reconstruction of Religious Thought in Islam* (Stanford University Press, 2013; part of the Encountering Traditions Series).
3 Muhammad Asad's (1980) English translation of the Quran, *The Message of the Quran*, (Gibraltar: Dar Al-Andalus, 1980) was mostly used for quotations from the Quran, with certain modifications and changes to align the passage more closely to the original Arabic, even if sometimes this compromised the poetic quality of the verses.
4 Sahih al Bukharri, from the book of "Bab al Fitan." Hadith No. 6665.

5 These Hadiths are found in the Sunnan of Abi Dawood (and in Sunnan Al-Bukhari and Sunnan Musslim).
6 Sunnan Ibn Majah, Kitab al Fitan, Hadith No. 3959.
7 For a further discussion on these Quranic passages and Hadith, see the work of the Syrian Scholar Jawdat Said, *Madhhab Ibn Adam al-Awal: Mushkilat al-Unf fi al-Amal al-Islami* [*The Path of Adam's First Son: The Question of Violence in Islamic Movements*] (Beirut: Dar Al Fikr, 1993[1966]).
8 There are several excellent biographies of Khan, but for a concise and short discussion of the highlights of Khan's life, the nonviolent army he organized and the education and recruitment of women in the movement, read Robert C. Johansen's (1997) excellent journal article, "Radical Islam and Nonviolence: A Case Study of Religious Empowerment and Constraint among the Pashtun," *Journal of Peace Research*, Vol. 34, no. 1 (Feb, 1997), pp. 53–71. Canadian filmmaker Teri McLuhan also made a documentary with important real archival footage on Khan titled *The Frontier Gandhi* (2008): www.thefrontiergandhi.com/
9 Eknath Easwaran (1999) discusses Khan's understanding of nonviolence and Islamic faith in his biography of Khan, *Nonviolent Soldier of Islam: Badshah Khan: A Man to Match His Mountains* (Tomales: Nilgiri Press, 1999).

References

Asad, Muhammad. *The Message of the Quran* (English translation of the Quran). Gibraltar: Dar Al-Andalus, 1980.
Easwaran, Eknath. *Nonviolent Soldier of Islam: Badshah Khan, a Man to Match His Mountains*. Berkeley: Blue Mountain Center of Meditation, 1999.
Iqbal, Muhammad. *The Reconstruction of Religious Thought in Islam*. Stanford: Stanford University Press, 2013.
Johansen, Robert C. "Radical Islam and Nonviolence: A Case Study of Religious Empowerment and Constraint Among Pashtuns." *Journal of Peace Research* 34, no. 1 (February 1, 1997): 53–71.
McLuhan, T. C. *The Frontier Gandhi Badshah Khan | A Film by T.C. McLuhan*. T. C. McLuhan Peace on Earth Productions, 2008. www.thefrontiergandhi.com/about.html.
Reda, Nevin. "The 'Good' Muslim, 'Bad' Muslim Puzzle? The Assertion of Muslim Women's Islamic Identity in the Sharia Debates in Canada." In *Debating Sharia: Islam, Gender Politics and Family Law Arbitration*, edited by Anna Korteweg and Jennifer Selby. Toronto: University of Toronto Press, 2012, pp. 231–256.
Said, Jawdat, *Madhhab Ibn Adam al-Awal: Mushkilat al-Unf fi al-Amal al-Islami* (*The Path of Adam's First Son: The Question of Violence in Islamic Movements*). Beirut: Dar Al Fikr, 1993 (first edition: 1966).

12

TRANSFORMING TERRORISM WITH MUSLIMS' NONVIOLENT ALTERNATIVES?

Chaiwat Satha-Anand

On the afternoon of December 1, 2001, a 24-year-old Palestinian named Nabil went to see his friend, chatted with him, paid him the $15 debt he owed, and handed him a petition he had written to the local council to tar the road outside his family home. Then he washed his car, went to prayer, and read the *Qur'an*. At 10 p.m. he drove off to pick up another friend, and together they went to detonate the bomb on their bodies at Ben Yehuda shopping mall on that fateful Saturday night, killing themselves, 11 Israelis, and wounded 37 others (Barker 2003, 11).

On September 7, 2003, Ariel Sharon gave the final order to an Israeli F-16 fighter plane to fire a laser-guided bomb at an apartment in Gaza in an effort to assassinate Shaykh Ahmed Yasin, the revered leader of Hamas. The shaykh managed to escape with a minor injury and Hamas threatened unprecedented revenge, declaring that any Israeli who occupies their land is a potential target and that this assassination attempt has "opened the gates of hell" (*Bangkok Post*, September 8, 2003).

AFP recently reported that on the second anniversary of the September 11, 2001, attack, the Muhajiroun, a British Islamic group, was planning a London rally dedicated to the terrorists/hijackers whom they called the "magnificent 19." The group spokesperson told BBC radio that "I believe the Muslim community around the world believes those 19 were magnificent" (*Bangkok Post*, September 9, 2003). Meanwhile, Abdul Hadi Awang, president of the opposition Pan-Malaysian Islamic Party, speaking to 2,000 supporters at his party's annual meeting in Kuala Lumpur on September 12, 2003, denounced the US as an enemy of Islam and voiced support for Palestinian suicide bombers (*Bangkok Post*, September 13, 2003).

These newspaper clippings indicate at least three points. First, violence related to Muslims will continue—some carried out with Muslims as targets, while others will be committed in the name of Islam. Second, terrorism, especially the 9/11 incident in which some 3,000 people were killed with 19 suicide killers, can be seen by some Muslims as justified and, in fact, celebrated. Third, given the above two conditions and the fact that there is a high percentage of Muslims that expresses support for the use of suicide bombing as a method to "defend Islam" in several countries—73 percent in Lebanon and 27 percent in Indonesia (Pew Global Attitudes Project 2002)—I do not think it would be difficult to find another "Nabil," an ordinary young Muslim who would sacrifice his/her life for the cause he/she believes in.

This chapter is an attempt to suggest that terrorism, seen as a form of political violence, grounded in its own reasons yet producing destructive results to all concerned, needs to be transformed into more productive/creative conflicts with Muslims' nonviolent alternatives. I would argue that this radical transformation is possible precisely because of the similarities, not differences, between terrorism used by some Muslims and "principled nonviolence." I will begin with an attempt to understand terrorism as a form of political violence and ask not what it is, but how it works. Then the religious edicts condemning and justifying terrorism by traditional religious scholars as against/supporting the tenets of Islam will be critically examined by drawing attention to three philosophic issues: questioning the supremacy of instrumental rationality, the absence of innocents, and the reduction of humans to objects. Then, examples of Muslims' nonviolent actions as a creative form of resistance aimed at and engaged to move conflicts in the world towards "truth and justice" will be explored as an alternative to terrorism, highlighting not only the obvious differences, but more importantly the similarities between principled nonviolence and religious-based terrorism.

Understanding Terrorism: Rationality and Dynamics

In the period leading up to and including September 11, from 1998–2002, there were 1,649 incidents that the US Department of State termed "international terrorist attacks." Contrary to conventional understanding, most of these occurred in Latin America, with 676 incidents compared to 387 in Asia and 135 in the Middle East. Business targets have been attacked 1,462 times, which accounts for more than 66 percent compared to diplomatic, governmental, military, and other targets. It goes without saying that civilians have been the primary victims, while the military accounted for only 1.7 percent of all targets. The highest number of casualties in the past five years, excluding the 9/11 incident, however, was in Asia with 4,161, compared with 283 in Latin America and 1,462 in the Middle East. The September 11, 2001 attack clearly contributed most significantly to the number of casualties in North America with 4,091 (U.S. Department of State 2003).

From 1980 to 2001, of 188 separate suicide terrorist attacks, 179 (or 95 percent) of them were part of organized campaigns, with the non-religious Marxist-Leninist Tamil Tigers of Sri Lanka becoming the world leader of this type of terrorism. More importantly, this phenomenon has been steadily on the rise since those who supported such practices have learned that "it pays." As a result of terrorism, American and French military forces were compelled to leave Lebanon in 1983, Israeli forces to quit Gaza Strip and the West Bank in 1994 and 1995, and the Sri Lankan government to work towards an independent Tamil state from 1990 on, among other cases (Pape 2003, 344). In addition, according to B'tselem, the Israeli Information Center for Human Rights in the Occupied Territories, between September 29, 2000 and November 30, 2002, the number of Israelis killed by Palestinians was 640, among which were 440 civilians, with 82 under the age of eighteen. The number of Palestinians killed by Israelis was 1,597, 300 of whom were minors. From the signing of the Oslo agreement in 1993 until the beginning of August 2002, there were 198 suicide-bombing missions; 136 of these ended with the attackers blowing up themselves and others (Margalit 2003, 36).

Terrorism as a phenomenon is therefore important to any analysis of present global trends and politics because it is increasingly prevalent. In addition, the American reaction to the 9/11 tragedy with the use of force, aiming to correct the wrong of terrorism, has plunged the world deeper into deadly conflicts. President George W. Bush spoke on the second anniversary of September 11 that

> The memories of Sept. 11 will never leave us. We will not forget the burning towers . . . We will not wait for further attacks on innocent Americans. The best way to protect the American people is to stay on the offensive, to stay on the offensive at home and to stay on the offensive overseas.
>
> *(Bush Virginia Speech, 2003)*

In the two years after the September 11 incident, the US started two wars in Afghanistan and Iraq. Reports of casualties from these deadly conflict sites came in almost daily, while George W. Bush and his vice-president were advised not to be present at Ground Zero memorial services in 2003; it seems the president was right when he said that his "war on terror" was not over. In fact, this war has in some ways transformed the world into a more dangerous place plagued with the specter of violence—where ordinary people are trapped between the deadly force of terrorism carried out by both state and non-state actors on the one hand, and the hardened arms of the state drowning out the call for rights and liberties on the other (International Council on Human Rights Policy 2002).

If the effects of terrorism are to be mitigated in the long run, the phenomenon needs to be critically construed. It is important to first underscore the fact that the term terrorism itself is extremely political. For example, the US government's policy in dealing with terrorism clearly states that while concession to terrorists will not be made, it will apply pressure on states that sponsor terrorism and enhance international collaboration against it. More importantly, it will try to bring terrorists "to justice for their crimes" (ibid.).

According to Richard Falk, terrorism in US and Israeli political discourse has been associated with anti-state forms of violence that were so criminal that "any method of enforcement and retaliation was viewed as acceptable, and not subject to criticism" (Falk 2003, xviii). However, those who use terror tactics normally avoid the term and claim they are resisting oppression and fighting for justice. But then most governments also exclude "state terrorism" and thereby relegate a major source of violence and fear suffered by civilians around the world to silence (International Council on Human Rights Policy 2002).

To better understand terrorism, therefore, it might be instructive to hear the voices of both a perpetrator and a victim.

On the morning of December 23, 1929, Lord Irwin, the British Viceroy, had just returned from a tour of South India. As he approached Delhi, a bomb had exploded under his train. Lord Irwin escaped injury and Gandhi congratulated him on his miraculous escape (Nanda 1997, 234). Gandhi also delivered a speech to a meeting of the Indian Congress party and drafted a resolution denouncing terrorism. He wrote that he would despair for nonviolence if he were not certain that bomb throwing was nothing but "froth coming to the surface in an agitated liquid." The danger of terrorism lies in its internal consequences: from violence committed against the foreign ruler, there was only an "easy, natural step to violence to our own people whom we may consider to be obstructing the country's progress."[1] He seemed to think of terrorism as a kind of delusional, irrational act. As a matter of fact, in January 1930, a small left-wing Indian terrorist group founded in 1928, the Hindustan Socialist Revolutionary Army (HSRA), published a manifesto titled "The Philosophy of the Bomb," attacking both Gandhi's policy of nonviolence and his criticism of terrorism, which was due to "sheer ignorance, misrepresent[ation], and misunderstand[ing]," and claiming that those who committed such acts are "delusional" and "past reason" (Charan 1979, 137).

Most of the HSRA members had previously been members of Gandhi's nonviolent movement, but they turned to the use of violence when their goals could not be realized. Their manifesto claimed that the terrorists do not ask for mercy nor compromise, that their war is a war to the end, and that the mission of the youth of India is to conduct not just "propaganda by deed" but "propaganda by death." It argued that a revolution cannot be completed without terrorism and that it was not an imported European product but homegrown. Most importantly, it claimed that a terrorist does not sacrifice his or her life out of the psychological need for appreciation or any other form of irrationality/insanity. Instead, the document emphatically stated that "it is to reason and reason alone that he (a terrorist) bows" (ibid., 139). Because of British domination, an Indian was forced by reason and dictated by conscience to go into violence by accepting terrorism. This is because terrorism instills fear in the hearts of the oppressors and brings hope of revenge and redemption to the oppressed masses. It gives courage and self-confidence to the wavering and shatters the spell of the subject race in the eyes of the world, because it is the most convincing proof of a nation's hunger for freedom (ibid.). According to Laura Blumenfeld, terrorism is "not so much about killing people as about dehumanizing them to make a political point." She should know because her father, a New York rabbi, was shot and wounded by a Palestinian in Jerusalem's old city in 1986. Twelve years later, she confronted Omar Khatib, the Arab gunman, in an Israeli courtroom; after several meetings, Omar wrote her father a letter stating that "Laura was the mirror that made me see your face as a human person [who] deserved to be admired and respected" (Sachs 2002).

From the perspectives suggested above, terrorism can be seen as a threat or an act of violence against civilians. Construed as a form of political violence, it can also be seen as a reaction to oppression and injustice and, hence, rational from the perspective of perpetrators. More importantly, the act of terror becomes possible when the victim has been dehumanized and is no longer recognized as a human being. But apart from specific conditions, such as organizational/technical skills or financial support for terrorists, it is also important to emphasize three other ways that terrorism works (Satha-Anand 2002).

First, it works by severing the link between the targets of violence and the reason for violence. This is perhaps the most glaring reason why it is often seen as irrational, since there seems to be no reason why the civilian victims, directly unrelated to the conflicts, are attacked. The point, however, is when that logical link is cut off, the question of innocent lives becomes irrelevant to the terrorists. The "enemy" society, already dehumanized, can be effectively turned into a monolith devoid of complexities that exist in reality, and thus anyone can be attacked.

Second, since terrorism can attack anyone at any time or place, it successfully robs a society of that precious sense of certainty that allows members to continue their lives in normality. I would argue that in the Hobbesian sense, terrorism retrogresses a political society to a "state of nature" when fear for one's own life replaces a sense of certainty grounded in a confidence that the state can protect its own citizens. When its ability to protect is compromised, if not altogether lost, its legitimacy to exist will be seriously called into question, since the protection of its citizens' lives is seen as the absolute minimum of the normal functioning of the state. This is one of the reasons why some scholars believe that the September 11 attack discloses a structural modification in the character of power and security, and hence a different approach to terrorism, guided perhaps by the framework of war and a reformulation of the limits of the use of force, is required. (Falk 2003)

Third, with the absence of normality amidst the hegemony of fear, it transforms the society that mourns the tragic fate of its victims into a society of possible victimizers bent on using violence against others. The purpose of terrorism as political violence is not exactly to create material or human destruction—though a case can be made for symbolic attack as in the September 11 incident—but to transform the very existence of the "enemy" society itself into an alienated collective facing internal contradiction at moral, cultural, and political levels that might eventually tear it apart.[2]

Treating Terrorism: Muslims' Condemnations and Justifications

A most curious little booklet circulated among Muslims that I have recently come across has two titles: *Clarification of the Truth in Light of Terrorism, Hijackings & Suicide Bombings* and *An Advice to Usaamah Ibn Laaden from Shaykhul Islam Ibn Baaz* (Ibn Baaz 2001).[3] As the former Mufti of the Kingdom of Saudi Arabia, Abdul Azeez Ibn Baaz (d. 1999 or 1420 AH) was considered by many a great scholar of "traditionalist" Islam and *Sunnah* (traditions of the Prophet). The booklet has two parts. The first is a religious-based argument in favor of obedience to the rulers. The second is a collection of various Islamic scholars' opinions on hijackings and suicide bombings.

Ibn Baaz called Bin Laden a *"khaarijee,"* a member of *Khawaarij*, which was a sect that appeared in the early history of Islam and was said to be responsible for the killings of many of the Prophet's companions.[4] They committed three major crimes: rebelling against Muslim rulers, declaring Muslims to be unbelievers due to sins, and making permissible the taking of human life unlawfully. Ibn Baaz cited a Hadith related by Ahmad and Tirmidhi that the Prophet said: "There are three things towards which the heart of a Muslim never shows hatred or rancor: Making one's actions sincerely for Allaah; giving obedience to the rulers (*wulaatul-umur*); and sticking to the *Jamaa'at* (united body)" (ibid., 2–3). It is interesting to note that in an interview with the *Nida'ul Islam* (no.15), bin Laden charged some of the Muslim leaders as well as the scholars, especially "in the country of the two sacred mosques," as engaging in the major *Kufr* (falling outside of the faith). This is another reason, if not a more important one, why Ibn Baaz regarded bin Laden as a *khaarijee*—because his statement was seen as a blanket *takfeer* (declaring Muslims to be unbelievers and therefore make allowable the spilling of their blood) (ibid., fn. 8, 7–8).

In an interview with *Al-Jazeerah* at the end of 1998, Osama bin Laden said:

> I look with great veneration and respect at those great men in that they lifted the humiliation from the forehead of our *Ummah* (community of believers), whether it was those who bombed in Riyaadh or those in Khobar or in East Africa, and whatever resembles these acts.

Ibn Baaz gave his *fatwah* (religious ruling) on "the terrorist attack in Riyadh" by stating:

> And there is no doubt that this act can only be undertaken by one who does not believe in Allah or the Last Day ... Only vile souls which are filled

with enmity, jealousy, evil, corruption and absence of faith in Allah and His Messenger can perform the likes of these acts.

Then he added his judgment: "And those who perform the likes of this are more deserving of being killed and being restrained on account of what they have committed of great sin" (ibid., 4).

Citing a Hadith compiled by Imam Muslim, Ibn Baaz made a point that a Muslim has to "hear and obey" his/her ruler even if "he flogs your back and takes your wealth," even if these leaders have "hearts of devils in the bodies of humans." He also cited the teaching of Imam al-Barbahaaree (d.329 AH), who taught that:

> If you find a man making supplication (*du'a*) against the ruler, know that he is a person of innovation (*bid'ah*). If you find a person making supplication for the ruler to be upright, know that he is a person of the *Sunnah* (traditions of the Prophet), if Allah wills.
>
> *(ibid., 12–13)*

Based on early Islamic history when Uthmaan Ibn Affaan (the third noble caliph) was killed as a result of discord (*fitnah*) among the elites of the time, especially between Ali and Mu'aawiya (the fourth and fifth caliphs after the Prophet), Ibn Baaz was extremely antagonistic to the idea of challenging or disobeying the rulers. In other words, Ibn Baaz claimed that discord and open rebellion resulted from "open proclamation of the faults of the rulers." Armed with hatred for the rulers, the people will kill them (ibid., 14–15).[5]

Ibn Baaz's concern could be illustrated by the Sadat assassination. Muhammad 'Abd al-Salam Faraj, who was tried and executed in 1982 for the October 6, 1981 assassination of President Sadat, wrote in his *Al-Farida Al-Gha'eba* (*The Neglected Duty*), a most important repository of his group's thought, that:

> Fighting the near enemy is more important than fighting the distant enemy ... The cause of the existence of imperialism in the lands of Islam lies in these self-same rulers.... There can be no doubt that the first battlefield of the *jihad* is the extirpation of these infidel leaderships.
>
> *(quoted in Lewis 2002, 107–108)*

When asked to explain his motive, Khalid al-Islambouli, an officer who was the instigator and executor of the Sadat assassination, stated in the Egyptian investigation file record that: "I did what I did, because the Shari'a was not applied, because of the peace treaty with the Jews and because of the arrest of Muslim 'Ulamaa without justification"(Guenena 1986, 44). It could be said that the killing of President Sadat was perceived as a necessity because he was *a heretic* (*Kufr*) since he did not rule in accordance with traditions of the Prophet (*Shari'a*); *a traitor* because he made peace with the enemy; and *an unjust ruler* because he arrested Islamic scholars (*Ulamaa*) unjustly (ibid).

In other words, Ibn Baaz's argument for obedience to rulers is based on the idea that disobedience, even criticism of the leaders, will eventually undermine their authority, create disunity among the Muslim community, and then lead to deadly conflicts, which in history appeared in the form of rightful rulers killed. This, in turn, would result in weakening and disunity, if not disintegration, among the Muslim *Ummah* (community). The theoretical question of limit to obedience, à la Aristotle's rights to revolt, was responded to with the words of Imam ash-Shawkaanee (d.1250 AH), who wrote that a believer can disobey the ruler if the latter disobeys God. Yet, "it is not permissible to revolt against the leaders even if they reach excessive levels of oppressions, as long as they establish the Prayer and no manifest disbelief appears from them" (Baaz 2001, 17).

This formulation of the ruler's disobedience to God, and therefore a justified pretext for disobeying him/her, is quite problematic for at least two reasons. First, it is a highly constricted notion of disobedience since only the sacred religious duty, prayer, is specified, while other duties—for example, treating scholars and citizens justly—are excluded as the basis for obedience among Muslims. Second, it seems that only "manifested" disobedience or glaring disbelief of God would justify Muslims' disobedience. This condition seems to establish the primacy of appearance over other types of "reality," easily concealed in the present times. Both conditions, including the fact that criticisms of Muslim rulers are discouraged, effectively result in a contracted space of politics. It is therefore not surprising that, in the eyes of Muslim assassins who claim to kill in the name of Islam, the most dangerous enemies of Islam are those within and that killing becomes a wedge driven into the texture of society to create a necessary space for desirable socio-political changes. In this sense, it could be argued that even with global-reach organizations such as Al-Qaeda, terrorism begins and exists in distinct contexts where local grievances are voiced. The interplay between local conditions such as the erosion of distributive capabilities of the states, perceptions of corrupt rulers, and the power of universal messages such as the Islamic call for social equity and moral piety would contribute significantly to the rise of violent alternatives in a constricted political space. I would therefore suggest that to treat terrorism as a purely "outside" or "international" phenomenon is insufficient for a critical understanding of the subject.[6]

The last part of the booklet, entitled "The Verdicts of the Major Scholars Regarding Hijackings & Suicide Bombings," mainly comprises the words of two religious scholars—Ibn Baaz and Ibn Al-Uthaymeen (d. 2000/1421 AH)—but a short section by Ibn Taymiyyah (d. 728 AH) on the "Seceders," or those who go out of the faith (*khawaarij*), is also included. It is divided into sections condemning "suicide bombings," "attacking the enemy by blowing oneself up in the car," "hijacking planes and kidnapping," and "those who partake in bombings, hijackings." Importantly, the document claims that the verdicts reflect "the true position of Islam and the people of *Sunnah* (traditions of the Prophet) towards the evils of those who hold permissible the shedding of blood without just cause" (Baaz 2001, 19). But it is the reasons given for these condemnations that shed light on the problematic nature of how terrorism is treated by Islamic scholars.

According to the booklet, there are three reasons why terrorists' actions, such as suicide bombings and hijackings, are wrong, judging from "the true position of Islam." First, suicide bombing is wrong because suicide itself is unacceptable in Islam. Citing the Holy *Qur'an* and a Hadith on the authorities of Bukhari and Muslim, Ibn Uthaymeen categorically states that one who commits *jihad* by means of suicide, such as attaching explosives to a car and storming the enemy, knowing full well that he/she who carries out the act will die, is regarded as "one who has killed himself, and as a result he shall be punished in Hell" (ibid., 23–24).[7] Suicide is a major sin because it is born out of desperation. In such a state, a Muslim calls for help from God and, with patience, God will assist him. To commit suicide, then, is a suspension of faith in God's infinite Mercy. In condemning suicide as a major sin, Ibn Uthaymeen quoted another verse from the *Qur'an*, which reads: "And whoever kills a believer intentionally, his recompense is Hell to abide therein, and the Wrath and the Curse of Allah are upon him, and a great punishment is prepared for him" (IV: 93). It is interesting to note that the content of this verse has very little to do with suicide but everything to do with homicide, unless one chooses to assume that the suicidal bomber is splitting his/her self into two, the self that was intentionally killed in "suicide" is seen as that of the believer, killed by another part of the self that has fallen from the faith. Hence, suicide in this sense is seen as taking the life of the believer, and he/she who commits it will be punished with a life in Hell.

Second, Ibn Uthaymeen suggests that suicide bombings will be acceptable if, according to Ibn Taymiyyah, it is a *jihad* in Allah's cause, "which caused a whole nation to truly believe (and become Muslims), and he did not really lose anything, since although he died he would have to die anyway, sooner or later" (ibid., 20). Death for a Muslim is not a negative state but a return to the Origin (*Al-Qur'an*, II: 156). But the act of tying explosives to themselves and then "approaching unbelievers and detonating them amongst them" is a clear case of suicide, and those who commit it will be in Hell because "this person has killed himself and has not benefited Islaam" (Baaz 2001, 21). The Shaykh advises against terrorism of this kind, because if the terrorist kills himself along with a large number of other people,

> then Islam will not benefit by that, since the people will not accept Islam ... Rather it will probably just make the enemy more determined, and this action will provoke malice and bitterness in his heart to such an extent that he may seek to wreak havoc upon the Muslims.
>
> *(Baaz 2001, 21)*

In other words, suicide bombing is condemned on the grounds that it would engender a stronger negative reaction from Muslims' opponents that would then adversely benefit their plight, as is the case in Palestine. Would this then mean that, had it furthered the Islamic cause, defined by practical and at times quantitative consequences to Muslims, it would have been acceptable "to the true position of Islam"?

Third, Ibn Baaz maintains that hijacking planes and kidnapping children, which now encompass the whole world, are great crimes. Governments and scholars must try to end "this evil," which has caused "great harm and inconvenience" to "the innocent." Those who partake in these acts of terror

> are not to be co-operated with, nor are they to be given salaams to. Rather, they are to be cut off from, and the people are to be warned against their evil. Since they are a *fitnah* (tribulation/trial) and are harmful to the Muslims, and they are the brothers of the Devil (*Shaytaan*).
>
> (ibid., 22, 26–27)

It seems that Ibn Baaz here condemns terrorism because of its harmful effects on *the innocents*. But then he instructs the Muslims to dissociate themselves from those who "partake in these acts" because of its harmful effects on *the Muslims*. A question can therefore be raised as to whether violent effects on innocents, and not necessarily Muslim innocents, constitute sufficient ground for believers to dissociate themselves from the perpetrators of these acts? This instruction to cut off the tie that binds Muslims in a community of faith because of the acts of terror committed is substantiated by the teaching of Ibn Taymiyyah (d. 728 AH), who said that Muslims must fight against those who strive to kill *every Muslim* who does not agree with their view, declaring the blood of the Muslims, their wealth, and the slaying of their children to be lawful, while making *takfeer* (declaring Muslims to be unbelievers) of them. This is because "they are more harmful to the Muslims than others, for there are none which are more harmful to the Muslims than them, neither the Jews and nor the Christians" (ibid., 26).

In the eyes of these scholars who condemn terrorism, terrorists are the enemies most harmful to Muslims because they are born from the bosom of Muslim communities. They were made into the "harmful" others, fallen from the ties of mercy that bind members together, and deserve to be destroyed. This last reason is strikingly similar to the argument made by those committed to acts of terror themselves, notably by some of those responsible for the 1981 Sadat assassination discussed earlier. In the final chapter of *Al-Farida Al-Gha'eba*, Faraj writes that the situation of Muslims resembled the time when they were under "the yoke of the Mongols." He then concluded that:

> Governments in the Islamic world today are in a state of apostasy . . . Our *Sunna* has determined that the apostate be punished more severely than he

who had always been an infidel. The apostate must be killed even if he is in no position to fight, while an infidel does not merit death in such a case.
(quoted in Sivan 1985, 128)

More important, perhaps, is to see how those Muslims who support violent acts and play their parts in committing such acts against civilians justify their terror.

Mahmoud Abouhalima, convicted for the 1993 World Trade Center bombing, explains that the act of terror was committed for "a very specific reason" and aimed at a "specific achievement." Commenting on the Oklahoma City federal building bombing, he said it was an attempt to "reach the government with the message that we are not tolerating the way that you are dealing with our citizens." Following Shaykh Abdul Rahman's teaching, Abouhalima condemns the US because it helped to create the state of Israel, supported secular Egyptian government, and sent its troops to Kuwait during the Gulf War. But he is against the US and its abhorrent policies not because he is anti-Christian, but because the American ideology of secularism is hostile towards religion, especially Islam. When asked if the US would be better off with a Christian government, he replied: "Yes, at least it would have morals" (Juergensmeyer 2000, 67–68). He also said that secular America did not understand him and people like him because "the soul of religion, that is what is missing." He compared a life without the soul of religion to a pen without ink; even if that pen is worth "two thousand dollars, gold and everything in it, it's useless if there's no ink in it." Religion as the soul revives the whole life, while secularism has none and, therefore, secular people "are just moving like dead bodies" (ibid., 69).

The feeling experienced by terrorists that others would not understand them is quite common. What is not are the explanations for this lack of understanding. While Abouhalima attributed this absence of understanding to the presence of secularism, others pointed to a lack of shared experience of suffering. Eyad Sarraj, a recipient of the Physicians for Human Rights Award, is a Palestinian psychiatrist who was detained three times by Arafat's forces in 1996. He expressed his shock when a BBC interviewer appeared to understand his comment that the struggle of the Palestinians is about how *not* to become a bomb, and that the amazing thing is not the occurrence of suicide bombing, but its rarity. He believed suicide bombings by Palestinians to be acts of desperation, a serious stage of "the seemingly perpetual conflict" after "we have tried everything." He explained what it means to live under Israeli occupation. Among other things, it means:

- identity number and permit to live as a resident, which will be lost if one leaves the country for more than three months;
- a traveling document that specifies that the holder is of an undefined nationality;
- being called twice a year by the intelligence for routine investigation and persuasion to work as an informer on "your brothers and sisters";

- leaving your home in the refugee camp in Gaza at 3 a.m., going through roadblocks and checkpoints to do the work that others won't and returning home in the evening to collapse in bed for a few hours before getting up for the following day;
- losing respect from one's own children when they see their father spat at and beaten before their eyes;
- seeing the (name of the) Prophet being spat on and called a pig by Israeli settlers in Hebron.

Sarraj concluded that this is why Palestinian children have been throwing stones, and as a result killed almost daily. When arrested, they were tortured and made to confess. Consequently, everyone in the community suspected one another of being spies. "We were exhausted, tormented and brutalized." He ended his account with a question: "I've told you a few things. Now do you understand why we have turned into suicide killers?" (Sarraj 1997, 1–2). But killing oneself as a result of an utterly exhausted and brutalized existence is one thing; killing others, including women and children who have nothing to do with the brutal life one has to endure, is quite another. How, then, could acts of terror that destroy the lives of innocents be justified?

Dr. Abdul Aziz Rantisi, one of the founders of Hamas, answered this question in an interview by saying: "We are at war"—a war not only with the Israeli government but also with the whole of Israeli society. He then clarified that this war is not against Jewish culture or religion. He said, "We're not against Jews just because they're Jews," but rather, and especially, because of Israel's stance towards the Hamas concept of an Islamic Palestine. It is "Islamic nationalism" that Israel wants to destroy. It is interesting to note the shift from Hamas' military operations aimed at military targets to the use of terror aimed at anyone anytime. Rantisi clearly stated that this shift took place when Palestinian demonstrators were attacked by Israeli police in front of Al-Aqsa mosque in 1990 and the massacre of Muslims in Hebron by Dr. Baruch Goldstein during the month of Ramadan in 1994, while Israeli soldiers were standing nearby. Rantisi concluded that these were "attacks on Islam as a religion as well as on Palestinians as a people." For this reason, the question posed about innocent lives lost was irrelevant because this war between Hamas and Israel is one with no innocent victims (Juergensmeyer 2000, 73). He added that the fact most misunderstood by others is that the Palestinians are seen as aggressors. Based on the reality of the occupation and the accompanying violence, he categorically stated that "we are not (the aggressors): we are the victims." In this sense, Rantisi thought of the bombings as a "necessary" moral lesson intended to make innocent Israelis feel the pain that innocent Palestinians had felt, to actually experience violence in order to understand what the Palestinians had gone through (ibid., 74).

In *Rehearsals for a Happy Death*, Anne Marie Oliver and Paul Steinberg recounted the statements of young volunteers for suicide-bombing missions in

Gaza using some of the data from videotapes. In one case, a smiling lad, no more than 18 years old, who would carry out a suicide bombing with plastic explosives attached to his body, stated that his act of terror would be committed

> for the sake of God, out of love for this homeland and for the sake of the freedom and honor of this people, in order that Palestine remain Islamic, and in order that Hamas remains a torch lighting the roads of all the perplexed and all the tormented and oppressed [and] that Palestine might be liberated.

Another young man said that "what a difference there is between one death and another ... Truly there is only one death, so let it be on the path of God" (quoted in ibid., 70–71). Seen from the perspective of these perpetrators, their acts are not irrational or aimless, wanton violence. Those who condemn it and even call it "suicide bombings" are wrong, since this conveys the meaning of an impulsive act by a deranged individual. These acts should instead be called, according to Rantisi, "self-chosen martyrdom" (*istishhadi*), because those who undertake them deliberately choose to carry them out as part of their religious obligation. Rantisi claims that Hamas does not order them to do it but "give[s] permission for them to do it at certain times" (ibid., 72–73).

It goes without saying that terrorists grow out of and operate in their specific contexts. But the accounts of those related to terrorism discussed above suggest some common threads that indicate that terrorism often grows out of a context of extreme injustice and is carried out to communicate those grievances in situations where other channels are absent or inadequate. People who commit "suicide bombing," for example, are young ordinary men (and women) who made their choices based on their sets of political and religious justifications. What is important, however, is that these deliberate decisions to kill or be killed in the name of Islam are made in a redefined world—a world at war without innocents. As a result, the logic of exclusivity assumes paramount significance. In the notebooks of some Uzbek students belonging to the Islamic Movement of Uzbekistan led by Soviet Army veteran Juma Namangani, who attended training courses on terrorism in the Fergana Valley during 1994–1996, *jihad* is considered "a cleansing act," where one of the aims is to raise popular awareness that the enemies are among them. A student writes:

> unbelievers and the government are oppressors; that they are connected with Russians, Americans and Jews, to whose music they are dancing; and that they don't think about their people ... We speak of the fate of faith betrayers, according to Islamic law and about how people should distance themselves from those who breach the faith and should side with the *mujahideen* ... it has to be announced that jihad is a necessary religious requirement, for all social groups of people. And in life, everyone must either be a Muslim or a non-Muslim, that is, no one can remain in the middle.
>
> (Olcott and Babajanov 2003, 36)[8]

Four groups of religious people were identified as targets for killing. They are:

> Those who try to gain converts to Christianity on Muslim soil. Spies who work as Christian clerics . . . Christians and Jews who speak against the *mujahideen* and those who propagate against Islam. Those Christians who collect money for the struggle against Muslims, and those who speak against Muslims.
>
> *(ibid., 38)*[9]

Reviewing these accounts of Muslims who chose the ways of terror as well as those who condemn them, I am struck not by the differences between these two groups but by the similarities. There is a drawing of a line between Muslims and the others at work here that makes violence/injustice against the other readily possible. Among the scholars working for the state, Muslims who disobey their rulers and become terrorists have fallen from the faith and therefore deserve to be punished, killed in this life, and will go to hell in the Hereafter. The world they live in, born out of their concrete experiences, is a world at war in which killing and violence can be justified. Yet this war is different because it is not a war between two armies or combatants (a place for non-combatants does exist). This is a war between two societies, Palestinian/Israeli or Muslim/non-Muslim, and therefore there are no innocents. The Muslims who use terror claim that they are the victims and that the terror is intended to communicate their grievances so that those who have inflicted pain on them will experience what they have been through. The people who commit and are committed to terror were deliberate in sacrificing their lives for the cause of something greater that they believe in.

If terrorism is construed as a form of political violence born out of structural causes, such as the absence of democracy and unjust distribution of national wealth, and is legitimized by religious convictions, among others, trying to put an end to it by military might is futile (Barker 2003, 138–140).[10] If terrorism poses a profound threat to the world, especially in terms of the ways that different people connect with one another with some degrees of certainty, then there is a need to deal with it. I would argue that violence is powerless against terrorism and condemnations are futile because their proponents ask the wrong questions. Perhaps a question that does not ask how to end terrorism, but instead how to transform it, will provide a more promising alternative.

Transforming Terrorism: Muslims' Nonviolent Alternatives?

Among my collection of newspaper clippings about violence in the Middle East, there is a picture of a man comforting another injured man in a road accident. The rescuer is gently patting the other's face with water. It would not be remarkable but for the fact that the injured man was an Israeli police officer on the way to the scene of clashes in Jerusalem, the place of accident was near a cliff in the

Jaber-al-Mukaber, Palestine, and the one who comforted him was a local Palestinian. In fact, local Palestinians came out to help all four Israeli officers.[11] This picture shows two things. First, a line drawn to divide humans into enemy camps that deserve only to be killed is not impervious to being crossed. Second, given the degree to which different groups of people have to stay together, it is possible to imagine that there are more crossings of such lines than what has been recorded in the press.[12]

A number of recent studies demonstrate that Muslims have found an alternative to terrorism in the use of nonviolent campaigns to address their grievances. In surveying 18 cases of unarmed insurrections against authoritarian governments in the Third World from 1978 to 1994, both successful and failed, Zunes found some that had taken place in Muslim societies, which naturally involved Muslim participation (Zunes 1994). There are also cases of Muslims' unarmed resistance in the Middle East and North Africa (Zunes 1999, 41–51; Dajani 1999, 52–74), as well as the use of communal nonviolent actions among Muslim minorities in Thailand (Satha-Anand 2003). Some years ago, there was a study on *sulha* (mediation/arbitration/ reconciliation), a Palestinian ceremony that is a positive symbol of reconciliation necessary for an alternative kind of cultural analysis highly important for Peace Studies (Smith 1989). A Palestinian academic has recently written a comprehensive study that identifies principles and values grounded in Islamic traditional sources for nonviolence, based on an indigenous Islamic context which could serve as guiding principles for a framework for the application of peacebuilding/nonviolence in the Islamic context (Abu-Nimer 2000–2001). Finally, Maria Stephan (2009) has compiled a collection of studies exploring *Civilian Jihad Nonviolent Struggle, Democratization, and Governance in the Middle East*, in which she notes that

> ordinary people across the Middle East, a region notorious for its many conflicts, have for decades fought for rights, freedoms, self-determination, and democracy without using violence. Khalid Kishtainy, an Iraqi intellectual, coined the term civilian jihad to describe a form of political struggle whose "weapons" include boycotts, strikes, protests, sit-downs, humor, and other acts of civil disobedience and nonviolent defiance.
>
> *(Stephan 2009, 1)*

The discussion of these studies is obviously beyond the scope of this chapter. But suffice it to suggest here that at a minimum, these studies show that Muslims' nonviolent actions do exist in contemporary societies.

Moreover, Muslims' nonviolence is by no means inactive nor passive but has evidently been part of spirited struggle against injustices in which Islamic scriptural sources continue to serve as fountains of justifications for them. The question here, however, is in what ways Muslims' nonviolent actions could become alternatives in transforming terrorism.

Based on a specific understanding of terrorism as a rational form of political violence and the justifications of terror given by perpetrators themselves discussed earlier, I would argue that similarities between terrorism and Muslims' nonviolent actions do exist, especially on two important issues: fighting injustice and death. However, two other important issues characterizing terrorism pose a hindrance to such transformation: the absence of innocents and the instrumental logic governing terrorism. By overcoming these important obstacles, given existing similarities, transforming terrorism becomes a distinctive possibility.

Existing Injustice

Understood as a form of political violence, terrorism is a response to perceived injustice, shaped by a fusion of local and global conditions. This is not that much different from the conditions faced by nonviolent movements around the world, especially a Muslim nonviolent movement fighting against British occupation in India from 1930 to 1947. In mobilizing support from the Pathans in the Northwest subcontinent to fight against the British with nonviolence, Abdul Ghaffar Khan (1890–1988), known to his people as *Badshah Khan* (emperor or king of kings) and to Indians as "the Frontier Gandhi," said:

> Fifty percent of the children in our country are ill. The hospitals are meant for the English. The country is ours, the money is ours, everything belongs to us, but we are hungry and naked in it. We have not got anything to eat, no houses. He has made *pukka* roads because he needs them for himself. These roads were built with our money. Their roads are in London. These are our roads but we are not allowed to walk on them . . . He excites the Hindus to fight the Muslims and the . . . Sikhs to fight the Muslims. Today these three are the sufferers. Who is the oppressor and who has been sucking our blood? The English.
>
> *(quoted in Banerjee 2000, 600)*

The 95-year-old Gurfaraz Khan who had listened to Badshah Khan's speech before joining him, said:

> He told us that it was wrong that this land was ours but rule was in British hands . . . he pointed out that injustice of our children running barefoot and they being in their suits . . . they could even afford to kick bread and we did not have enough to eat.
>
> *(ibid., 63)*

Listening to Khan's speeches, many of those who later joined his nonviolent movement admitted that they did not know that the British were ruling India at the time.

> He explained to us about the British and said how they had come from 80,000 miles away and were occupying our land that was not theirs. They were here to colonize us. He said that we must demand our independence and fight for it.
>
> *(ibid., 62)*

Another said,

> The mullahs (local Islamic religious leaders) and the *khans* were in the pay of the British so they never told people the truth. No one in the whole Frontier had the spirit or the guts to speak against the British other than Badshah Khan.
>
> *(ibid., 62)*

Not only did the British occupy and exploit India, they dealt with those who fought nonviolently for independence with imprisonment, forced labor, and sometimes direct killings. One example of direct killings was the Amritsar massacre at the order of General Dyer on April 13, 1919, when British troops fired into a nonviolent crowd, killing 379, and injuring more than a thousand notwithstanding (Ashe 1969, 194) in Kohat, 1932, following the arrest of Badshah Khan. British detachments opened fire at the people, killing some 300 Red Shirts (the *Khudai Khidmatgar*: the Pathan nonviolent movement in their uniforms) and injuring a thousand more (ibid., 114). The fact that these nonviolent Muslims could face the force of violence with nonviolence could be attributed to their organization, strict discipline not unlike a military organization (Ibid., 84–91), and strong commitment to nonviolence. This last quality is related to a specific understanding of death.

Death

Terrorists, especially suicide bombers or "self-chosen martyrs," commit their acts of terror for much larger causes, such as the liberation of their people. They are willing to sacrifice their lives because of their specific appreciation of "meaningful" death as a religious obligation in the Path of God. According to Gandhi, humans are advised to

> learn to love death as well as life, if not more so ... Life becomes livable only to the extent that death is treated as a friend, never as an enemy. To conquer life's temptations, summon death to your aid. In order to postpone death a coward surrenders honor, wife, daughter and all.
>
> *(Gandhi 1949, 338)*

For the Pathans, when Badshah Khan invited volunteers to join his nonviolent movement, he made it quite clear that given the authorities' brutality, death was a real possibility. Emphasizing the singularity and inevitability of death, he said, "As death will come only once therefore it is much better to die for the sake of one's nation and country." Then in a speech at a mosque on December 16, 1931, he added that

> a man is sure to die whether he is brave or not. But there is a difference between every sort of death. Do not forget your object—your object is to liberate your country. The best death is that when one dies the way of God and Holy Prophet.
>
> *(Banerjee 2000, 151)*

One of the reasons why a violent *jihad* is so problematic is not only because of different understandings between physical and spiritual *jihad* as often indicated (ibid., 148), but also because of its relationship with death. *Jihad* as a phenomenon has at times been reified and dehistoricized. As a result, the contradictions and ambivalence that have characterized its complex history have been erased; and the changing understandings of death as political action that have in part been revealed by history have been effaced. Seery argues that this situation is a result of how "Westerners" view non-Western cases of political suicide as "culturally pathological," where terrorists, guerrilla fighters, *sati* (Hindu women who followed their husbands to their deaths), and *satyagraha* (Gandhi's principled nonviolence) are lumped together as "crazed fanatics" (Seery 1996, 7; quoted in Euben 2002, 8). In a curious way, a Pathan's choice of using nonviolence against the British is remarkably similar to a suicide bomber's choice, because by renouncing violence while confronting the possibility of death, the death of a nonviolent Pathan would draw "the poison of violence" that was destroying the Frontier to himself literally and symbolically. Following Rene Girard's influential *Violence and the Sacred*, his death would become an act that "trick(s)" violence into spending itself on the victim whose death will provoke no reprisals and save others (Girard 1979, 36). But unlike Girard's notion, the nonviolent Pathan is not a ritualized scapegoat but a "self-chosen martyr" who chose to take up this burden with full awareness of the price he might have to pay in the name of purification and renewal. Far from pathological, death for a Muslim, especially a good death, is a return to the Origin and is hence taken as a next step closer to the End of Time and the Almighty (*Qur'an*, XLV: 24–26).

The Innocents

When a terrorist decides to blow up an airplane or a crowded bazaar, it is understood that the tie between the targets and the reasons for hurting the targets has been severed. But more important, perhaps, is the terrorists' conception of the world on the other side, on the "enemy's side." Rantisi, a Hamas founder, answered the question about justification for killing innocent victims by redefining the situation as a war situation. But even in war, not unlike just war theory, there are Islamic injunctions that stipulate that non-combatants, or innocent members of that society (such as women, children, and the elderly), are not to be harmed. In fact, this is one of my basic arguments for the affirmation of nonviolent actions in Islam because modern warfare with its destructive technology has blurred the line separating "enemies" from "innocent victims" (Satha-Anand 2001b). However, the world of terrorism is different. To justify such an indiscriminate act of terror, a redefined "world at war" is seen as a warring world without any innocents on the "enemy's side." This negative monolithic, and in a sense "essentialized" understanding of the others, renders violence against them easily justified and therefore highly probable.

My question is, what does Islam say when one looks at the world and sees no innocents, especially on the other side? Would this inability to see innocents among "the others" be reflective of an impaired faith in God as all Merciful? In his sadness and anger because his people went astray, Moses prayed to God asking to be forgiven:

> Admit us to Thy mercy!
> For Thou art the Most Merciful
> Of those who show mercy.
> (*Qur'an*, VII: 151)

When Jacob's sons came to ask his permission to bring his youngest son, Benjamin, with them to collect grain. Jacob was sad and afraid the same fate might await Benjamin because he had lost his beloved son, Joseph, once before. Then he said:

> But God is the best.
> To take care (of him),
> and He is the Most Merciful of those who show mercy!
> (*Qur'an*, XII: 64)

What these verses reflect, among other things, is the connection between God's Infinite Mercy and human's faith in it. Both Moses and Jacob could go on because they have faith in God's Mercy. If God's Mercy is Infinite, will it be possible to imagine a world where there is an absence of the innocents on the "other side" who would not, and will never, receive God's Mercy? What would be the consequences of such a perspective on a Muslim's faith? Umar Faruq Abd-Allah claims that the Mercy of God epitomizes Islam's ethos, noting that "the formula 'In the name of God, the All-Merciful, the Mercy-Giving' (bismi-Llahi 'r-Rahmani 'r-Rahim), occurs one hundred and fourteen times in the Qur'an" and is central to Islamic ritual (Abd-Allah 2004, 2).

Here is perhaps where nonviolent action is most different from terrorism. In the oath taken by recruits to be a member of Badshah Khan's Khudai Khidmatgars

(Servants of God), the Pathans have to pledge to refrain from violence and revenge; forgive those who oppress them or treat them with cruelty; refrain from taking part in feuds and quarrels, antisocial customs and practices; live a simple life; practice good manners; devote at least two hours a day to social work; and be fearless and prepare for any sacrifice. But most relevant to the present discussion is the very first pledge, which says: "I am a Servant of God, and as God needs no service, but serving his creation is serving him, I promise to serve humanity in the name of God" (Johansen 1997, 59).[13]

There are three important issues significant to Muslim nonviolent action within this pledge. First, it reaffirms God's Omnipotence and therefore needs no human service to Him. Second, it celebrates God's Mercy by the way in which serving humanity becomes a surrogate to serving Him. Third, it underscores God's universal magnanimity by identifying the target of service as "humanity," an inclusive category. This very last point is significant both theologically and historically. True, Qur'anic verses can be cited to support exclusivity and thereby be used to justify violence against the others who have fallen outside the faith, as is evident from the opinions of those who condemn and justify terrorism discussed earlier. But the theological ground for Muslim nonviolent action rests on Words of God that are inclusive. God says in the *Qur'an* that killing a person, who does not kill others or cause mischief, is like killing the whole people, while "if anyone saved a life, it would be as if he saved the life of the whole people" (V: 35).[14] The choice of action by Muslims, inspired or justified by the sacred text, is profoundly conducive to the kinds of Muslim one wishes to become, and by extension to the kinds of world Muslims seek to help create. Historically, Badshah Khan's Khudai Khidmatgars was different from the Maududi's *Jama'at-I-Islami* and Muhammad Ilyas' *Tablighi-Jama'at*. The Muslim nonviolent movement was non-sectarian since there were Hindus and Sikhs as members. It did not invite people to join the movement to improve themselves as good Muslims but to fight the British colonizer. And it did not seek to recreate the local community on the basis of early Islamic example (Banerjee 2000, 161–162). In this sense, I would argue that this Muslim nonviolent movement fought against the colonizer with nonviolence without impairing their faith in God's Omnipotence, Infinite Mercy, and Universality.

Instrumental Logic as Dehumanization

On August 16, 1946, declared "direct action day" by Muhammad Ali Jinnah, communal violence erupted in India. In Calcutta, more than 6,000 Muslims and Hindus were killed, while some 20,000 women and children were raped and maimed. Abdul Ghaffar Khan remarked: "I fail to understand how Islam can be served by setting fire to religious places and killing and looting innocent people" (Radhakrishnan 1998, 34; 31–35). I would argue that Islam cannot be served because the use of violence, in communal violence and especially in terrorism, is governed not only by the motives and desires of the perpetrators, but more importantly, by a specific kind of logic. The political theorist Hannah Arendt suggested some four decades ago that the very substance of violence is ruled by the "means-end category" where the end is always in danger of being overwhelmed by the means which it justifies. She clearly stated that "violence, finally . . . is distinguished by its instrumental character" (Arendt 1970, 46).

This instrumental character means that violence in general, and terrorism in particular, is but a tool. Its instrumental character is best described by Mahmud al-Zahar, a Hamas leader in Gaza. Following the cessation of suicide attacks in October 1995, he announced that: "We must calculate the benefit and cost of continued armed operations. If we can fulfill our goals without violence, we will do so. Violence is a means, not a goal" (quoted in Pape 2003, 348). As a tool, it is governed by an instrumental logic. This instrumental logic depends more on the specific character of the tool than on the intention of users. For example, if one decides to use terror against others, the nature of terrorism itself will dictate the way in which the act is to be carried out. Secrecy becomes part of the tool that would govern the user. Small and closed organization is another part of the tool that would make it possible to acquire the necessary C-4, for example. In other words, I would argue that it is the logic of the instrument that governs the users and the ways in which they perceive their targets. Although targets of terror can be conceptualized differently (see, e.g., Schmid 1992, 65), all share one thing in common: they have been turned into objects, at times through a complex dehumanization process that would make killing them easier.

This logic is markedly different from Muslim nonviolent action, where the opponents remain distinctively humans. In fighting against injustice, the logic of nonviolence dictates that the user is willing to sacrifice oneself without harming the others who are the opponents precisely because they are humans.

A Khudai Khidmatgar nonviolent soldier, Khalam Khan from Nowshera, said in an interview:

> We were hit on several occasions but never hit back. I had sworn against violence. Badshah Khan had explained to us that we are waging a war against the British with non-violence and patience . . . and we believed in him and followed him. Once a British police officer asked me why we followed Badshah Khan. He said: "Are you paid to do this?" I said, "no, we even have to take dry bread from our own houses to sustain us, and then go with Badshah Khan to oust you from our country." The officer patted me on the back.
>
> *(Banerjee 2000, 122)*

Turning humans into objects under the governing instrumental logic is also problematic from an Islamic point of view. Partaking in the most important article of faith, a Muslim believes that he/she is created by God, the Creator. God, the

Creator, created humans with a purpose (*Qur'an*, II: 30), while humankind "can have nothing but what he strives for" and most importantly, "thy Lord is the final Goal" (*Qur'an*, LIII: 39–42). If Muslims believe that God created humans with a purpose in search of God as their final goal, then to turn humans into objects is to rob them of their natures as the created with purpose. It also cuts the tie between humans and the pursuit of their final goal, which is God. In this sense, terrorism and violence in general, which turn humans into objects, effectively create a world in which the created have no purpose and the purposeful tie to the Divine cut off. Instrumental logic governing the use of violence, therefore, profoundly contradicts the Islamic cosmos governed by Purpose of the Divine.

Conclusion: Transforming Terrorism?

Terrorism as a form of political violence happens because injustice exists at local and sometimes global levels. In addition to addressing the structural causes that give rise to terrorism, it is important to transform it. I have argued that Muslim nonviolent action could serve as a platform for such transformation because of two important similarities: the imperative to fight injustice in the world and the willingness to die for a good cause. However, two profound differences do exist: the negation of the possibility of innocents among the opponent and instrumental logic governing terror. From a Muslim's point of view, neither the negation of the innocents on the other side nor turning humans into objects can be supported by a profound philosophic understanding of Islam where God's Mercy is Infinite and the creation of the universe, especially mankind, is done with a Divine Purpose.

Muslim nonviolent action, as evident from the examples of the Khudai Khidmatgar—a case of Muslim nonviolent soldiers who fought valiantly against the British colonizer with nonviolence—provides a possible alternative in which injustice can be corrected, self-sacrifice honored, and beliefs in God's Mercy and Divine Purpose not compromised. In this chapter, I have tried to understand terrorism as a rational phenomenon and have discussed the ways in which it was both condemned and justified by those most directly involved with the act in order to suggest that transforming terrorism with Muslim nonviolent action is not merely wishful thinking. The possibility that Muslim nonviolent action could present itself as an alternative to terrorism is distinctive because profound similarities do exist and important differences could be overcome such that the Muslims' struggle for justice, based on a critical Islamic understanding of the world, could continue.

Notes

* This chapter was originally presented at the International Conference on "Contemporary Islamic Synthesis," organized by the Center for Global Peace, American University, Alexandria, Egypt, October 4-5, 2003, an earlier version appeared in Said et al. (2006)
1 M.K.Gandhi, *Young India*, January 2, 1930.

2 It is interesting to note the militarized transformation of advanced democracies, which are increasingly undertaking prolonged military operations that include counter-terrorism and peacekeeping. See an insightful study on the repositioning of the Israeli military in the policymaking process which resulted from its engagement in warfare and other forms of military operations against the Palestinians in Yoram Peri (2002).
3 The inside cover indicated that it is translated into English by www.Fatwa-online.com, among others.
4 Called the "Seceders" because they regarded the succession of caliphs after the Prophet's death as unlawful. They later became disillusioned with Ali, the Prophet's son-in-law who was the closest male relative and the fourth caliph, for his compromise that one of them, Ibn Muljam, assassinated Ali. See a brief description of *khawaarij* in Ruthven 1997, 53, 59.
5 It could certainly be argued that the ardent support many Islamic scholars have given to the rulers in the Saudi Arabia is a result of a specific historical context of symbiotic relationship between the state and religious establishment, beginning in the mid-eighteenth century between Muhammad ibn' Abd-al-Wahhab (1703–1781), a puritan reformer, and Muhammad al-Sa'ud, a local ruler who ruled the area from 1745 to 1765. A useful, though brief, account of contesting sacred authority in Saudi Arabia is in Eickelman and Piscatori (1996, 60–63). But here I am concentrated on the rationality of justifications for obedience given by the religious scholars.
6 This is a modification of Barker's conclusion that "all terrorism is local." See Barker (2003, 120). See also a report on the rise of "religious extremism" in South Asia and the Middle East, which are consequences of the absence of democracy, the failure of governments to address social changes, and external support and the breakdown of *ijtihad* (independent interpretations of Islam under changing circumstances) within Islam itself.
7 *Al-Qur'an* cited is from "An-Nisaa": "And do not kill yourselves. Surely, Allah is Most Merciful to you." (IV: 29) The Hadith cited from both Bukhari and Muslim is the saying of the Prophet that "Indeed, whoever (intentionally) kills himself, then certainly he will be punished in the Fire of Hell, wherein he shall dwell forever."
8 It is interesting to note the subtitle of this article, which provocatively states: "During the mid-1990s, a group of young Uzbeks went to school to learn how to kill you. Here is what they were taught" (30).
9 See also what some Evangelicals are trying to do in Muslim lands at present in David Van Biema, "Missionaries Under Cover: Growing numbers of Evangelicals are trying to spread Christianity in Muslim lands. But is this what the world needs now?," *Time*, June 30, 2003, pp. 51–58. It is interesting to note some of these missionaries' prayers. One prays that "the weapon of mass destruction, Islam, be torn down" (52), while the other prays every early morning when he hears the muezzin's call the Muslims to prayer that "I pray against that call—that it would not affect their souls" (53).
10 See also Jason Burke (2003), who argues that the basis for support of terrorism among some Muslims is the sympathy felt for the cause worldwide and therefore fighting against terrorism by killing individual leaders or stopping their financial activities is "ludicrous" and will do nothing to solve the problem.
11 Reuters' photograph in *Bangkok Post*, September 30, 1996.
12 I have discussed this issue in Satha-Anand (2001a).
13 It is interesting to note that there are different versions of these oaths. See a different version by the 86-year-old Sarfaraz Nazim, a member of the Khudai Khidmatgars, in Banerjee (2000, 74).
14 *The Glorious Qur'an.* Translation and Commentary by A. Yusuf Ali, p. 252. It should be noted that in other translations, this text appears in verse 32 and not 35. See, for example, *The Koran.* N. J. Dawood (trans.) (London: Penguin Books, 1985), pp. 390–391.

References

Abd-Allah, Umar Faruq. "Mercy: The Stamp of Creation." *Nawawi Foundation Paper*, 2004. www.nawawi.org/wp-content/uploads/2013/01/Article1.pdf.

Abu-Nimer, Mohammed. "A Framework for Nonviolence and Peacebuilding in Islam." *Journal of Law and Religion* XV, nos. 1–2 (2000–2001): 217–265.

Arendt, Hannah. *On Violence*. New York: Harcourt, Brace & World, Inc., 1970.

Ashe, Geoffrey. *Gandhi*. New York: Stein and Day, 1969.

Baaz, Shaykhul Islaam Ibn. *Clarification of the Truth in Light of Terrorism, Hijackings & Suicide Bombings and an Advice to Usaamah Ibn Laaden (died 1420 AH/1999 CE)*. Birmingham: Salafi Publications, October 2001.

Banerjee, Mukulika. *The Pathan Unarmed*. Karachi, New Delhi and Oxford: Oxford University Press, 2000.

Barker, Jonathan. *The No-Nonsense Guide to Terrorism*. Oxford: New Internationalist in association with Verso, 2003.

Bhagwat Charan, "The Philosophy of the Bomb." In *The Terrorism Reader: A Historical Anthology*, edited by Walter Laqueur, 137, 139. London: Wildwood House, 1979.

Burke, Jason. *Al-Qaeda: Casting a Shadow of Terror*. London: I. B. Tauris, 2003. Cited in Nemat Guenena, *The 'Jihad': An 'Islamic Alternative' in Egypt* [*Cairo Papers in Social Science*, Vol. 9 Monograph 2 (Summer 1986)]. Cairo: The American University in Cairo Press, 1986, p. 44.

"Bush Virginia Speech: Excerpts." *BBC News*, 11 September 2003. http://news.bbc.co.uk/2/hi/americas/3100286.stm.

Dajani, Souad. "Nonviolent Resistance in the Occupied Territories: A Critical Reevaluation." In *Nonviolent Social Movements: A Geographical Perspective*, edited by Stephen Zunes, Lester R. Kurtz, and Sarah Beth Asher, 52–74. Oxford: Wiley-Blackwell, 1999.

Eickelman, Dale F. and James Piscatori. *Muslim Politics*. Princeton, NJ: Princeton University Press, 1996.

Euben, Roxanne L. "Killing (for) Politics: Jihad, Martyrdom and Political Action." *Political Theory* 30, no. 1 (February 2002).

Falk, Richard A. *The Great Terror War*. New York: Olive Branch Press, 2003.

Gandhi, M. K. *Non-Violence in Peace & War (Vol. II)*. Ahmedabad: Navajivan Publishing House, 1949.

Girard, Rene. *Violence and the Sacred*, Patrick Gregory (trans.). Baltimore and London: The Johns Hopkins University Press, 1979.

The Glorious Qur'an, translation and commentary by A. Yusuf Ali. n.p.: The Muslim Students' Association of the United States & Canada, 1977.

Guenena, Nemat. *The 'Jihad': An 'Islamic Alternative' in Egypt* [*Cairo Papers in Social Science*, Vol. 9 Monograph 2 (Summer 1986)]. Cairo: The American University in Cairo Press, 1986.

International Council on Human Rights Policy (ICHRP). *Human Rights After September 11*. Versoix, Switzerland: International Council on Human Rights Policy, 2002.

Johansen, Robert C. "Radical Islam and Nonviolence: A Case Study of Religious Empowerment and Constraint among Pashtuns." *Journal of Peace Research* 34, no. 1 (1997): 53–71.

Juergensmeyer, Mark. *Terror in the Mind of God: The Global Rise of Religious Violence*. Berkeley: University of California Press, 2000.

Lewis, Bernard. *What Went Wrong? The Clash Between Islam and Modernity in the Middle East*. New York: Perennial, 2002.

Margalit, Avishai. "The Suicide Bombers." *The New York Review of Books*, January 16, 2003. www.nybooks.com/articles/2003/01/16/the-suicide-bombers/.

Nanda, B. R. *Mahatma Gandhi: A Biography*. New Delhi: Oxford University Press, 1997.

Olcott, Martha Brill, and Bakhtiyar Babajanov. "The Terrorist Notebooks." *Foreign Policy*, November 4, 2003.

Pape, Robert A. "The Strategic Logic of Suicide Terrorism." *American Political Science Review* 97, no. 3 (2003): 343–361.

Peri, Yoram. *The Israeli Military and Israel's Palestinian Policy: From Oslo to the Al Aqsa Intifada*. Washington, DC: U.S. Institute of Peace, 2002.

The Pew Global Attitudes Project. *What the World Thinks in 2002: How Global Politics View Their Lives, Their Countries, Their World, America*. Washington, D.C.: The Pew Research Center for the People & the Press, 2002.

Radhakrishnan, N. *Khan Abdul Ghaffar Khan: The Apostle of Nonviolence*. New Delhi: Gandhi Smriti and Darshan Samiti, 1998.

Said, Abdul Aziz, Mohammed Abu-Nimer, and Meena Sharify-Funk, eds. *Contemporary Islam: Dynamic, Not Static*. London: Routledge, 2006.

Sarraj, Eyad. "Why We Have Turned Into Suicide Bombers: Understanding Palestinian Terror." *Just Commentary*, no. 3 (September 1997): 1–2.

Satha-Anand, Chaiwat. "Crossing the Enemy's Line: Helping the Others in Violent Situations Through Nonviolent Action." *Peace Research* 33, no. 2 (2001a): 105–114. doi:10.2307/23608078.

Satha-Anand, Chaiwat. "The Nonviolent Crescent: Eight Theses on Muslim Nonviolent Action," In *Peace and Conflict Resolution in Islam: Precept and Practice*, edited by Abdul Aziz Said, Nathan C. Funk and Ayse S. Kadayifci, 195–211. Lanham, New York and Oxford: University Press of America, 2001b.

Satha-Anand, Chaiwat. "Muslim Communal Nonviolent Actions: Minority Coexistence in a Non-Muslim Society." In *Cultural Diversity and Islam*, edited by Abdul Aziz Said and Meena Sharify-Funk, 195–207. Lanham, New York and Oxford: University Press of America, 2003.

Satha-Anand, Chaiwat. "Understanding the Success of Terrorism." *Inter-Asia Cultural Studies* 3, no. 1 (April 2002): 157–159.

Schmid, Alex. "The Strategy of Terrorism: The Role of Identification." A report of a seminar in *Transforming Struggle: Strategy and the Global Experience of Nonviolent Direct Action*. Cambridge, MA: Program on Nonviolent Sanctions in Conflict and Defense, Center for International Affairs, Harvard University, 1992.

Seery, John E. *Political Theory for Mortals: Shades of Justice, Images of Death*. Ithaca: Cornell University Press, 1996.

Sivan, Emmanuel. *Radical Islam: Medieval Theology and Modern Politics*. New Haven and London: Yale University Press, 1985.

Smith, Daniel L. "The Rewards of Allah." *Journal of Peace Research* 26, no. 4 (November 1989): 385–398.

Stephan, M. *Civilian Jihad—Nonviolent Struggle, Democratization*. Palgrave Macmillan, 2009. www.nonviolent-conflict.org/wp-content/uploads/2016/02/Maria.J.Stephan_Civilian-Jihad-EN.pdf.

Susan, Sachs. "Punishing a Terrorist by Showing Him His Victim's Humanity." *New York Times.com*, April 6, 2002.

U.S. Department of State. *Patterns of Global Terrorism 2003*. Washington, DC: U.S. Department of State, April 2004. www.state.gov/documents/organization/31912.pdf.

Zunes, Stephen. "Unarmed Insurrections Against Authoritarian Governments in the Third World: A New Kind of Revolution." *Third World Quarterly* 15, no. 3 (September 1, 1994): 403–426.

Zunes, Stephen. "Unarmed Resistance in the Middle East and North Africa." In *Nonviolent Social Movements: A Geographical Perspective*, edited by Lester R. Kurtz and Sarah Beth Asher, 41–51. Oxford: Wiley-Blackwell, 1999.

13
ISLAMIC APPROACHES TO NONVIOLENCE AND PEACEBUILDING

A Critical Examination

Mohammed Abu-Nimer

Introduction[1]

Since the later 1990s, the role of religion in conflicts, particularly in transforming and resolving conflicts, has increasingly become a point for scholarly and policy debates (Abu-Nimer 2003; Appleby 2000; Gopin 2000). On the one hand, much scholarship focuses on how violent conflict has been exercised through frameworks of religions, which operate through symbols, institutions and the possibility of "post-secular" alternatives. It often skirts discussion of the problematic aspects of the secular frameworks and "solutions" imposed upon traditional societies such as Iraq or Libya, failing to recognize that "the religious actors in a conflict are integral to the political and cultural structures of the societies in which they operate, and so religious identity often competes with the state to gain citizens' loyalty" (Abu-Nimer and Seidel 2017, 180). On the other hand, there has been an increase in the number of arguments for the inclusion of religion and religious leaders in promoting peace through nonviolence resistance, dialogue, education and the religious scriptures themselves (Abu-Nimer 2003, 2010; Abu-Nimer and Smith 2016).

Nevertheless, the reality is that most religious identities (symbols and rituals, etc.) are often misused to promote violence and violent conflict. Examples exist across religions, ranging from violent extremist Buddhist monks in Myanmar, Christian terror groups such as the Ku Klux Klan or Ilaga in the Philippines, Muslim terror groups such as Al-Qaeda or Boko Haram, Jewish violent extremists and terror groups in the Palestinian occupied territories (such as the Jewish Defense League or Terror Neged Terror), to the Saffron terror motivated by Hindu nationalism.

Yet each of these religions also exemplifies messages of peace, justice and coexistence. While some proponents argue in favor of secularism, maintaining that violence is inherent in religion, others contend that religion is peace and that those who commit violent acts in the name of religion are in fact misusing it. The issue is perhaps more complex.

Prevalent passages in the religious scriptures and histories of all of the world's major religions support peace; however, there are also examples within those same texts that depict battles (such as Azhab, Idra or Jericho), religious warriors (such as King David, Lord Krishna or Samson) and/or violent acts, whether self-inflicted (self-immolation) or inflicted on others (the prescription of a variety of forms of capital punishment for transgressions). While it is true that these passages are often taken out of context by extremists and terror groups for the purpose of justifying violence, it is hardly possible to deny their presence. It is thus important to examine not only the tension but also the relationship between peace and violence in religion.

This chapter explores this very tension in Arab and Muslim religious contexts and aims to build a better understanding of not only the inherent values of peace within the religion, but also the limited role prescribed for violence. Such an understanding has become increasingly important in efforts to incorporate religion and religious leaders in building a sustainable peace, as well as in the prevention of possibilities for violent incidents.

Islamic Teaching and Islamophobia

Islam, in particular, rose front and center into the spotlight following the terror attacks that took place on 11 September 2001 in New York.[2] These events manifested dangerous and violent potencies in some marginal Muslim extremist groups and individuals. And while the vast majority of Muslims condemned these events, the subsequent US- and European-led interventions in Iraq and Afghanistan only strengthened Al Qaeda and other terror organizations' violent campaigns supporting offensive and aggressive ideologies based on their own Islamic interpretations. In addition, the advent of social media as a platform for information sharing has created a deluge of information exacerbating the inherent connection of religion and violence, with no lack of focus on acts committed by Islamic extremists. These factors, combined with European and American policies motivated by secular and rightwing religious agendas aimed at securing economic and political strategic interests in Arab and Muslim countries, have created a global Islamophobic campaign and discourse that systematically links Islam with violence and war.

Another key factor that has contributed to the negative images associated with Islam and to Islamophobic reactions in western societies is the lack of research and visibility of information relating to Islam, peace and nonviolence. In contrast to the numerous resources available on Islam and violence, very few studies actively promote and explore the issue of nonviolence and peacebuilding in Islam. Three types of studies relate to Islam, nonviolence and peace. First, "offensive Islam" asserts that Islam as a religion and culture lends itself to the justification of war and violence in settling conflicts. Islam, in this perspective, is a religion of war, a "religion of the sword," and a fundamentalist religion. Another type of study focuses on several hypotheses related to the nature of justice and the conditions placed on the use of violence and force in Islam. Such research is conducted from a security studies and international power paradigm perspective and concludes that pacifism is a Christian concept alien to Islamic teachings. This "defensive Islam" group talks about the use of force as a defensive strategy and the duty of Muslims to defend their basic rights and pursue justice as a primary value in Islam.

A third type of study, which is still emerging, reinterprets Islamic teaching and reframes the issue of using force and violence to settle conflicts in moral, historical and contextual frameworks. The emphasis by this group is on values of peace, unity of human kind, nonviolence and justice. In other words, they emphasize that the overall message of Islam is peace and nonviolence. For these scholars, Islam as a religion carries and promotes only one primary universal and transcendent message of peace and nonviolent approaches to conflict. Such values constitute a solid foundation for political and social change in Muslim societies.

With the heightened media attention highlighting violent actions committed by terror groups in the name of Islam, much discussion has arisen in this context regarding violence in Islam, underscoring aspects of religious texts that could be deemed responsible for the justification of violence. To counter this portrayal, religious scholars highlight peaceful passages in the Hadith and Qur'an that show the promotion of peace, diversity, coexistence, forgiveness and reconciliation, among other positive qualities. These discussions underscore the tension in the Islam between the "warrior" and the "pacifist," or rather the nonviolent resister.[3] This tension becomes even more poignant when one examines the possibility of peacebuilding and conflict resolution in Muslim societies.

Examination of the tension and, consequently, the relationship is central to understanding how conflicts can be resolved in a sustainable way, how nonviolence is compatible with different cultural practices and the function and role of violent action—such as in defense or war. Since many of the militant Muslim organizations (such as Al-Qaeda and ISIS) heavily rely on narrow and exclusive interpretations of Muslim sources, it is imperative that an alternative narrative and perspective on the issues of war, violence, peace and relations with the other be put forth for Muslim and non-Muslim communities alike. Building this understanding will help with the prospect for a more peaceful coexistence. While some scholars have argued that cultural, and thus religious, differences do not play a significant role in developing conflict resolution techniques (Burton 1990), the way that cultural and religious norms influence life in societies strongly informs how people think and thus their acceptance of techniques that can not only be used in conflict resolution, but also in conflict prevention and the promotion of peace.

Mechanisms for building and maintaining peace, as well as peaceful activism, are present throughout Islam, transmitted through both religious and cultural beliefs within Muslim societies, notably Sulh (reconciliation), Wasata (mediation) and

Tahkim (Arbitration). However, there are fewer documentations of examples of Islamic nonviolence resistance. In addition, the need to deploy nonviolent action to achieve difficult goals in societies plagued by authoritarianism, poor education and structural barriers to the access of education, religious leaders that have been coopted by the government, a lack of economic opportunity and numerous other challenges creates frustration in the lives of many Muslims (Abu-Nimer 2003).

The current challenge in dealing with Muslim peace and nonviolent approaches is to move beyond the framing of peacebuilding objectives and interventions only to respect Muslim values, and to use it as a framework to address the realities of many Muslims' lives, especially those interested in resolving and preventing conflicts in the Muslim world. In order to do this, it is necessary to look at religious texts that serve as the building blocks of the faith, namely the Qur'an and Hadith, as well as examples within Muslim history and culture that support nonviolence, peace, justice and the peaceful resolution of conflict. At the same time, it is important to examine the instances in which violence was permitted and the limits to this violence.

Islamic Religious Foundations for Nonviolent Action

In the classical framing of nonviolent action and resistance, spiritual leaders such as Gandhi, Martin Luther King and the Dalai Lama have consistently articulated the religious path that led them to endorse and adopt nonviolence as a way of life and a path to fight injustice. Utilizing their own religious traditions, they have each identified the values and norms that called for the use of nonviolence over the use of violence. However, they did not deny the existence of religious teachings in their faith and scripture that justify the use of violence and aggression. On the contrary, they acknowledged it and preached for a higher moral ground to be taken, because in all religions nonviolence and reconciliation are regarded as higher virtues than the justified use of violence.

Such theological and moral groundings exist in Islam, too, reflected by a clear set of values that constitute the foundation for nonviolence. And while there are many values in Islamic teachings that support the endorsement and practice of nonviolent resistance (for full list of these values, see Abu-Nimer 2003), for the sake of this specific chapter, a few select central ones are highlighted as follows:

> **Peace in Islam:** Muslim and non-Muslim scholars alike have often recognized the many aspects inherent in Islam that support peace, frequently citing the numerous examples within the Qur'an and the Hadith. "Peace is one of the fundamental values of Islam. It carries a central position in the Islamic teaching. In fact, it is the crux of all Islamic injunctions that state that one should not create problems for others in any form, neither by words, nor by actions and even nor by gestures" (Ahmad 2015, 13). The root of the word Islam itself is related to the word for peace (*salam*)

signifying that peace is integral and indicative of the religion itself. The religious texts support the notion that affection, kindness, love and mercy are attributes carried by those of the faith. The faithful should be compassionate, just and use wisdom (*hikmah*) in one's actions and in making decisions. Compassion (*rahmah*), faith (*yakeen*), love (*muhabat*) and service (*amal*) to Allah and to one's fellow human beings all play an integral role in the way the faithful should act towards others. These qualities demonstrate examples of the "Qur'an commanding believers to be righteous and above passion in their dealings with their fellow beings" (Abu-Nimer 2010, 77).

Justice in Islam: The Qur'an requires believers to work for justice (*adl*) and reject injustice. Islam calls for believers to establish a just social reality and to measure any act or statement according to whether, how, and when it will accomplish that desired reality (Abu-Nimer 2003). In doing so, believers act for the cause of Allah (verses 5:8, 57:25, 16:90, 4:58, 42:15) by rejecting oppression and striving for justice within interpersonal relationships as well as the structural levels of society, such as governance structures. Speaking and acting in a just way is a Divine call that followers are obliged to pursue towards all people, not just Muslims: "Allah commands justice, the doing of good, and liberality to kith and kin, and he forbids all shameful deeds, and injustice and rebellion" (Qur'an 16:90). Further emphasizing the virtuosity in being a just person, verse 4:58 simply but powerfully states "God loves those who are just." In another verse: "worship God and associate naught with Him and behave benevolently towards parents, kinsmen, orphans, the needy, the neighbor that is a kinsman, the neighbor that is a stranger, the companion, by the roadside, the wayfarer and those who are under your authority" (4:36, 37). The Prophet described the best act of justice as a verbal expression of resistance against an unjust ruler. The Prophet (ﷺ) said, "The best type of Jihad (striving in the way of Allah) is speaking a true word in the presence of a tyrant ruler."[4]

Justice and peace have a symbiotic relationship. Not only are they intrinsically linked within Islam, but several scholars of peacebuilding argue that peace cannot exist without justice (Lederach 1994, 1997; Burgess 1994). In Islam, peace is achieved through the pursuit of justice. The pursuit of justice includes both economic and social justice, empowering both the weak and the poor. Some Islamic religious obligations to insure social justice include calling Muslims to the duty of giving of alms to the poor (*zakah*) and charity (*sadaqah*), duties that each believer has to perform within his/her capabilities/limits. The religion also provides for the inheritance of women and children and just treatment of debtors, orphans and widows.

Nonviolence and the Sacredness of Human Life: As peace and justice are interconnected within Islam, these two values, not to mention the sacredness of human life, also serve as a basis for nonviolent action within Islam. Often thought of as "intimately associated with certain ethical and religious traditions, notably Buddhism, Hinduism, and Christian pacifism" (Barash and Webel 2009, 458), nonviolence is not only present within Islam but an increasing number of nonviolent Islamic movements have also surfaced in Muslim societies in recent years. In fact, as argued by Khalis Jalabi, a pioneer in Islamic nonviolent approaches, "nonviolence is the Prophets' approach in forming societies" (Jalabi 1997, 1992).[5] Nonviolence is also not a new concept in Islam. Perhaps one of the strongest early historical examples dates back to the Prophet Mohammed himself, who undertook 13 years of nonviolent struggle in Mecca. During this period, the Prophet and his followers were actively persecuted by the Meccans. Rather than resist using violence, for 13 years they resisted nonviolently.[6]

Human life is deemed sacred, and the Qur'an speaks of the preservation of life and avoiding transgressing God:

> We ordained for the Children of Israel that if anyone killed a person not in retaliation of murder, or (and) to spread mischief in the land—it would be as if he killed all mankind, and if anyone saved a life, it would be as if he saved the life of all mankind.
>
> *(Qur'an 5:32)*

The verse clearly demonstrates not only that life is sacred but also that taking a human life unjustly disobeys the word of God. A further verse states: "And do not take a life which Allah has forbidden save in the course of justice. This he enjoins on you so that you may understand" (6:15). There is a meaning for the person's life. It is an integral part of the great cosmic purpose. Consequently, what the individual does matters profoundly. "Our Lord, Thou has not created all this in vain!" (3:191). In this vein, destroying and wasting resources that serve human life is prohibited, which was respected already by early Islamic leaders such as Abu Bakr (Sahih Muslim 839; al-Tabari 1969, 3: 226–227).

The Qur'anic story of the two sons of Adam, Abel and Cain, as highlighted by Jawdat Said (1996-Arabic), serves as an example of the foundation for the preference of nonviolence over violence. The verse states,

> Recite unto them with truth the story of the two sons of Adam, how they each offered a sacrifice. It was accepted from one of them, but not accepted from the other. The one whose sacrifice was not accepted said to his brother, "I will surely kill you." The other answered, "Allah accepts only from those who ward off evil. *Even if you stretch out your hand against me to kill me, I will not stretch out my hand against you to kill you, lo! I fear Allah, the Lord of the Worlds.*"
>
> *(Qur'an 5:27, emphasis added)*

In Islamic history, there is the example of Caliph Imam Ali, who, in reacting to his people's pressure to go to war, uttered the following words, exemplifying the preference for nonviolence over violence:

> If I order you to march on them on warm days, you say "this is the fire of summer. Give us time until the heat is over." If I ask you to march on them in winter, you say "this is the bite of the frost. Give us the time until the cold is over." All this and you fleeing from the heat and the cold, but, by God, you are more in flight from the sword.
>
> *(Kishtainy 1990, 12)*

Saving lives, patience and avoiding violence are the main values conveyed here by the Imam.

Patience (*Sabr*): Muslims are encouraged to be patient and to suspend their judgment of others, whether they are Muslims or non-Muslims. Patience is a virtue of the believers who can endure immense challenges and still maintain a strong belief in God. There are many Qur'anic verses that command the believers to be patient and practice patience in responding to injustice and others' wrongdoing (31:17; 70:05; 16:27; 08:46; 03:146; 11:49; 30:60). There is also the story of Ayoub, who is held in high regard for his belief and patience despite his experience of various tragedies (Kathir 17–19). Such a value is necessary in peacebuilding and nonviolence resistance due to the nature of those initiatives, which often produce few macro impacts or short-term changes, but are considered a long-term investment in the community. In addition, an intervener in such a community would need a great deal of patience to carry out initiatives for peace and development in the community. Patience is an important quality of the believers, as agents of change, in Islam. As the Prophet said:

> How wonderful is the case of a believer; there is good for him in everything and this applies only to a believer. If prosperity attends him, he expresses gratitude to Allah and that is good for him; and if adversity befalls him, he endures it patiently and that is better for him.[7]

The same characteristic is required for any conflict resolver and for those who engage in sustainable dialogue processes. Assisting people and promoting a peaceful coexistence in conflict areas requires patience among both the interveners and the receiver.

Collaborative Actions and Solidarity: Peacebuilding and nonviolence approaches assume that collaborative and joint efforts to resolve a problem are more productive than competitive efforts by individuals only. A well-known Hadith in Islam is: "God's hand with the *Jama'a* (group)," which is often utilized to motivate disputants to reach an agreement, achieve unity, gain strength and be empowered by working together. It also contains the underlying meaning of reducing cost and damage that might occur to individuals if they stand alone in a conflict. It is used to mobilize unity and support to stand against the outside enemy, and to motivate people to avoid political and social schisms or rivalries (*fitna*). Nevertheless, the saying encourages the collaborative approach to challenges. Such a concept has been easily utilized as a base for social and political mobilization, and can also be employed for collective action in a social or economic development context.

In Islam, the base for solidarity is extended beyond the Muslim community; God has created all humans equally and they have a common origin, and they should, therefore, assist and not neglect each other's' needs.

> O Mankind! Reverence your Guardian-Lord, Who created you from a single person, His mate, and form them twain scattered (like seeds) countless men and women. Fear Allah, through whom ye demand your mutual (right) and (reverence) the wombs (that bore you): for Allah ever watches over you.
>
> *(4:1)*

Solidarity among Muslims is also a central value. A well-known traditional says: "help your brother (Muslims) whether he is an aggressor or a victim of aggression." When the Prophet was asked: How can we assist our brother when he is an aggressor? He replied, "By doing your best to stop him from aggression" (Saiyidain, 199:159). This is a clear message to avoid the use of violence and prevent aggression by Muslims against other Muslims and non-Muslims. Solidarity in this context is the opposite of the tribal solidarity (*assabiyyah*—assisting members of the same tribe/clan/family against outsiders regardless of the conditions).[8]

Pluralism and Diversity: Pluralism and diversity are core values in Islamic tradition and religion. The Qur'an supports diversity and tolerance of differences based on gender (49:13; 53:45); skin color or language (30:23); different beliefs (64:2); different ranks (6:165); and different social grouping and communities (2:213; 10:19; 7:38 13:30; 16:63; 29:18; 35:42; 41:42; 64:18). It asserts that differences are inherent in human life. Thus ethnic, tribal and national differences are not accurate measurements of closeness to God; the extent and degree of faith is the sole criteria by which those groups will be judged. The existence of differences among people in general is a basic assumption and value in Islam (11:118–119; 10:99; 16:93). Scholars cite the saying of the Prophet: "My Ummah's difference is a mercy" (a highly disputed Hadith, however, very popular among Muslims) (Howadi 1993, 23).

Tolerance of the "other," non-Muslim believers (people of the book), is repeatedly accepted and emphasized in Islam. The equality of the followers of different religions is reiterated in both the Qur'an and Hadith many times. Muslims are asked to remember that there is no difference in the treatment of people of different religions except in their faith and deed (3:113–114; 2:62; 5:68).

The Qur'an calls to abandon fighting and live and coexist beside each other as different religions. It reaffirms the validity of the other religions and requires its followers to respect such scriptures (see 3:64; 5:68–69).

Among Muslims themselves, pluralism historically existed in early Muslim communities with the notion that there was no single Islamic law or constitution developed. There was no standardization of the Islamic law. In the Sunni tradition, when standardized, such laws came up with four theological schools, and were not limited to legal or jurisprudent aspects (Esack 1998). Moreover, the Qur'an is often used to legitimize the validity of differences (*ikhtilaf*). On the other hand, Islamic theological interpretations were least tolerant of the nonbelievers or infidels. Throughout history those who were cast as "*kufar*" (infidels) were persecuted and punished by rulers and followers.

Seven main principles or *ausul* can be derived from the Qur'an supporting coexistence and tolerance (Howadi 1993, 202):

1. The absolute protection of human dignity regardless of the person's religion, ethnicity and intellectual opinion orientation (17:70). This dignity has immunity from transgression by others given by God to each individual;
2. All humans come from the same origin and are thus related to one another (4:1; 6:98; 5:32);
3. The differences among people are designated by God in his universe. The differences in ethnicity, race, culture, etc., are factual and a natural part of life. (30:22; 10:99; 11:188, 199);
4. Acknowledgment of other religions and assertion of their unified origin (42:13; 2:136);
5. The freedom of choice and decision after the calling or the message has been delivered (2:256; 18:29; 17:107; 109:4–6);
6. Judgment is carried out by God only and this occurs on Judgment Day (42:48; 16:124; 31:23; 88:25, 26); and
7. Doing good, and acting justly, and with equity in dealing with all human beings (5:8; 4:135; 60:8).

The existence of differences is a given in Islam, and consequently there is no justification in violating a person's right to existence and movement due to different religious affiliations (42:15). Islam spread and coexisted in many different cultures and ethnic groups (Asia, Middle East, Africa and South East Asia). Islam was not consumed by those cultures; it did not reject them, either, but instead created a new civilization. Islam is multicultural and pluralist in its existence and practice. While Asian, African or European Muslims are different in their cultures, as Muslims they are nevertheless expected to tolerate each other's cultural differences as well as those of the non-Muslims in their communities.

In peacebuilding, diversity and tolerance of differences are core principles of practice. Islamic nonviolent and conflict resolution processes and models are based on the above assumptions to bring people to the realization that they are different,

Islamic Approaches to Nonviolence   **251**

and such differences should not be and are not a basis for discrimination or bias. Thus, it is harmful and unjust to deprive people of their rights because of their national, racial, religious or any other category affiliation. These values have been made integral parts of Islam since its inception.

Tensions with Nonviolent Action in the Context of Muslim Societies

While nonviolence indeed has a lengthy tradition within Islam, dating back to its very founding days, on the macro social and political levels there have been few intentional and systematic collective applications of this framework to settle conflicts of governance and wars. Opponents of nonviolent actions have equated it with pacifism and surrender, which is generally viewed negatively in a Muslim cultural context. Islamic scholars and *faqihs* (Islamic jurists) from the four main schools of Islamic *fiqh* have adopted the notion of justifying the use of violence as a strictly defensive mode of action (i.e., "Defensive Islam"). This Islamic religious scholarship is saturated with books and essays discussing the specific conditions that allow the use of violence, and they have articulated in detail the circumstances, scope and proportionality of using violence in response to injustice. However, the Muslim duty is to respond and not be passive or surrender, as the misperceived pacifist. It is against values in Islam not to react when an injustice has taken place.

The terms "pacifism" and "pacifist" not only imply that an individual or group should not act in a violent way, but can also be interpreted as not reacting to rectify the injustice or even as the portrayal of the victim or the oppressed sitting back in acceptance of his/her fate and thus simply waiting for his/her impending end at the hands of the oppressor. Unfortunately, this image has often been associated with peace work and peace groups, as well as with the term nonviolence.

This can be better understood by looking at the word for nonviolence in Arabic. *La unf*, literally translated as "no-violence," carries with it the negative connotation of surrender and passivity and invokes exactly the picture of the lamb waiting for the slaughter. In reaction to this, some pioneers of nonviolence in Islam, namely Khalid Kishtainy, Khalis Jalabi, Jawdat Said and Imam al-Shirazi, have entirely avoided the use of the word *la unf* by coining the term "civic jihad," creating a path towards the development of nonviolent frameworks of resistance. Maria Stephan (2010) uses the similar term, "civilian jihad," in her edited volume, which reviews campaigns for change in the Middle East. While to an outsider *jihad* may seem like an aggressive term to apply to nonviolent action, in fact "*jihad* has been interpreted as striving and struggling to live according to principles of faith" (Abu-Nimer 2010, 82).

War and violent action are permitted in Islam for the purpose of defense:

> there are circumstances in which Islam contemplates the possibility of war—for instance, to avert worse disasters like the denial of freedom to

human conscience ... the essential thing in life is peace. It is towards the achievement of peace that all human efforts must be sincerely diverted.
(Saiyidain 1994, 175)

However, it is important to note that violent action for the purpose of defense has limits prescribed within the holy texts. Several verses, often taken out of context within the Qur'an as a call to war or justification of violence against Christians, Jews and other non-Muslims, refer to specific events in Islamic history, when Muslims themselves were under attack and were called upon to defend themselves. For example, the Quraysh attempted to harm the Prophet, who was then saved by his uncle. After more than ten years of persecution of Muslims in Mecca, God first requires that they be patient and endure (Qur'an 4:77). Only after they are driven from their homes are they given the permission to fight:

> Those who have been attacked are permitted to take up arms because they have been wronged—God has the power to help them—those who have been driven unjustly from their homes only for saying, "Our Lord is God." If God did not repel some people by means of others, many monasteries, churches, synagogues, and mosques, where God's name is much invoked, would have been destroyed. God is sure to help those who help His cause— God is strong and mighty—those who, when We establish them in the land, keep up the prayer, pay the prescribed alms, command what is right, and forbid what is wrong: God controls the outcome of all events.
> (Qur'an 22:39–41)

Even though several battles took place during the lifetime of the Prophet himself, several scholars have examined these events and determined that none was waged for any other purpose than self-defense.

> [H]e [the Prophet Mohammed] only fought those who waged war against him and fought him first. As for those who made peace with him or conducted a truce, then he never fought them and he never compelled them to enter his religion.
> (Al-Jawziyyah 1996, 237)

Limitations to the Use of Violence

Even when violence for the purpose of defense or defensive war is permitted, the Qur'an prescribes limits on this violence. "Scholars agree that certain conditions permit the use of force, though there has been a massive amount of writing and lively debates, by Muslims and non-Muslims alike, regarding what Islamic teachings do and do not allow" (Abu-Nimer 2010, 82). For example, in deconstructing the phrase "Fight in God's cause against those who fight you, but do not overstep the limits: God does not love those who overstep the limits" (Qur'an 2:190), Haleem explains that "those who fight you" refers specifically to fighters or warriors and holds civilians exempt, thus not excusing the slaughter of civilians (Haleem 2001). Using Umar ibn Abd al Aziz's interpretation of this verse, Al-Tabari indicates that this forbids fighting women, children and monks (al-Qurtubi, 348). This is further reinforced by Abu Bakr, the first caliphate, who when he sent his army to the borders of Syria, famously placed a number of restrictions on the use of force:

> Stop, O people, that I may give you ten rules for your guidance in the battlefield. Do not commit treachery or deviate from the right path. You must not mutilate dead bodies. Neither kill a child, nor a woman or an aged man. Bring no harm to the trees, nor burn them with fire, especially those which are fruitful. Slay not any of the enemy's flock, save for your food. You are likely to pass by people who have devoted their lives to monastic services, leave them alone.
> *(Sahih Muslim, 839; al-Tabari 1969, 3:226–227)*

The foundations laid down in Islamic texts and throughout early Islamic history limit the type and nature of force that can be used in fighting the other. The strict conditions on how to treat innocent people beyond any doubt prohibit excessive force and violence as a means to resolve any conflict.

Once hostilities have been initiated, the Qur'an provides for peace and forgiveness. This takes place under several circumstances. If the enemy stops fighting, then Muslims should not continue to fight: "But if they cease, God is Oft-forgiving, Most Merciful" (2:192). The subsequent verse reiterates the command that one should cease fighting if the opposing forces surrender or cease to fight and indicates that peace should be established with all that do not oppress the Muslims: "And fight them on until there is no fitnah and the religion is only for God, but if they cease, let there be no hostility except to those who practice oppression" (2:193).

Once peace is achieved, there are precedents as to peace treaties that offer terms for the foundations of peaceful co-existence. One such peace treaty is the Covenant of Madinah, a treaty between the Muslims and the local Jews that offers terms of mutual help and solidarity should either community be attacked by outsiders, mutual effort towards justice and reciprocal respect and tolerance (Ahmad 2015, 17). Examples of such treaties display forgiveness to those who fought against the Muslims and lay down the foundations for peaceful co-existence in the same community.

Nonviolent Actions in the Current Reality of Muslim Societies

Considering the above solid Islamic theological and moral foundations for both "defensive Islam" and the clear preference for nonviolent action, it is obvious to pose the following questions: why and how can this be applied in Arab and Muslim communities or societies today? Is it feasible to expect nonviolent strategies to be the leading strategies in responding to violent extremism in the name of religion?

The so called "Arab Spring" experiences in Egypt, Tunisia, Yemen and Syria have provided an excellent example and illustration of both the potential success and serious obstacles that arise when deploying nonviolent strategies and actions in opposing current political regimes. There is no doubt that many nonviolent strategies have been utilized and that most were effective in contributing to the removal of the old repressive regimes. Nevertheless, the macro and micro (external and internal) forces and factors have proven to be too powerful in blocking the process of nonviolent change or action. Thus, in most of these cases, political and religious leaders either opted for a military option or withdrew from the scene, allowing the military and security branches to dictate violence and militarization as the way to attempt to bring the conflicts to an end. One of the outcomes of the collapse of the organized nonviolent action or campaigns in Syria, Iraq, Yemen and Egypt was that these countries slid into civil wars and paramilitary activity.

Nevertheless, when these nonviolent campaigns were in full swing in early stages of these revolutions (2010–2011), Arab and Islamic religious identity was a powerful source for mobilization and sustaining the action. The systematic use of various religious identity components (symbols, rituals, sites, text, etc.) was prevalent in all the cases. For example, the call for protest often emerges from the weekly Friday prayer in every mosque in the city or capitol; enlisting Allah's name in chanting slogans against the regimes, symbols of interreligious diversity, etc. These various deployments of religious nonviolent strategies provided solid proof that nonviolent action is neither contradictory to Islamic theology nor to cultural practices as has been argued by analysts and policy makers who link Islam with violence.

The failure to sustain the nonviolent action or campaigns in these contexts should help peacebuilding and nonviolent activists to further understand and acknowledge the power of inherent obstacles that block the nonviolent paradigm in the Islamic context.

Islamic Ideals and Muslim Reality: Explaining the Gap

It is important to note that Muslims who work for social and political change face difficulties in implementing these peaceful Islamic ideals and values. The obstacles to such implementation comes from both macro and micro challenges.

The macro challenges are both internal and external. Internally, they relate to political, social and cultural structural arrangements that prevent agents of change and ordinary people from accessing or implementing such values in massive social movements or in institutional changes. Among these structural challenges are systems of technocracy and bureaucracy that lead to political stagnancy. In such systems, there is a lack of imaginative and creative political leadership at the decision-making levels. Under these authoritarian control systems, civil liberties and public participation in the decision-making process are absent.

Another challenge is the cooptation of religious leaders by the government. The former tend to promote the interests of the leaders and ignore the people's interests and desires; this in turn leads to a lack of trust and credibility in the religious leadership. Such cooptation tendencies among religious intuitions and leaders became clear in their response to the pressure exercised by political leaders and regimes in the post revolutions. For example, the Syrian grand Mufti endorsing the Assad regime and his atrocities against civilians since 2011; the Yemeni religious leaders divided in their endorsement of the various military factions; Egyptian religious institutions providing a full endorsement of the use of military and security means to deal with wide ideological and religious opposition. The formal and religious institutions too have been coopted and shaped to serve the ruling elites in many Arab and Muslim societies. Thus, their religious leaders are often viewed as echoes of the ruling corrupt leadership, and contribute to the perpetuation of the social and political control system. In addition, their formal training continues to follow religious Madrasah systems, which have been in place for centuries without any major revisions or reforms.

A third challenge is the wide system of corruption, which is present at all levels and has worsened poverty conditions and blocked sustainable development in Muslim communities. For example, the current Tunisian civic and governmental system is facing a major challenge in fighting corruption in a post-revolutionary context. The wide scale of corruption significantly decreases people's hopes in effective means of nonviolent actions due to a lack of trust in the function of governance systems, although a number of nonviolent campaigns have targeted corruption, some of them quite successfully (Beyerle 2014).

A fourth challenge is the patriarchal Arab and Muslim social structure, which pays little attention to the equality and inclusion of women, especially in public spheres (Moghadam 2003; Sharabi 1988). This prevents sustainable and inclusive social change and nonviolent action efforts in the society. It is true that during the Arab Spring many women participated in the movements and led local campaigns; however, the full participation of women is a necessary condition for the sustainability of any outcome based on nonviolent social change actions.[9]

Hierarchy is the fifth challenge. The domination of hierarchal norms (due to tribal and traditional values) over egalitarian practices (sisterhood and brotherhood, Ummah, individual responsibility, etc.) results in and places more attention on ranking and association than on individual capacities (Hudson 1977; Barakat 1993). Hierarchy contradicts with the egalitarian values and equal participation in decision-making and conflict resolution processes and nonviolent actions. In Arab Muslim social and cultural contexts, hierarchical structures are central to regulating relations, while the nonviolent paradigm is based on principles of inclusion and equality.

Military or dictatorial regimes are another blocking factor in Arab and Muslim states (Guirguis 2016; Rohde 2010). Such dictatorial state regimes lack wide political legitimacy and as a result rely on "security apparatus." Thus, the introduction and application of genuine Islamic conflict resolution based on the values and principles discussed above are perceived to be a threat to such regimes. The historical survival of these political institutions has been based on and sustained by promoting values of tribal and clannish loyalty, a lack of any wide public accountability, authoritarian and hierarchical social and cultural arrangements, the exclusion of women from public leadership and the promotion of ethnic and sectarian policies of exclusions.[10]

Finally, the Arab and Islamic educational systems in most cases have been shaped by the same policies established by the ruling elites (Mehar 2010; Shaw 2006). Thus, they lack critical education curricula and often rely on frontal and information banking methods of teaching. In addition, due to either lack of economic resources or deliberate political policies, many Muslim countries have relatively little investment in their educational systems (Ali 2009; Looney 2003; Malik 2008).

Among the external challenges, colonialism and post-colonialism are two systems that had impacts on the development of Muslim and Arab countries, including: increased economic dependency on western systems (Englebert 2000); imposed cultural globalization trends of consumption that challenge the Islamic value system; support of militarization and oppressive security regimes; triggered war and humiliation (the Arab-Israeli conflict has left a huge and serious destructive imprint on Arab countries); exploitation of natural and human resources; imposition of foreign agenda over local and homegrown formulas of development and governance, etc. (see for example Young 2001). These residues of colonial heritage certainly contribute to blocking the implementation and adoption of Islamic nonviolence campaigns for change.

On the micro or individual level factors, the challenges of nonviolent action arise out of a set of beliefs that are often raised by participants in civil society and conflict resolution workshops. These beliefs or assumptions question the intention and legitimacy or credibility of agents of social change who call for nonviolence and conflict resolution methods of change. Some of these assumptions include: first, peace is a tool for cooptation and pacification (that it is used by the most powerful to suppress the weaker party); second, peace and nonviolence contradict justice; third, violence can eventually terminate conflicts. In this context, Arab participants often refer to Gamal Abdul Nasser's statement in reference to the Israeli occupation of Palestine: "What has been taken by force can only be returned by force"; fourth, nonviolence is a non-authentic method on a political level; fifth, in the past few years, Arab participants in peacebuilding capacity building workshops began saying: "we have tried it and it did not work, in fact it made things worse, just see the situation in Syria, Egypt, Yemen, and Tunisia."[11] The above are selected set of factors that constitute serious barriers and resistance to the adoption of nonviolent and peacebuilding approaches voiced by people in Muslim communities.

Promoting peacebuilding and nonviolent methods of social and political change in a Muslim community context requires that agencies of change attend to and address the individual's attitudes and fears that block the possibility of utilizing nonviolent paradigms. It is also important to invest further in approaches and methods that can reduce or contain the negative and destructive impact of the above external and internal factors, as well. These are examples of the many difficult questions and assumptions that ought to be identified and addressed prior to any study or articulation of Islamic sources of peace and nonviolence. Without addressing these concerns, scholars and practitioners will not be able to effectively reach out to the community and people in Muslim settings.

Conclusion

Islam promotes numerous nonviolent and peacebuilding values and expects Muslims to live by them. The difficulty arises not in the absence of these peaceful values and ideals but in their implementation and in the obstacles facing individuals and organizations who aim to generate institutional and structural political and social changes. The task of Muslim and non-Muslim scholars and practitioners is to continue the construction of an authentic and culturally based peacebuilding and nonviolent framework that can be applied on the policy as well as community level.

The Qur'an, the Hadith and other Islamic traditional sources provide plenty of evidence for the hypothesis that Islam is a religion of peace and justice, and that nonviolent practices are also well rooted in the religion. Educating people (Muslim and non-Muslim) around the world on the peaceful message of Islam and eradicating ignorance that leads to the negative stereotyping of Islam and to enmity between Muslims and non-Muslims is the first essential step toward peaceful and just relations between Muslim and non-Muslim communities. However, such efforts are not enough by themselves. Peacebuilders and agents of social change in Muslim communities also have to face the internal, social, cultural and political obstacles that exist in the structures present in Muslim communities. It is true that such structural obstacles are further maintained by external forces; however, individuals and organizations can resist and face such internal decay and its supporting structures. Every Muslim community should resort to self-examination and self-criticism of the role it has played in perpetuating the reality of stagnation, violence and sense of helplessness. This needs to occur in order for any genuine change to take place. Peacebuilding tools and approaches are effective methods to conduct such a process.

The discussion in this chapter identified important Islamic assumptions, principles and values that constitute the basic elements of an Islamic peacebuilding and nonviolent approach to all types and levels of conflicts (interpersonal, organizational, family, community and national, too). This framework, if applied in a community context, ought to incorporate and be guided by certain principles, such as to: (a) increase solidarity among members of the community; (b) bridge the gap of social and economic injustice; (c) relieve the suffering of people and save human lives; (d) empower people through participation and inclusivity; (e) insure the basic human rights for followers of all faith groups; (f) promote common citizenship based on equality among all members of the community; and (g) utilize and encourage the values of diversity and tolerance.

The need for an Islamic nonviolent paradigm for change stems from the massive degree of destruction, displacement and loss of human lives that has been experienced by the average person in Arab and Muslim societies. The region has suffered from millions killed, injured and traumatized, millions of refugees, trillions of dollars in property losses and economic damages. Militarization and violent security tools have not produced stability or order. On the contrary, violent extremist groups and their narrative have gained more visibility and the majority of populations are not engaged in the process of change, but rather are victims and avoiders of the conflict.

A framework of nonviolence based on the above set of principles and rooted in Islamic cultural and religious foundations can be the guiding map for processes of implementing nonviolent strategies and actions in Arab and Muslim settings—a strategy that will reengage communities and public in general.

Notes

1 The author is grateful to Renata Nelson for her assistance in researching materials and copy editing this chapter.
2 Obviously, the negative images and misperceptions of Islam and Muslim cultural practices have historically existed for many centuries in western and non-Muslim communities. Karen Armstrong has documented such images in her book on the history of religion and violence (2014).
3 The author has discussed the need to distinguish between pacifism and nonviolent resistance and has endorsed the notion that Islam does not support the practice of pacifism as a means for withdrawal from life or conflict, as it has been portrayed by certain Christian traditions (see Abu-Nimer 2003).
4 [Abu Dawud and At-Tirmidhi]. Book 1, Hadith 194. In another Hadith, the Prophet (ﷺ) said: "If anyone seeks the office of judge among Muslims till he gets it and his justice prevails over his tyranny, he will go to Paradise; but the man whose tyranny prevails over his justice will go to Hell." (Sunan Abi Dawud 3575; in English translation Book 24, Hadith 356).
5 Another pioneer of non-violence in Islam is Satha-Anand, who contributed a great deal to the early discussion Islam and nonviolence through his monograph and co-edited volume stemming from a seminar held in Bali in 1986 (Satha-Anand, Paige, and Cilliat 1993).
6 For example, when Quraysh leaders decided to wage a war against the Prophet, he opted for migration instead of retaliation or engaging in war. In another situation when Oqba Bin Moaet attacked the Prophet and tried strangling him in Kaaba area, however, Abu Bakr came and rescued him. The Prophet did not use any violence to

defend himself during this period (see Ibn Hisham, *Al Sira al Nabbawiya* [*The Prophet's Biography*] Beirut: Dar Almarifa, n.d.).
7 Sahih Muslim Arabic/English book reference Book 1, Hadith, 27. In another Hadith: some of the Ansar asked the Messenger of Allah (for help) and he gave them (something). Then they asked him and he gave them, then when he had run out he said: "Whatever I have of good, I will never keep it from you, but whoever wants to refrain from asking, Allah, the Mighty and Sublime, will help him to do so, and whoever wants to be patient, Allah will help him to be patient. None is ever given anything better and more far-reaching than patience." Sunan an-Nasa'i 2588; Sahih Al Bukhari: Book 23, Hadith 0; In English translation: Vol. 3, Book 23, Hadith 2589.
8 Bukhari: al-Adab al Nabawi, pp. 66, Tjrid al-Bukhari (Kitab al-Mazalim, chapter 22, No. 1–2, also Muslim book: 34 (cited in Saiyidain 1994, 159).
9 "High numbers of young people, particularly young women, are unemployed and excluded from the formal economy" (2016, 2) http://reliefweb.int/sites/reliefweb.int/files/resources/AHDR2016En.pdf
10 There are many studies that analyze the political and socio-cultural position of the Muslim states. See more details on many Arab regimes in Abu-Nimer 2003.
11 Based on capacity building training in peacebuilding conducted by the author within KAICIID programs for interreligious dialogue in Amman, Jordan; Cairo, Egypt, Tunisia between 2014 and 2016.

References

Abu-Nimer, Mohammed. 2003. *Nonviolence and Peace Building in Islam: Theory and Practice*. Gainesville, FL: University Press of Florida.
Abu-Nimer, Mohammed. 2010. "An Islamic Model of Conflict Resolution: Principles and Challenges," in *Crescent and Dove: Peace and Conflict Resolution in Islam*, ed. Wamar-ul Huda, 73–92. Washington, DC: United States Institute of Peace Press.
Abu-Nimer, Mohammed and Timothy Seidel. 2017. "Religion, Politics, and Conflict Transformation in Israel and the Occupied Palestinian Territory," in *Conflict Transformation and the Palestinians: The Dynamics of Peace and Justice Under Occupation*, eds. Alpaslan Özerdem, Chuck Thiessen, and Mufid Qassoum, 178–193. London and New York: Routledge.
Abu-Nimer, Mohammed and Renata Smith. 2016. "Interreligious and Intercultural Education for Dialogue, Peace and Social Cohesion," *International Review of Education*, 62(4): 393–405. (August 2016). doi:10.1007/s11159-016-9583-4
Ahmad, Rashid. 2015. "Doctrine of Peace: An Islamic Perspective," *Al-Idah* 31 December, 2015.
Ali, Saleem H. 2009. *Islam and Education: Conflict and Conformity in Pakistan's Madrassahs*. Oxford: Oxford University Press.
Al-Jawziyyah, Muhammad ibn Ibi Bakr Ibn al-Qaayyam. 1996. *Hidayat al-Hiyarah fi ajwibat al a-Yahood wa al_Nasarah* (Vol. 1). Jeddah: Dar al-Qalam.
Appleby, R. S. 2000. *The Ambivalence of the Sacred: Religion, Violence, and Reconciliation*. New York: Rowman & Littlefield.
Armstrong, Karen. 2014. *Fields of Blood: Religion and the History of Violence*. New York: Anchor Books.
Barakat, Halim. 1993. *The Arab World: Society, Culture and State*. Berkeley: University of California Press.
Baresh, David P. and Charles P. Webel. 2009. *Peace and Conflict Studies: 2nd Edition*. Thousand Oaks, CA: Sage.

Beyerle, Shaazka. 2014. *Curtailing Corruption: People Power for Accountability and Justice.* Boulder, CO: Lynne Rienner.
Burgess, Heidi and Paul Burgess. 1994. "Justice without Violence: A Theoretical Framework," in *Justice Without Violence,* eds. Paul Wehr, Heidi Burgess and Guy Burgess. Boulder, CO: Lynne Rienner.
Burton, J. W. 1990. *Conflict Resolution and Prevention.* New York: St. Martin's Press.
Englebert, Bert. 2000. Pre-Colonial Institutions, Post-Colonial States, and Economic Development in Tropical Africa. *Political Research Quarterly,* 53(1): 7–36.
Esack, Farid. 1998. *Islam and Politics.* London: Third World Foundation.
Gopin, Marc. 2000. *Between Eden and Armageddon: The Future of World Religions, Violence and Peacemaking.* Oxford: Oxford University Press.
Guirguis, Laure. 2016. *Copts and the Security State: Violence, Coercion, and Sectarianism in Contemporary Egypt.* Stanford, CA: Stanford University Press.
Haleem, Muhammad Abdel. 2001. "War and Peace in the Qur'an" from the book *Understanding the Qur'an Themes and Style.* www.islamawareness.net/Jihad/jihad_article001.html (Accessed 21 July 2017).
Howadi, Fahmi. 1993. *Islam and Democracy.* Cairo: Al Ahram Publication. (Arabic).
Hudson, Michael C. 1977. *Arab Politics: The Search for Legitimacy.* New Haven, CT: Yale University Press.
Jalabi Khalis. 1992. *Studies in Science and Peace.* Dar Al Kutub AL Rabiya. Damascus Min al-dharrah ilá al-majarrah wa-min al-khaliyah ilá al-dimagh (Arabic Edition).
Jalabi Khalis. 1997. *The Psychology of Violence and the Strategy of Peaceful Action.* Dar Aal Fikr: Beirut. (Arabic).
Kathir, Ibn. n.d. *Stories of the Prophet.* Mansura: Dar Al-Manarah, pp. 157–159.
Kishtainy, Khalid. 1990. "Violent and Nonviolent Struggle in Arab History," in *Arab Nonviolent Political Struggle in the Middle East,* eds. Ralph Crow, Philip Grant, and Saad I. Ibrahim, 9–24. Boulder, CO: Lynne Rienner Publishers.
Lederach, John Paul. 1994. *Preparing for Peace: Conflict Transformation Across Cultures.* Syracuse: Syracuse University Press.
Lederach, John Paul. 1997. *Building Peace: Sustainable Reconciliation in Divided Societies.* Washington, DC: United States Institute of Peace.
Looney, Robert. 2003. "Reforming Pakistan's Educational System: The Challenge of the Madrassas," *The Journal of Social, Political and Economic Studies,* 28(3): 257–274.
Malik, Jamal, ed. 2008. *Madrasas in South Asia: Teaching Terror?* London and New York: Routledge.
Mehar, Muhammad Ayub. 2010. *Is There a Vicious Circle in Muslim World? The Crisis of Institutional Governance, Competitiveness and Higher Education.* Saarbrücken: Lambert Academic Publishing.
Moghadam, Valentine M. 2003. *Modernizing Women: Gender and Social Change in the Middle East: Second Edition.* Boulder, CO: Lynne Rienner Publishers.
Rohde, Achim. 2010. *State-Society Relations in Ba'thist Iraq: Facing dictatorship.* Volume 11 of SOAS Routledge Studies on the Middle East. London: Routledge.
Sahih Muslim, vol. 3. 1976–1979. trans. Abdul Hambid Siddiqi. Lahore: Sh. Muhammad Ashraf.
Said, Jawdat.1996. *Be as the Son of Adam. Damascus.* (Arabic).
Saiyidain, Khwaja Gulam. 1994. *Islam: The Religion of Peace: 2nd edition.* New Delhi: Har-Anand Pub.
Satha-Anand, Chaiwat, Glen Paige, and Sarah Cilliat. 1993. *Islam and Nonviolence.* Honolulu: Center for Global Nonviolence Planning Project.

Sharabi, Hisham. 1988. *Neopatriarchy: A Theory of Distorted Change in Arab Society*. New York: Oxford University Press.
Shaw, Ken. 2006. "Muslim Education in the Gulf States and Saudi Arabia: Selected Issues," in *Education in the Muslim World: Different Perspectives*, ed. Rosarii Griffin. Oxford: Symposium Books.
Stephan, Maria, ed. 2010. *Civilian Jihad: Nonviolent Struggle, Democratization, and Governance in the Middle East*. 2009 edition. New York: Palgrave Macmillan.
Young, Robert J. 2001. *Postcolonialism: An Historical Introduction*. Oxford: Wiley-Blackwell.

PART V
Addressing the Issues Cross-Culturally

14

BUILDING PEACE WITH RELIGIOUS SUPPORT

The Case of Sri Lanka

Jehan Perera

Introduction

Seven years ago, in 2010, I was part of the small team that began to set up inter-religious groups to engage in peacebuilding in Sri Lanka. It was slow and hard work at the beginning. The political context was filled with intolerant and narrow nationalism. Civil society peace-building work was labelled as being anti-national by the nationalists in the government, who rejoiced in the war victory of the Sri Lankan security forces over the Liberation Tigers of Tamil Eelam. We ourselves did not know the religious clergy in many of the districts and they did not know us, and so it was difficult to get them to come for meetings and to commit their scarce time when their own religious duties took up so much of their time. It was discouraging to travel for hours to a distant district and find that only a handful had turned up for the meeting. But soon the value of those meetings spread by word of mouth. The religious clergy in a district who knew of each other, but had never had an opportunity to spend time with one another, now took that opportunity and began to value it.

The post-war period from May 2009 to January 2015 was one in which the government restricted the space for civil society. It was during this period that the district level inter-religious committees (DIRCs) we set up played a major role at the community level in mitigating local-level conflicts and addressing collective issues of concern to their communities. Due to constant interaction, the multi-ethnic and multi-religious members of these committees developed a greater degree of trust that is utilized to withstand the polarizations of the current day. Capacities of the members of DIRCs have been built over the years, and they are well trained on subjects of conflict resolution, early warning and mediation, conflict sensitivity and prioritization of humanitarian needs, pluralism, media, documentation and referrals, and they have also built linkages with media.

There is a great deal of work that these inter-religious committees have done together to improve their understanding of one another and of their religions. They have been engaged in a process of understanding the nature of the political problems that separate the ethnic communities and make their political leaders see each other as opponents instead of as partners. Today the DIRCs serve as focal points for inter-religious reconciliation and problem solving at the local level. Their work in the communities has helped resolve issues of inter-religious and inter-ethnic tension before they escalate into conflagrations, and has also contributed to building reconciliation through collective activities.

Those who formed inter-religious committees were conscious of both the need to be strong with regard to their aspirations and to temper what they said so that the entire group could accept it. They demonstrated on a micro level what is necessary to be done at the macro level by the large political actors. Each of the religions, and the individuals who are their adherents, see problems from different perspectives. But when they come together as an inter-religious group of Buddhists, Hindus, Muslims and Christians, they become problem solvers, each on the same side trying to reach the best solution. As the religious clergy are moral arbiters in Sri Lankan society, especially at the community level, they show the way in which the diversity of Sri Lanka's people can become a source of strength.

Setting

Sri Lanka has a plural society of several different ethnic communities, the two largest being Sinhalese and Tamil. The centralized state inherited by the newly independent country in 1948 effectively transferred political power into the hands of the Sinhalese majority, who comprise about three-fourths of the population. The inability of the political elites belonging to the different ethnic communities to share power equitably among themselves led to a series of broken agreements and to acute mistrust between the communities. The difficulty of protecting minority interests in a unitary system of government in which majority-minority relations are strained is exemplified by Sri Lanka's modern political history.[1]

As the Tamils from the north in particular were rarely represented in the higher rungs of the government, they were unable to sway government decisions to take their concerns into account. The inability of Tamil politicians to obtain adequate redress to their grievances eventually led to the build-up of separatist sentiment, militancy and war. For three decades from the late 1970s until May 2009, Sri Lanka was stalemated between governments that were not prepared to devolve power to the Tamil majority provinces and a Tamil militant movement that wanted a separate country. The Sri Lankan ethnic conflict was considered "one of the deadliest and most protracted conflicts of our time" (de Votta, 2004, 2) and was the longest running civil war in the Asian region at the time it ended.

In May 2009, Sri Lanka's 26-year war between government forces and LTTE came to a bloody end. But despite the end of the war, Sri Lanka continues to be deeply divided on lines of ethnicity, religion and politics. The overwhelming tendency in the literature on Sri Lanka is to label the conflict as 'ethnic' (Peleg 2007, 3–6). The cultural diversity found in Sri Lanka is undeniably an essential dimension of this conflict. The majority, at about 75% of the population, is Sinhala or Sinhalese, with about 94% of them Buddhist. The rest are divided among the Sri Lankan Tamils (11.4%), who compete with the Sinhalese for claims of historical entitlement to the land; the Sri Lankan Moors (8.2%), who trace their roots to Arab traders; and the Indian Tamils (5.0%), who were brought to the island as plantation workers by the British (Department of Census and Statistics 2008). However, it is important to note that ethnicity is one of multiple axes of identity and its importance in conflict varies over time.

Post-War Context

The last phase of the war was one of the most challenging in the annals of modern warfare. It ensured that the Sri Lankan war took the headlines of the international media. The Liberation Tigers of Tamil Eelam (LTTE) in their retreat herded the Tamil population of the northern territories it once controlled into a tiny patch of land. Using more 300,000 civilians as human shields, they sought to keep the Sri Lankan military forces at bay and buy time for some change to ensure their continued survival. When the LTTE was on the verge of being militarily annihilated, Western countries urged restraint, the non-use of heavy weapons that could cause indiscriminate casualties and the evacuation of the civilian population.

Sri Lanka is an example in which the military response was successful. However, the end of the war has left a difficult legacy of human rights violations and war crimes from which the country is trying to extricate itself. Horizontal inequalities, defined as severe inequalities in economic and political resources between culturally defined groups, were undoubtedly a contributing factor to the perpetuation of Sri Lanka's long-running conflict. No sooner had it won the war than the government asserted economic development to be the main engine of reconciliation. Contrary to hopes that the end of the conflict would lead to democratic reforms to enable greater devolution of power and accountability, the post-war period became characterized by the shrinking of political space for Sri Lankan civil society, an erosion of the rule of law and increasingly centralized authoritarian rule. Sri Lanka has come under intense international pressure and there have been four resolutions of the UN Human Rights Council in Geneva since 2009 on this account. Today Sri Lanka is a country that continues to be deeply divided on lines of ethnicity, religion and politics.

If Sri Lanka's success was its ability to annihilate the LTTE on the military battlefield, its failure came with the end of the war and an inability and unwillingness on the part of the victorious government to close the chapter on the war by seeking the truth regarding the past, requiring accountability for war crimes, compensating the victims and engaging in political reform that would heal the wounds of the war and win the hearts and minds of the people in the war zones. The over-centralization of power during the period of the war led to allegations of gross abuse of power, corruption and impunity. In particular, the period of governance of President Mahinda Rajapaksa (2005–2015) was also marked by non-adherence to systems of governance and by a willingness to obtain results without adequate consideration given to the costs. His political downfall at elections he called prematurely in 2015, with two years left in his presidency, was due to excesses that cost him key constituencies.

The use of Sinhalese nationalism to an excessive degree alienated the ethnic and religious minorities, especially the Muslims who had voted for the former president at previous elections. But they became subject to physical attacks by extremist Buddhists, who were backed by sections of the government. The level of corruption was also excessive, which alienated the Sinhalese intelligentsia, who were concerned about the growing indebtedness of the country. The government's refusal to take that course of action meant that Sri Lanka risked becoming an international outcast and the subject of economic and political sanctions that would have generated new divisions and hatreds within the country, and with the international community.

The presidential elections of January 2015 offered an opportunity for change. At stake in these elections was whether Sri Lanka continued on the path set by the Rajapaksa government or took a different path. In January 2015 and again in August of the same year, the majority of Sri Lankan voters cast their votes against the incumbent government. The main significance of the election verdict is that it paved the way for transition to take place in two key aspects of governance. The first was to take away the arbitrary power of individuals and vest them instead in systems. The sustainability of this process lies in the fact that virtually all the political parties have agreed that the systems of government need to be strengthened. The majority of people chose the rule of law over the rule of men epitomized by the previous government.

The lifting of the sense of fear in political dissenters and in ethnic and religious minorities has been the biggest improvement that the change of government brought to the country. The new government has charted a shift away from the highly centralized and national security-dominant state structure that the Rajapaksa government had constructed to a more consensual mode of governance. In keeping with his election promise, President Maithripala Sirisena, with the backing of Prime Minister Wickremesinghe, championed the passage of the 19th Amendment to the constitution, which reduced the power of the presidency and the scope for the abuse of power, and strengthened parliament and state institutions such as the judiciary, public service and police.

The second important transition that the country is taking is movement away from the continuation of militarization and rising governmental antipathy towards ethnic minorities of the previous period to a society that is truly multi-ethnic and multi-religious in its decision making and its choices. But as this still remains a transitional process, there will need to be a lot of compromise and patience. The main post-war failure of the Rajapaksa government in terms of resolving the ethnic conflict was its use of a strong military presence to keep the Tamil people in check rather than finding a mutually acceptable solution that would enable the military to be withdrawn from the Tamil majority areas and restore civilian rule. This failure continued to fuel Sinhalese nationalism, which then spilled over into anti-Muslim actions that appeared to have government cover.

During the last period of Rajapaksa rule, there was also a rise in attacks against Muslims and their places of religious worship and businesses, which made all minorities, including Sinhalese Christians, feel insecure. These attacks, often led by nationalist Buddhist monks, were accompanied by police inaction (National Christian Evangelical Alliance 2015). This smacked of government complicity. The very poor showing of the Buddhist People's Front (BJP), a Buddhist monk-led party, at the elections shows that the anti-Muslim sentiment of the past few years was not a bottom-up phenomenon, but rather one that was being politically cultivated at higher levels.

After the elections of 2015, Sri Lanka now has a government in which all parties and all communities are represented. The process of decision making will be slow and difficult, but the new government will represent the diversity of Sri Lanka's multi-ethnic and multi-religious population. In fact, the new Sri Lankan government has shown that it is possible to win hearts and minds even after a bloody and costly war. In terms of both war and peace, what to do and what not to do, Sri Lanka could provide lessons to an international community that is struggling to come to terms with terrorism and its spread.

The release of the UN Report on alleged war crimes and human rights violations in Sri Lanka's war in September 2015[2] has been an important step in the country's transition to reconciliation, as it requires the government and people to give their attention to unhealed wounds of the past that continue to fester in the body politic. The investigation team made strong indictments against both the government and LTTE forces for war crimes. The most contentious aspect of the report was its recommendation that the government should "adopt a specific legislation establishing an ad hoc hybrid special court, integrating international judges, prosecutors, lawyers and investigators, mandated to try war crimes and crimes against humanity, with its own independent investigative and prosecuting organ."[3]

Public opinion in Sri Lanka amongst the Sinhalese majority is against any international investigation into the past. It is to be noted that even prior to its release, the government had developed a complex and well thought out mechanism to be led by Sri Lankans. By co-sponsoring the UN Human Rights Council resolution on Promoting Reconciliation, Accountability and Human Rights in Sri Lanka in October 2015, the government has taken the initiative with regard to the implementation of its recommendations.[4]

Sri Lanka's foreign minister, Mangala Samaraweera, addressed the UNHRC in Geneva and laid down the parameters of the government's plan for post-war justice and reparation as follows:[5]

> The ideas that the Government has evolved for setting up independent, credible and empowered mechanisms for truth seeking, justice, reparations and guarantees of non-recurrence within the framework of the Constitution include the following:
> —For truth seeking, the establishment by statute, of two mechanisms:
>
> (i) a Commission for Truth, Justice, Reconciliation and Non-recurrence to be evolved in consultation with the relevant authorities of South Africa. This mechanism is envisaged as having a dual structure: a 'Compassionate Council' composed of religious dignitaries from all major religions in the country and a structure composed of Commissioners. For many victims of human rights abuses, from whichever community, where the perpetrators are unclear for a judicial mechanism to handle, or where the practices of the state and society have resulted in discrimination, this Commission will allow them to discover the truth, understand what happened and help remedy any sense of injustice.
> (ii) an Office on Missing Persons based on the principle of the families' right to know, to be set up by Statute with expertise from the ICRC, and in line with internationally accepted standards.
>
> —On the Right to Justice, what is being proposed is for a Judicial Mechanism with a Special Counsel to be set up by Statute. This takes into account the right of victims to a fair remedy and aims to address the problem of impunity for human rights violations suffered by all communities. There have been previous instances as well in Sri Lanka when criminal justice mechanisms of different kinds have been set up.[6] This, therefore, is not at all an alien concept. Neither is it aimed at a particularly group of persons, but something that is essential in terms of upholding the rule of law, and creating a society that respects the rule of law.
> —On the Right to Reparations, an Office for Reparations to be set up by Statute to facilitate the implementation of recommendations relating to reparations made by the proposed Commission on Truth, Justice, Reconciliation and Non-recurrence, the Office of the Missing Persons, the LLRC and any other entity.

As can be seen in the government's proposals, the positive impact that religious clergy has had on peace-building in Sri Lanka is reflected in the proposal to establish a Compassionate Council composed of religious dignitaries from all major religions in the country to accompany its Truth-seeking Commission.

Religious Mobilization[7]

The mobilization of religious identities, on the one hand, plays a key role in the war's social and political history. On the other hand, the politicization of religion has also become a major impediment to peace-building in Sri Lanka. The history of religious interference in political and social peace-building has impacted negatively on the potential of religions to advocate for reconciliation and forge peace. Religious mobilization, although not the direct cause of the Sri Lankan conflict, has increased the tensions that compelled the war. Sri Lankan history is replete with many instances where religious and ethnic concerns interacted to prevent peace. For example, one of the earliest negotiations between the Sinhala-dominated government and the Tamil political parties (the Bandaranaike-Chelvanayakam Pact 1957) was abrogated when Buddhist monks organized a protest on the Prime Minister's front lawn.[8]

This conflation of religious and ethnic identity has been a crucial dimension in Sri Lanka's civil war. Historical myths and narratives have been used to construct ideological justifications for Sinhala-Buddhist dominance. The sixth-century chronicle, Mahavamsa, for instance, is heavily influenced by the view of the Buddhist clergy as protectors of Buddhism and the island of Sri Lanka as the Buddhist Promised Land (Bartholomeus 2002). Since the country is construed as the sacred stronghold of Buddhism, it becomes vital that it is protected from conquest or adulteration. Sections of the Sinhalese political elite have employed this notion of a sacrosanct Sinhala-Buddhist heritage to unite and mobilize the Sinhala people; unfortunately, however, such politics also served to increase the country's ethnic divisions and precipitate its civil war.

The connections between ethnicity and religion in the Sri Lankan Tamil community are more complex. The Liberation Tigers of Tamil Eelam (LTTE), at least publicly, repudiated caste-based stratification, and as such, it was not always in its interests to incorporate the "traditional" Tamil heritage of Hinduism in its nationalistic rhetoric. Occasionally, however, the Hindu identity of the Tamils is utilized to speak out against the group's enemies—for instance, Muslims, on both ethnic and religious grounds, are excluded from the Tamil category, while Christians who disagree with the ideals of Tamil nationalism are sometimes targeted through their religion. Indeed, in many regards, Tamil Hindus have used their religious traditions to "energize and mobilise their cultural and political action against the dominant political structures" with continuing belief in an ancient heritage that lies in its connection to the land.[9]

Since both Sinhalese and Tamils feel that their existence is threatened, a large majority perceived the nationalistic conflict as a necessary evil. K. M. de Silva observes,

> there is the Sinhalese sense of historical destiny, of a small and embattled people who have preserved Theravada Buddhism when it was obliterated in India under a Hindu revivalist tide, and whose language despite its roots in

classical Indian languages, is uniquely Sri Lankan. Linked to this is their perception of the Tamils as a traditional "national" enemy against whom they have fought at various times over two thousand years of a common history.
(de Silva 2003)

The Sinhalese, though a majority in the country, feel threatened by the large population of Tamils who surround them in the region, especially in South India. This "minority complex" of the Sinhalese is theorized to contribute to their need for political power. Thus, the devolution of power, or federalism, is perceived as paving the way for Tamil secession, and unity with the larger Tamil polity living in South India and the eventual domination of the Sinhalese.

Since a political solution necessitates negotiating with those perceived as the "enemy" and maintaining a sustained collaboration, it is construed as diametrically opposed to the values of ethnic patriotism. Those who work for peace with justice and accountability to overcome the past legacy of human rights violations are thus branded as traitors, and are publicly vilified as such. Since religion has been so effectively conflated with the conflict, it becomes particularly difficult for religious leaders to abandon the norm and speak for peace. As representatives of their group's beliefs, their public personas are subject to both external and internal pressure. Precisely because the Buddhist establishment has a vested interest in the status quo, it is extremely difficult for monks to openly support a political peace in which there is sharing and devolution of power.

While it is often claimed that religious leaders want peace, this desire is often frustrated by their different, sometimes mutually exclusive understandings of peace as a process, a goal and an outcome. Many among the Buddhist leadership, for example, hold contradictory positions on the Sri Lankan conflict. The first is an avowed preference for non-violence. The other is a commitment to a centralized government and unitary state (a standpoint that also openly conflicts with the motivations of ethnic minorities and thus negates the monks' potential for being nonpartisan intermediaries). Unfortunately, these political beliefs currently hold more influence over the Buddhist clergy. Their view of peace does not correspond with the ideals of power-sharing that other religious leaders hold, while their past political affiliation with the war undermines the trust necessary for being intermediaries for peace.

In addition, the religious dimensions of conflict in Sri Lanka also take on a Buddhist-Christian dynamic, which renders it even more difficult for religious leaders to engage in inter-religious peace programmes. In recent years, Sri Lankan Christians have been accused of using dishonourable methods to persuade Buddhists and Hindus away from their traditional religious heritage. Evangelical Christians, who aim to convert, are perceived as particularly dangerous in Sri Lanka, and are even targeted by Christians of other denominations.[10] Since religion is so central to ethnic identity in Sri Lanka, it is easy to understand why the proselytizing themes of this "foreign" religion have inspired fear and suspicion.

It is this failure to find a common ground that is harming the institutional inter-religious peace-building effort the most. Members know that there are a number of differences between them, but they fear that addressing these differences will lead to conflict and damage the nascent movement. Since they have not been able to engage with each other and formulate a mutually inclusive ideal, they cannot take any decisive action or plan for the future. This failure to agree upon a mutual view of "peace" is also problematic since it reflects the incompatible attitudes within society—which are also the root of the civil war. If these organizations are to provide leadership in bringing peace to Sri Lanka, they must be able to reflect the solution within their own ranks to show that it is both possible and preferable. Otherwise, the unaddressed conflicts and growing division within them will become the very antithesis of the ideal they are seeking to project.

However, their lack of enthusiasm to take on such a symbolically controversial and time-consuming role means that these organizations tend to lie dormant unless prodded by external actors. Forming a movement that is both united in purpose and strengthened by resilient inter-religious relationships is a challenging task. Increasing the complexity of current efforts are members' high profiles. As prominent leaders of the country's various religious groups, their values or actions are exposed to both internal and external critique. Some are subject to political patronage, meaning that they must be careful when sanctioning an ideal that is both politically vilified and generally perceived to be unrealistic (at present, there is a widespread lack of faith in a negotiated political solution due to the recent military success, and the unsuccessful track-record of negotiations in the past). When coupled with the individual prejudices that members may hold, these political pressures further prohibit internal unity and restrict inter-religious peace-building.

The prominent position and varying political beliefs of these religious leaders not only hinder internal accord, but also make it difficult for them to fully commit to the time and mutual effort it takes to establish a religious movement. It is common for outside actors to organize meetings and identify issues for religious leaders to engage with and undertake. Interactions take place on an ad-hoc basis and have not developed into sustained, meaningful relationships between religious groups. Furthermore, some top religious leaders are reluctant to get involved in their organizations' activities unless they are persistently courted by community leaders. This lack of initiative and commitment among many of the top religious leaders significantly restricts the impact such a group could have. Not only does it prevent the group from developing into an independent body, but it also presents a model of apathy that contradicts the active social conscience they are trying to inspire.

This lack of motivation also inhibits religious leaders from committing to significant action. Most activities organized by these inter-religious organizations revolve around meetings and speeches, and occasional statements to address pressing national issues. Workshops, conferences and programmes which promote sustainable peace and inter-religious solidarity, however, are of no avail unless their ideas and plans are put into practice. As Douglas Johnson (2005, 8) argues,

> as popular as inter-religious dialogue has become as a proscribed remedy for reconciling strained relations . . . its perceived worth is probable overrated if it only amounts to ad hoc meetings and a sterile exchange of views about belief systems. If, however, it includes a mandate for action and a commitment to meet on an ongoing basis, then the relationships that result will likely lead to increased trust, at which point all things become possible.

In spite of these challenges, religious organizations also work to mitigate divisions and promote peace. It is important to emphasize that identity is fluid and dynamic; it is not fixed and immutable. As such, influential leaders and faith-based organizations have the power to shift identities towards a position that is more closely aligned with religious ideals of virtue. Inter-religious cooperation and dialogue could potentially promote this change. There are currently a number of different religious and inter-religious efforts that are attempting to create and promote peace in Sri Lanka. Their work ranges from development projects to humanitarian aid. Faith-based efforts hold immense potential to create peace in Sri Lanka.

Literature in the field of religious peacemaking identifies a number of specific, though not unique, strengths which faith-based actors possess. These include "strong faith-based motivation, long-term commitment, long-term presence on the ground, moral and spiritual authority, and a niche to mobilise others for peace" (Tsjeard et al. 2005, 8). Religious interventions can take many forms, involving local religious bodies, grassroots initiatives, or actions by religious leaders to bridge "the divide between faiths, to engage in dialogue, build relationships, and develop trust and work together to resolve common problems" (Johnson 2005, 8). One particular asset of faith-based peace-building in Sri Lanka is that most people in the country are oriented towards their own religious community; thus, when these interventions are framed by religious narratives and contexts, they become much more effective in persuading involved parties towards peace.

Religious peace-building in Sri Lanka is organized at two different levels. The inter-religious councils headed by leaders of national religious organizations hold interventions and publicly speak for humanitarianism and peace. Meanwhile, there are less publicized grassroots efforts which are also powerful advocates for a sustainable peace. Institutional faith-based peace-building efforts in Sri Lanka aim to harness the influence and action of prominent members of all religious communities. This is not an easy task given the obstacles. However, religious leaders also operate with distinct advantages when it comes to faith-based conflict resolution and peace-building. Indeed, Sri Lanka's religious leadership has access to several critical resources that could assist peace-building initiatives in Sri Lanka. The extensive, well-established religious networks and institutions in Sri Lanka are valuable channels of communication and action. In fact, religious leaders generally have extensive reach and influence in Sri Lankan society, as the majority of the population belongs to a religious community, and is thus accessible through religious infrastructure. Furthermore, these religious leaders occupy crucial intermediary roles in Sri Lankan society.

In the period immediately prior to the commencement of the Norwegian facilitated peace process in 2002, for example, Christian bishops acted as facilitators, carrying messages between the leadership of the Sri Lankan government and leaders of the LTTE. It is also important to note that their leadership is constant and durable, especially when contrasted with the country's political leaders, who are vulnerable to the pressures of a democratic electorate and thus change more frequently. Indigenous religious leaders are long-term players who have been present throughout the lengthy lifecycle of Sri Lanka's conflict. As a result, they are well poised to provide much needed continuity in approaches and commitment to peace-building initiatives and advocacy in Sri Lanka. The religious clergy maintains a very close relationship with the people of the country. Thus, they are well situated to undertake observatory and educational roles to discourage violence, corruption, human rights violations or other behaviour that impedes viable and sustainable peace-building initiatives.

In Sri Lanka religious leaders (especially Buddhist monks) can be particularly influential in political decision making processes due to the status and respect they hold in Sri Lankan society and their close links with the political establishment (Orjuela 2004, 181–182). This ability to influence politicians is a critical resource which can be drawn upon to initiate political and constitutional changes necessary for a sustainable solution to Sri Lanka's conflict. Additionally, Sri Lanka's religions are organized at local, national and international levels, and thus are a vital link to global resources and encouragement. Religious leaders thus possess the capability to mobilize widespread support for a peace process (Johnson 2005, 55). International support for peace could be a potential defence against the strong opposition of nationalist parties which discourages many religious leaders from taking up the cause. On the other hand, such international involvement may lead to perceptions of foreign interference and deter indigenous efforts.

Organizational Efforts

In light of the failure of successive governments to find a political solution to the Sri Lankan conflict, many civic and religious organizations have attempted to mobilize religious leaders in support of a sustainable social and political change. There are several multi-religious peace initiatives, such as the Congress of Religious, the Sri Lanka Council of Religions for Peace and the National Peace Council (NPC), that not only merge the strengths of the four Sri Lankan religions into one collective power, but also demonstrate first hand that unity and concord between groups is possible. At a time when the political leadership has failed to substantially alter the status quo, stronger inter-religious initiatives at the top level could become a very persuasive argument for peaceful dialogue and reconciliation.

The NPC started a project to promote cooperation among multi-religious communities in Sri Lanka, focusing on groups that have been divided by the conflict. The overall objective of the NPC is to create peaceful relations between all communities in Sri Lanka's diverse population, contributing to a healing society in a post-war context. The intention is to promote multi-religious community responsiveness of groups divided by the conflict and enable them to find appropriate humanitarian solutions to care for conflict-affected women and children.

While the political situation is much improved after the change of government in 2015, and the space for dissent has increased, there still remain concerns about the potential for instability and a return in some form of those influential under the former regime. In the present context, the DIRCs promote inter-ethnic and inter-religious dialogue. They identify participants for dialogue on current national reconciliation issues that have an impact on wider ethno-religious relations and work on issues around constitutional reform and transitional justice, which are two key areas of focus in relation to national reconciliation.

The NPC supports inter-faith and inter-ethnic dialogue to reduce ethno-religious tensions in selected locations and ensure that national reconciliation processes and policies take account of ethnic and religious viewpoints. The operational logic of these interventions is that if Sinhalese, Tamil and Muslim religious and civil society leaders interact collaboratively and problem solve around common interests, then inter-ethnic relations at the community level will improve. If religious leaders are empowered to better understand and contribute constructively to policy advocacy at the local and national level, then there will be a greater likelihood that such policies will be sensitive to ethno-religious sentiments. In addition, the promotion of such an approach to dialogue will demonstrate the opportunity for national replication that can contribute to the integration of pluralistic views in wider reconciliation reform efforts in Sri Lanka.

District inter-religious committees (DIRCs), which are presently active in 16 of the country's 25 districts, have direct access to grassroots communities, enabling them to understand and voice their concerns. The committee members have contacts with higher-level religious leaders and those with political command, and are in a position to inform and influence them. By having a structure so closely tied to a grassroots organizing structure, NPC has been able to empower local leaders and maintain a bottom-up approach in finding solutions to humanitarian needs through a multi-religious perspective.

DIRCs have two primary roles in furthering peace at the grassroots level. One is offering local religious communities opportunities to undertake multi-religious action and advocacy for peace, while their second objective is to help local communities create a strong internal solidarity regardless of ethnic or religious division.

At the community level, the DIRCs mediate in local conflicts between ethnic or religious groups, easing the tension and suspicion that is residual from the war. As leaders from the communities in which they mediate, DIRCs are attuned to the local dynamics of a larger national conflict, and are equipped with the moral and social relationships needed to sustainably intervene. DIRCs also often engage in national advocacy on issues that are informed by local voices and needs. A key goal of their peace-building activities lies in stimulating collective responsiveness to the humanitarian needs of those in one's own community. DIRCs thus build and work within inter-religious efforts towards finding sustainable solutions to the post-war effects of violence and disaster.

NPC addresses the unique challenges, constraints and opportunities with regard to post-war dialogue and conflict prevention efforts in Sri Lanka. It conducts baseline studies to better understand current perceptions on the status of ethno-religious relations in selected project districts. Thereafter, building on local partner expertise, it establishes inter-ethnic and inter-religious spaces that seek to mitigate the risk that local level disputes, incidents and tensions could escalate into violence. Religious leaders participate in these same spaces to enable them to better understand and engage constructively in discourse on national reconciliation policies. The outcomes of such discussions are channelled towards policy and decision makers at a local and national level, in order that such policies reflect and take into account all ethno-religious views.

NPC also focuses on the promotion of human rights as a fundamental cross-cutting issue. This approach is integrated into all training and dialogue events with members of the DIRCs. Through this project, members of the DIRCs receive training on concepts of pluralism and minority rights, which form the bedrock for national peace-building and reconciliation programmes. In addition, the content of proposals for transitional justice are discussed with the DIRCs, which many see as a process closely intertwined with the UN Human Rights Council Resolution on Sri Lanka in October 2015. While the NPC has had their own training and capacity building on human rights, they have also ensured that such training is cascaded to their local community-based partners. The NPC has also worked to ensure that religious and ethnic minorities are linked with existing human rights networks, victim organizations, and organizations dedicated to promoting and protecting human rights.

Inter-faith fora have been identified as a suitable entry point through which to encourage dialogue between ethno-religious communities. During the last decade, especially when people-to-people engagement was actively discouraged by the state, inter-faith fora provided a relatively safe space for local communities to come together to address local issues. It was also a safe space for discussion of national issues, such as the need for equitable humanitarian responses in the immediate post-war context, state occupation of land in conflict affected areas, militarization and the erosion of democratic norms. During both the time of war and in the post-war period up to 2015, the government restricted the space for civil society to engage in civil empowerment and human rights work in the former war zones, and even in the rest of the country.

NPC conducts training programs that range from non-violent communication, mediation, and conflict sensitivity to gender equality. In addition, the NPC conducts awareness-raising workshops on the history of conflict in Sri Lanka and religious tolerance. Building on this series of training programs, the DIRCs function as an early-warning and early-response mechanism, meeting on a monthly basis to share recent experiences of members, identify any incidents that have taken place and discuss ways and means to resolve them. DIRC representatives maintain a register of issues that are presented or brought to their notice at monthly meetings. Information on issues resolved or unresolved for that period are shared with the NPC, and follow up is monitored. If any serious unexpected incidents take place that have or could have an immediate negative impact on community relations, the DIRCs are mandated to meet quickly to discuss and find solutions to mitigate the risk of escalation into violence.

Case Studies (National Peace Council 2016a)

What is evident from the work of NPC is the reservoir of untapped goodwill that exists between the religious communities at the grassroots level. When religious leaders are brought together in structured initiatives they begin to better understand each other and to work together. In the northern capital of Jaffna, the Buddhist monk who is a member of the Jaffna DIRC has helped his colleagues from other religions to network with government authorities, including the army that effectively runs the north even after the war. The Jaffna DIRC has also gone as a group to make representations before the Governor of the Northern Province and make appeals on behalf of people affected by problems that they cannot solve on their own. Another very successful activity has been exchange visits, whereby members of the inter-religious committees go on cross-country visits to gain awareness of the issues that exist in other parts of the country.

In 2012, in Balapitiya, a town in the Galle district in the deep south of Sri Lanka, two groups—majority Sinhala and minority Muslim—clashed. The clash followed an incident of suspected robbery. The youth of one community was suspected of robbing a shop belonging to a member of the other community. A dispute between two individuals took on ethnic dimensions and led to an inter-community conflict. Members of a DIRC—convened and nurtured by a local non-governmental organization, the National Peace Council—were concerned at the turn of events. They wanted to ensure that the tension and unease did not spread to other villages in the area. Among key issues identified by the group for action was the desire to counter the increasing tension between Sinhala and Muslim communities in the south of the country. Mono-ethnic villages abutted each other and had existed peacefully for years. There was concern that tension in proximate areas would lead to conflict in others, too. This is all too possible in an environment where ethno-religious Sinhala groups are trying to sow discontent against religious minorities, especially Muslims.

The principal of a local Sinhala school—Kotawela Primary School, a member of the Galle DIRC and the teaching advisor to the Education Department for the area—devised a plan. They organized a visit to a Muslim school in the district. The exchange was framed within activities schools were empowered to undertake on their own, without too much protocol. The Ministry of Education encouraged activities promoting social cohesion. So the students of Kotawela Primary School planned a visit to the Panapitiya Muslim Maha Vidyalaya (school). Panapitiya borders Balapitiya, where the Sinhalese and Muslim communities clashed in 2012.

Members of the Galle DIRC made personal contributions and collected money from leading business people in the area. The parents of students also contributed. In February 2014, 40 Sinhala students, with their parents and teachers, visited the Muslim school. They took traditional Sinhala sweetmeats and gifts for the children of the Muslim school. The Muslim village too treated the visitors with great ceremony. They were treated to traditional Muslim food and gifts. Activities during the exchange included a program that highlighted Buddhist and Muslim religious teachings. "Peace and reconciliation are significant concerns for all of us. It is after I joined the DIRC that I realized that I too could play a role," said Sudath Premalal, a DIRC-member who played a key role in organizing the visit.

The Kandy Dalada Perahara is an event of immense religious and cultural value to Buddhists and all Sri Lankans. It is held over ten days in August every year and has been an annual fixture since the time the sacred tooth relic of Buddha was brought to the country; Kandy was designated as a UNESCO World Heritage Site in 1988 due to this cultural and religious significance. Over one hundred elephants accompanied by dancers go on parade. The Dalada Perahara is viewed by thousands of people, including a large number of foreigners who specially come to Sri Lanka for the event. However, it was brought to the notice of the Kandy DIRC that the commentaries during the event are only carried out in Sinhala and English. This left out a large group of Tamil-speaking communities who come to Kandy from all parts of the country to see the Perahara. Having identified the issue and recognized the need to address the situation immediately at the meeting held on 2 August 2016, members of the Kandy DIRC met with the relevant persons who were in a position to address this issue. Their recommendation was readily accepted by the relevant authorities, and as a result a commentary in Tamil was carried out during the Kandy Dalada Perahara, facilitating thousands of Tamil-speaking visitors coming to Kandy specifically for the event.

Such work may be more effective in changing attitudes and promoting peace than similar work among those at the public level. It de-ethnicizes relationships as the group gets involved in a common peace-building or conflict resolution task. It helps build mutual empathy. Unlike the political leadership, the religious clergy have no concrete roles or agendas that prevent them from committing to a whole-hearted stand for peace. Peace through grassroots is also comparatively more stable, since it builds up a movement rather than trying to persuade multiple levels of political, social and religious hierarchies from the leadership down. Most importantly, working at the grassroots level bypasses the need to work through the very political structure that opposes peace; at the same time, it promotes a change in the hearts of the people, who together have the power to elect new leadership and change the state of the nation.

Sustaining Efforts

The sustained efforts of religious leaders in post-conflict peace-building are crucial to the successful resolution of conflict. Inter-religious peace initiatives offer a way to break down social boundaries and reconcile alienated communities. Religious leaders who occupy lower rungs of the religious hierarchy prove crucial to these organizations and to the movement as a whole. Not only are they able to mobilize many of the same resources as their leadership, but they are also more available to take part in the intensive peace-building activities that the future will require. Furthermore, as the segment of the religious leadership that works most closely with the people, they will have the personal and influential relationships necessary to encourage peaceful values at the grassroots.

The Sri Lankan government has affirmed that it will establish a Truth-Seeking Mechanism, one key component of which will be a Compassionate Council consisting of religious leaders. For the past seven years, the National Peace Council has been strengthening and expanding DIRCs, which are now active in 21 of the country's 25 districts and seek to empower local level sub-sectoral groups to support people-to-people interactions; such interactions increase citizens' ability to learn about, contribute to and engage in the government's transitional justice process, and build acceptance for an inclusive pluralistic national identity founded on shared values and respect for diversity. More recently, the government itself has decided to establish district-level committees to address issues of inter-religious and ethnic tension in the country. These committees would be set up in all 25 districts of the country. The District-Level Reconciliation Committee is to undertake a study on the background and causes of religious and ethnic tensions in the locality; formulate a suitable strategy and approach to mediate the problems; provide rapid response to resolve conflicts and tensions invite the perpetrators and victims and mediate conflict resolution; maintain a database on incidences of tension and attacks on religious places; mediate, negotiate and resolve conflicts; and prevent hate attacks ("Sri Lanka to set up regional committees" 2017).

Religious leaders have the social legitimacy and moral influence to engage key influencers and grassroots constituencies to lead social change, while the faiths they practice can promote tolerance and acceptance of pluralistic identities that connect groups through shared values and aspirations across other conflict divides.

In Sri Lanka, religious leaders are also uniquely positioned to address local issues of conflict and vulnerability amidst social and political stress; they can channel community concerns to influencers and decision-makers (i.e., connecting more people to key people), thereby functioning to transform everyday interventions into peace-writ-large.

In a submission to the Consultation Task Force appointed by the government to ascertain the appropriate reconciliation mechanisms in terms of the UN Human Rights Council resolution of October 2015 (National Peace Council 2016b), NPC recommended the increase of citizen engagement and support for the government's reform process amongst divided ethno-religious groups. It also urged greater support to civil society community initiatives to promote reconciliation and an inclusive national identity that would break down barriers and stereotypes and nurture deeper understanding, tolerance and trust. NPC also recommended that the religious leaders associated with its DIRCs should be brought into the proposed Compassionate Council as a district-level tier that can actively engage with the general population and support the Truth-Seeking Commission in its work (National Peace Council 2016a).

Ultimately, successful policy implementation will depend upon the infrastructure available at national, sub-national and grassroots levels. Thus, without first strengthening this infrastructure, inter-religious initiatives have little hope of extending the scope of any movement for peace. However, with religious values one of the few commonalities between the divided ethnic groups, such movements will be essential in encouraging dialogue and fostering peace. The next stage of this movement, its organizational development, coincides with a critical period in the country's history. The inter-religious peace movement will thus be more necessary than ever. If the organizations driving this movement could encourage an internal unity based on mutual values and work together towards building peace at all levels of society, they could become an influential force in the field of post-conflict reconciliation.

Capacitating second tier civil society organizations so that there is a regional resource available on peace, reconciliation and human rights related work is crucial as it will serve to increase the scope and depth of peacebuilding work that is being done currently. NPC finds that it is especially important to build their profiles and confidence to enhance the spread of peacebuilding work. A key lesson for NPC in its current engagement is that messaging is a key component of peace work, in terms of both content and the message bearer. NPC focuses on tapping into groups with moral authority and leadership in local communities to build trust in processes not readily acceptable to the public, especially in Sinhala areas. In effect, the NPC's fundamental approach is a 'more people through key people' engagement.

The core element of peacebuilding work in Sri Lanka at this current time is generating consensus for the government's transitional justice and reconciliation process. The need to create public awareness on the process and thereby build support for it is an urgent one. If Sri Lanka's reconciliation project is to be successful, peacebuilding work, especially in the rural sector, has to increase significantly and urgently. For best impact, the work has to be carried out systematically and cohesively with collaboration among civil society organizations which have a long presence in advocacy work on the ground. With the moral authority to decry conflict, and the social networks to mobilize support and public action, religious groups could spread the message of peace in effective and sustainable ways. In particular, inter-religious initiatives which aim to bridge ethno-religious divides and establish a discourse of understanding even in the face of severe opposition provide evidence that the religious commitment to peace with justice is strong.

Notes

1 The Sinhalese, though a majority in the nation, feel threatened by the large population of Tamils who surround them in the region. This "minority complex" of the Sinhalese is theorized to contribute to their need for political power (de Silva 2003, 513).
2 The report is divided into two parts which are interlinked:

   1) The overarching Report of the Office of the United Nations High Commissioner for Human Rights on Promoting Reconciliation, Accountability and Human Rights (A/HRC/30/61), which can be found here: www.ohchr.org/EN/HRBodies/HRC/RegularSessions/Session30/Documents/A_HRC_30_61_ENG.docx
   2) The accompanying report of the OHCHR Investigation on Sri Lanka (A/HRC/30/CRP.2), which can be found here: www.ohchr.org/EN/HRBodies/HRC/RegularSessions/Session30/Documents/A_HRC_30_CRP_2.docx

   The response sent by the Sri Lankan Government can be found here: www.ohchr.org/Documents/HRBodies/HRCouncil/OISL/ResponseSriLanka15092015.pdf
3 UNHRC Resolution (A_HRC_30_L.29) on promoting reconciliation, accountability and human rights in Sri Lanka, October 1, 2015.www.ohchr.org/en/NewsEvents/Pages/DisplayNews.aspx?NewsID=16553&LangID=E
4 Ibid.
5 Statement delivered by Mangala Samaraweera, Minister of Foreign Affairs of Sri Lanka at the 30th Session of the UN Human Rights Council, Geneva, on 14 September 2015. www.news.lk/fetures/item/9742-statement-by-mangala-samaraweera-at-the-30th-session-of-the-unhrc-geneva
6 In the aftermath of the abortive Marxist-inspired JVP insurrection of 1971, a Criminal Justice Commission comprising five judges of the Supreme Court was set up, dispensing with the normal laws of evidence to deal with large number of cases.
7 The discussion in this section is based on "Religion, Conflict and Peacebuilding: The case of Sri Lanka," by Mariyahl Hoole et al. (2013). See also Nordquist (2013).
8 For a detailed discussion of the *Bandaranaike-Chelvanayagam Pact* see: DeVotta (2005); De Silva 1993. See also https://peacemaker.un.org/sites/peacemaker.un.org/files/LK_570726_Bandranayaki%20Chelvanayakam%20Pact.pdf
9 Juergensmeyer, quoted in Wellman and Tokuno (2004, 292).
10 Wanigaratne, quoted in Flanigan (2008).

References

Bartholomeusz, T. *In Defense of Dharma: Just War Ideology in Buddhist Sri Lanka*. New York: Routledge, 2002.

Department of Census and Statistics. *Population by Ethnicity, Census Years*. Colombo: Department of Census and Statistics, 2008.
de Silva, K. M. *A History of Sri Lanka*. Colombo: Vijitha Yapa Publications, 2003.
de Silva, K. M. 'Regionalism and Decentralisation of Power,' in *Sri Lanka: Problems of Governance*, ed. K. M. De Silva. New Delhi: Centre for Policy Research, 1993, 103–108.
De Votta, N. *Blowback: Linguistic Nationalism, Institutional Decay, and Ethnic Conflict in Sri Lanka*. Stanford: Stanford University Press, 2004.
De Votta, N. 'From Ethnic Outbidding to Ethnic Conflict: The Institutional Bases for Sri Lanka's Separatist War,' *Nations and Nationalism*, Vol.11 No.1, 2005, 150–159.
Flanigan, S. T. 'Faith and Fear in Development: The Role of Religion in Sri Lanka's NGO Sector,' Paper Presented at the ISA's 49th Annual Convention: Bridging Multiple Divides, San Francisco, 2008. Accessed www.allacademic.com/meta/p254098_index.html
Hoole, Mariyahl, Nari Senanayake and Jehan Perera. 'Religion, Conflict and Peacebuilding: The case of Sri Lanka,' in *Gods and Arms: On Religion and Armed Conflict*, ed. Kjell-Ake Nordquist, Church of Sweden Research Series, 2013, 95–120. Eugene, OR: Pickwick Publications.
Johnson, Douglas. 'The Religious Dimensions of Peacebuilding,' in *People Building Peace II: Successful Stories of Civil Society*. European Centre for Conflict Prevention, Boulder, CO: L. Rienner Publishers, 2005. www.peoplebuildingpeace.org/thestories/article.php?id=91&typ=theme&pid=21
Kjell-Ake Nordquist, ed. *Gods and Arms: On Religion and Armed Conflict*. Church of Sweden Research Series. Eugene, OR: Pickwick Publications, 2013.
National Christian Evangelical Alliance of Sri Lanka. *Silent Suppression: Restrictions on Religious Freedoms of Christians 1994–2014*. Colombo: Author, 2015.
National Peace Council of Sri Lanka. *Working Religiously for Peace*. Colombo: Author, 2016a.
National Peace Council of Sri Lanka. 'Proposal of the National Peace Council to the Consultation Task Force on Truth Seeking and Institutional Reform to meet the imperatives of Transitional Justice', 26 July 2016b.
Nordquist, Kjell-Ake, ed. *Gods and Arms: On Religion and Armed Conflict*. Church of Sweden Research Series. Eugene, OR: Pickwick Publications, 2013.
Orjuela, C., *Civil Society in Civil War—Peace Work and Identity Politics in Sri Lanka*. Gothenberg: Department of Peace and Development Research, 2004.
Peleg, I. *Democratising the Hegemonic State: Political Transformation in the Age of Identity*. Cambridge: Cambridge University Press, 2007.
'Sri Lanka to Set Up Regional Committees to Address Interreligious Violence,' *Xinhua News Agency* | Wed, 2017–2006–2021, Colombo.
Tsjeard, Bouta, S., A. Kadayifci-Orellana, and M. Abu-Nimer. *Faith-Based Peace-Building: Mapping and Analysis of Christian, Muslim and Multi-Faith Actors*. Clingendael and Washington, DC: Clingendael Institute and Salam Institute for Peace and Justice, 2005.
'UNHRC Resolution (A_HRC_30_L.29) on Promoting Reconciliation, Accountability and Human Rights in Sri Lanka', October 1, 2015. www.ohchr.org/en/NewsEvents/Pages/DisplayNews.aspx?NewsID=16553&LangID=E
Wellman, Jr., K. James, and Kyoko Tokuno. 'Is Religious Violence Inevitable?' *Journal for the Scientific Study of Religion*, Vol. 43 No. 3 September 1, 2004, 291–296. doi:10.1111/j.1468-5906.2004.00234.x

15

INTERRELIGIOUS DIALOGUE

Lisa Schirch

Introduction

In communities around the world, people with different spiritual practices and theological beliefs have met to talk with each other for a variety of purposes and through a variety of forms. People may come together through shared location, shared history, or shared problems or conflicts. They may come together to build understanding of theological and scriptural reasoning, to explore spiritual and cultural practices, or to engage in joint problem solving with the goal of developing a plan of action together. Regardless of the type of interreligious dialogue, there are a number of preconditions that allow dialogue to take place, ranging from a belief in dignity of and respect for all people to skills in building relationships.

As a dialogue facilitator and participant in interreligious dialogues in dozens of countries, and as author of a book on dialogue, this chapter grows out of both my personal experience and scholarship. This chapter addresses the structure of interreligious dialogue processes, to indicate common models for how they work. Interreligious dialogue often includes a sharing of experience, confession, and repentance of wrongdoing, as well as acts to symbolize forgiveness and reconciliation. Interreligious dialogue can result in a variety of outcomes. It can improve understanding, reduce antagonism, or create joint statements or actions to address a problem. This chapter attempts to paint a landscape map illustrating the vast territory of interreligious dialogue while also using a spotlight to highlight key elements and characteristics.

What Is Interreligious Dialogue?

Dialogue is distinct from other forms of communication. Fundamentally, dialogue is an exchange between two or more people or groups. A dialogue can be an informal conversation or a formal meeting or event. Interreligious dialogue is a formal or informal exchange between two or more people to share, learn, and understand different religious traditions and practices and/or to find ways to work together to address shared problems. Interreligious dialogue is as old as religion itself, as religion is essentially a result of people being in dialogue with each other on the most profound questions facing humanity: Who are we? Where did we come from? What are we here to do? How shall we treat each other?

Religion itself is a set of ideas that aim to "connect" people through dialogue and action. The Latin root of the word "religion" is ligar—the same root of the word ligament, the connective tissue binding muscle and bone. In this sense, the word "religion" means connecting, or reconnecting.[1] Sociologist Émile Durkheim refers to the experience of "wholeness" or "holiness" in sacred, religious experience as the "collective effervescence" or the inherent social nature of religion set apart from everyday life's "profane" or nonreligious experience (Durkheim [1912] 1965). Religion is and always has been a dialogue between people with different experiences and beliefs.

Dialogue is a distinct way of communicating that differs most significantly from debate. Table 15.1 highlights some of the most essential differences between dialogue and debate.

Effective dialogue between people of diverse experiences and beliefs usually requires the guidance of a facilitator. The role of the facilitator in guiding the conversation makes dialogue different from other communication forms. Facilitators help create a safe space by setting ground rules or guidelines to keep dialogue

TABLE 15.1 Debate vs. Dialogue

DEBATE	DIALOGUE
The goal is to "win" the argument by affirming one's own views and discrediting other views.	The goal is to understand different perspectives and learn about other views.
People listen to the other to find flaws in their arguments.	People listen to the other to understand how their experiences shape their beliefs.
People critique the experiences of others as distorted and invalid.	People accept the experiences of others as real and valid.
People appear to be determined not to change their own views on the issue.	People appear to be somewhat open to changing their understanding of the issue.
People speak based on assumptions made about the others' positions and motivations.	People speak only about their own understanding and experience.
People oppose each other and attempt to prove each other wrong.	People work together toward common understanding.
Strong emotions like anger are often used to intimidate the other side.	Strong emotions like anger and sadness are appropriate when they convey the intensity of an experience or belief.

participants focused on listening to and working with each other. Facilitators guide the dialogue process without deciding who is right or wrong, or declaring a "winner" as a moderator does in a debate.

Types of Interreligious Dialogue

Dialogue takes place both within religions and between religions. Intra-religious dialogue takes place between different denominations or streams within a religion. For example, interreligious dialogue has taken place between Catholics and Mennonites within Christianity, and between Sunni and Shia traditions of Islam. The differences within religious traditions may be just as significant as those between religious traditions. For that reason, this chapter uses the term "interreligious dialogue" in reference to any type of dialogue involving religious acts with different belief systems and spiritual practices.

There are at least five types of interreligious dialogue. These include the following:

Geography	Dialogue between people in a specific geographical region
History	Dialogue between people with a shared or linked history
Theology	Dialogue between people on theology
Scriptural Reasoning	Dialogue between people reading the same set of scriptures
Spiritual and Cultural Practices	Dialogue between people to compare, contrast, or learn from each other's spiritual and cultural practices

In practice, some interreligious dialogue may be purely in one category, or fit into more than one category. Examples of each type illustrate these schemata.

The television show *Little Mosque on the Prairie* illustrates a *geography-based interreligious dialogue*. Muslim immigrants living in the Canadian prairie province of Saskatchewan rent space from the local Anglican church. In a variety of the show's episodes, Muslims and Christians living side by side and sharing the same religious space live with and learn from each other. In communities around the globe, people of different faiths live side by side and even share their religious spaces with other groups. While in some places, there is great hostility and people do not speak to one another, it is not uncommon for people to have informal and formal dialogues with religious groups in close geographical proximity. As mass migration increases, bringing, for example new waves of Muslim immigrants to Europe and North America, the need for geography-based interreligious dialogue increases.

While geographical proximity does not always mean there are deep historical connections, in some places, geography coincides with history. History-based interreligious dialogues examine how relationships shift over time, and what allowed good relationships to take root. The Iberian Peninsula has been the sight of tremendous interreligious violence and the illumination of the possibility of *"conviviencia,"* or a state of interreligious harmony and synergy. The narrative claims that Muslim rule in Spain enabled Muslim and Jewish communities to reach their best potential of interreligious dialogue and coexistence. Some scholars point out *conviviencia* or peaceful coexistence was exaggerated in large part to shame Christians for their brutal intolerance of people of other religions (Cohen 2013). While the portrait of Jewish-Muslim relations in Spain was not always perfect and did have serious crises, there were significant exchanges between the two communities based on their shared history, especially a history of shared persecution by Christians.

In Charlottesville, Virginia, Jews, Muslims, and Christians take part in an interreligious dialogue they call "*scriptural reasoning.*" Jewish scholar Peter Ochs, a professor at the University of Virginia, has helped to popularize the idea of scriptural reasoning, where people of different religious traditions read scripture together, with the aim of gaining new insights on texts by hearing how people with different religious backgrounds make sense of scripture (Ochs 2012). According to the website for the Scriptural Reasoning Network, a key idea of scriptural reasoning dialogue processes is to "create an expansive network of interfaith friendships that would create a firewall against religiously motivated prejudice and violence" (Scriptural Reasoning Network).

In Ireland, Christians and Muslim engage in an ongoing dialogue of "religious experience" based on understanding spiritual and cultural practices such as music and prayer with people of different faiths. The dialogue includes learning about each faith's approach to spiritual practice but also finding prayers, music, and rituals that feel comfortable to people of both religions. A website and resource manual called "A Journey Together" (2007–2017) illustrates how an interreligious group to explore spiritual practices can help build "respect, understanding and cooperation" (A Journey Together).

In Iran and Indonesia, Shia and Sunni groups have a dialogue on public issues facing their communities as well as broader tensions between the two sects of Islam. Recognizing the common threats facing both sects, Muslims dialogue with each other on how to develop their communities, address violent extremism, and learn to foster coexistence with each other.

These five types of inter and intra-religious dialogue illustrate the wide range engagement already underway. In each of these contexts, there are fundamental preconditions for engagement.

Preconditions of Interreligious Dialogue

Taking part in a dialogue with a person or group that is different from oneself is a contested idea and practice. Not all religious actors believe that dialogue is beneficial. Many consciously or unconsciously believe that there is only one right way to believe or act. Institutionalized religion attempts to shape and socialize a religion's doctrine and spiritual practice. For some, this is an experience of indoctrination that requires overcoming and excluding all other forms of belief and practice. In this approach to religion, dialogue is dangerous, for it introduces a challenge or doubt to a religion's beliefs and practices. In this approach, religious actors who value purity of thought and action may believe that dialogue "dirties" the pool of religious thought and action. For some, dialogue with people of different beliefs is a polluting force, threatening the integrity of one's own belief system and integrity. For some religious actors, keeping a distance from others who are different is a religious practice intended to keep a purity of thought and action. For those who view religion as strict adherence to specific doctrine, a dialogue experience of learning from others might be seen as threatening or undermining that doctrine. When people believe they alone hold the whole truth, there is no need to listen to others. Some disavow dialogue because it requires them to recognize that they may be able to learn from people who believe differently.

In contrast, dialogue requires an intention to be open to the process of learning and changing. Those religious actors that are open to dialogue tend to have similar characteristics. Dialogue requires a fundamental belief in the dignity of all human beings. Dialogue itself translates a belief in the dignity of all humanity into an action that illustrates respect for others. Respect is shown through the act of listening to another person from a different religious orientation. Listening and learning from others is central to interreligious dialogue. For many, the goal is not to change the other religion, but to understand the other religion. For some, their own religious beliefs come into clearer focus or advance to a deeper level when they listen to and learn from other people of a different religious background.

Finally, dialogue is a "theory of change." Religious actors who take part in dialogue presume that dialogue affects relationships between groups. For some, dialogue is an alternative to coercion, judgment, isolation, or the use of force against other religious groups. These punitive efforts also attempt to affect relationships between groups. While some believe coercive force is more powerful that persuasive appeal, religious actors who engage in dialogue tend to see the limits of coercive action and place more hope in dialogue as an instigator of change.

Organizing Interreligious Dialogues[2]

Planning a formal interreligious dialogue requires multiple roles, including organizers/promoters, designers, facilitators, and, of course, participants from the relevant faith traditions. It also requires paying special attention to a variety of factors, including who is on the organizing committee, where the dialogue will take place, and what types of food or drink are offered. While these may seem like simple logistics, every element of planning an interreligious dialogue weakens or strengthens the likelihood that the dialogue will be helpful instead of hurtful.

Dialogue organizers/promoters coordinate invitations for people to attend the dialogue. The organizing role also involves managing the logistics and atmosphere of the dialogue process. *Dialogue designers* sequence the steps in the dialogue process. This includes developing the questions for leading the group through the topic. It also involves planning other interactions for the participants, such as introductions, a discussion of ground rules, or group meals and activities. *Dialogue facilitators* guide participants through the dialogue process. Usually the facilitator works from a dialogue plan created by the designer, and carefully makes decisions about when to stray from that design.

A diverse organizing committee, with members representing diverse stakeholder groups that will be invited to the dialogue, creates legitimacy and helps with outreach as "co-sponsors" and "co-facilitators" of an interreligious dialogue. Sometimes significant care and resources must be expended on outreach to ensure all stakeholders in a community are present. A diverse organizing committee can assist in developing marketing messages to invite other stakeholders to the dialogue. A diverse organizing committee can also assist in thinking through the facilitation and design of the dialogue process.

A diverse organizing group can help to select and train dialogue facilitators who represent different religious groups taking part in the dialogue. A Catholic-Hindu dialogue should include both a Catholic and a Hindu facilitator. Highly trained and experienced facilitators greatly increase the chances that an interreligious dialogue will go well. Without facilitation training and experience, many interreligious dialogues have failed and actually worsened tensions between religious groups. Co-facilitators representing diverse groups will add to the safety each group feels. Furthermore, people tend to come to dialogues with people like themselves, and will be hesitant to sit down at a table of strangers. Diverse organizers and facilitators can help to make sure that people sit in diverse groups in a dialogue.

Using flyers, posters, or email solicitations to invite people to a dialogue usually does not work. Face-to-face persuasion and invitation are the best ways to invite people to a dialogue process. Organizers can invite key leaders first, then invite others using the commitment of participation from key people as a way to persuade people to participate. Committed participants can be asked to suggest names or extend invitations to others they think should be included.

Choosing the space or venue for an interreligious dialogue requires great care. The space should be neutral, both symbolically and logistically, to communicate a sense of fairness and equality before the process even begins. Dialogue participants will question the location of the dialogue and whether it gives some members more of an advantage than others. Even neutral institutions may have a historical association with one side or another of a dialogue. Sometimes dialogues may require more than one venue. For example, in a sustained dialogue between Muslims and Jews, it may be wise to alternate between meeting in a synagogue and a mosque.

Scheduling interreligious dialogue sessions requires a sensitivity to members' varying religious schedules related to sacred days of the week as well as holidays or times of the year when people may be fasting. At the more mundane level, scheduling also requires thinking about job schedules, childcare availability, transportation options, and other aspects that may affect equal participation by all groups.

Ideally, an interreligious dialogue is more than a one-off event. It is usually difficult and unwise, however, to try to sign people up for a longer process than that to which they initially agreed. Transparency about the duration of the dialogue is important. But it is better to start with an invitation to an initial dialogue and generate enthusiasm for an ongoing process once people have experienced the power of dialogue.

Finally, it is important to pay attention to hospitality. Providing appropriate food and drink helps people to relax and gives them something to do as they interact with each other at breaks. Beauty and comfort in a space also help people relax enough to consider multiple points of view and to see the humanity in others. The book *Ritual and Symbol in Peacebuilding* provides more detail on the symbolic role of space in dialogue processes. (Schirch 2005).

Structuring an Interreligious Dialogue

Structuring an interreligious dialogue requires careful thought and planning. The outline for how to structure a dialogue described here has been tested through a variety of processes on many issues with many different groups (Campt and Schirch 2007). Ideally, dialogue organizers choose their facilitators early in the process, so the facilitators can be involved in the design of the dialogue—the focus of the next lesson.

Phase 1: Establishing Common Intentions and Norms

The first phase of an interreligious dialogue should help to clarify a group's common intention to listen to and learn from each other. This phase is important because people tend to question other people's motives when they are in conflict with them.

A dialogue facilitator is essential to help create a space where people can both identify their differences and find common ground. A facilitator guides people through a dialogue process. A facilitator helps each person feel emotionally safe and reassures them that the facilitator's role is to guard against verbal attacks or humiliation of participants during the dialogue. People's perceptions of a facilitator's personality and skills in creating this safe space are important. For example, the dialogue designer may call for the facilitator to greet participants upon arriving and connect one-on-one with them before the session starts. Facilitators are "process experts" rather than experts on a subject area. They keep a dialogue focused, help participants consider a variety of views, and summarize group discussions. They make sure all participants have an opportunity to contribute. They model active listening and respectful speaking.

Next, a facilitator introduces the dialogue's goal and focus. Understanding the dialogue's purpose helps people to understand what is expected of them.

Participant introductions are an important element in creating an environment where people trust each other. Introductions can include name and an organizational affinity as well as personal information such as family life or hobbies. Most importantly, participants want an opportunity to say something about their motivations and goals for being part of the dialogue as well as hear from others. Understanding these motivations can help build trust among participants. These types of introductions also set the stage for each person talking throughout the rest of the dialogue.

A facilitator can then help participants identify group agreements—sometimes also called dialogue guidelines or ground rules. Group agreements are a set of behavioral standards and goals that the group agrees to follow to create the best possible experience. Group agreements are important for several reasons.

First, setting group agreements can help people understand what can feel like an unusual process. In dialogue, the group designs and agrees to its own set of cultural norms. Participants decide to be in the process and choose what behaviors to honor and protect.

Second, the process of setting group agreements helps people understand that everyone in the group is essentially equal. This is unusual because in most settings, there is some degree of hierarchy where someone is in an authoritative role over others. Participants learn that dialogue is an opportunity to both share their own truths and learn from others.

Groups set group agreements in a number of ways. When facing time constraints, one approach is to list the group agreements and ask if people can comply with them. It is important that each person has a chance to modify or raise concerns about the rules. After ample opportunity to change the proposed group agreements, the facilitator can invite public agreement that the group is willing to hold. A better approach is to elicit the group agreement from the group. This method allows the group more opportunity to own the dialogue process and heightens their commitment to the group agreements. See Table 15.2 for a sample of basic group agreements.

Phase 2: Sharing Experiences and Perceptions

Dialogue is essentially a forum for people to share their life experiences. People often do not recognize that every person experiences life in a unique way. Learning in dialogue comes through exploring the similarities and differences in the experiences of people from different backgrounds. Dialogue participants come to understand that their beliefs about an issue are shaped by their unique experiences, and that others' different understandings or opinions often grow out of different experiences. For example, it might be helpful for the facilitator to

TABLE 15.2 Sample of Basic Group Agreements

1. *Recognize the power of deep listening.* Listen to understand the other's point of view rather than to prepare a defense of your own view. Try to listen more than you speak.
2. *Respect others, and refuse to engage in name-calling.* Resist the temptation to call people names. People have the right to define themselves, but not others.
3. *Speak about personal experiences.* Start your sentences with "I" rather than "you." "I experienced ..."
4. *Minimize interruptions and distractions.* In general people should be allowed to finish what they are saying without being interrupted directly or with side-talk between other participants. Also, people should silence their cell phones.
5. *Maintain confidentiality.* Outside the group, discuss the content of what was said, not who said what.
6. *Ask questions.* Ask honest, thought-provoking questions that give people the opportunity to explore and explain their underlying assumptions.
7. *Stay through the hard times.* Make a commitment to stay in the dialogue despite the tensions.
8. *Aim to understand.* The goal of dialogue is to increase understanding between individuals. The goal is not to solve the problem or agree on everything.
9. *Recognize common ground.* Every two people share something in common. Find it!
10. *"Ouch," then educate.* If someone says something hurtful, don't just disengage. Let the individual and the group know why it was hurtful.

begin the dialogue by asking each participant to share an example of when they felt like an outsider. This helps each participant understand that vulnerability is a common human experience. While some participants may feel like a minority in the dialogue, it can be important to recognize that others in the group have had a similar experience.

Dialogue requires clear and open-ended questions that allow every participant to share an experience that is relevant to the topic. A dialogue on interreligious understanding might begin with a neutral question such as "What do you appreciate about your religion?" Or ask a question that creates an opportunity to learn to know one another, such as "Share a story about a time when this community really worked well together to understand people of other religions." The questions should elicit an entire set of stories that highlights the diversity of the issues. It is essential that the questions help the group honor every person's experience. An interreligious dialogue might ask "What do you appreciate about other religions?" This is generally more helpful than asking, "What are specific problems with other religious groups?" The second question creates a tense situation. The phrasing of the question itself suggests that certain people in the room have experiences that are more real and/or relevant to the topic than other participants.

It is common in a dialogue for some participants to add their analysis or opinions of a problem when they share their personal experiences. Facilitators can carefully encourage participants to stay focused on describing their own experiences while listening and asking questions of other participants' experiences. If this phase is handled well, participants recognize how experiences shape perceptions or opinions of the issue at hand.

Phase 3: Exploring Differences and Commonalities

After having an opportunity to share their experiences, this phase of dialogue allows participants to ask the question together, "Why are our experiences and perceptions so different?" If the group has built trust with each other, shared honestly, and listened closely to each other, participants will likely have heard perspectives that do not fit easily into their worldview or set of preconceived notions. They may begin searching for a larger understanding of the truth. It may be helpful to have a notetaker write on large sheet paper to identify the main differences and commonalities.

Table 15.3 lists questions that can help participants recognize differences and similarities between individuals and sub-groups within a dialogue. They raise awareness about how people's perceptions affect their interpretations of reality and begin to see their own role in a problem or conflict.

In some situations, it may be helpful to separate dialogue participants into sub-groups or "caucuses" of people with similar experiences. Caucuses can help participants more fully explore potentially sensitive dialogue themes. In an interreligious dialogue, for example, a facilitator could caucus with members of each religion separately to ensure that each group is equally empowered to be able to articulate their experiences and needs. In a dialogue on religious divisions, caucuses may help groups explore facts, ideas, and/or behaviors in a comfortable group before they discuss them with the "other" group.

When discussing particularly difficult subjects, the greater level of honesty in a caucus can help move a dialogue forward. For example, a caucus used in

TABLE 15.3 Sample Questions for Exploring Diversity (Campt and Schirch 2007)

Sample Questions for Exploring the Diversity of Experiences
How is interreligious conflict affecting our community?
What changes to interreligious relationships are we seeing?
How have religious issues affected how we work together? Are there new tensions among us?
What are three main issues that keep us from improving relationships between religions?
What values in our community can we draw on to address this problem?
What are the causes or history of the issues?
Do we have different understandings of the history of interreligious relationships?

Suggested Caucus Questions
What do we need to know from an opposing point of view in order to address this issue?
How does our group benefit and suffer from the status quo?

a dialogue between Christian police forces and Muslim community members could ask each subgroup to develop three questions they would like to ask the other group. Caucus discussions can be summarized and brought back to the large group to accelerate progress on key issues.

Before probing these questions directly, the facilitator should make sure that participants acknowledge the group's diverse experiences and perspectives. As people begin to sort out the diversity of narratives expressed in Phase 2, they often raise the issue of *perception*. Participants may suggest that others are "paranoid," and thus see mistreatment where there might be other explanations for people's behavior. On the other hand, it is also common for some participants to assert that other groups just don't "get it" and are blind to oppression. A facilitator can ask participants to hold together the complexity that people's experiences are valid, people do have perceptions that shape their experience of reality, and, most importantly, there is likely a much longer history and set of institutional patterns that contribute to the sense of the problem. A final task in Phase 3 is for facilitators to help participants see their role as agents for change to help address the problems or conflicts that they may have inherited.

Phase 4: Exploring Possibilities for Action

Ideally, dialogue energizes a group to take action. The final phase of a dialogue explores the personal or collective actions to address the issues. If the dialogue has reached its potential for transformation, people often feel energized and motivated to enact change. Sometimes, people make plans or begin projects to work together. Sometimes a dialogue groups commits to continuing to build relationships across lines of division. Table 15.4 identifies some possible dialogue questions to help participants move from dialogue to action.

TABLE 15.4 Sample Questions for Action Planning (Campt and Schirch 2007)

Sample Questions for Action Planning
What should we do about this issue now that we have built relationships with each other, shared our experiences, and deepened our understanding of the issues?
What can we do individually and as a community to improve relationships among ourselves and address the needs in our community?
Of all the ideas shared, which 2 or 3 ideas seem most practical for us to work on together?
What resources do we already have available to us?
If there are existing options to address this issue, what do we think of these existing options? (Facilitators can offer a handout with 3–5 policy options to address the problem. The group can take turns reading the options aloud to the group.)
Which of these policies do you think will address everyone's needs in this issue?
What other policy options can we brainstorm together?

At the end of a dialogue, facilitators can ask people to reflect on the positive qualities of the dialogue. For example, a facilitator can ask: "What are one or two positive things that you have gotten out of this process?" Participants may also want to express appreciation to each other. Facilitators can ask people to thank people individually, exchange phone numbers or emails, or find another way to keep in contact with each other to continue the informal dialogue.

Dialogue and Social Change

Dialogue may not always be possible or productive if power is unbalanced and awareness of a conflict is low. Often people within the more powerful group have little interest in meeting with members of the less powerful group. Those with less political advantage may see dialogue as passive, or even a distraction from the real work for change. Some people with political advantage may see dialogue as an opportunity to reach across the lines of conflict and bring people into their own political agenda.

In Nashville, Tennessee in the 1960s, African American students were not able to set up a meeting with the mayor to discuss racial integration. The students first had to use nonviolent action to demonstrate their ability to bring pressure upon city and business leaders. Black students increased their power by organizing, training themselves in nonviolent action, and carrying out sit-ins, marches, and boycotts of stores that promoted racial segregation. These actions brought media attention, public sympathy for their cause, and pressure on white leaders to do something about the boycotts, which were affecting white businesses. A successful dialogue that led to desegregation became possible only after there was a rough balance of power between the white leaders and African American community.

Dialogue is useful for information gathering, analysis, relationship-building, and decision-making. Dialogue is also a method of social change. Adam Curle's diagram (Table 15.5) illustrates how some methods like dialogue are better able to contribute to social change if power is roughly balanced between groups (Curle 1971). Nonviolent actions raise awareness of key issues and help to balance power. They increase the willingness of all groups to engage in dialogue. Dialogue is more productive if participants from all sides of a conflict are committed to understanding the issues better. When power is unbalanced and public awareness of an issue is low, it may be important to first raise public awareness and demonstrate collective power through petitions, marches, or some other type of nonviolent action.

The goal of an interreligious dialogue is to create greater understanding and/ or to build trust between diverse people and groups. Participants will become active if they personally feel motivated to take action or want to act collectively with others. But dialogue organizers and facilitators cannot mandate action. Participants only "buy in" to the idea of action themselves. Ideally, an interreligious dialogue process creates a space for people to build relationships and create new networks that increase people's vision and desire to take collective action.

TABLE 15.5 Power, Dialogue, and Social Change (Curle 1971; adapted by Schirch 2004)

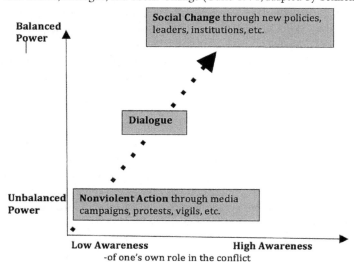

While dialogue planners and facilitators cannot promise joint action at the outset of a dialogue, they can create the space for it to happen. Creating enough time and space in the dialogue agenda for this phase is important. If people view the last "action planning" phase of dialogue as an add-on or as something to get through after a long day, it is less likely that it will indeed lead to effective action.

How and when does dialogue effectively translate into structural change? What is the tipping point for creating change that transforms an issue (Gladwell 2002)? Is it the sheer number of people that need to go through a dialogue process in order to build relationships across the lines of a conflict and understand more deeply the issues involved? Or is it the involvement of key community leaders in a dialogue process? Or is the dialogue process itself something that can foster change?

Mahatma Gandhi and Martin Luther King both taught that dialogue should be tried first, before any other strategies. When Gandhi became determined to end British colonialism, he invited and engaged in dialogue with Muslim and Hindu leaders as well as British leadership. But he also understood that at many points along the journey, the British representatives were not interested in talking with him or that when they did talk with him, they were sometimes just trying to dissuade him from pursuing change. Likewise, sometimes the conflict between Muslim and Hindu leaders was intense and dialogue was unproductive. Gandhi pushed for change through a wide variety of nonviolent tactics and strategies, but took every opportunity to engage in dialogue with those who opposed him or opposed the idea of coexistence.

Interreligious dialogue is an important facet of building peace in a divided world. Religious leaders can come together to share experiences related to their shared geography or history, their shared desire to understand theological issues, scriptural reasoning, and spiritual and cultural practices. The practical dimensions of this exchange require thoughtful preparation and careful facilitation. Interreligious dialogue is itself a sacred practice; it brings people with different experiences and beliefs into conversation and relationship with one another.

Notes

1 There is some debate about which Latin root forms the basis of the word "religion." Some say *religare*, meaning similarly "to fasten or bind," is the root. Other interpretations purport that *relegere* is the root, meaning "to re-read or go over a text." A third option, *re-eligere*, means "to choose again." See Philogos (2007).
2 This section of the chapter is summarized from *The Little Book of Dialogue on Difficult Subjects* (Schirch 2004).

References

Campt, David, and Lisa Schirch. *The Little Book of Dialogue on Difficult Subjects*. Intercourse, PA: Good Books, 2007.
Cohen, Mark. "The 'Golden Age' of Jewish-Muslim Relations: Myth and Reality." In *A History of Jewish-Muslim Relations*. Princeton: Princeton University Press, 2013.
Curle, Adam. *Making Peace*. London: Tavistock, 1971.
Durkheim, Émile. *The Elementary Forms of the Religious Life*, trans. Joseph Swain. New York: The Free Press, [1912] 1965.
Gladwell, Malcolm. *The Tipping Point: How Little Things Can Make a Big Difference*. New York: Little, Brown, and Company, 2002.
"A Journey Together." 2007–1017. www.coistine.ie/dialogue-resource.
Philogos. "Roots of 'Religion.'" *Jewish Daily Forward*, May 25, 2007, www.forward.com/articles/10776/roots-of-religion Accessed March 3, 2018.
"A Journey Together." www.coistine.ie/different-kinds-of-dialogue. Accessed September 1, 2016.
Ochs, Peter. "An Introduction to Scriptural Reasoning: From Practice to Theory." *Journal of Renmin University of China* (2012) Vol. 26.5: 16–22.
"The Scriptural Reasoning Network." www.srnetwork.org/history/ Accessed July 28, 2017.
Schirch, Lisa. *Little Book of Strategic Peacebuilding*. Intercourse, PA: Good Books, 2004.
Schirch, Lisa. *Ritual and Symbol in Peacebuilding*. Connecticut: Kumarian Press, 2005.

16

WARRIORS AND PACIFISTS

Dilemmas, Paradoxes, Alternatives[1]

Lester R. Kurtz

Warrior and Pacifist Dilemmas

The ruthless King Ashoka apparently murdered at least one of his brothers and conquered much of the South Asian subcontinent 2,400 years ago. According to legend, he was overwhelmed with grief at the carnage of his war after his troops had overrun Kalinga. He converted to Buddhism, became a vegetarian, and spent the rest of his life promoting public works, tolerance, and justice. His edicts, inscribed on stone tablets discovered and deciphered at the beginning of humanity's bloodiest century thus far (the twentieth) show the possibility of religion as a positive force to create a peaceful culture and turn warriors from destruction to preservation (Ashoka 1993).

Ashoka's story is a historical lesson in the turn from violence to nonviolence as a result of a spiritual experience, although it comes after the king has already consolidated his rule by killing his adversaries. This tension between the warrior and the pacifist—and the role of the faith traditions in promoting both motifs—has been explored in some detail throughout this volume. In this final chapter, I wish to review some of these issues and propose that Mohandas K. Gandhi has created a potential way out of our current conundrum.

We are familiar with the centuries of battles blessed by priests and popes, shaman and gurus, rabbis and muftis. That is the side of history most often remembered, but perhaps the least valuable for our time. King Ashoka's dramatic conversion from warrior to pacifist is the opposite of what we often see in the faith traditions. Many founders of the world's religions promote some variant of pacifism, only to have their teachings used to justify the use of violence and war, even the Buddhists (see Frydenlund and Perera, Chapters 2 and 14 in this volume). The tension between warrior and pacifist motifs that run through the world's scriptures and faith traditions results in a paradox: religious institutions are the major carriers of both violence and peace, of revenge and reconciliation.

Virtually all of the world's dominant faith traditions emphasize both contradictory themes of the warrior and the pacifist; when religious institutions are aligned with state power, the balance shifts toward the warrior. The warrior motif sacralizes violence and posits it as a necessary, sometimes obligatory, action and legitimizes it when confronting evil or on behalf of transcendent causes. The pacifist motif insists on refraining from the use of violence even for self-defense.

Both motifs present moral dilemmas to individuals and cultures, however. The warrior may have moral qualms about killing others, or even a physiological or psychological resistance to doing so, as modern combat research demonstrates (see Grossman and Siddle 2008), as does the visibility of post-traumatic stress disorder (PTSD) or, more precisely, Perpetration-Induced Traumatic Stress (PITS; see MacNair 2002, 2018). The pacifist may escape those moral dilemmas, but at the expense of others—mainly the duty to act in the face of evil, injustice, or other conditions that seem to call for active resistance.

The underlying argument of this final chapter is that Mohandas K. Gandhi and others in recent decades have produced a cultural innovation by synthesizing elements of these two motifs, addressing the dilemmas that each presents. From the warrior motif Gandhi takes the idea of standing up and fighting against evil, injustice, and systems of exploitation. From the pacifist motif he incorporates the idea of *ahimsa*, or nonharmfulness, so that the nonviolent activist engages in struggle but without harming the adversary (cf. Kurtz 2008; Kurtz and Kurtz 2005). Indeed, the purpose of Gandhian nonviolence is not to destroy enemies, but bring them around to seeing the injustice of their actions, or at least to change the behavior being challenged. This approach is underscored in the "love your enemies" theme that runs through the world's faith traditions ("Love Your Enemies").

Religious leaders and people of faith continue to play a key role, as they have through the centuries, in legitimating either nonviolent or violent means for confronting large-scale human conflict. One of the most significant cultural developments of the late twentieth century was the increasingly activist role of religious institutions and leaders in public discourse about the legitimacy and morality of violence and warfare. The struggles faced by religious people in the nuclear age are neither new nor unique—they were faced by the ancient Hebrew prophets and the early church, for example, and have been faced by men and women of many faiths in many epochs. Now even the Roman papacy, with a long history of promoting warfare, is explicitly condemning war and promoting nonviolence (see Pope Francis, Chapter 9). The stakes are higher, however, and religious rhetoric may play a pivotal role in legitimating the various paths proposed for the future.

Violence and the Sacred

The paradox of violence is that humans are often determined to repel violence with violence, thus simultaneously condemning and condoning it. A remarkable ambivalence about violence pervades our global culture—it is both widely abhorred and ubiquitously used as a basis for social control, from the household to global socio-economic order.

René Girard (1977, 15) contends that it is precisely *because* they detest violence that people make a duty of vengeance. If we wish to prevent an interminable outbreak of vengeance, it is not enough to convince people that violence is detestable; they know that already. As a result of our ambivalence toward violence, elaborate social mechanisms are institutionalized to distinguish between legitimate and illegitimate violence. The use of violence (or its threat) is a mechanism of social boundary maintenance; it is an expression of attempts to gain or retain power, which requires a rhetoric of justification (see Weber 1968; cf. Arendt 1970, 2013). That is where the faith traditions play a prominent role. Throughout the centuries and across cultures, religious beliefs and institutions have been used to legitimate radically opposing positions in the debate. How are religious doctrines used to provide justifications for everything from absolute pacifism to the idea of an imminent nuclear holocaust as God's will? Such matters are part of the larger issue of the rhetoric and structure of violence, especially as they pertain to issues of war and peace.

Violence and the sacred are intimately linked. Violence, in religious terms, becomes a sacrificial act designed to appease the Gods, and a matter of duty. "In many rituals," Girard (1977, 1) observes, "the sacrificial act assumes two opposing aspects, appearing at times as a sacred obligation to be neglected at grave peril, at other times as a sort of criminal activity entailing perils of equal gravity." A sacred animal whose life is protected under normal conditions must be killed in the liminal period of religious rituals (cf. Turner 1969).

Religious beliefs and institutions are so significant in such matters, because they are often the arbiters for moral decision-making, or at least affect the process. At the very least, they provide the basis for accounts of such decisions. Challenges posed by the threats faced in the nuclear age have precipitated a reevaluation of moral teachings about warfare within many religious traditions.

As Max Weber (1968) pointed out, the state is usually considered to have a monopoly on the legitimate use of violence. Within a global social order, where weapons of mass destruction are widely criticized even by those who have them, the legitimacy of state-sanctioned violence is often challenged, but the predominant non-state group using violence on the global stage in the early twenty-first century claims to be a state, the so-called Islamic State, underscoring Weber's argument. Even secular political elites who shape state policies often feel compelled to use religious arguments to justify their wars and military budgets. This problem is compounded by the lack of any formal global political system beyond a weak United Nations, within which guidelines are established and agreed upon by elites and a sanctioning system that maintains order. The role of major religious institutions is heightened by this fact because they are simultaneously national and transnational. Girard (1977, 18) argues that "ritual in general, and sacrificial rites in particular, assume essential roles in societies that lack a firm judicial system." That is precisely the nature of the current global situation in which, despite efforts of the United Nations and the World Court, there is no formal system for imposing certain sanctions against those who violate even agreed-upon norms.

Debates over the legitimacy of particular forms of violence are framed, of course, within the context of specific political contexts and social hierarchies. Frames (see Goffman 1974) for fashioning positions on security issues are constructed from different positions within the decision-making structure of a society. These different frames have what Max Weber calls "elective affinities" (*Wahlverwandtschaften*) with the interests of the adherents. Although institutions are, no doubt, established and maintained on the basis of particular interests, they seem to take on lives of their own, as Weber notes (e.g., Weber 1958). They become "iron cages" and entrap even those individuals who dominate them. The institutional apparatus of the modern nuclear armed forces has become a "nuclear cage" (Kurtz 1988) that subverts the very security it is allegedly providing. The military-industrial complex often controls even those who are ostensibly in charge of it, and becomes part of what C. Wright Mills ([1959] 2000) calls the "drift and thrust" toward World War III.

The pages that follow provide an illustrative social history of this set of motifs, looking at key moments in religious history when they emerged or were employed.

From the Warrior and Pacifist to the Nonviolent Activist

We first examine the warrior motif in some of its major manifestations, beginning with the notion of the G-d as warrior among the ancient Hebrews and the warrior dharma in ancient South Asian culture. The idea of engaging in warfare as a Divine duty may be as old as what we call civilization; all of the arguments both for and against that idea can be found in the famous Exodus narrative in the Jewish Torah and in the *Bhagavad Gita*, a story embedded in the world's longest epic, the *Mahabharata*. In the bible narrative,[2] God frees the Hebrew slaves from their bondage in Egypt with the help of a reluctant prophet and natural disasters, then enables them to conquer existing peoples in a "Promised Land" to give the freed slaves a homeland. In the *Gita*, the warrior Arjuna loses his will to fight when he sees his kinsmen and teachers facing him on the battlefield. God in the *Gita* takes the form of Krishna, who also serves as Arjuna's charioteer, and explains to him he must fight because he is a warrior, and that the consequences of his actions should not be his concern nor are they what they appear.

The idea of G-d as warrior in ancient Judaism is the foundation narrative for the use of violence on behalf of justice and freedom in Western civilization and is thus a central theme for our exploration as it becomes central to the recurring warrior theme in the West. The turning point is the exodus of the Hebrew slaves from Egypt, the liberation from slavery attributed to G-d by the ancient Hebrews and carried out by various means of violence that include natural pestilence and even the killing of the Egyptians' first-born sons. This theme from the Hebrew *Tanach* is explicitly echoed in the Christian "just war" tradition precipitated by the alliance between early Christianity and the Roman Empire and later the medieval crusades, when the Roman Catholic Pope issued a call to arms for Christians to liberate the Holy Land from the "infidels."

Living alongside the warrior motif, however, is the ancient tradition of pacifism, elements of which enrich the world's faith traditions. In ancient South Asia, the idea of *ahimsa*, or nonharmfulness, becomes a cornerstone of the Vedic religions, a concept emphasized and embellished by the Buddha in his efforts to reform and demilitarize the culture of his time. In East Asia the teachings of the sage Lao Tzu (1988) promoted peaceful coexistence among all elements of the universe as the law of existence, laying the groundwork for a tradition that paralleled the *ahimsa* of South Asia and later became intertwined with it. West Asian (or Middle Eastern) pacifism has its roots in the Hebrew prophets and the early Christian church in which violence even in self-defense was thought by some to contradict the teachings of Jesus.

In the twentieth century, Gandhi brings together elements of Hinduism, Buddhism, Jainism, Islam, and Christianity, along with his observation of various modern social movements, to make explicit an implicit spiritual alternative to violence in nonviolent civil resistance and lifestyles. Paralleling the development of nuclear weapons and other weapons of mass destruction is the institutionalization of mass protest and sophisticated nonviolent civil resistance to tyranny and injustice, from the anti-colonial movements of the first half of the century through the civil rights, human rights, and pro-democracy movements that followed. Nonviolent direct action emerges as a major force in late twentieth- and early twenty-first-century politics. In an age of not only untold destruction in violent conflict and warfare but also violence toward nature and the environment, nonviolent lifestyles emerge as a counterpoint movement to construct a more peaceful world. Religious beliefs, rituals, and institutions are at the core of this development, with its roots in ancient faith traditions, but develop in historically unprecedented ways.

Beliefs, Rituals, and Institutions

Religion plays a major role in contemporary life, despite predictions to the contrary in the early modern period. It motivates and legitimates a culture of violence, but also nonviolent solutions and movements. Religious symbols and issues become "conflict symbols," serving like lightning rods to attract the energy of many social conflicts that become defined in religious terms and interpreted with religious rhetoric, even if they involve other underlying causes and issues. Most major conflicts in the world today have a religious component—almost always intertwined with other factors and forces.

Religious involvement in a conflict brings it to a new level of intensity (or an increased intensity of a conflict leads to religious interpretations and rhetorical frames) because by nature religion is about ultimate concerns and fundamental life issues. Not only have religious traditions promoted and legitimated war over the centuries, they have also provided many of the most significant alternatives to war and critiques of violence. In the nuclear age, the existence of a significant anti-war segment among religious leaders brings anti-war perspectives into the mainstream of public policy discourse in a way that would not be otherwise possible. Prominent religious authorities have access to the halls of power that most peace activists do not. It is interesting, for example, to note U.S. President George W. Bush's homage to Roman Catholic Pope John Paul II, despite the latter's denunciation of war and violence, including explicit criticism of the president's foreign policies and the American invasion of Iraq.

Three major dimensions of religions support each of the three motifs—the warrior, the pacifist, and the nonviolent activist. By exploring beliefs, rituals, and institutions systematically within each of these motifs, we can observe nine aspects or dimensions of the relationship between religion and conflict, as suggested in Table 16.1, and better understand how religion and violence are interrelated.

First, every religious tradition has a set of systematically interrelated beliefs. They are generally presented in narrative form—myths, legends, and stories that run the gamut from worldviews (pictures of the nature of the cosmos) to details about the ethos (lifestyle) of the people who hold the beliefs (see Geertz 1973). From the war stories of the world's scriptures to religious prohibitions against killings, beliefs provide motivations and moral guidelines for behavior. Contradictory elements are brought together within a single narrative framework (Kurtz 1979); however, they often lead to conflicting interpretations about the meaning of the narrative and its implications for life in the present. Consequently, a single narrative in a sacred text might contain both warrior and pacifist motifs, but the contradiction is not always immediately apparent to believers because it is woven into the texture of a story that is accepted as a whole.

Beliefs about the legitimacy and efficacy of violence are central to the warrior motif, often linking its use to higher purposes and powers, sacred duties, and themes of sacrifice for God, nation, family, comrades in arms, and so forth. Specific beliefs about violence come together as a package, constructed over time within a culture or a faith tradition, usually transculturally, and contain elements

TABLE 16.1 Dimensions of Religious and Conflict Motifs

	Warrior	Pacifist	Nonviolent Activist
Beliefs			
Rituals			
Institutions			

of many cultural groups and traditions. Stories about a people's history and the moral lessons they provide, either explicitly or implicitly, are often linked not only to ethical systems but also to a people's sense of identity and social construction of their history.

Beliefs about these motifs are embedded in ritual behavior performed as a central part of a people's collective action. Rituals are a regularly repeated, traditional, and carefully prescribed set of behaviors that symbolize a value or a belief and may or may not have sacred significance (Kurtz 2016). When issues of violence, life, and death are at stake, rituals—such as engaging in battle or protest—are usually sacralized.

Although the content of rituals varies across cultures and over time, as a form of human interaction, they usually have a number of characteristics:

1. They provide solutions to problems; e.g., the problem of death is addressed by funeral rituals in every tradition. Rituals of combat actualize beliefs in patterns of behavior, as do rituals of protest.
2. Rituals are rooted in experience, so appear empirically verifiable—belief in their efficacy persists even when they appear to fail, which may be attributed to flaws in its performance rather than the ritual itself.
3. They involve a demarcation of social and ethical boundaries and the identification of evil. What individual, group, or force is responsible for our troubles? What can be done to remedy the situation or counter their actions? Ritual actions are believed to identify and eliminate, denounce, or mitigate evil.
4. Rituals re-enforce, or reify, social processes and institutions. Religious authorities who direct or carry out the rituals and the institutions that host them gain new authority. When security is threatened, people may turn to the experts in military rituals. Ritual experts gain new power when people believe in the efficacy of the rituals. War chiefs and weapons experts, but not anti-war activists, are usually consulted when the war ritual does not work. The use of violence to address social problems is highly ritualized and objections about its efficacy are often suppressed; it is not war itself that does not work, but how it is being performed. The institutions of war that sponsor and sustain its rituals are ironically strengthened when war is *not* working, on the one hand, but heroes of nonviolence (like King) are ritually cited as examples whose behavior should be emulated in prescribed ways, on the other.

Many of the rituals that sustain nonviolence have their roots in the various faith traditions—from the direct nonviolence of civil disobedience, marches and demonstrations, petitions and speeches—to the structural and cultural nonviolence of institutions that promote and sustain love, respect, and equality of opportunity. Not all nonviolent leaders are also religious figures, of course, but many are, like the iconic King and Gandhi. Moreover, religious leaders regularly bring nonviolent options into the mainstream of political discourse (Goran and Kurtz 2003), often by refashioning traditional rituals into tools for protest.

Rituals are sustained by institutions, which regularize the behavior of individuals and communities over time and sponsor warrior and pacifist rituals. Wars have been blessed traditionally by shamans, priests, pastors, imams, and rabbis across the millennia, but they have also organized movements for justice and preached nonviolent behavior and beliefs to their congregations, from the ground up, from the family to the community and globe. The military-industrial complex, religious and cultural institutions, and the broader state are interwoven, as are nonviolent social movements, nongovernmental organizations, and faith institutions working to bring about change nonviolently. Military officers and anti-war protestors often share a pew in worship.

Faith institutions have multiple functions in any given society, and it is the role of religious leaders in those central rituals and aspects of personal, family, and social life that indirectly gives them authority to speak on issues of violence and nonviolence. Faith institutions and receive a sort of "halo effect," if you will, that confers authority on religious leaders because of what they have done for their congregants, especially in times of crisis or ceremonies in the life cycle such as births, deaths, marriages, and rites of passage. When a family turns to a faith leader in times of crisis, that person earns their respect and family members may be more willing to listen to that leader's advice regarding the use of violence when the question arises, making it as much of a spiritual issue as a political one.

Indeed, the histories of the warrior motifs and various faith communities are inextricably intertwined; organized warfare emerges at the beginning of the agricultural era, which also gives birth to the Abrahamic religions.

The Warrior Motif

> The Lord is a warrior: the Lord is his name.
> The chariots of Pharaoh and his army
> he has cast into the sea;
> the flower of his officers
> are engulfed in the Red Sea.
> The watery abyss has covered them,
> they sank in the depths like a stone.
> Thy right hand, O Lord, is majestic in strength.
> thy right hand, O Lord, shattered the enemy.
> Exodus 15.3–6

Perhaps the most common theme is that God is a protector and champion of God's worshippers. (Note that the terms "God" and "the gods" are used here without explicit definition and are intended to refer to the appropriate deity or deities when discussing each tradition.) Such protection often requires, of course, military obligation, because the deity is frequently reliant upon humans to engage in battle. One of the most ancient and well-known of these traditions is that of the ancient Hebrews, where the warrior tradition is intertwined with an alternative tradition of what Rabbi Tirzah Firestone calls "active peace" (Chapter 5).

Ancient Hebrews: G-d as Warrior

The most significant narrative in the history of Judaism is the story of the Exodus—the delivery of the Hebrew slaves from bondage under the pharaoh. It was made possible by the use of violence against both the Egyptians (including the deaths of children) and the residents of the territory which the Israelites believed they were promised by G-d. Although subsequently appropriated by the powerful, and countered elsewhere in the Jewish tradition with calls for peace and protection of human life, the G-d of the Talmud is the champion of the oppressed and a defender of justice. The military prowess of the ancient Hebrews is provided by Adonai to a band of poor slaves who forged a covenant with their deity. According to the book of Joshua (24.8–13), the Lord told the Israelites,

> Then I brought you into the land of the Amorites who lived east of the Jordan; they fought against you, but I delivered them into your hands; you took possession of their country and I destroyed them for your sake.

After a series of natural calamities—plagues and the death of the Egyptian first-born, the ancient Hebrews escaped, wandered in the wilderness, and were then commanded to conquer the residents of the territory where they settled. This development, presented in narrative form in the Torah, was not unique to the ancient Hebrews; it was part of a larger social process in the Fertile Crescent as humans moved from being hunter-gatherers to farmers and pastoralists, settling more permanently in villages and cities, and for the first time developing systematic means of warfare. The Jewish tradition also developed a powerful counter-narrative that opposed the violence and promoted a dream of a peaceful culture—these themes are presented as counterpoints in this ancient tradition, as other chapters in this volume demonstrate (see Firestone, Scham, and Zion, Chapters 5–7).

Not only were the Israelites led to conquer existing peoples with G-d's help, according to their scriptures, they were often commanded to exterminate defeated populations, sometimes sparing the women and children, at other times destroying everything and everyone. The protection and battle victories offered were conditional—they were dependent upon continued adherence to the terms of the covenant, and according to the prophets. The Babylonian Empire, according to the tradition, later carried out the Lord's will by destroying the Israelites themselves because of their domestic injustice and failure to carry out the terms of their covenant with G-d.

The ancient Hebrews were also the inspiration for some of the most eloquent dreams of peace, such as the famous passage in Isaiah (2.4; cf. Micah 4.3) enshrined in a statue in front of the United Nations donated by the Soviet Union: "They shall beat their swords into plowshares, and their spears into pruning-hooks; nation shall not lift sword against nation nor ever again be trained for war." Those eloquent words are placed in a context, however, in which all nations and peoples are united under the Hebrew G-d's command. The proud and lofty should hide in caves "from the dread of the Lord and the splendour of his majesty, when he rises to inspire the earth with fear" (Isaiah 2.19). It is precisely because the God is so powerful, and can vanquish any enemy, that an era of peace is ushered in on the "day of doom" (Isaiah 2.12), a point often ignored by those who have adopted the "swords into plowshares" vision as a slogan for the contemporary peace movement.

It is not humans, but G-d, according to the Hebrew scriptures, who provides protection and makes decisions about who will win or lose in battle, often depending on whether or not they are a faithful people. The people are often warned against reliance upon their own military prowess and are to take no pride or consolation in it:

> A King is not saved by a great army,
> nor a warrior delivered by great strength.
> A man cannot trust his horse to save him,
> nor can it deliver him for all its strength.
> The Lord's eyes are turned towards those who fear him.
> (Psalms 33.16)

Indeed, the contradictions of the warrior and the pacifist are interwoven in the Hebrew scriptures (see Firestone, Chapter 5), and some would argue, as does Spiegel (1989, 243), that the Torah's view is that G-d is also merciful, motherly and tender, forgiving and nonviolent. Spiegel claims that the violent passages have more to do with what humans bring upon themselves rather than acts of God as acts of violence backfire, citing the karma-like proverb, "Whoever digs a trench for other people falls into it himself" (ibid.).

Constantine and the Crusades

The Hebrew notion of G-d as protector and warrior was adopted and embellished by medieval Christians. Although the early church was probably a pacifist religious community (see the discussion below and Bainton 1960), as Christianity became closely associated with the power structure of Western civilization, God became increasingly associated by the church with military might. The most significant turning point in the history of Christianity in terms of attitudes toward war came in 312 C.E. (Common Era) with the conversion of Emperor Constantine to the faith. He reportedly had a vision in which he saw the sign of a cross in the heavens, and the words "In This Sign Conquer," a scene represented by

Raphael in a Vatican painting (Fehl 1993). The sign was painted on his troops' shields; he won the decisive Battle of Molveno, consolidated his power, and became convinced that the Christian God was a great God of War.

Following the forcible Christianization of the Roman armies, Constantine built a portable altar to carry into battle, and the pacifism of the early church became a minority position. "Just war" theories emerged at that time, first (traditionally) from the pen of Augustine, with strict proscriptions around warfare, but allowing for it under certain circumstances. The loopholes were subsequently expanded so enormously that by the eleventh century, Christians believed that God had commanded them to engage in warfare as an act of obedience. In *The Story of Civilization*, Will Durant (1950, Book V) calls the crusades "the climax of Christianity."

Bemoaning the control of Jerusalem (and, in fact, the Near East), and responding to stories of oppression and desecration by the Turks in the eleventh century, the ambitious Pope Urban II believed that he was called by God to "free" the Holy Land from the infidels. In November of 1095, he delivered a famous speech in Auvergne, in which (according to one version) he called upon the French to

> enter upon the road to the Holy Sepulchre; wrest that land from the wicked race, and subject it to yourselves. That land which as the Scripture says "floweth with milk and honey," was given by God into the possession of the children of Israel Jerusalem is the navel of the world . . . This royal city, therefore, situated at the centre of the world, is now held captive . . . From you especially she asks succor, because, as we have already said, God has conferred upon you above all nations great glory in arms. Accordingly undertake this journey for the remission of your sins, with the assurance of the imperishable glory of the kingdom of heaven.
>
> *(Urban II)*

The crowd reportedly shouted "Dieu le veut" (God wills it), and thousands adorned their brow or breast with the cross of Christ and set forth to engage in battle. For the next two centuries, Europe was united more than it had been since the Roman Empire, behind the banners of the Crusades. According to Hale (1957, 259),

> The Church, by supporting the institutions of chivalry and the knightly orders, had blessed weapons that were not always to be used against the oppressor or the infidel, and by admitting that it was permissible to wage a just war, she had in effect sanctioned all wars. . . . The Church, too, needed war to support her authority and punish those who defied it.

As Luard (1986, 332) observes, "guns were sometimes named after the apostles; swords and halberds were engraved with religious scenes; and generals launched attacks in the name of their patron saint." Following the Crusades (and no doubt while they were in progress), there was no unanimity among Christians about the morality of war. Erasmus accused the leaders for that "madness of war that has persisted so long and so disgracefully among Christians" and Sir Thomas More believed that "the common folk do not go to war of their own accord, but are driven to it by the madness of kings." As a consequence, the rulers were compelled to find reasons to justify their wars (ibid., 333).

As John Ferguson (1978, 108) contends, "the Crusaders in general left Muslims with the picture of Christians as militaristic imperialists, and the life in the Crusaders' camps did much to increase their contempt for Christian moral indiscipline." Although probably no religious tradition ever engaged in such an intensive holy war campaign as Christianity, the Muslims have their own holy war tradition and practice.

> Say to those who disbelieve, if they cease He will forgive them what has passed, but if they turn again, then usages of the ancients are past! And fight them until there is no temptation and religion is entirely unto God. And if they give over, God shall surely see what they are doing, but if they turn again, then know that God is your Protector—best Protector, and best Helper!
>
> *(Qur'an 8:38–40)*

Judeo-Christian support for "just wars" was incorporated early on in their successor tradition, Islam, founded by Prophet Muhammad (born about 570 C.E.), which I will discuss below.

The Western religions of Judaism, Christianity, and Islam have the most elaborated doctrines of warfare. The Eastern religions are not without their justifications of war as well, however, the most famous of which is the story told in the *Bhagavad Gita*.

Krishna and Arjuna: The Warrior Dharma

Despite the strong emphasis on *ahimsa*—nonharmfulness—in Hinduism, the *Bhagavad Gita* tells the story of Arjuna, who loses his will to fight on the battlefield of a conflict over succession to the throne. Faced by the sight of his kinfolk in the opposing army, Arjuna lays down his weapons. He is finally convinced to fight by Krishna, an incarnation of the God Vishnu. There are two reasons why he must do so when ordered to: (1) because the body is not important, but a temporary container of the soul and (2) because it is his *dharma* (duty) as a warrior to fight. Moreover, Krishna tells Arjuna that, just as a person puts on new garments, giving up old ones, the soul similarly accepts new material bodies, giving up the old ones.

> The soul can never be cut into pieces by any weapon, nor can he be burned by fire, nor moistened by water, nor withered by the wind. This individual

> soul is unbreakable and insoluble, and can be neither burned nor dried.... It is said that the soul is invisible, inconceivable, immutable and unchangeable. Knowing this, you should not grieve for the body.
>
> *(Bhagavad Gita 2.22–25)*

According to A. C. Bhaktivedanta Swami Prabhupada (1972, 28),

> when Krsna orders fighting, it must be concluded that violence is for supreme justice and, as such, Arjuna should follow the instruction, knowing well that such violence, committed in the act of fighting for justice, is not at all violence because, at any rate, the man, or rather the soul, cannot be killed.

Arjuna is thus given much the same justification for violence as the ancient Hebrews: it is divinely sanctioned action on behalf of justice; what is forbidden becomes obligatory (see Girard 1977). When what is morally forbidden—the taking of life—becomes expected by the gods as a sacrificial ritual, it is imbued with a cosmic justification that serves the purposes not only of the gods, but also (or primarily?) their "representatives" on earth. Moreover, the consequences of his actions are minimized by the theory of reincarnation. Killing is not as significant as it might seem, since it merely releases the soul to transmigrate to another body, providing a mechanism of "moral disengagement" (Bandura 1999) that enables the warrior to address potential self-sanctions for engaging in behavior normally forbidden.

Themes and Dilemmas in the Warrior Motif

"And do ye abide without the camp seven days: whosoever hath killed any person, and whosoever hath touched any slain, purify both yourselves and your captives on the third day, and on the seventh day," the ancient Hebrew warriors are advised (Numbers 31:17). They apparently understood that the act of killing can cause psychological trauma to the perpetrator, what Rachel MacNair (2002, 2018) calls PITS—Perpetration-Induced Traumatic Stress. As the social history of the warrior motif demonstrates in case after case, the warrior is faced with significant ethical dilemmas. Having been taught from childhood not to kill others, sometimes not to harm them, the warrior in combat is faced with an anguished choice between competing ethical demands: adherence to duty to a higher cause and one's comrades-in-arms, on the one hand, and the widespread condemnation of killing on the other.

The most striking empirical evidence of the warrior's internal dilemma is found in combat research, some of it sponsored by the U.S. military and labeled post-traumatic stress disorder (PTSD) or, more precisely, PITS. Dave Grossman and Bruce K. Siddle (2008, 1797) note that "the killing that lies at the heart of combat, is an extraordinarily traumatic and psychologically costly endeavor that profoundly impacts all who participate in it." This cost is not only felt by the individual soldier, but by the spouses and families of those in combat (Edmunds 2015) as well as the larger society, especially when large numbers of wounded warriors return from the battlefront (Grossman and Siddle 2008, 1797).

How is this profound warrior dilemma addressed? A number of strategies have emerged over the centuries: the sacralization of violence, providing it with a Divine sanction; the use of purification rituals, from those used by the ancient Hebrews and other early faith communities (Girard 1977) to the sweat lodge rituals for returning American veterans by Native American chaplain Arnold Thomas (Telonidis 2012). The contemporary secular equivalent of those rituals is the psychological counseling that many PTSD sufferers receive. Warrior narratives in the faith traditions become an important strategy for overriding objections to killing (see Rubenstein 2010).

Finally, social psychologist Albert Bandura contends that individuals who use violence undertake a psychological process he calls "moral disengagement": "moral reasoning is translated into actions through self-regulatory mechanisms rooted in moral stands and self-sanctions by which moral agency is exercised" (1999, 193). In order to engage in "reprehensible conduct," individuals have to go through a process of moral disengagement, by which they do not employ the moral self-sanctions that normally prevent them from engaging in inhumane conduct. These mechanisms of moral disengagement include moral justification; palliative comparison; euphemistic labeling; minimizing, displacement, and diffusion of responsibility; ignoring or misconstruing the consequences; attribution of blame; and—one of the most common—dehumanization of the adversary.

Another solution, of course, for the warrior's dilemma is to become a pacifist (as a friend of mine fighting as an American soldier in the Vietnam War did). That position raises its own dilemmas, as we shall see as we examine the pacifist motif.

The Pacifist Motif

Like the warrior, the pacifist believes in a sacred obligation, but in this case *not* to kill—for some even not harming—any other person. In its most extensive versions, the taboo against harming and killing is extended to other sentient beings, an idea most developed in Jainism and Buddhism.

Nonviolence in the Eastern Religions

One of the clearest nonviolent traditions in the world's religions comes from the Buddha, who seemed unequivocal in his denunciation of the use of violence in any form, although subsequent followers managed to find justification for killing under extraordinary circumstances (usually to defend Buddhist institutions), as we see in chapters by Iselin Frydenlund and Jehan Perera (Chapters 2 and 14).

The Eightfold Path that guides the Buddhist's life contains a set of Five Precepts, the first of which is "not to kill, but to practice a love which does no harm to any" (Ferguson 1978, 43; cf. Philips 2008; Subramuniyaswami 2004). "Everyone is afraid of violence; everyone likes life," insists the Buddha. "If one compares oneself with others one would never take life or be involved in the taking of life" (*Dhammapada*, 130; cf. Buddha 1959). Similar ethical principles are found in Taoism (see Lao Tzu 1988) and Moism (see Mo Tzu 1963).

The injunction against killing applies to war, murder, the killing of animals for food, and ritual sacrifice (Ferguson 1978, 47), and the consequence of taking life is an inferior incarnation. "He who destroys the life of any being may, in his next birth, meet death unexpectedly while in the prime of life" (Telakatahagatha 78). Violence is overcome through meditation and thereby the cultivation of compassion, benevolence, and loving kindness (*metta*). The precept not to kill in Buddhism involves *ahimsa*—nonviolence or nonharmfulness—also present in Jainism and Hinduism, and is related to a belief in the unity of all being. When there is no subject-object split, harming the other is no different from harming oneself. This concept also lies at the basis of Gandhi's notion of *satyagraha*, or truth-force, although Gandhi himself was not a pure pacifist. According to Gandhi (1967, 153–154),

> Ahimsa is not merely a negative state of harmlessness, but it is a positive state of love, of doing good even to the evildoer. But it does not mean helping the evildoer to continue the wrong or tolerating it by passive acquiescence.... If I am a follower of Ahimsa I must love my enemy. I must apply the same rules to the wrongdoer, who is my enemy or a stranger to me, as I would to my wrongdoing father or son.

The notion of *ahimsa* is an interesting test case in religious teachings about war and peace. It seems sufficiently straightforward to prevent the justification of any participation in warfare whatsoever, and yet it has been modified to allow exceptions to its seeming rigidity. According to some, *ahimsa* is a relative obligation—e.g., a soldier might take a vow to do injury only in battle (Ferguson 1978, 32). Moreover, the prohibition against the taking of life, according to some, does not extend to circumstances in which the Doctrine of the Buddha itself is in danger. In a number of situations in which the rare instances of apparent sanctioning of violence by the Buddha have been highlighted, such as the Sri Lankan civil war (see Perera and Frydenlund in this volume, Chapters 2 and 14), the Buddha is said by some to have encouraged his disciples to defend the Order even with arms, and there are historical instances in which even monks participated directly in battle.

A second circumstance in which killing is deemed acceptable by some applies a principle of proportionality. In one story, the Buddha himself is said to have killed a bandit in order to save five hundred merchants. A third Buddhist argument for killing is similar to that given to Arjuna: since existence itself is illusory, when one appears to kill, that too is an illusion. There are other examples, and in all instances "the person killing must act either out of compassion and charity, or thoughtlessly, so that the inner peace is not disturbed; the monks of Hiei-zan when arming for war would cover their eyes" (Ferguson 1978, 55–56).

Other Buddhists take the injunction in the opposite direction, however, such as Vietnamese monk Thich Nhat Hanh (1993, 5), whose commentary on the First Precept suggests it means

> aware of the suffering caused by the destruction of life, I vow to cultivate compassion and learn ways to protect the lives of people, animals, plants and minerals. I am determined not to kill, not to let others kill, and not to condone any act of killing in the world, in my thinking, and in my way of life.

It is born, he says,

> from the awareness that lives everywhere are being destroyed. We see the suffering caused by the destruction of life, and we undertake to cultivate compassion and use it as a source of energy for the protection of people, animals, plants, and minerals.
>
> *(ibid., 9)*

Compassion is the only safe energy and, since we are made of non-human elements such as plants, minerals, and sunshine, to practice that precept in a way that is deep and true, it must be extended to the ecosystem (ibid.). A famous opponent in the war in his homeland, Vietnam, Thich Nhat Hanh declares, "I am determined not to kill, not to let others kill, and not to condone any act of killing in the world, in my thinking, and in my way of life" (ibid.).

In the final analysis, the use of Buddhism to justify violence and warfare suggests that it is not so much the content of the teaching as the position of the religious leaders in the social hierarchy of a society. If allied with ruling elites who require both force and legitimation, virtually any religious tradition can be called upon to justify the use of violence, no matter how repugnant it may be to the religion's founders. Similarly, if allied with a group attempting the violent overthrow of what is perceived to be an unjust order, religious teachings provide justification for the use of arms in rebellion.

It is precisely this ambivalence of religious doctrine that makes it so powerful. The same symbols, myth structure, and beliefs can be used to legitimate opposite positions on issues of violence, war, and peace, giving each side a sense of righteous indignation in the service of their cause.

Given the millennia of religious justification of warfare, what is surprising is not the continued legitimation of various "sacred causes," but the extent to which the name of the gods is being used to challenge the very foundations of power in the contemporary world.

Christian Pacifism

The evidence for the pacifism of the early church is, according to some scholars, overwhelming, although Nigel Biggar's analysis in this volume (Chapter 8) develops a careful scholarly critique of a prominent advocate of that position and concludes that the early church was not a pacifist community. The primary (but not exclusive) reasons for that stance were the example of Jesus' life and teachings, and the Christian principle of *agape* (love directed toward all humanity), as suggested by a number of the Church Fathers (see Bainton 1960; Hays 1996). The argument for pacifism in Christianity begins with Jesus's own admonition to "love your enemies and pray for those who persecute you" (Mt. 5:43) and his asking God to forgive his executioners as he was dying on the cross "for they know not what they do" (Lk 23:34).

Jesus's pacifism was embellished by many of the prominent early "church fathers"; Tertullian, for example, asked: "Whom have we to hate? If injured, forbidden to retaliate, ... who can suffer injury at our hands?" (*Apology*). He believed that love and killing were incompatible with one another and that the injunction to love one's enemies was the final test of one's relationship to God. Origen argued (in *Against Celsius*, III.7) that Jesus "did not consider it compatible with his inspired legislation to allow the taking of human life in any form at all." Saint Cyprian of Carthage, in the third century, praised the Christians of his day by noting,

> They do not even fight against those who are attacking since it is not granted to the innocent to kill even the aggressor, but promptly to deliver up their souls and blood that, since so much malice and cruelty are rampant in the world, they may more quickly withdraw from the malicious and the cruel.
>
> *(National Conference of Catholic Bishops 1983, 35)*

Soldiers who converted to the early church were allowed to remain in the military, but under the strict condition that they were not to kill or they would be excommunicated. Thus, Saint Martin of Tours lay down his arms after his conversion, reportedly telling Caesar, "Hitherto I have served you as a soldier. Allow me now to become a soldier of God ... I am a soldier of Christ. It is not lawful for me to fight" (Severus 2007, 6).

Liu Cheng and Egon Spiegel (2015) note that Jesus chooses to ride into Jerusalem on a donkey "because he intends to demonstrate that violence is not a way to solve conflict." The point is that "a donkey isn't suited for war like a horse is." Moreover, "By riding into Jerusalem on the ass's foal," they contend, "Jesus focuses a whole peace program: He is demonstrating that he practices what he preaches throughout all his short life" (Cheng and Spiegel 2015, 370). Moreover, Spiegel contends that Jesus's renunciation of violence is primarily a result of his trust in

God and that "the use of violence on the one hand and trust in God on the other exclude each other" (Spiegel 1989, 244). It is a theme picked up by the United Methodist bishops in their renunciation of nuclear weapons, reliance on which they label "idolatry" (United Methodist Bishops 1986).

Since the early 1980s, increasing numbers of official bodies and unofficial Christian groups have denounced the possibility of carrying out a just war with existing weapons of mass destruction, especially with nuclear weapons. The U.S. Catholic bishops reach some sobering conclusions in their pastoral letter on nuclear weapons. Christian pacifism has emerged from the biblical and early church tradition, and from the historic peace churches: the Society of Friends (Quakers), the Brethren, and the Mennonites (Chatfield 1973). The nonviolence of these small groups has been embellished in the latter half of the twentieth century through the church itself, but also through a burgeoning global peace movement, and the inspiration of the great preachers of nonviolence: Gandhi, King, Jr., and Thomas Merton. Both King and Merton were profoundly influenced by Gandhi and the Eastern traditions (especially Hinduism and Jainism), but Gandhi himself was inspired by the nonviolent teachings of Christ.

Contemporary Christian pacifism is just as diverse as that of the early church, but it is out of this radical commitment to nonviolence and pacifism that the most dedicated struggles of protest against warfare in the twentieth century have emerged. Although he does not explicitly affirm pacifism, Pope Francis's invitation certainly moves in that direction: "In 2017, may we dedicate ourselves prayerfully and actively to banishing violence from our hearts, words and deeds, and to becoming nonviolent people and to building nonviolent communities that care for our common home" (Chapter 9).

The Pacifist's Dilemmas

"Pacifism is objectively pro-Fascist," George Orwell (1942, 419) insisted, writing during World War II. "This is elementary common sense. If you hamper the war effort of one side you automatically help that of the other."

The most obvious dilemma pacifists face is their apparent inability to address social problems, injustice, or evil—perhaps the possibility that they are aiding the wrong side. The pure pacifists who insist that the use of violence is forbidden under all circumstances may find themselves on the sidelines of resistance. Now, admittedly, that "ideal type" of pacifist here might not describe many who would self-identify as pacifists, but it does exist historically and provides a helpful contrast to the more ubiquitous warrior. From the Jain monks and nuns who do not even wish to inhale insects, to the church father Tertullian, who believes "it is better to be slain than to slay" even in self-defense, a strict ethical adherence to pacifism may paralyze one in the face of evil and injustice, creating a cognitive contradiction just as severe as the ethical contradictions warriors may face in the midst of battle.

The argument of the pure pacifist is that because every thought, word, and deed has consequences that reverberate through larger society and the environment, acts of violence ultimately have negative consequences, whereas acts of compassion build up a more peaceful world. That may be of little comfort to pacifists paralyzed by ethical constraints in the face of immediate danger to their families or vulnerable populations whom they might see as requiring protection.

It is in response to those difficult kinds of situations that faith communities over the ages have developed elaborate ethical constructs that permit the use of violence under certain specific circumstances, while still setting boundaries on when and how it is used. Whether it is the leaders of the Christian church after it came under the emperor's protection in the fourth century, the Prophet Mohammed giving moral guidance when the Islamic community was under violent attack, or the modern Israeli army attempting to instill ethical boundaries on the use of force (see Zion and Biggar, Chapters 7 and 8 this volume), the effort to set limits on the use of violence is a common, dilemma-fraught effort existing throughout the religious world.

Religious violence, Joseph Camilleri argues (Chapter 10) "is generally marginal to the religious life (Juergensmeyer 2003)." Although every tradition has "elements that justify and even encourage violence, most religious actors do not engage in violence or, if they do, they do not invoke religious belief to justify their violence" (ibid.).

Taboos: Religious Limits on Violence

Religious institutions and leadership are not always rallying the troops to battle and justifying the war campaigns of political elites. They also define the boundary lines around both the decision to go to war and the conduct of war.

Take No Spoils

One of the most significant elements of religious teaching on warfare is that it is almost always to be conducted for the deity, rather than for those mortals going into battle. This teaching is, of course, a double-edged sword, because it draws boundaries, on the one hand, around the conduct of war, but on the other hand it provides the ultimate justification for war: if it is not for the political or military leaders who make the decision, but only "for the glory of God," then how could it be wrong? Most efforts to draw taboo lines around warfare do diminish the carnage, at least initially, but once the guidelines are established for a "just war," there seems to be an infinite variety of reasons for engaging in battle on an infinite number of occasions.

The unanticipated consequences of taboo lines are often quite dramatic. The injunctions of the ancient Hebrew God not to take spoils, so that individual participants would not profit from war, in some cases led to widespread slaughter.

The battles described in the book of Joshua, for example, explain how the ancient Hebrews took possession of the Promised Land. There were strict rules about taking booty from the victories they were "given by the Lord," and all silver, gold vessels of copper and iron, etc., were to be put in the "Lord's treasury" (Joshua 6:19). In city after city, they "captured the city with its king, and all its villages, put them to the sword and destroyed every living thing; they left no survivors" (Joshua 10:39).

Social Boundaries and Killing

Taboo lines are often created in order to protect the religious community from using violence internally, so that (except under the proper aegis of the authorities) warfare is to be waged against those on the outside. The Islamic jihad, for example, is to be carried out within very strict guidelines. According to Abdel-Ati (1963, 7), it "does not mean violating the rights of others or killing them or plundering their properties; rather, it means offering one's own self to be killed." Jihad is only to be carried out against three categories of people: "(1) those who rebel against the Imam; (2) protected minorities such as Jews, Christians and Zoroastrians, if they violate the conditions of protection; and (3) whoever is hostile, among the various kinds of unbelievers" (from the [Twelver] Ordinances of Islam by Najm al-Din al-Muhaqqiq al-Hilli (d. 1278 C.E.); Williams 1971, 269). It is only to be carried out against non-Muslims (Williams 1971, 257), is not to be undertaken during the sacred month (ibid., 258), and has other strict limitations (ibid., 270).

This establishing of taboo lines around believers or around tribal lines is probably the most significant of religious boundaries around violence, and it is found in many of the world's religions. Despite the fact that injunctions against killing are often against killing either within the tribe or within the community of believers, taboo lines are often much more complex than they originally appear. One of the most enigmatic events surrounds what appears to be a straightforward command (one of ten) not to kill, given by Adonai to the ancient Hebrews. After Moses encounters the Lord on Mount Sinai and receives the commandments, he descends the mountain only to find the Israelites engaging in idolatrous worship, singing and dancing around a bull-calf. Moses angrily shatters the tablets, rallies the Levites to him and instructs them, saying,

> These are the words of the Lord the God of Israel: "Arm yourselves, each of you, with his sword. Go through the camp from gate to gate and back again. Each of you kill his brother, his friend, his neighbour." The Levites obeyed, and about three thousand of the people died that day. Moses then said, "Today you have consecrated yourselves to the Lord completely, because you have turned each against his own son and his own brother and so have this day brought a blessing upon yourselves."
>
> *(Exodus 32:28)*

Religious prohibitions always seem to have an exception that is believed sanctioned by the deity. In the Jewish tradition, the commandment not to kill is often interpreted as prohibiting murder and leaving open the door for justified killing under certain circumstances, as Rabbi Firestone (Chapter 5) notes. Thus, even religious teachings apparently intended to prohibit warfare, or to draw firm boundaries around violence, are reinterpreted so as to legitimate it. The classic example is "just war" theory in the Christian tradition, which Nigel Biggar (Chapter 8) outlines and supports in his chapter in this volume. He develops a well-documented case for the just war position having earlier origins in the church, and even that the New Testament does not support the idea of a pacifist Jesus as argued by Richard Hays (196) and others.

Just War Theory

Drawing upon the Hebrew scriptures (the "Old Testament"), Ambrose, bishop of Milan, prayed for the victory of the Roman armies after the church and the empire became intertwined with Constantine's "Christianization" (see Ferguson 1978, 105). Ambrose drew upon both the Old Testament and Cicero's just war doctrines to develop a Christian philosophy of war, later embellished by Augustine, bishop of Hippo Regius in Africa. According to the U.S. Catholic bishops (see National Conference of Catholic Bishops [NCCB] 1983, 26ff.), the just war doctrine as it developed over the centuries in the Christian tradition

> begins with the presumption which binds all Christians, we should do no harm to our neighbors; how we treat our enemy is the key test of whether we love our neighbor; and the possibility of taking even one human life is a prospect we should consider in fear and trembling.

In short, the original purpose of just war teaching was an effort to prevent war: the decision to go to war should require "extraordinarily strong reasons for overriding a presumption in favor of peace and against war" (ibid., 27).[3] Two types of criteria must be applied to determine if the conditions for a just war exist: those relating to the decision to fight—*jus ad bellum* criteria—as well as standards for the conduct of war once the decision to fight has been made—*jus in bello* criteria (see Johnson 2010, 2014).

In the early days of the Judeo-Christian-Islamic tradition, during the Exodus, warfare had been brought by God for protection of God's people and as a means of fulfilling a Divine promise. It was strictly delineated, however, with specific rules of procedure. When approaching a city, the Israelites were to make an offer of peace before going to war against them. If it were refused, there were clear procedures as to what to do in battle (e.g., trees that yield food are not to be cut down) and after the city had been "delivered by the Lord" (see Deuteronomy 20).

The God of Isaac and Jacob was seen by Jesus and the early church as a Protector, but not as a God of war. As members of a persecuted minority sect, the early

Christians were enjoined to serve God by loving their enemies. Following the conversion of Constantine, Christianity became the establishment religion and the loving of enemies gave way to killing them under certain strict guidelines. The idea that God sometimes allowed battle for a just cause gradually gave way, as the church grew in power, to the notion that God called Christians to do battle in God's name, setting the stage for centuries of armed conflict and hostilities between the two Abrahamic religions of Christianity and Islam.

The criteria governing the decision to go to war rely primarily on the issue of proportionality: i.e., is the good to be gained from the battle proportionate to the cost to be incurred? According to the U.S. Catholic Bishops (National Conference of Catholic Bishops 1983), a decision to go to war is possible only when the following conditions are met: (1) just cause, (2) competent authority, (3) comparative justice, (4) right intention, (5) last resort, (6) probability of success, and (7) proportionality. It is especially with the final two criteria that many Christian authorities have been forced to reevaluate the traditional legitimation of warfare in the latter part of the twentieth century. It is impossible to envision any way in which a total war, such as a nuclear war, could meet the criteria of the probability of success and proportionality. Except in the most limited of nuclear conflicts, how could any party waging the war be successful in preserving the values for which the war was allegedly waged? The purpose of this criterion is "to prevent irrational resort to force or hopeless resistance when the outcome of either will be clearly disproportionate or futile" (ibid.). According to German theologian Egon Spiegel, the most important is the "last resort" criterion because "under the aspects of nonviolence there are endless . . . possibilities before reaching the last resort, [so it can] . . . never be reached."[4]

Finally, the "damage to be inflicted and the costs incurred by war must be proportionate to the good expected by taking up arms" (ibid., 31). As with the probability of success, proportionality in a nuclear war is possible only in a strictly limited nuclear war. One must ask, therefore, in the most optimistic scenarios, what objectives would legitimate the destruction of a nation's heartland, or several major cities? Nuclear winter theories suggest, of course, that it is unlikely that a catastrophe of enormous proportions could be prevented even in a limited nuclear exchange.

Even after the decision is made to go to war, the conduct of war itself must be subject to two principles: proportionality and discrimination. As the U.S. bishops put it,

> Response to aggression must not exceed the nature of the aggression. To destroy civilization as we know it by waging a 'total war' as today it could be waged would be a monstrously disproportionate response to aggression on the part of any nation.
>
> *(ibid., 33)*

The principle of discrimination prohibits action against innocent civilians (see Ramsey 2002, 2010; Johnson 2010. As the Vatican Council stated, "Any act of war aimed indiscriminately at the destruction of entire cities or of extensive areas along with their population is a crime against God and man himself. It merits unequivocal and unhesitating condemnation" (Paul VI 1965).

On the basis of these principles, and the qualitatively different nature of modern warfare, the possibility of waging a nuclear war is impossible within the just-war criteria. For these reasons, the Second Vatican Council reaffirmed "the condemnation of total war already pronounced by recent popes" (National Conference of Catholic Bishops 1983, 33).

As with most principles, however, there are loopholes in just-war theory, especially in the principle of discrimination, which prohibits directly *intended* attacks on noncombatants. Does the fact that there are sixty potential military targets in Moscow mean that the city is a military target and that the deaths of millions of civilian inhabitants as "collateral damage" would be "unintended" (see ibid., 57; Walzer 1977, 276–277)? Others argue that there are no innocents in a society mobilized for war. Although admitting that the issues are not easily resolved, the bishops contend that "entire classes of human beings such as schoolchildren, hospital patients, the elderly, the ill, the average industrial worker . . . may never be directly attacked" (NCCB 1983, 34).

The Catholic bishops thus conclude that the nature of modern war requires, in the words of the Vatican Council, "a completely fresh reappraisal of war," with attention to both the just-war teaching and nonviolence. These two elements of the Christian tradition "diverge on some specific conclusions, but they share a common presumption against the use of force as a means of settling disputes" (ibid., 37).

Islamic Riffs on the Just War Theme

Intertribal raiding was a common practice among the Arabs in the Prophet's time and he could attempt to abolish it, continue to allow it, or control it among his followers; the only logical choice seemed to be the latter (Ferguson 1978, 126). His decision was to ban intertribal raiding within the umma of Islam, but he himself engaged in raids on the caravans going to and from Mecca, in the belief that business practices in Mecca were at the root of the social evils of the time. The term used to designate such practices, Jihad, is often translated as "holy war," and that is the primary way in which the early Muslims regarded it (Williams 1971, 266), but it refers more generally to religious struggle. According to one apologist, Hammudah Abdel-Ati (1963, 6),

> there are two kinds of Jihad: great Jihad, which means conducting [a] fight against one's own evils or wrong inclinations and caprices instigated by the inner self in man; small Jihad, which means campaigning against the outer enemy of faith or nation.

As in the Christian crusade tradition, jihad is a source of glory, and those who die in its service die as martyrs and go directly to eternal paradise. "Violence is not preferred," in Islam, Williams notes (ibid., 262), "but in view of the nature of the world, it is not to be shunned either. And finally, because struggle is a moral activity, even violence must be conducted by rules." Moreover, "as a religious activity, . . . [*jihad*] was subject to the Law just as were prayer, sacrifice, or pilgrimage" (ibid., 266). The stated purpose of jihad is not self-aggrandizement, but part of a reciprocal relation with God. As the Qur'an (22:39–42) puts it, "Verily God helpeth one who helpeth Him. Verily God is strong. Almighty—Those who, if we give them power on earth establish worship and pay the poor-due and enjoin kindness and forbid iniquity." Furthermore, tribes under attack by the armies of Islam were given a choice: either they could accept the protection of the umma of Islam by converting, or they could suffer the consequences of war. Following the death of Muhammad in 632 C.E., the Muslim armies swept across southern Europe, Northern Africa, and into northern India.

Born out of a "tribal" context, the leaders of early Islam attempted to mitigate the negative effects of incessant intertribal warfare in the region by establishing strict boundaries around the use of violence—when to go to war, and how to conduct it. Those boundaries were, in large part, adapted from those established by Moses and the ancient Hebrews, who also constituted a migratory tribal society, and attempted to minimize the impact of ongoing warfare and conflicts with hostile societies. As the Islamic community became the establishment in their region, however, the guidelines for fighting became gradually relaxed, and the use of warfare more frequent. Acts of aggression for self-aggrandizement became defined, as among the Crusaders, as battle for the glory of God, and the prohibitions become construed as justifications, because "this war" is an exception to the rule and is fought for high moral purposes.

That is not to say that Islam is a warrior-dominated religion, however; as Afra Jalabi notes (Chapter 11), the Qur'an also has anti-violence themes and promotes active peacemaking. Moreover, Chaiwat Satha-Anand (Chapter 12) and Mohammed Abu-Nimer (Chapter 13) both argue that Islam has a strong nonviolent tradition in its scripture and tradition. Moreover, Richard Bonney (2004) in his thorough treatment in *Jihad: From Qur'an to bin Laden*, goes so far as to argue that

> *There is no such thing, in our view, as Islamic terrorism, There is terrorism perpetrated by violent Islamists*, that is to say, by those who are acting in a political cause but who seek to motivate people . . . by using the terminology of the faith of Islam.
>
> *(ibid., xii)*

If "just war," and perhaps jihad, might not be moral options given the nature of modern warfare, and pacifism seems to leave one on the sideline helpless to act, we might turn to Gandhi or an alternative to the warrior and pacifist options.

The Nonviolent Activist

In an effort to address the dilemmas faced by the warrior—including the "just warrior"—and the pacifist, Mahatma Gandhi cultivated a dramatic cultural innovation by combining the two motifs in a paradoxical new motif. Gandhi's nonviolent activist—the *satyagrahi* (holder to the Truth)—fights like the warrior, but like the pacifist avoids harming or killing the adversary. It is this key insight, drawn from multiple spiritual traditions and his insights into practical political dynamics that led Gandhi to develop a new paradigm of conflict that I consider transformative. Gandhi's approach allows both individuals and groups to fight for just causes without facing the self-sanctions that Bandura (1999) identifies, or the moral condemnation by others of acts of violence.

This paradoxical bringing together of these contradictory motifs produces a dramatic cultural innovation. It is reminiscent of the concept of *Shalom* in Judaism, which Firestone (Chapter 5) observes is composed of Hebrew letters that signify the paradoxical co-mingling of fire and water. Gandhi's cultural innovation set off a karmic chain of events from his South African ashrams through the Indian Independence movement to the U.S. civil rights movement, the anti-apartheid movement in South Africa, and numerous nonviolent movements bringing down dictators and facilitating social change throughout the world in subsequent decades.

In addition to Gene Sharp (1974), who systematized and secularized the strategic aspect of Gandhi's paradigm, many other scholars (e.g., Bondurant 1958; Bell 2008; Nagler 2004) observe that Gandhi's theory of power provides a new framework for understanding the dynamics of both domination and rebellion. The power of nonviolence—sometimes dubbed "people power"—allows resisters to bring down the pillars of support for an unjust system by refusing to cooperate with it and mounting a multi-pronged resistance. Power is thus not simply, as feminist theorists later put it, "power over," or domination, but also "power to," or empowerment (see Bell 2008), and is no longer a zero-sum game in which one party gains power only at the expense of another. Power does not grow simply out of the barrel of a gun, as Mao and many others argue, but from a variety of sources.

Thus, Gandhi's approach to the question of violence as a weapon of conflict reshapes the battlefield. The *Satyagrahi* fights not against people who are enemies, but behaviors, ideas, and structures that result in harm. He drew upon multiple faith traditions, research on successful uses of nonviolence, and what he called his "experiments with Truth," his own efforts to bring about change through nonviolent resistance of various forms of domination. To Hindu and Buddhist conceptions of *ahimsa*, Gandhi added elements from the bible—especially Jesus's so-called Sermon on the Mount and the *Qur'an*, insisting that nonviolence was a fundamental law of the universe and more powerful than violence. "Nonviolence," he insisted, "is the greatest force at the disposal of mankind. It is mightier than the mightiest weapon of destruction" (Gandhi 1967, 122).

Nonviolent civil resistance has a strong elective affinity (Weber 1968) with spiritual disciplines. As Thomas Merton (1968, 14) puts it,

> Non-violence is perhaps the most exacting of all forms of struggle, not only because it demands first of all that one be ready to suffer evil and even face the threat of death without violent retaliation, but because it excludes mere transient self-interest, even political, from its considerations. In a very real sense, he who practices non-violent resistance must commit himself not to the defense of his own interests or even those of a particular group; he must commit himself to the defense of objective truth and right and above all of man. His aim is then not simply to "prevail" or to prove that he is right and the adversary wrong, or to make the adversary give in and yield what is demanded of him.

The most prominent recent reinterpretation of Christianity as a religion of nonviolence is Pope Francis, who in his 2017 New Year's message, "Nonviolence: A Style of Politics for Peace," declared that "Jesus marked out the path of nonviolence. He walked that path to the very end, to the cross, whereby he became our peace and put an end to hostility (cf. *Eph* 2:14–16) (Pope Francis 2017; Chapter 9 this volume). For this pope, nonviolence is a "style of politics" that runs the gamut from the psychological and micro level to the global. He protests what he calls

> "piecemeal" violence, of different kinds and levels, [that] causes great suffering: wars in different countries and continents; terrorism, organized crime and unforeseen acts of violence; the abuses suffered by migrants and victims of human trafficking; and the devastation of the environment. Where does this lead?
>
> *(Pope Francis, Chapter 9 [this volume])*

This position is consistent with Speigel's understanding of Jesus's teachings and actions so such much as a pacifist, but as radically nonviolent—"Jesus not only rejected a political-structural system of violence; he denied himself the revolutionary and violent reach for power" (Speigel 1989, 242). He followed instead a "strategy of non-violent action" (ibid.).

On a sociological level, Gandhi's application of *ahimsa* to conflict serves to contain conflict escalation. For Gandhi, it means that one respects one's adversary as a person, while resisting their behavior. Gandhi extends what is a moral guide for personal behavior to a strategy for organized collective behavior. As Margaret Chatterjee (1984) suggests, Gandhi transforms the concept from a pathway to individual liberation into a means for social change. At the psychological level, it also serves a strategic advantage as well—*Satyagrahi* are, as Gene Sharp puts it, "able to apply something like jiu-jitsu to their opponent, throwing him off balance politically, causing his repression to rebound" and changing the power dynamics of an asymmetrical struggle (Sharp 2005, 110; cf. Kurtz and Smithey 2018). Finally, *ahimsa* as an element of conflict strategies reduces motivations for harmful reciprocity on either side of a conflict and opens up the possibility for creative conflict transformation (Kurtz 2008, 841–842).

From Structuring Violence to Structuring Nonviolence

Given the dilemmas of both the warrior and pacifist motifs—and the danger of not solving the issue of widespread violence in an age when our means of destruction are so effective—we should be re-constructing our cultural paradigms, and faith traditions, which will play a key role in that process, as they have all along.

Johan Galtung (1990) provides a crucial new paradigm for understanding violence in all its forms; his conceptual scheme, represented as a violence triangle, notes the distinction among three interrelated types of violence:

1. Direct violence, which is what we usually think of as violence—explicit, usually physical attacks;
2. Structural violence, which is the harm done to people by social structures, such as a food distribution system that results in millions of child deaths from malnutrition and related causes every year; and
3. Cultural violence, that is, the cultural themes such as ethnocentrism, homophobia, sexism, and racism that demean groups of people and make them vulnerable to both structural and direct violence.

To these three, I have added ecoviolence, that is, violence against the environment, which has become more significant since Galtung's 1990 article (see Figure 16.1).

The annual death of millions of children by malnutrition and related causes is just as harmful to those children and their families as direct violence, but it is hidden from our view and often subtly—or overtly—legitimated by cultural violence that essentially renders the lives of poor, nonwhite children "less valuable" than white, privileged children. As Kathleen Maas Weigert (2008) puts it in her lucid explanation of Galtung's concept, structural violence refers to preventable harm or damage to persons (and by extension to things) where there is no actor committing the violence or where it is not practical to search for the actor(s); such violence emerges from the unequal distribution of power and resources or, in other words, is said to be built into the structure(s).

These different kinds of violence, according to Galtung (1990, 292), result largely from the failure to meet various types of human needs: survival, wellbeing, identity, and freedom. Galtung has suggested that Gandhi is to conflict what Einstein and Newton are to physics. That is, he has helped us to reconceptualize the means of conflict and recognize the possibility of nonviolent conflict and means of social change and human development. We believe that "nonviolence is

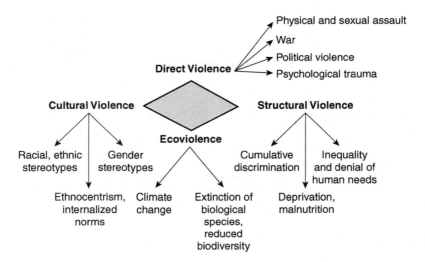

FIGURE 16.1 The Violence Diamond: Expanding Galtung's Triangle

Source: Galtung (1990), adapted in Kurtz (2015)

as much about 'processes' as it is about the 'outcomes' of human action and social order" (Mack and Kurtz 2017).

When we invert Galtung's triangle, with the addition of ecoviolence, we derive four types of nonviolence that give us a much broader picture of nonviolence than is usually called upon for bringing about social change, and one that more approximates the Kingian nonviolence that we are trying to elaborate: direct, cultural, and structural nonviolence, as well as eco-nonviolence (Mack and Kurtz 2017; see Figure 16.2).[5] Moreover, with this conceptual reframing of nonviolence, we can see its multiple dimensions and develop a more comprehensive understanding of how nonviolence can be constructed socially in the same way as violence has been.

As Camilleri notes elsewhere in this volume, the "advocacy of non-violence has been far more articulate when diagnosing and resisting evil than when propounding an alternative to ailing institutions and faltering policies and practices." To begin that task is the goal of this re-framing of Galtung's understanding of violence. To structure nonviolence, we need to develop not only direct action—or civil resistance—as one aspect of nonviolence, but also to find ways of cultivating structural and cultural nonviolence, as well as eco-nonviolence (see Figure 16.2).

The faith traditions will play a key role in the transformation from a culture of violence to a culture of peace; promoting cultural nonviolent themes; sponsoring rituals that cut across social, economic, and religious divisions; and promoting justice, peaceful societies, and just economic systems. Much of the creation of a

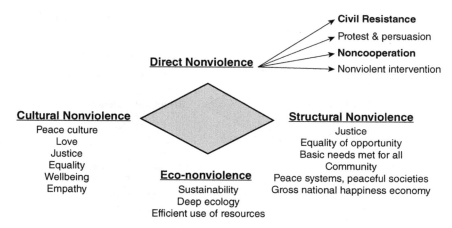

FIGURE 16.2 The Nonviolence Diamond

nonviolent society is cultural work that is the realm of religious beliefs, rituals, and institutions. No other social organizations have the same reach, from the micro level of interpersonal interactions and family life, to broader community, national, and global level impacts. In addition to mitigating direct violence in many dimensions, from the family and congregational level to global institutions, the faith traditions could play a major role in constructing nonviolence, just as they have often cultivated violence.

The cultural values undergirding a nonviolent social order such as love, justice, empathy, and peace (see Boulding 2008) are universally and explicitly preached by faith traditions on a scale and scope of no other social sphere, with the possible exception of educational institutions, which are not explicitly organized around the promotion of such values. The structural prerequisites of nonviolence have long been a priority for many (although admittedly not all) religious institutions, not only in their social work, but in advocating public and political policies that care for the poor and disadvantaged. Finally, direct nonviolence has been sustained and sponsored by people of faith and also by religious institutions, which are the most common place for recruitment of nonviolent activists along with educational institutions and labor organizations (see, e.g., Chatfield 1999). Nonviolent direct action from a faith perspective provides an alternative to terrorism as a way of confronting injustice without violence that turns humans into objects, denying the purposeful tie of humans to the Divine (see Satha-Anand's recounting of Muslim nonviolent freedom fighter Abdul Gaffar Khan, Chapter 12).

Nonviolence has been a mainstay of human social organization, values, and behavior throughout the centuries, often less visible than the violence that appears in the news precisely because violence is a violation of the normal and thus more "newsworthy." If we listen to the overwhelming message of compassion in Buddhism, of justice in Judaism, and love in Christianity, we can have the active peacemaking Jalabi suggests makes someone a Muslim. The paths of nonviolence converge in the spiritual teaching of all of these faith traditions when we listen beyond the drums of war. If we were to address the construction of nonviolence with the same commitment of human and material resources as we have the structures of violence, we might see a shift in the organization of life on the planet and an increase in the happiness and wellbeing of its inhabitants. Such a transformation is as much a spiritual as a political or economic task.

So, where do we go from here? Dr. King (1967) asks this in his final book, before his assassination. Will it be "chaos or community?" What emphasizes and energizes one motif or another, Firestone asks in her discussion of Judaism, noting the historical trauma in the Jewish tradition and its unhealed wounds. She quotes the poet W.H. Auden, "Those to whom evil is done/Do evil in return." Galtung (1997, 201) asks if it is possible for a civilization to undergo some sort of collective therapy similar to individual therapy in order to overcome its traumatic experiences; but warns that the precondition for any therapy is to know one's self, linking violence to the problem of chosenness, just as Firestone does (cf. Firestone 2008 and Erikson 1966).

The faith traditions all have a strong thread of self-criticism, confession, and self-awareness woven into their system-supporting roles in society. It is precisely because they are—like Simmel's "stranger" (1972)—simultaneously near to and remote from centers of power that they have the potential to bring about a transformation to a peaceful society in which nonviolence is constructed as deliberately as violence has been in human history.

Notes

1 I am grateful to Egon Spiegel for extensive comments and suggestions to improve this chapter.
2 I am avoiding the scholarly debate (see, e.g., Grabbe 2017) about whether or not a group of Israelites was actually enslaved in Egypt and led out by Moses in an empirically demonstrable event. What is important here is that it has been a significant narrative in the Judeo-Christian-Islamic tradition, used to justify the use of violence over the centuries.
3 Please see my discussion in Kurtz (1988, 223–225), from which the following section draws heavily.
4 Personal communication, 10 August, 2017.
5 The following discussion draws from a paper by Johnny J. Mack and myself prepared for the American Sociological Association (Mack and Kurtz 2017), which brings together his more detailed work on a Kingian approach to nonviolence and my own work in a similar direction. The diagram is from my class lectures at George Mason University, and he has a much more elaborate and sophisticated version in his doctoral dissertation (Mack 2013).

References

Abdel-Ati, Ḥammūdah. *Al-Jihad (Holy War) in Islam*. Bolgar, Indonesia: al-Azhar Press, 1963.
Arendt, Hannah. *On Violence*. Orlando: Houghton Mifflin Harcourt, 1970.
Arendt, Hannah. "Reflections on Violence," *New York Review of Books*, July 11, 2013. Available online at http://www.nybooks.com/articles/archives/2013/jul/11/hannah-arendt-reflections-violence/
Ashoka, "King Ashoka His Edicts and His Times," translated by Ven. S. Dhammika Kanda. Sri Lanka: Buddhist Publication Society, 1993. Available online at www.cs.colostate.edu/~malaiya/ashoka.html, 11 June 2004.
Bainton, Roland. *Christian Attitudes Toward War and Peace*. Nashville: Abingdon Press, 1960.
Bandura, Albert. "Moral Disengagement in the Perpetration of Inhumanities." *Personality and Social Psychology Review* 3, no. 3 (1999): 193–209.
Bell, Nance. "Power, Alternative Theories of." In *The Encyclopedia of Violence, Peace, & Conflict*, 2nd edn., edited by Lester Kurtz. Amsterdam: Elsevier, 2008, pp. 1703–1709.
Bondurant, J. V. *Conquest of Violence: The Gandhian Philosophy of Conflict*. Princeton, NJ: Princeton University Press, 1958.
Bonney, Richard. *Jihad: From Qur'an to Bin Laden*. New York: Palgrave Macmillan, 2004.
Boulding, Elise. "Peace Culture." In *Encyclopedia of Violence, Peace, and Conflict*, edited by Lester R. Kurtz. Amsterdam: Elsevier, 2008, pp. 1452–1465.
Buddha. *Buddhist Scriptures*, trans. Edward Conze. London: Penguin, 1959.
Chatfield, Charles. *Peace Movements in America*. New York: Schocken Books, 1973.
Chatfield, Charles. "Nonviolent Social Movements in the United States." In *Nonviolent Social Movements*, edited by Stephen Zunes, Lester Kurtz & Sarah Beth Asher. Maiden: Blackwell, 1999, pp. 283–301.
Chatterjee, Margaret. "Gandhi and the Critique of Civil society." In *Subtaltern Studies III*, edited by R. Guha, 153–195. New Delhi: Oxford University Press, 1984.
Cheng, Liu, and Egon Spiegel. *Peacebuilding in a Globalized World: An Illustrated Introduction to Peace Studies*, 1st edn. Beijing: People's Publishing House, 2015.
Durant, Will. *The Story of Civilization IV: The Age of Faith*. New York: Simon and Schuster, 1950, pp. 582ff. https://archive.org/stream/TheStoryOfCivilizationcomplete/Durant_Will_-_The_story_of_civilization_4#page/n9/mode/2up
Edmunds, Jonathan. "Spousal PTSD: Eradicating the Cycle of Violence." In *Women, War, and Violence: Topography, Resistance, and Hope [2 Volumes]*, edited by Mariam M. Kurtz and Lester R. Kurtz. Santa Barbara: Praeger, 2015, 1:367–381.
Erikson, Eric. "Ontogeny of Ritualization." In *Psychoanalysis: A General Psychology*, edited by R. M. Lowenstein, L. M. Newman, M. Schur, and A. J. Solnit. New York: International Universities Press, 1966, pp. 232–254.
Fehl, Philipp P. "Raphael as a Historian: Poetry and Historical Accuracy in the Sala Di Costantino." *Artibus et Historiae* 14, no. 28 (1993): 9–76.
Ferguson, J. *War and Peace in the World's Religions*. Oxford: Oxford University Press, 1978.
Firestone, Reuven. *Who Are the Real Chosen People? The Meaning of Chosenness in Judaism, Christianity, and Islam*. Woodstock, VT: SkyLight Paths Publishing, 2008.
Galtung, Johan. "Cultural Violence." *Journal of Peace Research* 27, no. 3 (1990): 291–305.
Galtung, Johan. "Is There a Therapy for Pathological Cosmologies?" In *The Web of Violence: From Interpersonal to Global*, edited by Jennifer Turpin and Lester R. Kurtz. Urbana: University of Illinois Press, 1997, pp. 187–206.

Gandhi, M. K. *The Mind of Mahatma Gandhi*, ed. R. K. Prabhu and U. R. Rao. Ahmedabad: Navajivan Press, 1967.

Geertz, Clifford. *The Interpretation of Cultures: Selected Essays*. New York: Basic Books, 1973.

Girard, René. *Violence and the Sacred*. Baltimore: John Hopkins University Press, 1977.

Goffman, Erving. *Frame Analysis: An Essay on the Organization of Experience*. Cambridge, MA: Harvard University Press, 1974.

Goran, Kelly, and Lester R. Kurtz. "Love Your Enemies? Mainline Protestantism and U.S. Foreign Policy." In *The Quiet Hand of God*, edited by Robert Wuthnow and John Evan. Berkeley: University of California Press, 2003.

Grabbe, Lester L. *Ancient Israel: What Do We Know and How Do We Know It?*, rev. edn. Bloomsbury Publishing, 2017.

Grossman, Dave, and Bruce Siddle. "Psychological Effects of Combat." In *Encyclopedia of Violence, Peace and Conflict*, 2nd edn., edited by Lester R. Kurtz. Amsterdam: Elsevier, 2008, pp. 1796–1805.

Hale, J.R. "International Relations in the West: Diplomacy and War." In *The New Cambridge Modern History Volume I: The Renaissance 1493-1520*, edited by Denys Hays, 259–91. Cambridge: Cambridge University Press, 1957. https://archive.org/stream/iB_CMH/01_djvu.txt.

Hays, Richard B. *Moral Vision of the New Testament: A Contemporary Introduction to New Testament Ethics*. Edinburgh: T & T Clark, 1996.

Johnson, James Turner. *Holy War Idea in Western and Islamic Traditions*. University Park, PA: Pennsylvania State University Press, 2010.

Johnson, James Turner. *Just War Tradition and the Restraint of War: A Moral and Historical Inquiry*. Princeton, NJ: Princeton University Press, 2014.

Juergensmeyer, Mark. *Terror in the Mind of God: The Global Rise of Religious Violence*. Berkeley, CA: University of California Press, 2003.

King, Martin Luther. *Where Do We Go from Here: Chaos or Community?* Boston: Beacon Press, 1967. Accessed 3 March 2018 http://kingencyclopedia.stanford.edu/encyclopedia/documentsentry/where_do_we_go_from_here_delivered_at_the_11th_annual_sclc_convention/index.html.

Kurtz, Lester R. "Fighting Violence against Women: A Toolkit." In *Women, War, and Violence: Topography, Resistance, and Hope*, edited by Mariam M. Kurtz and Lester R. Kurtz. Santa Barbara, CA: Praeger, 2015, 2:555–591.

Kurtz, Lester R. "Freedom and Domination: The Garden of Eden and the Social Order." *Social Forces* 58 (December, 1979): 443–464.

Kurtz, Lester R., ed. *The Encyclopedia of Violence, Peace, and Conflict*, 2nd edn. 3 volumes. Amsterdam: Elsevier, 2008.

Kurtz, Lester R. "Gandhi and His Legacies." In *Encyclopedia of Violence, Peace, and Conflict*, edited by Lester R. Kurtz. Amsterdam: Elsevier, 2008.

Kurtz, Lester R. *Gods in the Global Village: The World's Religions in Sociological Perspective*, 4th edn. Thousand Oaks, CA: Sage, 2016.

Kurtz, Lester R. *The Nuclear Cage: A Sociology of the Arms Race*. Englewood Cliffs, NJ: Prentice Hall, 1988.

Kurtz, Lester R., and Mariam R. Kurtz. "Solving the Qur'anic Paradox." *Ahimsa Nonviolence* 1 (July–August 2005): 350–358.

Lao Tzu. "Tao de Ching," translated by Stephen Mitchell. New York: HarperPerennial, 1988.

"Love Your Enemies: Selections from the World's Scriptures." http://origin.org/ucs/ws/theme144.cfm, 31 May 2003.

Luard, Evan. *War in International Society: A Study in International Sociology*. London: I.B. Tauris, 1986.

Mack, Johnny J. "A Discourse on Nonviolence as a Theory of Change for Peace and Conflict." PhD Thesis, George Mason University School for Conflict Analysis and Resolution, 2014.

Mack, Johnny, and Lester R. Kurtz. "Rethinking Nonviolence," with American Sociological Association, Montréal, Canada, August, 2017. file:///Users/lesterkurtz/Downloads/asa17_proceeding_1255461.pdf.

MacNair, Rachel. *Perpetration-Induced Traumatic Stress: The Psychological Consequences of Killing*. Psychological Dimensions to War and Peace. London; Westport, CO: Praeger, 2002.

MacNair, Rachel. "The Psychology of Agents of Repression: The Paradox of Defection." In *The Paradox of Repression and Its Management*, edited by Lester R. Kurtz and Lee Smithey. Syracuse, NY: Syracuse University Press, 2018, pp. 74–101.

Merton, Thomas. *Faith and Violence: Christian Teaching and Christian Practice*. Notre Dame, IN: University of Notre Dame Press, 1968.

Mills, C. Wright. *The Sociological Imagination*. Oxford: Oxford University Press, 2000 [1959].

Mo Tzu. "Mo Tzu's Doctrines of Universal Love, and Social Welfare." In *A Sourcebook of Chinese Philosophy*, ed. Wing-Tsit Chan. Princeton, NJ: Princeton University Press, 1963, pp. 211–217.

Nagler, Michael N. *The Search for a Nonviolent Future: A Promise of Peace for Ourselves, Our Families, and Our World*. Rev. and updated. Maui, HI: Inner Ocean Pub, 2004.

National Conference of Catholic Bishops. *The Challenge of Peace*. Washington, DC: NCCB. http://www.usccb.org/upload/challenge-peace-gods-promise-our-response-1983.pdf.

Nhat Hanh, Thich. *For a Future to Be Possible: Buddhist Ethics for Everyday Life*. Revised edition. Berkeley, CA: Parallax Press, 2007.

Orwell, George. "Pacifism and the War." *Partisan Review* 9 (August-September 1942): 419–25. Accessed March 3, 2018. http://www.orwell.ru/library/articles/pacifism/english/e_patw.

Paul VI, Pope. Pastoral Constitution on the Church in the Modern World, Gaudium et Spes. Accessed 3 March 2018 http://www.vatican.va/archive/hist_councils/ii_vatican_council/documents/vat-ii_const_19651207_gaudium-et-spes_en.html

Philips, Stephen. "Ahimsa." In *Encyclopedia of Violence, Peace and Conflict*, edited by Lester R. Kurtz. Amsterdam: Elsevier, 2008.

Pope Francis. "Nonviolence: A Style of Politics for Peace." January 1, 2017. https://w2.vatican.va/content/francesco/en/messages/peace/documents/papa-francesco_20161208_messaggio-l-giornata-mondiale-pace-2017.html

Prabhupāda, A. C. Bhaktivedanta Swami. *Bhagavad-gītā as It Is: With Original Sanskrit Text, Roman Transliteration, English Equivalents, Translation and Elaborate Purports*. New York: Macmillan, 1972.

The Qur'an (selections).

Rabia Terri. "Nonviolence in Islam: The Alternative Community Tradition." In *Subverting Hatred*, edited by Daniel L. Smith-Christopher. New York: Orbis Books, 2000, pp. 95–114.

Ramsey, Paul. *The Just War: Force and Political Responsibility*. Rowman & Littlefield, 2002.

Ramsey, Paul. *Speak Up for Just War or Pacifism: A Critique of the United Methodist Bishops' Pastoral Letter in Defense of Creation*. Pennsylvania State University Press, 2010.

Rubenstein, Richard E. *Reasons to Kill: Why Americans Choose War*. London: Bloomsbury Publishing, 2010.
Severus, Sulpitius. "Life of St. Martin." In *A Select Library of Nicene and Post-Nicene Fathers of the Christian Church, Second Series*, edited by Philip Schaff and Henry Wace, translated by Alexander Roberts, Vol. 11. New York: Charles Scribner's Sons, 1894. www.users.csbsju.edu/~eknuth/npnf2-11/sulpitiu/lifeofst.html.
Severus, Sulpitius. *The Works of Sulpitius Severus*, edited by Philip S. Schaff and Henry Wallace, translated by Alexander Roberts. New York: Cosimo, Inc., 2007.
Sharp, Gene. "The Methods of Nonviolent Action." From *The Politics of Nonviolent Action*. Vol. 2. Boston: Porter Sargent, 1974.
Sharp, Gene. *Waging Nonviolent Struggle*. Boston: Porter-Sargent, 2005.
Simmel, Georg. *On Individuality and Social Forms: Selected Writings*, edited by Donald Nathan Levine. Chicago: University of Chicago Press, 1971.
Spiegel, Egon. *Gewaltverzicht: Grundlagen einer biblischen Friedenstheologie*, 2nd edn. Kassel: WeZuCo, 1989.
Subramuniyaswami, Satguru Sivaya. "Sacred Texts Speak on Ahimsa." www.himalayanacademy.com/books/pamphlets/AhimsaNonViolence.html 27 May 2004
Telonidis, Taki. "In Sweat Lodge, Vets Find Healing 'Down To The Core.'" *NPR.org*, 28 May 2012. Accessed July 13, 2017. www.npr.org/2012/05/28/153875444/in-sweat-lodge-vets-find-healing-down-to-the-core.
Turner, Victor. *The Ritual Process*. Chicago: Aldine, 1969.
The United Methodist Council of Bishops. *In Defense of Creation*. Nashville: Graded Press, 1986.
Urban II, Pope. "Speech at Council of Clermont, 1095: Five Versions of the Speech". https://sourcebooks.fordham.edu/source/urban2-5vers.html.
Walzer, Michael. *Just and Unjust Wars: A Moral Argument with Historical Illustrations*. New York: Basic Books, 1977.
Weber, Max. *The Protestant Ethic and the Spirit of Capitalism*, translated by Talcott Parsons. New York: Free Press, 1958.
Weber, Max. *Economy and Society*. 2 vols. New York: Bedminster Press, 1968.
Weigert, Kathleen M. "Structural Violence." In *Encyclopedia of Violence, Peace, & Conflict*, 2nd edn., edited by Lester R. Kurtz. Amsterdam: Elsevier, 2008, pp. 2004–2011.
Williams, John Alden. *Themes of Islamic Civilization*. Berkeley: University of California Press, 1971.

INDEX

Note: figures are denoted with *italicized* page numbers; tables are denoted with **bold** page numbers.

Abouhalima, Mahmoud 226
active nonviolence: Christian 162–7, 177–8, 323, 327; Engaged Buddhist 53; interfaith initiatives using 295, 299, 302–5, 315, 322–7; Islamic 208–14, 229–37, 245; rethinking religion and violence with 2, 3, 4, 6, 8–9; terrorism transformation with 229–37
active peacemaking 196–9, 201, 203–4, 208–14, 244–5, 327
Age of Transition: Christianity in 170, 171, *172*, 173–9, 185–90; global context for religion in 169–70; Islam in 169–70, 171, *172*, 179–90; religious domain interpretation in 170–1; vision of human future in 185–90
ahiṃsā 24–5, 26, 31, 299, 302, 309, 312, 322–4
al-Islambouli, Khalid 222
Amalek/Amalekites 72–3, 94, 124
Ambedkar, Bhimrao Ramji 39–40
Amiel, Moshe 95
anger: Buddhist stance on 45, 46; Christian New Testament on 136, 137, 144–5, 151; compassion as response to 46, 204
Aquinas, Thomas 155, 176
Arab Spring 210–11, 254–5
Arjuna 309–10
Ashoka 26, 298
ash-Shawkaanee 223

atheists and agnostics 100, 159n20, 170
atonement: Christian views on 146–9, 174; Yom Kippur as Day of Atonement 123
Augustine, Saint 153, 154–5, 175–6, 308
Aung San Su Kyi 41, 53
Awakening Leadership Program 63
awareness, Buddhist stance on 46

bakesh shalom v' rodfehu 78–80
Bangladesh: Engaged Buddhism in 59
Bartholomew, Patriarch 189
Begin, Menachem 90
Ben-Gurion, David 101
Bennett, Naftali 95
Berrigan, Daniel 49
Bible: Christian 135–52, 171, 173–4; Jewish/Hebrew 93–4, 301, 305–7
bin Laden, Osama 221
Brazil: evangelical Christianity 170
Brit Shalom (Covenant of Peace) 92
Buber, Martin 92, 104, 105, 117, 128
Buddha: ethics for enlightenment practiced by 38, 46; foundational teachings of 43–4, 46, 47; interdependence awareness of 43, 51; karma realization by 57–8; Middle Way path discovery by 57; political and royal history of 22; violence allowances by 4; violence condemnation and nonviolence advocacy by 4, 25, 57–8, 64–5

Buddhadasa 41
Buddhism: *ahiṃsā* in 24–5, 26, 31, 312; comparative ethics and 17–20, 212–14; compartmentalization of values in 30–1; compassionate killing in 19; compassion in 19, 20–1, 31, 36, 43, 44, 46, 60, 64–5, 312, 313, 327; conflict approach in 16; degeneration theory on 17, 28, 32; diversity in 18; early history of 26–7; Engaged 4–5, 36–55, 57–65; ethical particularism in 18, 30–1; ethics of 17–20, 24, 29–32, 32n6, 38, 46, 212–14; Five Precepts of 46–7, 58, 312; foundational teachings of 42–8, 57–8; Four Noble Truths of 43–4; global context for 170; interdependence in 38, 43, 45–6, 49, 50–1, 53; interfaith initiatives with 47, 58–9, 61–3, 266, 272, 278–9; *jus in bello* ideals in 17, 26; just-war ideology in 14, 16–22, 27–8, 31; karmic consequences in 25–6, 57–8; killing stance in 19, 24–6, 27–8, 46–7, 312–13; *Mahāvaṃsa* use in 27–8, 29; meditation in 37–8, 40–1, 43, 44, 49–50, 54, 63, 312; merit ideals in 23–4; Middle Way Path in 57; militarism in 14, 20–2; mindfulness in 44, 45, 46, 63; Noble Eightfold Path in 44, 312; nonviolence tenets of 16, 24, 25, 26, 28–30, 31, 36, 47, 53, 54, 57, 60, 64–5, 177, 311–13, 327; number of followers of 37; pacifism associated with 14–15, 16, 24–5, 26, 28–30, 31, 302, 311–13; Pāli canon in 16–17, 22–6, 31–2; peace associated with 15–6, 36, 44, 46, 49–50, 54, 57, 58–63; political activism and paradigms in 13–14, 15–7, 22–7, 30–2, 268, 269, 271; proportionality of force in 312; royal ideology in 22–4; social engagement and 4–5, 36–55, 57–65; Three Poisons or Afflictions in 44–6; two wheels theory applied in 23, 27; utilitarianism in 20; violence advocacy and allowances in 4, 13–32, 39, 242, 268, 269, 271, 312–13
Buddhist Peace Fellowship, US 50, 59
Burma/Myanmar: Engaged Buddhism in 41, 51, 53, 59; Saffron Revolution in 53; violence in 55, 242

Cambodia: Engaged Buddhism in 59–60; violence in 54
capital punishment 147–9, 158–9n17, 159nn19–20

cherem 71–3
China: Christianity in 170; Engaged Buddhism in 51
chosenness 69, 72, 83, 118, 143,
Christianity: Age of Transition for 170, 171, *172*, 173–9, 185–90; Anabaptist distinction in 141–2, 157n6; anger in 136, 137, 144–5, 151; atonement in 146–9, 174; Bible as sacred text of 135–52, 171, 173–4; capital punishment views in 147–9, 158–9n17, 159nn19–20; comparative Buddhist ethics *vs*. 17, 19; Crusades in name of 155, 176, 302, 307–9; discriminate use of violence in 144–6, 156, 319–20; ethics of 171; evangelical 170, 272; fusion of religion and state with 188; global context for 170; interfaith initiatives with 266, 272, 275, 286–7, 289, 294; Islam comparison with 6, 170–90, *172*; just-war doctrine in 5, 135, 139–52, 154–7, 174–7, 178, 302, 308–9, 315, 318–20; killing taboos in 173, 314; military service views in 135, 138, 139–41, 151, 153, 314; motive for violence in 144–6, 151, 154–5, 156; nationalism views in 142–3, 158n9; New Testament as moral authority for 135–52; nonviolence embraced in 5–6, 135–9, 162–7, 174, 177–8, 314–15, 323, 327; number of followers of 171, *172*; pacifists in 5, 135–9, 152–3, 158nn8–9, 173, 174, 302, 314–15, 323; peace goals in 5, 135, 152, 154, 156, 162–7, 173, 177–9, 185; political context for 138–9, 162–7, 185, 187–90; practical application of vision in 187–90; proportionate use of force in 144–6, 156, 175, 176, 319; religious institutions in 187; research methodology for analysis of 149–52; retribution and vengeance in 141–2, 144, 145–6, 154, 156; self-interested advocacy in 188–9; separation of church and state with 188; soldier narratives in 139–40; suffering views in 146, 158n14, 163; supremacy over other faiths assumed in 189; violence and war engagement in 5, 135, 139–59, 163, 173–7, 178, 185–6, 242, 302, 307–9, 319–20; vision of human future in 185–90; war and peace intertwinement in 5, 135–59, 173–9, 185–6
Chungprampree, Somboon 60

civil rights movement: Jewish participation in 77–8; nonviolent activism in 3, 9, 164, 177, 245, 295, 315
collaborative actions, Islamic value of 248–9
colonialism: Buddhist social engagement against 37, 41, 47; interreligious dialogue on 296; legacy of, in Arab countries 256; nonviolence and peace viewed as passivity under 7; nonviolent activism against 8, 231–2, 235, 236; terrorism in response to 219–20
compassion: Buddhist stance on 19, 20–1, 31, 36, 43, 44, 46, 60, 64–5, 312, 313, 327; Christian views of 186; compassionate killing 19; Engaged Buddhism goals for 36, 43, 44, 46; Islamic stance on 180, 186, 204, 212–13; Purity of Arms honor code on 105
Compassionate Council 270, 280
conflict: Buddhist approach to 16; interfaith initiatives addressing 61–2; Islamic conflict resolution 244, 250–1; nonviolent activism as creative resolution of 323–4; religion and 2–3, 302–5; sacred 3
Congress of Religious 275
conquest and extermination, Jewish 71–3
Constantine 307–8
Conviviencia 286
corruption: interfaith initiatives affected by 268; Islam on 202, 255
Covenant of Madinah 253
Crusades 155, 176, 302, 307–9
Curle, Adam 295–296

Dalai Lama 37, 48–9, 59, 245
Day, Dorothy 9, 177
death, views of 224, 232–3; *see also* killing taboos
debate, dialogue *vs.* **285**, 285–6
Decade to Overcome Violence: Churches Seeking Reconciliation and Peace 2001–2010 179
degeneration theory 17, 28, 32
deliberative ethics 115–17
delusion or ignorance, Buddhist stance on 45–6
Dhammapada 64–5
dialogue: *definition of,* 284; *debate versus,* 285; *types of interreligious,* 286; *preconditions,* 287; *organizing steps,* 288; *structuring,* 290
Dicastery for Promoting Integral Human Development 166–7

dignity *see* human dignity
discrimination and oppression: Buddhist participation in 55; Buddhist social engagement against 37, 50; civil rights movement opposing 3, 9, 77–8, 164, 177, 245, 295, 315; Islamic opposition to 181, 186, 249–51; Islamophobia as 7, 55, 243–4, 269; Jewish experience of 69, 81–3, 87, 96; Jewish initiation of 91–2, 97; Programme to Combat Racism on 179; terrorism fighting 220
diversity: Buddhist 18; interreligious dialogue exploring **293**, 293–4; Islamic value of 249–51
double effect doctrine 150, 151

Eban, Abba 96
Eckhart, Meister 177
Egypt: Arab Spring in 254–5; Israeli relations with 90; Jewish people in 71, 73, 80, 301–2, 306, 327n2; Sadat assassination in 222–3
Engaged Buddhism: changing Asia and evolution of 39–43; Dalai Lama practicing 37, 48–9, 59; ethics of 38, 46; exemplars of 48–54, 57; Five Precepts of 46–7, 58; foundational Buddhist teachings applied in 42–8, 57–8; Four Noble Truths of 43–4; Nichidatsu Fujii practicing 53–4; Maha Ghosananda practicing 57, 59–60; Thich Nhat Hanh practicing 36, 46, 47, 49–50, 51, 59; interdependence in 38, 43, 45–6, 49, 50–1, 53; interfaith initiatives in 47, 58–9, 61–3; International Network of Engaged Buddhists espousing 4–5, 41, 51–2, 57, 59, 60–3; killing taboos in 46–7; Joanna Macy practicing 37, 50; meditation in 38, 40–1, 43, 44, 49–50, 54, 63; mindfulness in 44, 45, 46, 63; Nipponzan Myohoji practicing 53–4; Noble Eightfold Path in 44; nonviolence goals in 36, 47, 53, 54, 57, 60; overview of 36, 57–8; peace goals in 36, 44, 46, 49–50, 54, 57, 58–63; shadows and challenges for 54–5; Sulak Sivaraksa practicing 41, 46, 47, 51–2, 57, 58–9; social engagement in 4–5, 36–55, 57–65; Three Poisons or Afflictions in 44–6; traditional Buddhism *vs.* 36–8
environmental issues: Buddhist social engagement on 42, 43, 47, 50–1, 52; eco-nonviolence and 325, *326*; ecoviolence and 324, *325*

ethical theory: Buddhist 17–20, 24, 29–32, 32n6, 38, 46, 212–14; Christian 171; deliberative ethics and 115–17; ethical particularism as 18, 30–1; Islamic 171, 212–14; Jewish 5, 95, 105–30; professional ethics and 120; Purity of Arms honor code reflecting 5, 105–30; secular ethics and 48–9; self-other relationship in 123–5, 127; social engagement and 38; utilitarian 20, 118; virtue ethics and 29, 117–18, 274; *see also* moral theory
extermination *see* conquest and extermination; killing taboos

facilitation 289, 297
false speech, Buddhist stance on 47, 61
families: conflict in 3; Islamic valuing of 180; nonviolence in 165–6; religious institutions supporting 305
Faraj, Muhammad'Abd al-Salam 222, 225–6
Fellowship of Reconciliation, US 50
France: atheists and agnostics in 170; Christianity in 308; terrorism and terrorism response in 218
Francis, Pope 162–7, 178, 189, 190, 315, 323
Francis of Assisi 177
Froman, Menachem 97
Fujii, Nichidatsu 53–4

Galtung, Johan 15
Gandhi, Mohandas: on death acceptance 232; Fujii's ties to 54; interreligious dialogue support of 296; nonviolent activism by 2, 3, 4, 8, 164, 177, 203, 208, 245, 299, 302, 315, 322–4; terrorism response of 219; on dialogue, 296
Gbowee, Leymah 164
gender issues: Buddhist social engagement on 47, 50; Islamic stance on 205, 209, 255; *see also* women
generosity, Buddhist stance on 46, 47
Ghosananda, Maha 57, 59–60
Goenka, S.M. 40–1
Gopin, Marc 100
greed, Buddhist stance on 44–5, 46

Hamas 91, 124, 216, 227–8, 233–4
Hanh, Thich Nhat 36, 46, 47, 49–50, 51, 59, 177, 313
Hays, Richard 135–49, 151–2, 153, 157nn2–5, 158nn8–9

Hillel the Elder 78–9, 116
Hinduism: caste system in 39–40; comparative Buddhist ethics *vs.* 19; interfaith initiatives with 266, 289, 296; manuals of law/statecraft in 19, 24; nationalism in 242; nonviolence and nonviolent activism in 235, 312; violence engagement in 242, 309–10
Hindustan Socialist Revolutionary Army (HSRA) 219
historical trauma, 69, 81–83, 327
Holy War 73, 135, 155, 180; *see also* Crusades; *jihad*
human dignity: Buddhism on 40, 62; Christianity on 146, 162, 164; Islam on 62; Judaism on 77, 80, 126, 130n7; Purity of Arms honor code on 105, 106, 107, 108, 111–12, 126, 127
humanity: dehumanization of 220, 235–7, 311; Islam on malaise of 201–6; nonviolent service to 235; Purity of Arms honor code on 118, 121, 123–5, 128; universality of, in the Qur'an 201
human life: sacredness of, in Islam 246–8; saving of, as Jewish tenet 76–7, 116; taboo on taking of (*see* killing taboos)
human rights: Buddhist social activism for 37; *imago Dei* foundation of 77; interfaith initiatives addressing 8, 277–8; Jewish commitment to 77–8, 99, 100; killing taboos as foundation of 5; Purity of Arms honor code foundation of 126; Sri Lankan civil war impacting 267, 269–70

Ibn Al-Uthaymeen 223–4
Ibn Baaz, Abdul Azeez 221–3, 225
Ibn Taymiyyah 223, 224
Ilouz, Eva 100–1
imago Dei or image of God 77–8, 162
inclusiveness, Engaged Buddhist goal of 51
India: Ashoka as emperor of 26, 298; caste system in 39–40; conflict in 3; Engaged Buddhism in 39–41, 51; Hinduism in 39–40; Islam in 39; nonviolent activism in 2, 3, 4, 8, 164, 177, 231–2; politics and statecraft in 27, 30; terrorism in 219–20, 235
injustice: Buddhist social engagement against 37, 44, 47; Christian views of remedying 142, 144, 152, 154, 164–5; nonviolence fighting 8–9, 164–5, 231–2, 299; terrorism fighting 7–8, 220, 228, 231–2

interfaith initiatives: Buddhists in 47, 58–9, 61–3, 266, 272, 278–9; Christians in 266, 272, 275, 286–7, 289, 294; interreligious dialogue as 8, 284–97; Jews in 92, 97, 287, 289; Muslims in 5, 61–2, 266, 278–9, 286–7, 289, 294, 296; peacebuilding as 8, 59, 265–82, 297; political context for 265–75; in Sri Lanka 8, 265–82

intergenerational trauma *see* historical trauma

International Forum on Buddhist-Muslim Relations 5, 61–2

international law: Islam and 184, 185; Purity of Arms honor code and 107, 113–14, 125, 126–7

International Network of Engaged Buddhists (INEB): Awakening Leadership Program 63; founding of 41, 59; INEB Institute of 62–3; peace initiatives of 57, 59, 60–3; Sivaraksa's ties to 51–2; tenets of 4–5, 51, 60–1

interreligious dialogue: action planning and exploration in **294**, 294–6; caucuses in 293–4; common intentions and norms established in 290–1, **292**; debate *vs.* **285**, 285–6; definition and description of 284–6; differences and commonalties explored in **293**, 293–4; experiences and perceptions shared in 291–3; facilitation of 289, 290–5; geography-based 286; group agreements for 291, **292**; history-based 286–7; intra-religious dialogue as 286; invitations to 289; nonviolent activism encouraging 295, **296**; organizing of 288–90; overview of 8, 284; peacebuilding via 297; preconditions of 287–8; scheduling of 289–90; scriptural reasoning-based 286, 287; setting or venue for 289; social change and 295–7, **296**; spiritual and cultural practices-based 286, 287; structuring or design of 288–9, 290–5; theology-based 286; types of 286–7

intoxication, Buddhist stance on 47

Islam: active peacemaking in 196–9, 201, 203–4, 208–14, 244–5, 327; Age of Transition for 169–70, 171, *172*, 179–90; attachments in 200–1; Christianity comparison with 6, 170–90, *172*; collaborative actions and solidarity in 248–9; comparative Buddhist ethics *vs.* 19, 212–14; creation story in 7, 201–2; current reality for nonviolence in Muslim society 253–4; death views in 224, 232–3; ethics of 171, 212–14; fundamentalist or extremist 170, 179, 243–4, 321; fusion of religion and state with 188, 255; global context for 169–70; humanity or human condition malaise in 201–6; ideal-reality gap in 254–7; interfaith initiatives with 5, 61–2, 266, 278–9, 286–7, 289, 294, 296; international law and 184, 185; Islamophobia against 7, 55, 243–4, 269; Jewish relations with 73, 88–92, 95–8, 100, 112, 127, 216, 218–19, 226–8, 229–30, 253, 287; *jihad* in 180, 181, 183, 205, 211, 224, 228, 233, 251, 317, 320–1; justice valued in 246; just-war doctrine in 181–5, 205, 320–1; killing or bloodshed stance in 202–5, 221–9, 235, 317; light concealed and sought in 200–1; limitations to use of violence in 252–3, 320–1; nationalism of 227; non-resistance narratives in 203–4, 205, 206–8; nonviolence central to 6–7, 8, 198–9, 202–11, 217, 229–37, 242–59, 321, 327; number of followers of 171, *172*; pacifists in 198, 251, 258n3; patience valued in 248; peace embraced in 6–7, 179–81, 185, 186, 195–215, 242–59, 327; pluralism and diversity valued in 249–51; political context for 7–8, 183–4, 185, 187–90, 195–6, 204–5, 206–8, 217–21, 223, 226, 229, 231, 242, 254–7; practical application of vision in 187–90, 253–4; proportionality of force in 183; Qur'an as sacred text of 171, 179–82, 183–4, 197–9, 201–8, 235, 245–51, 252; religious foundations for nonviolence in 245–51; religious institutions in 187, 255; sacredness of human life in 246–8; self-defense stance in 182–3, 204, 206, 244, 251–2; self-interested advocacy in 188–9; separation of church and state with 188; Shariah law in 179, 184–5, 198; studies of teachings of 243–5; Sunnah or Hadith in 179, 183, 184, 198, 201, 205, 245–51; supremacy over other faiths assumed in 189, 200; tensions with nonviolence in 251–2; terrorism in 7–8, 112, 179, 216–38, 242, 243–4, 321, 326; twenty-first century 199–200, 253–4; universality of humanity in 201; values supporting nonviolence in 245–51; violence and war engagement in 7–8, 112, 179–86, 199–200, 202–6, 216–38, 242–5, 251–3, 309, 317, 320–1, 326; vision of human future in 185–90; war and peace intertwinement in 179–86, 242–3, 251–2

Israel: Basic Law of Human Dignity and Freedom in 126, 130n7; Declaration of Independence of 125–6, 129–30n6; establishment as state 89; Haganah in 88; historical trauma leading to foundation of 82, 83, 87, 96; Israeli Defense Force in 5, 104–30; military services in 88–90, 91, 95–6 (*see also* Israeli Defense Force); national identity or chosenness in 81, 83, 87, 88; National Religious in 89–90, 91, 95, 96, 97; Palestinian relations with 88–92, 95–8, 102n4, 112, 124–5, 127, 226–8, 229–30, 242; peace goals in 90, 91–2, 94–95, 97, 98–101; political context of 87, 89–92, 98–101; self-defense stance in 75–6, 82, 88–9, 104–5, 111–13, 126; Temple Mount conflict in 96–7, 98; terrorism and terrorism response in 216, 218–9, 226–8; violence use in 73, 75–6, 88–92, 94–8, 104–30, 216, 218–19, 226–8, 242; war and peace intertwinement in 73, 75–6, 81, 82, 83, 87, 88–92, 94–8; West Bank settlement in 90–1, 95, 97; Zionist movement in 86–7, 88–92, 94–8, 99, 106, 112

Israeli Defense Force (IDF): authority and wisdom sources for 125–6; code of ethics for 105, 108; deliberative ethics in 115–17; dignity goals for 105, 106, 107, 108, 111–12, 126, 127; disciplinary actions in 127; ethical education for 114–22, 126–7; ethical problematics for 107–11; harm prevention goals for 107, 111, 113, 120; historical background for 106–7; honor code for 120–2; humanity in 118, 121, 123–5, 128; international law and 107, 113–14, 125, 126–7; mission statement of 105; moral judgment development in 106, 108, 110–14, 115–17, 127–8; nationalism stance in 128–9; professional ethics in 120; proportionality of force in 113, 120; Purity of Arms honor code of 5, 104–30; rule-based obedience in 114–22; self-corrective mechanisms in 122–3; self-defense stance of 104–5, 111–13, 126; self-other relationship in 123–5, 127; sensitivity and moral courage in 118; utilitarian ethics in 118; virtue ethics in 117–18

Jainism 302, 311, 312, 315
Japan: Engaged Buddhism in 42, 51, 53–4
Jayewardene, J. R. 29–30
Jesus: just-war interpretation references to 139–40, 142–3, 144–5; nationalist revolt repudiation by 142–3, 158n9; nonviolence and active nonviolence practiced by 6, 163–4, 166, 177, 323; pacifist portrayal of 5, 136–8, 158nn8–9, 173, 174, 302, 314–5, 323; violent portrayal of 173, 174
jihad 180, 181, 183, 205, 211, 224, 228, 233, 251, 317, 320–1
Jordan: Israeli relations with 90
Judaism: Ashkenazi 95, 99; *bakesh shalom v' rodfehu* in 78–80; Bible in 93–4, 301, 305–7; *cherem* in 71–3; conquest and extermination in 71–3; ethical theory in 5, 95, 105–30; God as warrior in 301–2, 305–7; historical trauma effects in 69, 81–3, 87, 96; *imago Dei* tenet in 77–8; interfaith initiatives with 92, 97, 287, 289; Israel and (*see* Israel); killing taboos in 5, 69, 76, 77, 111, 310, 317–18; *kol demama daka* in 69–70, 83–4; *La'amod al Naphsham* in 74–6; *Milchemet Mitzvah* in 73; Mizrachi 99, 100–1; in modern times 87–92; Muslim relations with 73, 88–92, 95–8, 100, 112, 127, 216, 218–19, 226–8, 229–30, 253, 287; national identity or chosenness in 69, 80–1, 83, 86–7, 88; *nekamah* in 70–1; nonviolence stance in 92, 94, 99, 327; obligatory war in 73, 94; pacifist views in 69, 80, 86, 92, 98–101, 102n8, 302; peace tenets in 69, 76–80, 86, 90, 91–2, 94–95, 97, 98–101; *pikuach nephesh* in 76–7; Purity of Arms honor code in 5, 104–30; retribution and vengeance in 70–1; saving a life tenet in 76–7, 116; self-defense in 74–6, 82, 86, 88–9, 102n2, 104–5, 111–13, 126; silence reverence in 69–70, 83–4; sources of tradition of 93–4; take no spoils taboos in 316–17; Talmud in 93, 94; tapestry or woven image of 70, 80; Torah in 93, 126, 301, 307; violence and war stance in 5, 69, 70–6, 82–3, 86, 87–98, 104–30, 216, 218–19, 226–8, 242,

301–2, 305–7, 316–18; war and peace intertwinement in 5, 69–84, 86–102, 307; Zionist movement in 86–7, 88–92, 94–8, 99, 106, 112
jus ad bellum 17, 19, 318; *see also* just-war doctrine
jus in bello 17, 19, 26, 318
justice *see* injustice; social justice
just-war doctrine: Anabaptist distinction in 141–2, 157n26; atonement and capital punishment in 146–9; Buddhist 14, 16–22, 27–8, 31; Christian 5, 135, 139–52, 154–7, 174–7, 178, 302, 308–9, 315, 318–20; criteria justifying 156, 318, 319; discriminate use of violence in 144–6, 156, 319–20; Holy War distinction from 135, 155; Islamic 181–5, 205, 320–1; research methodology for analysis of 149–52; self-other ethical dilemma with 124; soldier narratives in 139–40

Kahane, Meir 97
karma 25–6, 57–8
Katznelson, Berl 112–13
Khan, Abdul Ghaffar "Badshah" 164, 208–11, 212, 214, 231–3, 234–5, 236
Khatami, Mohamed 189
killing taboos: Buddhist stance on 19, 24–6, 27–8, 46–7, 312–13; Christian 173, 314; compassionate killing vs. 19; Islamic stance on 202–5, 221–9, 235, 317; Jewish 5, 69, 76, 77, 111, 310, 317–18; justified sacrifice vs. 310; pacifists adhering to (*see* pacifists); psychological issues due to 2, 299, 310–11; self-other relationship and 123; social boundaries and 317–18; suicide and 29, 33n17, 224–5
kindness *see* loving kindness
King, Martin Luther, Jr.: Hanh relationship with 49; interreligious dialogue support of 296; nonviolent activism by 3, 9, 164, 177, 245, 315; on dialogue 296
kol demama daka 69–70, 83–4
Kook, Avraham Yitzhak HaCohen 95
Kook, Zvi Yehudah 95
Krishna 309–10

La'amod al Naphsham 74–6
Liberia: nonviolent activism in 164
loving kindness: Buddhist tenets of 16, 23, 44, 46, 53, 60, 312; Christian views of 146–7, 154, 163–4, 165, 173, 185, 186, 327; Islamic views of 185, 186

Macy, Joanna 37, 50
Magnes, Judah 92
Maharsha (Shmuel Eideles) 80, 84n6
Mahāvaṃsa 27–8, 29
Maimonides (Moshe ben Maimon) 75
media: conflict coverage by 3; interfaith initiatives using 265; Islam portrayal in 7, 199, 244; Sri Lankan civil war coverage by 267; violence as newsworthy in 327
meditation, Buddhist 37–8, 40–1, 43, 44, 49–50, 54, 63, 312
Melchior, Michael 100
Merton, Thomas 177, 315, 323
Milchemet Mitzvah 73
mindfulness, Buddhist 44, 45, 46, 63
Moism 312
moral theory: Buddhist 17–20, 46, 51; Christian 135–52, 309; moral accounting 123; moral authority 125–6, 135–52, 281–2; moral disengagement 310, 311; Purity of Arms honor code including 106, 108, 110–4, 115–7, 127–8; *see also* ethical theory
murder taboos *see* killing taboos
Myanmar *see* Burma/Myanmar

national identity: Jewish/Israeli 69, 80–1, 83, 86–7, 88; Sri Lankan interfaith peacebuilding initiatives creating 280–1
nationalism: Buddhist 39; Christian views of 142–3, 158n9; Hindu 242; interfaith initiatives in context of 265, 268, 271–2; Islamic 227; Jewish/Israeli 96, 99, 105, 128–9; moral and immoral 105; Purity of Arms honor code on 128–9
National Peace Council (NPC) 275–81
nekamah 70–1
Netanyahu, Benjamin 97
Nipponzan Myohoji 53–4
nonviolence: active (*see* active nonviolence); Arab Spring use of 210–11, 254; Buddhist 16, 24, 25, 26, 28–30, 31, 36, 47, 53, 54, 57, 60, 64–5, 177, 311–13, 327; Christianity embracing 5–6, 135–9, 162–7, 174, 177–8, 314–15, 323, 327; collaborative actions and solidarity for 248–9; conflict and 2–3, 323–4; as creative tool of prophets 206; cultural 325–6, *326*; death acceptance with 232–3; dehumanization avoidance

with 235–7; diamond of 325–6, *326*; direct 325, 326, *326*; eco-nonviolence 325, *326*; Hindu stance on 235, 312; ideal-reality gap for 254–7; injustice fought via 8–9, 164–5, 231–2, 299; the innocents not harmed with 233–5; interreligious dialogue encouraged via 295, **296**; Islamic tenets of 6–7, 8, 198–9, 202–11, 217, 229–37, 242–59, 321, 327; Jewish stance on 92, 94, 99, 327; religion and 302–5, 311–27 (*see also specific religions*); sacredness of human life and belief in 246–8; structural 325, 326, *326*; terrorism transformation via 217, 229–37, 326; *see also* pacifists; peace
Nonviolence and Just Peace conference 189

Organisation of Islamic Cooperation 189
Oz, Amos 105, 128–9
Oz v'Shalom/Netivot Shalom 99, 100

pacifists: Buddhist 14–15, 16, 24–5, 26, 28–30, 31, 302, 311–13; Christian 5, 135–9, 152–3, 158nn8–9, 173, 174, 302, 314–15, 323; definition of 31; dilemmas for 315–16; Islamic 198, 251, 258n3; Jesus as 5, 136–8, 158nn8–9, 173, 174, 302, 314–15, 323; Judaism on 69, 80, 86, 92, 98–101, 102n8, 302; motif of 302–5, 311–16; nonviolent activists as 2, 3, 4, 6, 8–9, 299; political 31; religious support for 302–5, 311–16 (*see also specific religions*); Tokyo conference exploring 1; warriors and 298–327 (*see also* war and peace intertwinement); *see also* nonviolence; peace
patience, Islamic value of 248
Pax Christi International 178
peace: active peacemaking 196–9, 201, 203–4, 208–14, 244–5, 327; Buddhism on 15–6, 36, 44, 46, 49–50, 54, 57, 58–63; Christianity on 5, 135, 152, 154, 156, 162–7, 173, 177–9, 185; collaborative actions and solidarity for 248–9; Dhammayietra or peace walks for 60; Engaged Buddhism agenda for 36, 44, 46, 49–50, 54, 57, 58–63; ideal-reality gap for 254–7; inner, meditation and 38; interfaith initiatives for building 8, 59, 265–82, 297; interreligious dialogue for 297; Islam embracing 6–7, 179–81, 185, 186, 195–215, 242–59, 327; Judaism on 69, 76–80, 86, 90, 91–2, 94–5, 97, 98–101; justice symbiosis with 246; just peace as goal of just-war doctrine 152, 154, 156; war intertwined with 5, 69–84, 86–102, 135–59, 173–86, 242–3, 251–2, 298–327; World Day of Peace 162, 190; *see also* nonviolence; pacifists
Perpetrator-Induced Traumatic Stress (PITS) 2, 299, 310
pikuach nephesh 76–7
pluralism: Islamic value of 249–51
politics: Buddhist violence and 13–14, 15–17, 22–7, 30–2, 268, 269, 271; Christianity in context of 138–9, 162–7, 185, 187–90; colonial (*see* colonialism); conflict related to 3; fusion of religion and state in 188, 255, 271–2; interfaith initiatives in context of 265–75; Islam in context of 7–8, 183–4, 185, 187–90, 195–6, 204–5, 206–8, 217–21, 223, 226, 229, 231, 242, 254–7; Israeli 87, 89–92, 98–101; nonviolent action in response to 7, 162–7, 177–8, 209, 322–4; political pacifism 31; religion intertwinement with 188, 195–6 (*see also specific religions*); royal ideology in 22–4; separation of church and state in 188; social engagement in (*see* social engagement); terrorism as political violence 7–8, 217–21, 223, 226, 229, 231 (*see also* terrorism); two wheels theory of 23, 27
Pontifical Council for Justice and Peace 178, 189
Post-Traumatic Stress Disorder (PTSD) 2, 299, 310–11
professional ethics 120
Programme to Combat Racism 179
proportionality of force: Buddhist 312; Christian 144–6, 156, 175, 176, 319; Islamic 183; Israeli 113, 120
psychological issues: Buddhist ethics reflecting 17, 32n6; Buddhist insight into 42; conflicts due to 3, 16; Jewish historical trauma affecting 81–3, 87; killing taboos affecting 2, 299, 310–11; nonviolent activism using 323–4
Purity of Arms honor code: authority and wisdom sources for 125–6; civilian warnings and flight opportunities in 114; code of ethics underlying 105, 108; deliberative ethics in 115–17; dignity goals in 105, 106, 107, 108, 111–12, 126,

127; disciplinary actions under 127; ethical education in 114–22, 126–7; ethical problematics for 107–11; harm prevention goals in 107, 111, 113, 120; historical background for 106–7, 112–13; honor code in 120–2; humanity in 118, 121, 123–5, 128; international law and 107, 113–14, 125, 126–7; Israeli Defense Force application of 5, 104–30; moral judgment development in 106, 108, 110–14, 115–17, 127–8; nationalism stance in 128–9; overview of 104–6, 126–9; principle of limitations in 114; professional ethics in 120; proportionality of force in 113, 120; rule-based obedience in 114–22; self-corrective mechanisms in 122–3; self-defense stance in 104–5, 111–13, 126; self-other relationship in 123–5, 127; sensitivity and moral courage in 118; utilitarian ethics in 118; virtue ethics in 117–18

Qur'an 171, 179–82, 183–4, 197–9, 201–8, 235, 245–51, 252

Rabbis for Human Rights *(T'ruah)* 99, 100
Rabin, Yitzhak 90, 91, 129
Rahula, Walpola 21–2, 27–8, 39
Rajapaksa, Mahinda 268, 269
Rantisi, Abdul Aziz 227–8, 233–4
religion: Age of Transition for 169–90; atheists and agnostics not practicing 100, 159n20, 170; beliefs in 303–4; Buddhism as (*see* Buddhism); Christianity as (*see* Christianity); conflict and 2–3, 302–5; fusion of religion and state with 188, 255, 271–2; global context for 169–70; Hinduism as (*see* Hinduism); institutions sustaining 187, 255, 305; interfaith initiatives (*see* interfaith initiatives); Islam as (*see* Islam); Judaism as (*see* Judaism); killing taboos in (*see* killing taboos); nonviolence and 302–5, 311–27 (*see also* nonviolence; pacifists; peace); political intertwinement with 188, 195–6 (*see also* politics); religious domain interpretation 170–1; rituals in 304–5; separation of church and state with 188; symbols of 3, 302; violence and 1–9, 242–3, 302–11, 316–21 (*see also* violence; war; warriors)
retribution and vengeance: Christian views on 141–2, 144, 145–6, 154, 156; Jewish views on 70–1; Purity of Arms honor code not embracing 105, 125
Roshi, Aitkin 50
Russia: Orthodox Church in 170

sacredness of human life 246–8
Sadat, Anwar 222–3
Saffron Revolution 53
Sarraj, Eyad 226–7
saving a life 76–7, 116
scriptural reasoning 284, 286–7
secular ethics 48–9
self-corrective mechanisms 122–3
self-defense: Christian pacifist views of 136; Islamic stance on 182–3, 204, 206, 244, 251–2; Jewish stance on 74–6, 82, 86, 88–9, 102n2; Purity of Arms honor code on 104–5, 111–13, 126
separation of church and state 188
sexual behavior 47, 189
silence: Christianity argument based on 150; Jewish reverence for 69–70, 83–4; *see also* meditation
Sirisena, Maithripala 268
Sirisamghabodhi, King 28–31
Sivaraksa, Sulak 41, 46, 47, 51–2, 57, 58–9
social boundaries and killing 317–18
social engagement: active nonviolence as (*see* active nonviolence); active peacemaking as 196–9, 201, 203–4, 208–14, 244–5, 327; Engaged Buddhism and 4–5, 36–55, 57–65; foundational Buddhist teachings applied to 42–8; shadows and challenges for 54–5; traditional Buddhism and 36–8
social justice: Buddhist social engagement for 37, 40, 50; Christian active nonviolence in pursuit of 162–7; Christian just-war doctrine in defense of 139; *imago Dei* foundation of 77; interfaith initiatives addressing 8; Islamic values of 246; Jewish goals of 77–8, 80, 327; killing taboos as foundation of 5; peace symbiosis with 246
socioeconomic status: Buddhist social engagement on inequality of 47, 50; caste system determining 39–40; conflict related to 3; interfaith initiatives addressing inequalities in 8; Islamic justice goals for 246
solidarity, Islamic value of 248–9
Sri Lanka: Buddhism in 13–22, 24, 27–8, 31–2, 36, 39, 51, 59, 268, 269, 271–2,

278–9; civil war in 8, 13–22, 24, 27–8, 31–2, 39, 54–5, 266–7; Engaged Buddhism in 36, 39, 51, 59; interfaith peacebuilding initiatives in 8, 265–82; nationalism in 265, 268, 271–2; post-war context in 267–70; suicide rates in 33n17; terrorism in 13, 20, 217–18
Sri Lanka Council of Religions for Peace 275
Sri Lankan interfaith peacebuilding initiatives: case studies of 278–80; Compassionate Council role in 270, 280; Congress of Religious in 275; district level interreligious committees in 8, 265–6, 276–80; human rights considerations in 8, 267, 269–70, 277–8; nationalism affecting 265, 268, 271–2; National Peace Council in 275–81; organizational efforts in 275–8; overview of 265–6; political context for 265–75; post-war context for 267–70; religious mobilization for 271–80; setting for 266–7; Sri Lanka Council of Religions for Peace in 275; sustaining efforts of 280–2
stealing or theft: Buddhist stance on 47; self-defense in cases of 75
suffering: Christian views on 146, 158n14, 163; terrorism as response to 226–8
Sunnah or Hadith 179, 183, 184, 198, 201, 205, 245–51
Sutta Nipata 64
symbols, religious 3, 302
Syria: Arab Spring in 211, 254–5; Islamic violence and 211; Israeli relations with 90; just-war doctrine applied to 177

taboos 316–21; *see also* killing taboos
take no spoils taboos 316–17
Talmud 93, 94
Taoism 312
Teresa, Mother/Saint 164
terrorism: condemnations and justifications of 221–9; death embraced by 224, 232–3; dehumanization via 220, 235–7; injustice fought via 7–8, 220, 228, 231–2; the innocents harmed by 220, 225, 233–5; instrumental logic governing 236; Islamic 7–8, 112, 179, 216–38, 242, 243–4, 321, 326; nonviolence for resisting and transforming 217, 229–37, 326; political nature of 7–8, 217–21, 223, 226, 229, 231; prevalence of 217–18;

Purity of Arms honor code challenges with 107–8, 112, 126; rationality and dynamics of 217–21; religion in context of 169; self-other characterization of 124, 127; Sri Lankan 13, 20, 217–18; war on terror 169, 218
Thailand: Engaged Buddhism in 41–2, 51–2, 58–9
Torah 93, 126, 301, 307
Tunisia: Arab Spring in 210, 254–5
two wheels theory 23, 27

United Nations 61, 89, 92, 113, 126, 177, 178, 267, 269–70, 300–1, 307
United States: atheists and agnostics in 170; Buddhist Peace Fellowship in 50, 59; Christianity in 170; civil rights movement in 3, 9, 77–8, 164, 177, 245, 295, 315; Fellowship of Reconciliation in 50; Jewish emigrants from 92, 99, 100, 101; Judaism in 99, 100; nonviolent activism in 3, 9, 164, 177; terrorism and terrorism response in 216–17, 218–19, 220, 226, 243
utilitarianism: Buddhist 20; Purity of Arms honor code on 118

values: Buddhist compartmentalization of 30–1; Islamic nonviolent 245–51
vengeance *see* retribution and vengeance
violence: ambivalent or bi-valent attitude toward 1–2, 299–301, 313; Buddhist advocacy and allowances for 4, 13–32, 39, 242, 268, 269, 271, 312–13; Buddhist social engagement against 44, 45, 47, 50, 53–4; Christian engagement with 5, 135, 139–59, 163, 173–7, 178, 185–6, 242, 302, 307–9, 319–20; compassionate 19; conflict and 2–3, 302–5; cultural 324, *325*; direct 324, *325*; ecoviolence 324, *325*; Hinduism engagement with 242, 309–10; Islamic engagement with 7–8, 112, 179–86, 199–200, 202–6, 216–38, 242–5, 251–3, 309, 317, 320–1, 326; Jewish engagement with 5, 69, 70–6, 82–3, 86, 87–98, 104–30, 216, 218–19, 226–8, 242, 301–2, 305–7, 316–8; legitimate *vs.* illegitimate 300–1; proportionality of 113, 120, 144–6, 156, 175, 176, 183, 312, 319; religion and 1–9, 242–3, 302–11, 316–21 (*see also specific religions*); retribution and vengeance-based (*see* retribution and vengeance); the sacred and 299–301;

self-defense as basis for (*see* self-defense); structural 324, *325*; taboos as religious limits on 316–21 (*see also* killing taboos); terrorism as (*see* terrorism); triangle or diamond of 324–5, *325*; unavoidable 20; *see also* war; warriors

virtue ethics: Buddhist 29; interfaith initiatives based on 274; Purity of Arms honor code on 117–18

war: Buddhist advocacy and allowance for 4, 13–32, 39, 242, 268, 269, 271, 312–13; Buddhist social engagement against 37, 44, 55; Christian engagement in 5, 135, 139–59, 163, 173–7, 178, 185–6, 242, 302, 307–9, 319–20; commanded or obligatory 73, 94; Holy War 73, 135, 155, 180 (*see also* Crusades; *jihad*); Islamic engagement in 7–8, 112, 179–86, 199–200, 202–6, 216–38, 242–5, 251–3, 309, 317, 320–1, 326; Jewish engagement in 5, 69, 70–6, 82–3, 86, 87–98, 104–30, 216, 218–19, 226–8, 242, 301–2, 305–7, 316–18; *jus ad bellum* ideals for 17, 19, 318 (*see also* just-war doctrine); *jus in bello* ideals for 17, 19, 26, 318; just-war doctrine (*see* just-war doctrine); karmic consequences for soldiers in 25–6; peace intertwined with 5, 69–84, 86–102, 135–59, 173–86, 242–3, 251–2, 298–327; self-defense as basis for (*see* self-defense); Sri Lankan civil 8, 13–22, 24, 27–8, 31–2, 39, 54–5, 266–7; unavoidable 20

war and peace intertwinement: in Christianity 5, 135–59, 173–9, 185–6; complexities of 80–4, 242–3; in Islam 179–86, 242–3, 251–2; in Judaism 5, 69–84, 86–102, 307; silence for discerning balance of 83–4; tapestry or woven image of 70, 80; warrior and pacifist motifs in 298–327

warriors: Buddhist stance on 4, 13–32, 39, 242, 268, 269, 271, 312–13; Christian images of 5, 135, 139–59, 163, 173–7, 178, 185–6, 242, 302, 307–9, 319–20; dilemmas for 310–11; God as 301–2, 305–7; Islamic images of 7–8, 112, 179–86, 199–200, 202–6, 208–14, 216–38, 242–5, 251–3, 309, 317, 320–1, 326; Jewish views of 5, 69, 70–6, 82–3, 86, 87–98, 104–30, 216, 218–19, 226–8, 242, 301–2, 305–7, 316–18; motif of 301–11; nonviolent activists as (*see* active nonviolence); pacifists and 298–327 (*see also* war and peace intertwinement); peacemaking activists as 196–9, 201, 203–4, 208–14, 244–5, 327; psychological issues for 2, 299, 310–11; Purity of Arms honor code for 5, 104–30; religious support for 302–5 (*see also specific religions*); self-defense of (*see* self-defense); Tokyo conference exploring 1; *see also* violence; war

Williams, Rowan 189

wisdom: Buddhist stance on 20–1, 43; Purity of Arms honor code sources of 125–6

women: Buddhist social engagement supporting 47, 50; Christian active nonviolence supporting 166; Islam on treatment of 205, 209, 255; nonviolent activism by 164, 209

World Conference on Church and Society 179

World Council of Churches 179, 189

World Court 301

World Day of Peace 162, 190

Yemen: Arab Spring in 210, 254–5

Zionist movement 86–7, 88–92, 94–8, 99, 106, 112